Modern Approach to Artificial Intelligence

Volume I

Modern Approach to Artificial Intelligence
Volume I

Edited by **Akira Hanako**

CLANRYE INTERNATIONAL

New Jersey

Published by Clanrye International,
55 Van Reypen Street,
Jersey City, NJ 07306, USA
www.clanryeinternational.com

Modern Approach to Artificial Intelligence: Volume I
Edited by Akira Hanako

© 2015 Clanrye International

International Standard Book Number: 978-1-63240-357-5 (Hardback)

Contents

Preface

Artificial intelligence is the term given to the intelligence that is seen to be exhibited by machines or software. It has emerged as an independent academic field of study. One can define this arena as the study and design of intelligent agents, where an intelligent agent is a system that comprehends its environment and takes actions that increase its chances of success. The term is also applicable to the task of developing systems gifted with the logical processes that are characteristic of humans, such as the ability to discover meaning, reason, generalize and learn from experience. The field is based on the foundational claim that the central property of humans, that is, intelligence, can be so accurately expressed that a machine can be made to simulate and imitate it. Artificial Intelligence research is a highly technical and specialized field, and can be divided into various branches. The goals of AI research include planning, learning, reasoning, natural language processing or communication, knowledge, perception as well as the ability to move and manipulate objects. The field of artificial intelligence is an interdisciplinary one, in which numerous scientific and social science disciplines converge such as psychology, computer science, linguistics, neuroscience, philosophy as well as other specialized fields such as artificial psychology. This is a highly scientific field that is undergoing constant and rapid changes and thus needs skilled researchers and engineers in its ranks.

This book lists and discusses the research compiled on the advances that artificial intelligence has undergone recently. I am thankful to those scientists and researchers whose toil and hard work helped make this effort a success as well as those outside the scientific community who have been unwavering in their support.

Editor

Imprecise Imputation as a Tool for Solving Classification Problems with Mean Values of Unobserved Features

Lev V. Utkin and Yulia A. Zhuk

Department of Control, Automation and System Analysis, St. Petersburg State Forest Technical University, Institutski per. 5, St. Petersburg 194021, Russia

Correspondence should be addressed to Lev V. Utkin; lev.utkin@gmail.com

Academic Editor: Wolfgang Faber

A method for solving a classification problem when there is only partial information about some features is proposed. This partial information comprises the mean values of features for every class and the bounds of the features. In order to maximally exploit the available information, a set of probability distributions is constructed such that two distributions are selected from the set which define the minimax and minimin strategies. Random values of features are generated in accordance with the selected distributions by using the Monte Carlo technique. As a result, the classification problem is reduced to the standard model which is solved by means of the support vector machine. Numerical examples illustrate the proposed method.

1. Introduction

There are several major data mining techniques including classification, clustering, and novelty detection. We consider classification as a data mining technique used to predict an unobserved output value y based on an observed input vector $\mathbf{x}$. This requires us to estimate a predictor f from training data or a set of example pairs of $(\mathbf{x}, y)$. A special very important problem of the statistical machine learning is the binary classification problem which can be regarded as a task of classifying some objects into two classes (groups) in accordance with their properties or features. In other words, we have to classify each pattern $\mathbf{x}$ into one of the classes by means of a discriminant function f.

A common assumption in supervised learning is that training and predicted data are drawn from the same (unknown) probability distribution; that is, training and predicted data come from the same statistical model. As a result, most machine learning algorithms and methods exploit this assumption which, unfortunately, does not often hold in practice. This may lead to a performance deterioration in the induced classifiers [1, 2]. This problem may arise if we have imbalanced data [3] or in case of rare events or observations [4]. The assumption does not hold also in case

of partially known or observed features. For instance, it may take place when we know only some mean values of the features but cannot get their actual values during training.

One of the approaches to handle the above problem and to cope with the imbalance and possible inconsistencies of training and predicted data is the minimax strategy for which the classification parameters are determined by minimizing the maximum possible risk of misclassification [1, 2]. This is an "extreme" strategy of decision making. As pointed out in [1], the minimax classifiers may be seen as overconservative since its goal is to optimize the performance under the least favorable conditions. Therefore, it is interesting to simultaneously study the so-called minimin or optimistic strategy for which the classification parameters are determined by minimizing the minimum possible risk of misclassification. This is another "extreme" strategy.

By taking into account the above, we propose a classification model using the minimax and minimin strategies for situations when a part of features are observed and there are precise values of the features corresponding to different classified classes, but our initial information about other parts of features is restricted by mean values of the features for every class. In other words, we know only mean values (expectations) of some features and do not have any observations. This is a very restrictive piece of information which should be exploited. The features with this information will be called unobserved for simplicity. A typical example of the above situation is a mode of production of reinforced concrete beams whose quality and strength depend on a number of parameters such as the weight of reinforcement bars and concrete materials. If we have not observed or measured some of the parameters before, it is difficult to reject new beams or to classify them into two classes: defective (rejected) or of high quality, because we do not have the learning set of beams with the measured parameters. However, if we know, for instance, how much steel has been used up by manufacturing N beams, then we are able to evaluate the average weight of steel in a beam. The information can be elicited, for instance, from experts. Often, it is easy for experts to provide judgments about some average values of a feature for every class because this information is the most simple and understandable.

One of the simplest ways to solve the classification problem with the partial information is to assume that the mean values are observed values. In fact, we replace in this case an unknown probability distribution of data of a feature by the deterministic variable which takes one value corresponding to the mean value of this feature. Of course, we accept here a very strong assumption which may lead to a significant performance deterioration especially if the underlying probability distribution is not symmetric. Another way is to find the mean values of every observed feature and use the simplest classification algorithm considered by many authors, for instance, by [5]. However, we lose some useful information in this case, which can be inferred from the observations.

In order to maximally exploit the available information about features, we propose another approach whose underlying ideas can be formulated with a combination of multiple imputation [6] and imprecise models of features.

As indicated in [7], imputation is a class of methods by which an estimation of the missing value or its distribution is used to generate predictions from a given model. In particular, either a missing value is replaced with an estimation of the value or alternatively the distribution of possible missing values is estimated, and corresponding model predictions are combined probabilistically. Various imputation treatments for missing values in training data are available that may be deployed at prediction time [8–13]. However, some treatments such as multiple imputation [6] are particularly suitable to induction. In particular, multiple imputation (or repeated imputation) is a Monte Carlo approach that generates multiple simulated versions of a dataset such that each is analyzed, and the results are combined to generate inference.

We do not know the probability distributions of data for unobserved features. However, the mean values of features and their boundary values produce a set of probability distributions bounded by some lower and upper cumulative distribution functions (CDFs). This way leads to constructing the so-called p-boxes [14, 15] from data. It should be noted that the considered set of distributions is not the set of parametric distributions having the same parametric form

as the bounding distributions, but it is the set of all possible distributions restricted by the lower and upper bounds. This is an important feature of the proposed approach in this paper. A probability distribution is selected from the p-box in order to make a pessimistic decision, which maximizes the risk function as a measure of the classification error. In other words, the well-known minimax strategy is applied for solving the classification problem, which appears as an insurance against the worst case [16]. Another probability distribution is selected from the p-box in order to make an optimistic or minimin decision. The similar idea applied to regression models has been considered in [17–19]. So, the first idea is to consider the lower and upper probability distributions of feature data produced by the corresponding mean values and bounds for the feature values.

It should be noted that the obtained bounding probability distributions do not belong to standard types of probability distributions and their convolution for combining features and for computing parameters of the discriminant function is an extremely hard problem. Therefore, in order to cope with this problem, the second idea is proposed. We can apply the Monte Carlo technique for generating random values of features, which are governed by the probability distributions selected from the p-boxes in accordance with the minimax and minimin strategies [20, 21]. In a nutshell, for every example of the training set, we generate a (large) number of random values for unobserved features. It is a multiple imputation technique which has been applied to classification problems [7, 22, 23]. But the main distinction of the proposed approach from the available ones is that it is based on some partial information about unobserved features and uses the p-boxes for generating random values of features.

After carrying out this procedure, the classification problem can be solved by means of standard methods, for instance, by means of the support vector machine (SVM). The Monte Carlo technique has also been applied to general classification problems [24, 25]. It has been successfully applied to reliability analysis problems in the framework of classification models [26, 27]. Of course, the Monte Carlo technique requires additional computation efforts. However, its main advantage is its simplicity. Moreover, we get the standard classification problem solved by standard available software tools.

We have to stress that there is no sense in applying the proposed model when we have some missing values among the observed values of a feature. The model has to be used when we do not have observations for some features at all and only mean values of the features and their bounds are known.

The paper is organized as follows. A statement of the well-known standard classification problem is given in Section 2. This statement is extended on the case of a set of probability distributions of training data in Section 3. In this section, two strategies, minimax and minimin, are formally introduced. The classification problem with mean values for a part of unobserved features is considered in Section 4. A general method for constructing the classification model by partial information about some features with using the set of probability distributions is described in the same section. A question of the training data generation for realizing the Monte

Carlo simulation is solved in Section 5. A way for reducing the classification problem with partial information about features to the standard problem and its solution by means of the SVM method is given in Section 6. Numerical examples with synthetic data and with the real datasets, including Iris, Pima Indian Diabetes, Mammographic Masses, Parkinsons, Indian Liver Patient, Breast Cancer Wisconsin (Original), Breast Cancer Wisconsin (Diagnostic), Musk, and Lung-Cancer datasets from UCI machine learning repository [28], are provided in Section 7.

2. The Standard Classification Problem

The binary-classification problem can be formulated as follows. There are predictor-response data with a binary response y representing the observation of classes $y = -1$ and $y = 1$. The binary-classification problem is to estimate a region in predictor space in which class 1 is observed with the greatest possible majority. Suppose we are given empirical data

$$(\mathbf{x}_1, y_1), (\mathbf{x}_2, y_2), \ldots, (\mathbf{x}_n, y_n) \in \mathbb{R}^l \times \{-1, +1\}. \quad (1)$$

Here, $\{\mathbf{x}_1, \mathbf{x}_2, \ldots, \mathbf{x}_n\}$ is some nonempty set of the patterns or examples; $y_1, \ldots, y_n$ are labels or outputs taking the values -1 and $+1$; l is the number of features. It is supposed that the number of elements in the training set belonging to the class y is n_y and their indices form the set of indices $N(y)$; that is, we can write $n_{-1} + n_1 = n$ and $N(y) = \{i : y_i = y\}$.

Classification problem is usually characterized by an unknown CDF $F_0(\mathbf{x}, y)$ on $\mathbb{R}^l \times \{-1, +1\}$ defined by the training set or examples $\mathbf{x}_i$ and their corresponding class labels y_i.

The main problem is to find a decision function $g(\mathbf{x})$, which predicts accurately the class label y of any example $\mathbf{x}$ that may or may not belong to the training set. In other words, we seek a function g that minimizes the classification error, which is given by the probability that $g(\mathbf{x}) \neq y$. One of the possible approaches for solving the problem is the discriminant function approach which uses a real valued function $f(\mathbf{x})$ called the discriminant function whose sign determines the class label prediction: $g(\mathbf{x}) = \text{sgn}(f(\mathbf{x}))$. The discriminant function $f(\mathbf{x})$ may be parametrized with some parameters $\mathbf{w} = (w_0, w)$, $w = (w_1, \ldots, w_l)$, that are determined from the training examples by means of a learning algorithm. In particular, the function $f(\mathbf{x})$ may be linear; that is, $f(\mathbf{x}) = \langle w, \mathbf{x} \rangle + w_0$. Introduce also the notation $x_i^{(k)}$ for the ith element of the vector $\mathbf{x}_k$.

Given the training data, the linear discriminant training problem is to minimize the following risk measure [29]:

$$R(\mathbf{w}) = \int_{\mathbb{R}^l \times \{-1,1\}} L(\mathbf{x}, y) \, dF_0(\mathbf{x}, y). \quad (2)$$

Here, the loss function $L(\mathbf{x}, y)$ usually takes a nonzero value when the sign of the discriminant function (the class label prediction) does not coincide with the class label y. The minimization of the risk measure is carried out over the parametric class of functions $f(\mathbf{x})$. In other words, the function $f(\mathbf{x})$ provides the minimum of $R(\mathbf{w})$ such that $R(\mathbf{w}_{\text{opt}}) = \min_{\mathbf{w}} R(\mathbf{w})$.

3. The Classification Problem under a Set of Probability Distributions

Let us represent the joint probability as $F_0(\mathbf{x}, y) = F_0(\mathbf{x} \mid y) \cdot P(y)$. Here, $P(y)$ is the prior probability that an example $\mathbf{x}$ belongs to the class y. Then, we can rewrite the risk measure taking into account two values of y

$$R(\mathbf{w}) = P(-1) R_{-1}(\mathbf{w}) + P(1) R_1(\mathbf{w}). \quad (3)$$

Here,

$$R_{-1}(\mathbf{w}) = \int_{\mathbb{R}^l} L(\mathbf{x}, -1) \, dF_0(\mathbf{x} \mid -1),$$
$$R_1(\mathbf{w}) = \int_{\mathbb{R}^l} L(\mathbf{x}, 1) \, dF_0(\mathbf{x} \mid 1). \quad (4)$$

By assuming that features are independent, we can rewrite the above risk measures as

$$R_y(\mathbf{w}) = \int_{\mathbb{R}^l} L(\mathbf{x}, y) \prod_{i=1}^{l} dF_i(x_i \mid y), \quad y = -1, 1. \quad (5)$$

Suppose that the distributions F_i are unknown. However, we assume that some lower and upper bounds for a set $\mathcal{F}_i(y)$ of the CDFs $F_i(x \mid y)$ are known to be accurate to $\mathbf{w}$ and they are $\underline{F}_i(x \mid y)$ and $\overline{F}_i(x \mid y)$, respectively. We can write

$$\mathcal{F}_i(y) = \left\{ F_i(x \mid y) \mid \underline{F}_i(x \mid y) \le F_i(x \mid y) \le \overline{F}_i(x \mid y) \right\}. \quad (6)$$

In other words, there is an unknown precise "true" CDF $F_i(x \mid y) \in \mathcal{F}_i(y)$ for every $y \in \{-1, +1\}$ and every $i = 1, \ldots, l$, but we do not know it and only know that it belongs to the set $\mathcal{F}_i(y)$. It has been mentioned that the set $\mathcal{F}_i(y)$ is not the set of parametric distributions having the same parametric form as the bounding distributions, but it is the set of all possible distributions restricted by the lower and upper bounds.

3.1. The Minimax Strategy. One of the possible strategies to derive an estimator is the minimax (pessimistic) strategy. According to the minimax strategy, we select a CDF from the set $\mathcal{F}_i(-1)$ and a CDF from the set $\mathcal{F}_i(1)$ such that the risk measures $R_{-1}(\mathbf{w})$ and $R_1(\mathbf{w})$ achieve their maximum for every fixed $\mathbf{w}$. The minimax strategy can be explained in a simple way. We do not know a precise CDF F_i, and every CDF from $\mathcal{F}_i(y)$ can be selected. Therefore, we should take the "worst" distribution providing the largest value of the risk measure. The minimax criterion appears as an insurance against the worst case because it aims at minimizing the expected loss in the least favorable case [16].

Denote $\mathscr{F}(y) = \mathscr{F}_1(y) \times \cdots \times \mathscr{F}_l(y)$. Since the sets $\mathscr{F}(-1)$ and $\mathscr{F}(+1)$ are obtained independently for $y = -1$ and $y = 1$, respectively, then

$$\overline{R}(\mathbf{w}) = \max_{F(\mathbf{x}|y) \in \mathscr{F}(y)} R(\mathbf{w})$$

$$= \sum_{y=-1,1} P(y) \max_{F(\mathbf{x}|y) \in \mathscr{F}(y)} R_y(\mathbf{w}). \tag{7}$$

The minimax risk functional with respect to the minimax strategy is now of the form:

$$\overline{R}(\mathbf{w}_{\text{opt}}) = \min_{\mathbf{w}} \overline{R}(\mathbf{w}). \tag{8}$$

Let us consider in detail the first problem $\max_{F(\mathbf{x}|-1) \in \mathscr{F}(-1)} R_{-1}(\mathbf{w})$. Most loss functions $L(\mathbf{x}, -1)$ applied in classification are increasing with f. This implies that the upper bound for $R_{-1}(\mathbf{w})$, that is, the maximum of $R_{-1}(\mathbf{w})$ over all distributions from $\mathscr{F}(-1)$, is achieved at the CDFs $\underline{F}(\mathbf{x} \mid -1)$ (see, e.g., Walley's paper [30]). Hence, there holds

$$\overline{R}_{-1}(\mathbf{w}) = \int_{\mathbb{R}^l} L(\mathbf{x}, -1) \, d\underline{F}(\mathbf{x} \mid -1). \tag{9}$$

Here,

$$\underline{F}(\mathbf{x} \mid y) = \prod_{i=1}^{l} \widetilde{F}_i(x_i \mid y), \tag{10}$$

where

$$\widetilde{F}_i(x_i \mid y) = \begin{cases} \underline{F}_i(x_i \mid y), & L(\mathbf{x}, y) \text{ increases with } x_i, \\ \overline{F}_i(x_i \mid y), & L(\mathbf{x}, y) \text{ decreases with } x_i. \end{cases} \tag{11}$$

The above condition can be rewritten in terms of the function f instead of L

$$\widetilde{F}_i(x_i \mid -1) = \begin{cases} \underline{F}_i(x_i \mid -1), & f(\mathbf{x}) \text{ increases with } x_i, \\ \overline{F}_i(x_i \mid -1), & f(\mathbf{x}) \text{ decreases with } x_i, \end{cases}$$

$$\widetilde{F}_i(x_i \mid 1) = \begin{cases} \underline{F}_i(x_i \mid 1), & f(\mathbf{x}) \text{ decreases with } x_i, \\ \overline{F}_i(x_i \mid 1), & f(\mathbf{x}) \text{ increases with } x_i. \end{cases} \tag{12}$$

In the same way, we can consider the second problem $\max_{F(\mathbf{x}|1) \in \mathscr{F}(1)} R_1(\mathbf{w})$. Most of loss functions $L(\mathbf{x}, 1)$ are decreasing with f. Therefore, the upper bound for $R_1(\mathbf{w})$ is achieved at the distribution $\overline{F}(\mathbf{x} \mid 1)$. This implies that

$$\overline{R}_1(\mathbf{w}) = \int_{\mathbb{R}^l} L(\mathbf{x}, 1) \, d\overline{F}(\mathbf{x} \mid 1). \tag{13}$$

Finally, we get the upper bound for the risk measure $R(\mathbf{w})$, which is of the form

$$\overline{R}(\mathbf{w}) = \sum_{y=-1,1} P(y) \int_{\mathbb{R}^l} L(\mathbf{x}, y) \prod_{i=1}^{l} d\widetilde{F}_i(x_i \mid y). \tag{14}$$

Now we have two tasks. First, we have to define CDFs $\underline{F}_i(x \mid y)$ and $\overline{F}_i(x \mid y)$ from the available information for every $y = -1, 1$ and for every $i = 1, \ldots, l$. Second, we have to define the prior probabilities of classes $P(-1)$ and $P(1)$.

3.2. The Minimin Strategy. The minimin strategy can be regarded as a direct opposite of the minimax strategy. According to the minimin strategy, the risk measure R is minimized over all probability distributions from the set $\mathscr{F}$ as well as over all values of parameters. The strategy can be called optimistic because it selects the "best" probability distribution from the set $\mathscr{F}$. Of course, the minimin strategy is of little interest. Nevertheless, we study it in order to compare "extreme" cases (minimax and minimin strategies).

Similarly to the minimax strategy, we can write

$$\underline{R}(\mathbf{w}) = \min_{F(\mathbf{x}|y) \in \mathscr{F}(y)} R(\mathbf{w})$$

$$= \sum_{y=-1,1} P(y) \min_{F(\mathbf{x}|y) \in \mathscr{F}(y)} R_y(\mathbf{w}). \tag{15}$$

Since loss functions $L(\mathbf{x}, -1)$ applied in classification are increasing with f, then the lower bound for $R_{-1}(\mathbf{w})$, that is, the minimum of $R_{-1}(\mathbf{w})$ over all distributions from $\mathscr{F}(-1)$, is achieved at the distribution $\overline{F}(\mathbf{x} \mid -1)$. The loss function $L(\mathbf{x}, 1)$ is decreasing. Therefore, the lower bound for $R_1(\mathbf{w})$ is achieved at the distribution $\underline{F}(\mathbf{x} \mid 1)$. Hence, there holds

$$\underline{R}(\mathbf{w}) = \sum_{y=-1,1} P(y) \int_{\mathbb{R}^l} L(\mathbf{x}, y) \prod_{i=1}^{l} d\widehat{F}_i(x_i \mid y), \tag{16}$$

where

$$\widehat{F}_i(x_i \mid y) = \begin{cases} \underline{F}_i(x_i \mid y), & L(\mathbf{x}, y) \text{ decreases with } x_i, \\ \overline{F}_i(x_i \mid y), & L(\mathbf{x}, y) \text{ increases with } x_i. \end{cases} \tag{17}$$

The optimization problem for computing the optimal values of parameters $\mathbf{w}$ for the minimin strategy can be written as

$$\underline{R}(\mathbf{w}_{\text{opt}}) = \min_{\mathbf{w}} \underline{R}(\mathbf{w}). \tag{18}$$

4. Mean Values of Features and a Method for Constructing the Model

Suppose that an object is characterized by l features. Moreover, we have the training set (1). Every observation $\mathbf{x}_i$ contains the observed values of t features $x_1^{(i)}, \ldots, x_t^{(i)}$. We assume that features with numbers $1, \ldots, t$ are observed without loss of generality. However, other $l - t$ features are unobserved, and we know only the conditional mean values $m_i(y)$ of the features for every class and their bounds a_i and b_i, $i = t + 1, \ldots, l$. How to classify the objects in this case?

One of the simplest ways is to assume that the mean values are observed values. In other words, we can write $x_j^{(i)} = m_j(y)$, $j = t + 1, \ldots, l$, for all $i = 1, \ldots, n$, that is, for all observations. This way can be applied when there are a lot of observations. However, when the amount of statistical data is small, the above replacement of observations by mean values may lead to incorrect classification. Moreover, we do not take into account the information about bounds of feature values here, which might be useful.

Another way is to find the mean values of every observed feature with the number $j = 1, \ldots, t$, for every class as

$$m_j(-1) = \frac{1}{n_{-1}} \sum_{i: y_i = -1} x_j^{(i)},$$

$$m_j(1) = \frac{1}{n_1} \sum_{i: y_i = 1} x_j^{(i)}. \tag{19}$$

Then we can exploit the simplest classification algorithm considered by many authors, for instance, by [5]. The algorithm is based on analyzing the distances between a predicted vector $\mathbf{x}$ and two vectors of mean values of features. The smallest distance determines the class of $\mathbf{x}$. It has been noted in [5] that the proposed decision is the best we can do if we have no prior information about the probabilities of the two classes. However, we lose some useful information in this case, which can be inferred from the observations.

Therefore, we have to develop a classification method which maximally exploits the available information about features.

The first important assumption we use below is that the values of t observed features are governed by the nonparametric or empirical distribution.

By dealing with the unobserved features, we consider two cases or two important assumptions. The first one is that we have conditional expectations $m_j(y)$ defined for every class. The second one is that we have unconditional expectation for every feature, which does not depend on the class. This case is less informative, but it is typical for many applications. It is reduced to the first case by accepting the equality $m_j(-1) = m_j(1)$.

Let us divide the discriminant function into two parts:

$$f^{(1)}\left(\mathbf{x}^{(1)}\right) = w_0 + \sum_{i=1}^{t} w_i x_i = w_0 + \left\langle \mathbf{x}^{(1)}, w^{(1)} \right\rangle,$$

$$f^{(2)}\left(\mathbf{x}^{(2)}\right) = \sum_{i=t+1}^{l} w_i x_i = \left\langle \mathbf{x}^{(2)}, w^{(2)} \right\rangle. \tag{20}$$

Here, $\mathbf{x}^{(1)} = (x_1, \ldots, x_t)$, $\mathbf{x}^{(2)} = (x_{t+1}, \ldots, x_l)$, $w^{(1)} = (w_1, \ldots, w_t)$, and $w^{(2)} = (w_{t+1}, \ldots, w_l)$.

The whole discriminant function is the sum $f^{(1)}(\mathbf{x}^{(1)}) + f^{(2)}(\mathbf{x}^{(2)})$. We assume that every function $f^{(1)}$ and $f^{(2)}$ has some conditional CDFs $F_1(f^{(1)} \mid y)$ and $F_2(f^{(2)} \mid y)$ for every $y = -1, 1$, respectively.

Let us return to the risk measure $R_y(\mathbf{w})$ defined in (4). It can be rewritten as follows:

$$R_y(\mathbf{w})$$

$$= \int_{\mathbb{R}^2} L\left(f^{(1)} + f^{(2)}, y\right) dF^{(1)}\left(f^{(1)} \mid y\right) dF^{(2)}\left(f^{(2)} \mid y\right)$$

$$= \int_{\mathbb{R}^{l-t+1}} L\left(f^{(1)} + f^{(2)}, y\right) dF^{(1)}\left(f^{(1)} \mid y\right) \prod_{j=t+1}^{l} d\tilde{F}_j\left(x_j \mid y\right). \tag{21}$$

Here, $F_j(x_j \mid y)$ is the conditional CDF of the jth feature for the class y.

By assuming that the observed features are governed by the empirical distribution, we can conclude that the distribution of the function $f^{(1)}$ is also empirical; that is, its PDF is the weighted sum of Dirac functions $\delta(f^{(1)} - f_i^{(1)})$ with weights $1/n_y$. Hence, we obtain

$$R_y(\mathbf{w}) = \int_{\mathbb{R}^{l-t+1}} L(f, y) \frac{1}{n_y}$$

$$\times \sum_{i \in N(y)} \delta\left(x - f_i^{(1)}\right) dx \prod_{j=t+1}^{l} d\tilde{F}_j\left(x_j \mid y\right)$$

$$= \frac{1}{n_y} \sum_{i \in N(y)} \int_{\mathbb{R}^{l-t}} L\left(f_i^{(1)} + f^{(2)}, y\right)$$

$$\times \prod_{j=t+1}^{l} d\tilde{F}_j\left(x_j \mid y\right). \tag{22}$$

The precise CDFs F_j, $j = t + 1, \ldots, l$, are unknown. However, we know the mean values of every feature with numbers $t + 1, \ldots, l$ for every class y and the bounds of their values. Therefore, we can construct a set of CDFs with some lower and upper bounds. Given the mean value $m_i(y)$ of the ith feature and its bounds a_i, b_i, the lower $\underline{F}_i(x \mid y)$ and upper $\overline{F}_i(x \mid y)$ conditional CDFs of the ith feature values are

$$\underline{F}_i(x \mid y) = \begin{cases} 0, & x < a_i, \\ \max\left(0, \dfrac{x - m_i(y)}{x - a_i}\right), & a_i \le x < b_i, \\ 1, & x \ge b_i, \end{cases} \tag{23}$$

$$\overline{F}_i(x \mid y) = \begin{cases} 0, & x < a_i, \\ \min\left(1, \dfrac{b_i - m_i(y)}{b_i - x}\right), & a_i \le x < b_i, \\ 1, & x \ge b_i. \end{cases}$$

It should be noted that the expression for the upper bound $\overline{F}_i(x \mid y)$ can be obtained by using the natural extension [31, 32] which can be represented as the following linear programming problem:

$$\overline{F}_i(x \mid y) = \min_{c,d}(c + d \cdot m_i(y)), \tag{24}$$

subject to $c, d \in \mathbb{R}$, $c + d \cdot z \ge \mathbf{1}\{z \le x\}$, for all $z \in [a_i, b_i]$.

Here, $\mathbf{1}\{z \le x\}$ is the indicator function taking the value 1 if $z \le x$. The lower bound $\underline{F}_i(x \mid y)$ can be obtained in the same way by solving the following programming problem:

$$\underline{F}_i(x \mid y) = \max_{c,d}(c + d \cdot m_i(y)), \tag{25}$$

subject to $c, d \in \mathbb{R}$, $c + d \cdot z \le \mathbf{1}\{z \le x\}$, for all $z \in [a_i, b_i]$.

The same bounds have been differently obtained in the work [33].

The lower and upper CDFs are shown in Figure 1, where $M = m(y) = 2$, $a = -1$, and $b = 8$. The resulting bounds are

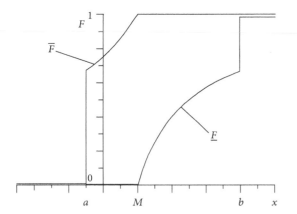

FIGURE 1: The lower and upper probability distributions.

optimal in the sense that they could not be any tighter under the given information. However, this does not mean that any distribution whose CDF is inscribed within this bounded probability region would have the same expectations $m_i(y)$. The obtained set is more rich and produces the p-box. This leads to a more conservative and cautious solution of the classification problem.

Now we have two problems. The first one is to determine the CDFs F_j, $j = t+1, \ldots, l$. The second problem is to solve an optimization problem for computing parameters $\mathbf{w}$ by using the above expressions for the risk measure.

Since the function $L(f, -1)$ is increasing, then the upper bound for $R_{-1}(\mathbf{w})$ can be written as

$$\overline{R}_{-1}(\mathbf{w}) = \frac{1}{n_{-1}} \sum_{i \in N(-1)} \int_{\mathbb{R}^{l-t}} L\left(f_i^{(1)} + f^{(2)}, -1\right) \times \prod_{j=t+1}^{l} d\widetilde{F}_j\left(x_j \mid -1\right). \tag{26}$$

Here, the upper bound $\overline{R}_{-1}(\mathbf{w})$ depends only on the bounds for CDFs $\widetilde{F}_j(x_j \mid -1)$. This is a very important property which will be used later.

The function $L(f, 1)$ is decreasing. This implies that the upper bound for $R_1(\mathbf{w})$ is

$$\overline{R}_1(\mathbf{w}) = \frac{1}{n_1} \sum_{i \in N(1)} \int_{\mathbb{R}^{l-t}} L\left(f_i^{(1)} + f^{(2)}, 1\right) \times \prod_{j=t+1}^{l} d\widetilde{F}_j\left(x_j \mid 1\right). \tag{27}$$

Here, the upper bound $\overline{R}_1(\mathbf{w})$ depends also only on the bounds for CDFs $\widetilde{F}_j(x_j \mid 1)$.

It should be noted that it is difficult to integrate in (26)-(27) in an explicit form in order to get some functions of parameters w even for the simplest loss functions L. However, we can apply the standard Monte Carlo technique. By using this technique, random values of features with the indices $j = t + 1, \ldots, l$, are generated in accordance with the CDFs $\widetilde{F}_j(x_j \mid 1)$ for the class $y = 1$ and with the CDFs $\widetilde{F}_j(x_j \mid -1)$

for the class $y = -1$. By generating K_i random vectors of features $\mathbf{x}_{i,k}^{(2)} = (x_{t+1}^{(i,k)}, \ldots, x_l^{(i,k)})$, $k = 1, \ldots, K_i$, for every $i = 1, \ldots, N(y)$ and every $y = -1, 1$ in accordance with the CDF $\widetilde{F}_j(x_j \mid -1)$ and the CDF $\widetilde{F}_j(x_j \mid 1)$, we rewrite (26)-(27) as follows:

$$\overline{R}_{-1}(\mathbf{w}) = \frac{1}{n_{-1}} \sum_{i \in N(-1)} \frac{1}{K_i} \sum_{k=1}^{K_i} L\left(f_i^{(1)} + \left\langle \mathbf{x}_{i,k}^{(2)}, w^{(2)} \right\rangle, -1\right),$$

$$\overline{R}_1(\mathbf{w}) = \frac{1}{n_1} \sum_{i \in N(1)} \frac{1}{K_i} \sum_{k=1}^{K_i} L\left(f_i^{(1)} + \left\langle \mathbf{x}_{i,k}^{(2)}, w^{(2)} \right\rangle, 1\right). \tag{28}$$

Finally, we obtain the upper risk measure as a function of parameters w as

$$\overline{R}(\mathbf{w}) = \sum_{y=-1,1} \frac{P(y)}{n_y}$$

$$\times \sum_{i \in N(y)} \frac{1}{K_i} \sum_{k=1}^{K_i} L\left(f_i^{(1)} + \left\langle \mathbf{x}_{i,k}^{(2)}, w^{(2)} \right\rangle, y_i\right), \tag{29}$$

where $x_j^{(i,k)} \sim \widetilde{F}_j(x_j \mid -1)$ for $i \in N(-1)$ and $x_j^{(i,k)} \sim \widetilde{F}_j(x_j \mid 1)$ for $i \in N(1)$.

In fact, we extend the training set by generating the "missing" values of features. We reduce the learning problem with combined types of the training information to the standard problem when there are training data in the form of real and generated observations of all features. It is important to note that we do not replace here the "missing" features by their mean values $m_i(-1)$, $i = t + 1, \ldots, l$. The "missing" values are replaced by a set of random values of features generated in accordance with the corresponding lower and upper CDFs.

The optimization problem for computing parameters w for the minimin strategy is of the same form as (29). However, the value $x_j^{(i,k)}$ is governed by the CDF $\widehat{F}_j(x_j \mid -1)$ for $i \in N(-1)$, and $x_j^{(i,k)}$ is governed by the CDF $\widehat{F}_j(x_j \mid 1)$ for $i \in N(1)$. This is just one distinction of optimization problems by the minimax and minimin strategies.

An important question is how to determine the functions $\widetilde{F}_j$ and $\widehat{F}_j$ or how to determine the type of dependence between L and x_j. We can propose two possible ways for doing that. First, the dependence can be determined by experts or by a decision maker on the basis of a preliminary analysis of features and classes. Very often, we can evaluate how possible changes of the feature values impact on the output variable y on the basis of physical meaning of the analyzed classification problem. Of course, this way is simple, but, generally, it cannot be always applied to classification problems. Second, we can enumerate 2^{l-t+1} variants of the CDFs $\widetilde{F}_j$ and $\widehat{F}_j$ by taking different lower and upper CDFs instead of $\widetilde{F}_j$ and $\widehat{F}_j$. In accordance with the minimax strategy, the optimal risk measure is the largest value of the risk measure $R(\mathbf{w})$ by optimal parameters $\mathbf{w}_{\text{opt}}$. The same procedure can be applied to the minimin strategy. However, we search for the smallest value of the risk measure $R(\mathbf{w})$ by optimal parameters $\mathbf{w}_{\text{opt}}$ in this case.

5. A Procedure for Generation of Random Feature Values

Let us consider how to generate random feature values in accordance with the above CDFs. First, we analyze the lower CDF. It can be seen from its form that the corresponding random variable is concentrated on two subsets. The first subset is the interval from $m_i(y)$ till b_i. The second is the point b_i. The probability that the random variable is in the interval $[m_i(y), b_i]$ is equal to $(b_i - m_i(y))/(b_i - a_i)$. The probability of the point b_i is $(m_i(y) - a_i)/(b_i - a_i)$. Therefore, a random number is generated in two steps. First, a random variable r uniformly distributed in interval $[0, 1]$ is generated. If r is larger than $(b_i - m_i(y))/(b_i - a_i)$, then $x = b_i$; that is, the generated number at the second step is b_i. If r is smaller than $(b_i - m_i(y))/(b_i - a_i)$, then we use the well-known inverse transformation method. According to the method, the random number x is computed through the inverse lower CDF; that is,

$$x = \frac{m_i(y) - a_i \cdot r}{1 - r}. \tag{30}$$

The right side of the above equality is obtained by means of the inverse transformation of the lower CDF.

The same simulation procedure can be provided for the upper probability distribution. A random variable r uniformly distributed in interval $[0, 1]$ is generated. If r is smaller than $(b_i - m_i(y))/(b_i - a_i)$, then $x = a_i$; that is, the generated number at the second step is a_i. If r is larger than $(b_i - m_i(y))/(b_i - a_i)$, then, according to the inverse transformation method, the random number x is computed through the inverse upper CDF; that is,

$$x = \frac{m_i(y) - b_i \cdot (1 - r)}{r}. \tag{31}$$

6. Hinge Loss Function and SVM

A procedure for computing optimal values of parameters $\mathbf{w}$ depends on the loss function L. We consider the so-called hinge loss function which is of the form $L(f, y) = \max(0, 1 - yf)$. This function is taken for the consideration in order to reduce the classification problem to the SVM method which gives the opportunity to construct nonlinear classification models in a rather simple way.

After substituting the hinge loss function into the objective function (29), we get the following optimization problem:

$$\overline{R}(\mathbf{w})$$

$$= \sum_{y=-1,1} \frac{P(y)}{n_y}$$

$$\times \sum_{i \in N(y)} \frac{1}{K_i}$$

$$\times \sum_{k=1}^{K_i} \max\left(0, 1 - y_i\left(\left\langle\left(\mathbf{x}_i^{(1)}, \mathbf{x}_{i,k}^{(2)}\right), w\right\rangle + w_0\right)\right). \tag{32}$$

It can be rewritten in a more dense form:

$$\overline{R}(\mathbf{w}) = \sum_{i=1}^{n} \frac{P(y_i)}{n_{y_i} K_i}$$

$$\times \sum_{k=1}^{K_i} \max\left(0, 1 - y_i\left(\left\langle\left(\mathbf{x}_i^{(1)}, \mathbf{x}_{i,k}^{(2)}\right), w\right\rangle + w_0\right)\right). \tag{33}$$

Let us introduce a new optimization variable

$$G_{i,k} = \max\left(0, 1 - y_i\left(\left\langle\left(\mathbf{x}_i^{(1)}, \mathbf{x}_{i,k}^{(2)}\right), w\right\rangle + w_0\right)\right). \tag{34}$$

Then we get the optimization problem

$$\overline{R}(\mathbf{w}_{\text{opt}}) = \min_w \left(\sum_{i=1}^{n} \frac{P(y_i)}{n_{y_i} K_i} \sum_{k=1}^{K_i} G_{i,k}\right), \tag{35}$$

subject to

$$G_{i,k} \geq 1 - y_i\left(\left\langle\left(\mathbf{x}_i^{(1)}, \mathbf{x}_{i,k}^{(2)}\right), w\right\rangle + w_0\right),$$

$$G_{i,k} \geq 0, \quad \forall i = 1, \ldots, n, \ k = 1, \ldots, K_i. \tag{36}$$

So, we have the linear optimization problem having $(l + 1) + \sum_{i=1}^{n} K_i$ optimization variables and $2\sum_{i=1}^{n} K_i$ constraints.

Let us add the standard Tikhonov regularization term $(1/2)\langle w, w\rangle$ (the most popular penalty or smoothness term) [34] to the objective function (35) and the constant "cost" parameter C. The smoothness (Tikhonov) term can be regarded as a constraint which enforces uniqueness by penalizing functions with wild oscillation and effectively restricting the space of admissible solutions. The detailed analysis of regularization methods can be found also in the work [35]. Then we get the following quadratic programming problem:

$$\overline{R}(\mathbf{w}_{\text{opt}}) = \min\left(\frac{1}{2}\langle w, w\rangle + C\sum_{i=1}^{n} \frac{P(y_i)}{n_{y_i} K_i} \sum_{k=1}^{K_i} G_{i,k}\right), \tag{37}$$

subject to (36).

Instead of minimizing the primary objective function (37), a dual objective function, the so-called Lagrangian, can be formed of which the saddle point is the optimum. The Lagrangian is

$$L = \frac{1}{2}\langle w, w\rangle + C\sum_{i=1}^{n}\sum_{k=1}^{K_i} \frac{P(y_i)}{n_{y_i} K_i} G_{i,k} - \sum_{i=1}^{n}\sum_{k=1}^{K_i} \eta_{i,k} G_{i,k}$$

$$- \sum_{i=1}^{n}\sum_{k=1}^{K_i} \varphi_{i,k}\left(G_{i,k} - 1 + y_i\left\langle\left(\mathbf{x}_i^{(1)}, \mathbf{x}_{i,k}^{(2)}\right), w\right\rangle + y_i w_0\right). \tag{38}$$

Here, $\eta_{i,k}, \varphi_{i,k}, i = 1, \ldots, n, k = 1, \ldots, K_i$ are Lagrange multipliers. Hence, the dual variables have to satisfy positivity constraints $\eta_{i,k} \geq 0, \varphi_{i,k} \geq 0$ for all i, k.

Hence, we get the simplified Lagrangian

$$L = \frac{1}{2}\langle w, w\rangle - \sum_{i=1}^{n}\sum_{k=1}^{K_i} \varphi_{i,k}\left(y_i\left\langle\left(\mathbf{x}_i^{(1)}, \mathbf{x}_{i,k}^{(2)}\right), w\right\rangle - 1\right). \tag{39}$$

Now we can divide all terms of the above objective function into two parts corresponding to the observed and unobserved features, respectively,

$$
\begin{aligned}
L = & \sum_{i=1}^{n} \sum_{k=1}^{K_i} \varphi_{i,k} + \frac{1}{2} \left\langle w^{(1)}, w^{(1)} \right\rangle \\
& - \sum_{i=1}^{n} \sum_{k=1}^{K_i} \varphi_{i,k} \left(y_i \left\langle \mathbf{x}_i^{(1)}, w^{(1)} \right\rangle \right) \\
& + \frac{1}{2} \left\langle w^{(2)}, w^{(2)} \right\rangle \\
& - \sum_{i=1}^{n} \sum_{k=1}^{K_i} \varphi_{i,k} \left(y_i \left\langle \mathbf{x}_{i,k}^{(2)}, w^{(2)} \right\rangle \right).
\end{aligned}
\tag{40}
$$

Hence, we obtain the dual optimization problem

$$
\begin{aligned}
\max_{\varphi_{i,k}} L \\
= & \sum_{i=1}^{n} \sum_{k=1}^{K_i} \varphi_{i,k} \\
& - \frac{1}{2} \sum_{i=1}^{n} \sum_{j=1}^{n} y_i y_j \left\langle \mathbf{x}_i^{(1)}, \mathbf{x}_j^{(1)} \right\rangle \sum_{k=1}^{K_i} \sum_{u=1}^{K_j} \varphi_{i,k} \varphi_{j,u} \\
& - \frac{1}{2} \sum_{i=1}^{n} \sum_{j=1}^{n} y_i y_j \sum_{k=1}^{K_i} \sum_{u=1}^{K_j} \varphi_{i,k} \varphi_{j,u} \left\langle \mathbf{x}_{i,k}^{(2)}, \mathbf{x}_{j,u}^{(2)} \right\rangle,
\end{aligned}
\tag{41}
$$

subject to

$$
0 \le \varphi_{i,k} \le \frac{C \cdot P(y_i)}{n_{y_i} K_i}, \quad i = 1, \ldots, n, \ k = 1, \ldots, K_i. \tag{42}
$$

Any data point for which $\varphi_{i,k} > 0$ is called a support vector. Let S and N_S denote the set of indices of the support vectors and their total number, respectively. Then one of the ways for computing the parameter w_0 is

$$
w_0 = \frac{1}{N_S} \sum_{s \in S} \left(y_s - \sum_{i=1}^{n} \sum_{k=1}^{K_i} y_i \varphi_{i,k} \left\langle \left(\mathbf{x}_i^{(1)}, \mathbf{x}_{i,k}^{(2)} \right), \left(\mathbf{x}_s^{(1)}, \mathbf{x}_s^{(2)} \right) \right\rangle \right),
\tag{43}
$$

where $(y_s, \mathbf{x}_s)$ is one of the support vectors.

If we assume that $K_i = K$ for all $i = 1, \ldots, n$, the prior probabilities are defined as $P(y) = n_y / n$, then we rewrite the optimization problem as

$$
\begin{aligned}
\max_{\varphi_{i,k}} L = & \sum_{i=1}^{n} \sum_{k=1}^{K} \varphi_{i,k} \\
& - \frac{1}{2} \sum_{i,j=1}^{n} \sum_{k,u=1}^{K} y_i y_j \left\langle \left(\mathbf{x}_i^{(1)}, \mathbf{x}_{i,k}^{(2)} \right), \left(\mathbf{x}_j^{(1)}, \mathbf{x}_{j,u}^{(2)} \right) \right\rangle \varphi_{i,k} \varphi_{j,u},
\end{aligned}
\tag{44}
$$

subject to

$$
0 \le \varphi_{i,k} \le \frac{C}{nK}, \quad i = 1, \ldots, n, \ k = 1, \ldots, K. \tag{45}
$$

Finally, we can write the discriminant function

$$
f(\mathbf{x}) = \sum_{i=1}^{n} \sum_{k=1}^{K} y_i \varphi_{i,k} \left\langle \left(\mathbf{x}_i^{(1)}, \mathbf{x}_{i,k}^{(2)} \right), \left(\mathbf{x}^{(1)}, \mathbf{x}^{(2)} \right) \right\rangle + w_0. \tag{46}
$$

The main advantage of the SVM is the use of kernels which are functions that transform the input data to a high-dimensional space where the learning problem is solved. There are many types of kernel that may be used in an SVM. Acceptable kernels must satisfy Mercer's condition. Commonly used forms of kernels are linear $K(\mathbf{x}_i, \mathbf{x}_j) = \langle \mathbf{x}_i, \mathbf{x}_j \rangle$, polynomial $K(\mathbf{x}_i, \mathbf{x}_j) = (\gamma \langle \mathbf{x}_i, \mathbf{x}_j \rangle + r)^d$, $\gamma > 0$, radial basis function (RBF) $K(\mathbf{x}_i, \mathbf{x}_j) = \exp(-\gamma \|\mathbf{x}_i - \mathbf{x}_j\|^2)$, $\gamma > 0$, and sigmoid $K(\mathbf{x}_i, \mathbf{x}_j) = \tanh(\gamma \langle \mathbf{x}_i, \mathbf{x}_j \rangle + r)$. Here, γ, r, and d are kernel parameters. The kernel functions allow us to significantly extend the class of discriminant functions that can be used in this approach.

7. Experimental Design

We illustrate the method proposed in this paper via several examples; all computations have been performed using the statistical software R [36]. We investigate the performance of the proposed method and compare it with other methods dealing with missing data by considering the accuracy measure (ACC), which is the proportion of correctly classified cases on a sample of data; that is, ACC is an estimate of a classifier's probability of a correct response. This measure is often used to quantify the predictive performance of classification methods, and it is an important statistical measure of the performance of a binary classification test. It can formally be written as ACC $= N_T / N$. Here, N_T is the number of test data for which the predicted class for an example coincides with its true class, and N is the total number of test data.

First, we consider a numerical example with synthetic data. In this example, we generate instances with two features ($l = 2$) such that the second feature is unobserved. We generate 500 normally distributed random values for every feature with the expectations $m_1(-1) = 4$, $m_1(1) = 6$, $m_2(-1) = 5$, and $m_2(1) = 10$ and the standard deviations $\sigma_1 = 1$ and $\sigma_2 = 3$, respectively. We take identical standard deviations for both classes in order to simplify the example. Moreover, we state the lower and upper bounds for values of the second feature $a_2 = 4$ and $b_2 = 14$. Then we randomly select $n = 10$ points (instances) with identical numbers of points (5) for both classes and get three training sets. The first and the second training sets are obtained in the following way. We generate the values of the second feature $K = 20$ times for every example. In sum, we have 200 examples. At that, the values for the first training set are generated in accordance with the CDFs $\widetilde{F}_j(x_j \mid 1)$ for the class $y = 1$ and with the CDFs $\widetilde{F}_j(x_j \mid -1)$ for the class $y = -1$.

TABLE 1: The ACC measures for linear and RBF kernels by normally distributed values of features.

	Linear kernel			RBF kernel		
n	ACC1	ACC2	ACC3	ACC1	ACC2	ACC3
10	0.41	0.85	0.85	0.59	0.87	0.82

TABLE 2: The ACC measures for linear and RBF kernels by exponentially distributed values of the second feature.

	Linear kernel			RBF kernel		
n	ACC1	ACC2	ACC3	ACC1	ACC2	ACC3
10	0.63	0.61	0.59	0.65	0.65	0.62

This training set corresponds to the minimax strategy. The values for the second training set are generated in accordance with the CDFs $\widehat{F}_j(x_j \mid -1)$ for the class $y = -1$ and with the CDFs $\widehat{F}_j(x_j \mid 1)$ for the class $y = 1$. The second training set corresponds to the minimin strategy. For getting the third training set, we replace all values of the second feature in the set of $n = 10$ examples by the expectations $m_2(y)$ for $y = -1$ and $y = 1$. Here, we use the available mean values of the second feature as values of the feature. We will call this strategy as direct for short. The initially generated 500 normally distributed random values will be used for testing resulting discriminant functions.

The ACC measures and the discriminant functions for the above three training sets will be indexed by numbers 1, 2, and 3 corresponding to the minimax, minimin, and direct strategies, respectively.

We will use the linear and RBF kernels with the parameter $\gamma = 1/l$. By applying the above initial data, we get three discriminant functions corresponding to three strategies (minimax, minimin, and direct):

$$f_1(\mathbf{x}) = -1.18x_1 + 0.445x_2 + 2.24,$$

$$f_2(\mathbf{x}) = 0.009x_1 - 0.49x_2 + 3.91, \qquad (47)$$

$$f_3(\mathbf{x}) = -0.00004x_1 - 0.5x_2 + 4.$$

The corresponding ACCs for linear and RBF kernels are shown in Table 1. One can see from the table that the optimistic and direct strategies provide better results in comparison with the minimax strategy. This can be explained by exploiting the normal distribution (symmetric and unimodal) with rather small standard deviations for generating the random values of the second feature.

We replace the normal distribution of the second feature values by the truncated exponential distribution with the CDF $1 - \exp((x - a_2)/m_2(y))$ if $x < b_2$ and 1 if $x \geq b_2$. This distribution is not symmetric, and its mean value cannot replace the corresponding random values. By taking the linear and RBF kernels, $n = 10$ and $K = 20$, we get the following discriminant functions:

$$f_1(\mathbf{x}) = -1.96x_1 + 0.2x_2 + 7.91,$$

$$f_2(\mathbf{x}) = -0.09x_1 - 0.47x_2 + 4.2, \qquad (48)$$

$$f_3(\mathbf{x}) = -0.5x_2 + 4.$$

The corresponding ACCs for linear and RBF kernels are shown in Table 2. It can be seen from the table that the minimax strategy provides better results. It follows from the fact that the minimax strategy takes into account the worst cases of the probability distribution of feature values. Of course,

TABLE 3: A brief introduction about datasets.

Dataset	N	l	n_{-1}	n_{+1}
Iris	150	4	50	150
Pima Indian Diabetes	768	8	268	500
Mammographic Masses	961	4	445	516
Parkinsons	195	23	48	147
Breast Cancer Wisconsin (Original)	699	9	458	241
Breast Cancer Wisconsin (Diagnostic)	569	32	212	357
Musk	476	166	207	269
Indian Liver Patients	583	10	167	416
Lung-Cancer	32	57	9	23

the exploited exponential distribution is not the worst case, but it is not the best case too. We can immediately observe that change for the worse of the probability distribution leads to improving the minimax strategy in comparison with the minimin and direct strategies.

The proposed method has been evaluated and investigated by the following publicly available datasets: Iris, Pima Indian Diabetes, Mammographic Masses, Parkinsons, Indian Liver Patient, Breast Cancer Wisconsin (Original), Breast Cancer Wisconsin (Diagnostic), Musk, and Lung-Cancer. All datasets are from the UCI machine learning repository [28]. Table 3 is a brief introduction about these datasets, while more detailed information can be found from, respectively, the data resources.

For all data, we use the repeated random subsampling validation procedure; that is, we randomly split the dataset into two subsets. One of them (training set having n instances) is used to train the model while the other (test set having $N - n$ instances) is used to validate the model. The number of instances for training will be denoted as n. Moreover, we take $n/2$ instances from every class for training. They are randomly selected from the classes. The remaining instances in the dataset are used for validation. The parameter of the RBF kernel γ for every dataset is chosen in order to maximize the accuracy measure. It is carried out by means of the following procedure. It is well known that letting the C and γ grow exponentially is a practical method to identify good parameters. An $r \times r$ uniform grid in the logarithmic coordinate space ($C' = \log_2 C$, $\gamma' = \log_2 \gamma$) is usually used. The point in the grid represents a parameter pair (C', γ'). However, we fix the value of $C = 100$ in order to reduce the number of experiments because our main aim is to compare the proposed models with known models. So, we perform

Table 4: The ACC measures for real datasets by different values of n.

Dataset	n	ACC1	ACC2	ACC3	ACC4
Iris	20	0.961	0.982	0.977	0.998
	40	0.944	0.963	0.986	0.998
Pima	20	0.501	0.598	0.502	0.573
Indian Diabetes	40	0.532	0.655	0.590	0.621
Mammographic	20	0.642	0.769	0.750	0.722
Masses	40	0.654	0.781	0.778	0.739
Parkinsons	20	0.567	0.721	0.706	0.637
	40	0.56	0.721	0.713	0.644
Breast Cancer	20	0.885	0.923	0.937	0.963
Wisconsin (Original)	40	0.832	0.919	0.815	0.962
Breast Cancer	20	0.820	0.835	0.885	0.921
Wisconsin (Diagnostic)	40	0.785	0.851	0.825	0.926
Musk	20	0.565	0.648	0.625	0.629
	40	0.606	0.678	0.689	0.658
Indian Liver	20	0.508	0.674	0.666	0.614
Patients	40	0.519	0.682	0.660	0.621
Lung-Cancer	12	0.647	0.709	0.693	0.637
	16	0.666	0.679	0.637	0.786

experiments on a 13 uniform grid where γ' has a range of $2^{-6}, \ldots, 2^6$.

From every dataset, we randomly select a feature corresponding to missing values and compute its mean values for negative and positive labels, respectively. Moreover, we find the smallest and largest values of the selected feature which will be used for determining the lower and upper cumulative distribution functions. Then we generate the random values of the selected feature $K = 20$ times for every instance. In sum, we have nK instances. The above procedure is repeated $N = 50$ times such that the selected feature with missing values is chosen randomly in every iteration. In addition to the minimin (ACC1), minimax (ACC2), and direct (ACC3) strategies, we generate random values of the "missing" feature in accordance with the normal distribution and compute the corresponding accuracy measure ACC4. By using the RBF kernels and the cost parameter $C = 100$, we get the ACC measures for different values of n, whose values are shown in Table 4. These measures are mean values of the corresponding ACCs computed for every iteration.

One can see from Table 4 that the proposed minimax strategy (ACC2) outperforms the direct strategy and the normal distribution imputation procedure for some real datasets. Of course, there are datasets for which the measures ACC3 or ACC4 are larger than ACC2. If we have seen from the experiments with synthetic data that the minimax strategy provides better results when the distribution of the feature values is not symmetric and its mean value cannot replace the corresponding random values, then it is difficult to determine clear conditions of using the proposed model with real data. We can say that these conditions directly depend on a probability distribution of the feature values in real data.

When we do not have this information, the proposed method should be used jointly with other models dealing with missing data.

8. Conclusion

A classification problem under partial information about some features in the form of conditional expectations or mean values of features for every class has been studied in the paper. Its solution is based on the pessimistic (minimax) and optimistic (minimin) decision strategies.

What are the main advantages of the proposed method? First, the classification algorithm totally exploits the available information in the form of mean values of some features and the bounds of these features. At the same time, it does not employ any additional information which may be unjustified and incorrect. It does not use also additional assumption which may lead to incorrect prediction results. Second, the proposed method has a strong probabilistic background, and this fact allows us to use it in arbitrary applications where the initial information is scarce. Third, the method exploits the well-known minimax and minimin strategies which have a strong explanation. A cautious decision strategy as an intermediate case between pessimistic and optimistic strategies with a predefined caution parameter can also be studied in the same way. However, this is a direction for further research. Fourth, the method is reduced to the SVM. This fact allows us to simply construct nonlinear classification models by using suitable kernels. Fifth, the method allows us to reduce the classification problem to the standard form. This implies that a standard software can be applied for its implementation. The algorithm for computing the optimal parameters of every classification model can be easily implemented with standard functions of the statistical software package R or by using the well-known software library LIBSVM (a library for support vector machines) [37].

The numerical examples have illustrated that the minimax classifiers can provide more accurate results in many cases in spite of their over-conservative decisions. At the same time, the given experiments can be viewed as a preliminary study of the proposed framework for applying the imprecise models to classification problems with missing values. An additional study has to be carried out in order to totally figure out when the proposed classifiers outperform the available classification models.

One can also see from the paper that the Monte Carlo technique is a versatile tool for dealing with partial information. Various classification problems under different types of partial and unreliable information could be solved in the same way. A detailed analysis of the corresponding classification models is another direction for further research.

At the same time, it is well known that one possible limitation of the Monte Carlo methods is the strong dependence of computational effort (proportional to the number of samplings). This implies that the learning of large datasets may lead to a hard computational problem. However, first of all, the minimax strategy should be used when the number of instances in training sets is rather small in order to provide the robust classification. When the training set consists of a large number of instances, other models might give better results. Second, variance reduction techniques can be applied to the classification procedures to decrease the computational effort. This is also a topic of further research.

The proposed method can be also extended on the case of interval-valued mean values of unobserved features. In this case, the lower and upper CDFs are determined by the lower and upper mean values of features.

Acknowledgment

The authors would like to express their appreciation to the anonymous referees whose very valuable comments have improved the paper.

References

[1] R. Alaiz-Rodríguez, A. Guerrero-Curieses, and J. Cid-Sueiro, "Minimax regret classifier for imprecise class distributions," *Journal of Machine Learning Research*, vol. 8, pp. 103–130, 2007.

[2] R. Alaiz-Rodríguez, A. Guerrero-Curieses, and J. Cid-Sueiro, "Improving classification under changes in class and within-class distributions," in *Systems: Computational and Ambient Intelligence*, J. Cabestany, F. Sandoval, A. Prieto, and J. Corchado, Eds., vol. 5517 of *Lecture Notes in Computer Science*, pp. 122—-130, Springer, Berlin, Germany, 2009.

[3] S. Kotsiantis, D. Kanellopoulos, and P. Pintelas, "Handling imbalanced datasets: a review," *GESTS International Transactions on Computer Science and Engineering*, vol. 30, no. 1, p. 25–36, 2006.

[4] G. M. Weiss, "Mining with rarity: a unifying framework," *ACM SIGKDD Explorations Newsletter*, vol. 6, no. 1, pp. 7–19, 2004.

[5] B. Scholkopf and A. J. Smola, *Learning with Kernels: Support Vector Machines, Regularization, Optimization, and Beyond*, The MIT Press, Cambridge, Mass, USA, 2002.

[6] D. B. Rubin, "Multiple Imputation after 18+ Years," *Journal of the American Statistical Association*, vol. 91, no. 434, pp. 473–489, 1996.

[7] M. Saar-Tsechansky and F. Provost, "Handling missing values when applying classification models," *Journal of Machine Learning Research*, vol. 8, pp. 1625–1657, 2007.

[8] G. E. A. P. A. Batista and M. C. Monard, "An analysis of four missing data treatment methods for supervised learning," *Applied Artificial Intelligence*, vol. 17, no. 5-6, pp. 519–533, 2003.

[9] A. Farhangfar, L. Kurgan, and J. Dy, "Impact of imputation of missing values on classification error for discrete data," *Pattern Recognition*, vol. 41, no. 12, pp. 3692–3705, 2008.

[10] S. Garcia and F. Herrera, "An extension on "Statistical comparisons of classifiers over multiple data sets" for all pairwise comparisons," *Journal of Machine Learning Research*, vol. 9, pp. 2677–2694, 2008.

[11] J. Grzymala-Busse and M. Hu, "A comparison of several approaches to missing attribute values in data mining," in *Rough Sets and Current Trends in Computing*, pp. 378–385, Springer, Berlin, Germany, 2001.

[12] J. Luengo, S. Garcia, and F. Herrera, "On the choice of the best imputation methods for missing values considering three groups of classification methods," *Knowledge and Information Systems*, vol. 32, no. 1, p. 77–108, 2012.

[13] J. Ning and P. E. Cheng, "A comparison study of nonparametric imputation methods," *Statistics and Computing*, vol. 22, no. 1, pp. 273–285, 2012.

[14] S. Destercke, D. Dubois, and E. Chojnacki, "Unifying practical uncertainty representations. II: clouds," *International Journal of Approximate Reasoning*, vol. 49, no. 3, pp. 664–677, 2008.

[15] S. Ferson, V. Kreinovich, L. Ginzburg, D. S. Myers, and K. Sentz, "Constructing probability boxes and Dempster-Shafer structures," Tech. Rep. SAND2002-4015, Sandia National Laboratories, January 2003.

[16] C. P. Robert, *The Bayesian Choice*, Springer, New York, NY, USA, 1994.

[17] L.V. Utkin, "Regression analysis using the imprecise Bayesian normal model," *International Journal of Data Analysis Techniques and Strategies*, vol. 2, no. 4, pp. 356–372, 2010.

[18] L. V. Utkin and F. P. A. Coolen, "On reliability growth models using Kolmogorov-Smirnov bounds," *International Journal of Performability Engineering*, vol. 7, no. 1, pp. 5–19, 2011.

[19] L.V. Utkin and Y. A. Zhuk, "A machine learning algorithm for classification under extremely scarce information," *International Journal of Data Analysis Techniques and Strategies*, vol. 4, no. 2, pp. 115–133, 2012.

[20] J. O. Berger and G. Salinetti, "Approximations of Bayes decision problems: the epigraphical approach," *Annals of Operations Research*, vol. 56, no. 1, pp. 1–13, 1995.

[21] J. Shao, "Monte Carlo approximations in Bayesian decision theory," *Journal of the American Statistical Association*, vol. 84, no. 407, pp. 727–732, 1989.

[22] A. Farhangfar, L. Kurgan, and J. Dy, "Impact of imputation of missing values on classification error for discrete data," *Pattern Recognition*, vol. 41, no. 12, pp. 3692–3705, 2008.

[23] D. Williams, X. Liao, Y. Xue, L. Carin, and B. Krishnapuram, "On classification with incomplete data," *IEEE Transactions on Pattern Analysis and Machine Intelligence*, vol. 29, no. 3, pp. 427–436, 2007.

[24] R. Esposito and L. Saitta, "Monte Carlo theory as an explanation of bagging and boosting," in *Proceedings of the 18th International Joint Conference on Artificial Intelligence (IJCAI '03)*, pp. 499–504, 2003.

[25] P. Sollich, "Bayesian methods for support vector machines: evidence and predictive class probabilities," *Machine Learning*, vol. 46, no. 1–3, pp. 21–52, 2002.

[26] J. E. Hurtado, "An examination of methods for approximating implicit limit state functions from the viewpoint of statistical learning theory," *Structural Safety*, vol. 26, no. 3, pp. 271–293, 2004.

[27] J. E. Hurtado and D. A. Alvarez, "Classification approach for reliability analysis with stochastic finite-element modeling," *Journal of Structural Engineering*, vol. 129, no. 8, pp. 1141–1149, 2003.

[28] A. Frank and A. Asuncion, *UCI Machine Learning Repository*, 2010.

[29] V. Vapnik, *Statistical Learning Theory*, Wiley, New York, NY, USA, 1998.

[30] P. Walley, "Measures of uncertainty in expert systems," *Artificial Intelligence*, vol. 83, no. 1, pp. 1–58, 1996.

[31] V. P. Kuznetsov, *Interval Statistical Models. Radio and Communication*, Moscow, Russia, 1991, in Russian.

[32] P. Walley, *Statistical Reasoning with Imprecise Probabilities*, Chapman and Hall, London, UK, 1991.

[33] S. Ferson, L. Ginzburg, and R. Akcakaya, "Whereof one cannot speak: when input distributions are unknown," Applied Biomathematics Report, 2001, http://www.ramas.com/whereof.pdf.

[34] A. N. Tikhonov and V. Y. Arsenin, *Solution of Ill-Posed Problems*, W.H. Winston, Washington, DC, USA, 1977.

[35] T. Evgeniou, T. Poggio, M. Pontil, and A. Verri, "Regularization and statistical learning theory for data analysis," *Computational Statistics and Data Analysis*, vol. 38, no. 4, pp. 421–432, 2002.

[36] R Development Core Team, *R: A Language and Environment for Statistical Computing*, R Foundation for Statistical Computing, Vienna, Austria, 2005.

[37] C.-C. Chang and C.-J. Lin, LIBSVM: a library for support vector machines, 2001, http://www.csie.ntu.edu.tw/~cjlin/libsvm/.

2

Chaotic Neural Network for Biometric Pattern Recognition

Kushan Ahmadian and Marina Gavrilova

Department of Computer Science, University of Calgary, Calgary, AB, Canada T2N 1N4

Correspondence should be addressed to Kushan Ahmadian, kahmadia@ucalgary.ca

Academic Editor: Sheryl Brahnam

Biometric pattern recognition emerged as one of the predominant research directions in modern security systems. It plays a crucial role in authentication of both real-world and virtual reality entities to allow system to make an informed decision on granting access privileges or providing specialized services. The major issues tackled by the researchers are arising from the ever-growing demands on precision and performance of security systems and at the same time increasing complexity of data and/or behavioral patterns to be recognized. In this paper, we propose to deal with both issues by introducing the new approach to biometric pattern recognition, based on chaotic neural network (CNN). The proposed method allows learning the complex data patterns easily while concentrating on the most important for correct authentication features and employs a unique method to train different classifiers based on each feature set. The aggregation result depicts the final decision over the recognized identity. In order to train accurate set of classifiers, the subspace clustering method has been used to overcome the problem of high dimensionality of the feature space. The experimental results show the superior performance of the proposed method.

1. Introduction

Growing efforts are devoted to develop and implement new security systems based on biometric features. System subjects could be either human or virtual reality entities, and they are accepted or rejected by the system based on biological or behavioral biometric features. Biometric pattern recognition includes recognition of fingerprint, face, gait, signature, voice, ear, iris, or other physiological or behavioral features.

As one of the key biometric features, facial biometrics plays a key role in user authentication. It consists of a set of high-dimensional vectors representing topological, color, or texture information. The feature set is very complex and may contain hundreds of features. This makes it a difficult biometric pattern recognition problem to deal with [1]. Many of the earlier face recognition algorithms are based on feature-based methods. These methods identify a set of geometrical features on the face such as eyes, eyebrows, mouth, and nose [2].

Properties and relations between the feature points, such as areas, distances, and angles are used as descriptors for face recognition. Statistical methods are usually used to lower the number of dimensions; however, there are no universal answers to the problem of how many points give the best performance. In addition, there is no clear answer on what the important features are or how to extract those features (Figure 1).

Alternative face recognition techniques based on elastic graph matching [3] and support vector machines (SVMs) [4] have been investigated as well.

On the other hand, appearance-based face recognition algorithms are used as a tool to project an image into the subspace and finding the closest point set [5]. One of the very well-known linear transformation methods that are used vastly for dimensionality reduction and feature extraction is the principal component analysis (PCA) [6]. In this method, object classes that are closer together in the output space are often weighted in the input space to reduce potential misclassification. PCA can be used over raw face image to extract the Fisherface or by similar manner on the eigenface to obtain the discriminant eigenfeatures [6]. Many variations of PCA combining feature representation methods that utilize the strengths of different realizations have been developed recently. LDA (Linear discriminant

FIGURE 1: Data samples for FERET facial database.

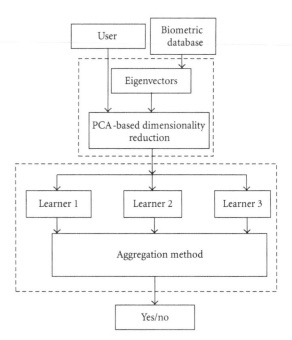

FIGURE 2: Traditional biometric system architecture.

analysis) [7], Kernel PCA [8], and generalized discriminant analysis (GDA) using a kernel approach [3] are among such methods.

However, a simple modification of PCA features or attempts to find a better fitting of those features onto linear or nonlinear subspaces alone is not sufficient to deal with high dimensionality of data. Thus, hybrid approaches were recently introduced to overcome shortcomings of individual methods. For example, a combination of support vector machines with skin color regression model was successfully used for face recognition from video sequences. Line edge map approach [2] to extract lines from a face edge map as features is based on a combination of template matching and geometrical feature matching. The nearest feature line classifier method [9] attempts to extend the capacity covering variations of pose, illumination, and expression for a face class by finding the candidate person owning the minimum distance between the feature point of query face and the feature lines connecting any two prototype feature points.

Among new approaches, learning techniques have emerged very recently. Some of the promising new approaches incorporate neural-network-based learning methods for biometric feature processing or fuzzy-logic-based multimodal biometric pattern classification systems [10, 11]. However, direct application of neural-network method is not sufficient to overcome the main obstacle, high complexity and high dimensionality of biometric data, especially if various features of a single or multiple biometrics must be taken into account. Dimensionality reduction methods are ideal for this task. The goal is to transform data from a high-dimensional space into a lower-dimensional one without loss of important information. Normally, the lower dimension maximizes the variance of data. High dimensionality of data is a common problem in recognition systems where a set of features from the training samples are used to create a learner. The complexity of designing algorithms for the recognition purpose grows significantly as the number of dimensions grows. A common set of methods to reduce the dimensionality of space is the clustering approach. In clustering, the objects are grouped according to their similarity by some similarity measures. Usually clustering is used to design a set of boundaries to

better understand the data (based on structured data). Other usage of clustering involves indexing and data compression. We aim to target the second goal in order to create a meaningful subspace of the original space.

The high dimensionality problem arises when the feature set comes either from a single complex resource (such as combination of geometric, appearance-based, and color-based facial features) or from different resources (face/ear). In this paper, we utilize the concepts discussed above in order to create a secure and precise system for face recognition. The unique characteristic of such system is that it is based on chaotic neural network for feature selection and training. In the next section we describe the proposed neural-network methodology with focus on the dimensionality-reducing methods. In Section 3, experimental results are presented. Concluding summary is found in Section 4.

2. Proposed Methodology

The proposed system consists of training different chaotic learners based on unimodal biometric data coming from a single source (i.e., a single subject). We start by proposing to use the chaotic Hopfield neural network for storing the biometric patterns. When a new pattern is introduced to the network, the network tries to convert the introduced pattern to the closest pattern saved in the memory and thus arrives to the user whose biometric is the closest to one given as an input. In order to train the network, we first obtain a set of vectors from user input (i.e., facial biometric) and then feed them as features of the new pattern to the CNN-based learning engine. Clustering is performed to group feature vectors with similar features and to further reduce complexity of feature vector space. Having the vector of weights from the candidate clusters, the next step in the

FIGURE 3: Proposed biometric recognition system.

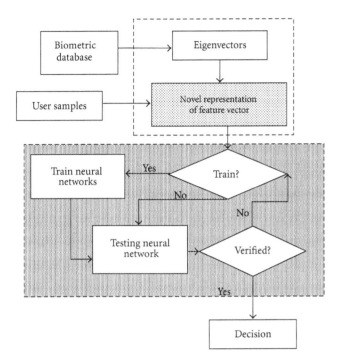

FIGURE 4: Face detection: detecting the area of interest based on the skin color tone. On the left, the candidate areas are selected and the eye templates are applied to find the correct face area. Then, the face area is selected and normalized.

proposed methodology is defining an energy model for the associative memory to learn the data patterns. The benefit of this approach is that this is a learner system that converges the given set of vectors to the stored pattern. In the classical formulation of Hopfield network for optimization problem, the method usually traps in one of many local minima of the energy function since no simulated annealing or noise injection policies have been applied. To remedy this problem, we take benefit from chaotic noise injection policy.

2.1. Overall System Architecture. One of the objectives of this paper is to investigate if neural networks combined with dimension analysis provide benefits in improving biometric system performance and circumvention, that is, resistance

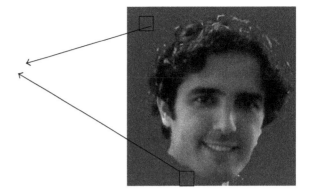

FIGURE 5: Removing the redundant areas.

to low-quality data or absence of one of biometric traits all together.

First, we aim to find the best subset of biometric features derived from the original dataset. The new subset could be either a portion of the original dataset or a reconstructed set of samples with a reduced dimensionality. As an example, when using the principal component analysis method (PCA), the main goal is to find the principal components of the distribution of features (such as faces, ears, and other biometrics utilized in the system), which are eigenvectors of the covariance matrix of the set of biometric images. These eigenvectors can be considered as a set of features that together characterizes the variation between biometric samples.

Here, we propose an alternative system. As the primary biometric sample, we chose face images due to significant variability of image quality and also popularity of the biometric for testing data analyzing methods.

Next, we propose a new principle for subspace analysis and dimensionality reduction based on a generalized description of spherical coordinates. Each face image in the training set can be represented in terms of a linear combination of the original images. The number of possible classes is equal to the number of face image groups in the training set. However, the faces can also be approximated using only the "best" eigenfaces—those that have the largest eigenvalues, and which therefore account for the most variance within the set of face images. The primary reason for using fewer eigenfaces is computational efficiency. This approach allows not only move compact space representation, but also a convenient tool for subsequent clustering and learning of common patterns. Next, we propose to use neural networks as a fast and reliable way for a biometric system to learn the pattern from the previously extracted subspaces. The neural network approach is based on my chaotic noise injection strategy which is the leading strategy for neural network training. In experimental section, I show that this approach has a high potential for success in biometric research studies. The advantages are the ability to learn and later recognize new biometric samples in an unsupervised manner and that method is easy to implement using the proposed neural network architecture. The traditional architecture is shown in Figure 2.

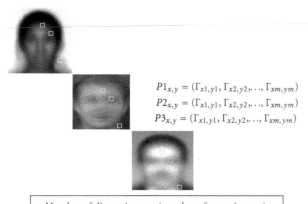

$$P1_{x,y} = (\Gamma_{x1,y1}, \Gamma_{x2,y2}, \ldots, \Gamma_{xm,ym})$$
$$P2_{x,y} = (\Gamma_{x1,y1}, \Gamma_{x2,y2}, \ldots, \Gamma_{xm,ym})$$
$$P3_{x,y} = (\Gamma_{x1,y1}, \Gamma_{x2,y2}, \ldots, \Gamma_{xm,ym})$$

Number of dimensions: m (number of mean images)
Number of points in the high dimensional space: $x * y$

FIGURE 6: Transforming points into vectors in d-dimensional space.

The new system architecture that we propose is based on neural network representation (see Figure 3).

The novelty of the proposed system relies on the representation of the feature space, which is not limited to single biometrics nor to the number of dimensions. While the system is capable of handling large number of feature vectors, it makes it also capable of learning complex biometric patters faster using neural network learner.

2.2. Chaotic Neural Networks.

Having the vector of weights from the candidate clusters, the next step in our methodology is defining an energy model for the associative memory to learn the data patterns. As it will be shown in Section 2.4, the inputs of the neural network are the obtained candidate vectors from the dimensionality reduction phase. The candidate vectors are generated from the original vectors of images each of which consists of a set of grayscale pixels.

The nature of associative network is based on minimizing the energy function assigned to the neural network. The energy function simply shows the distance of the stored pattern to the introduced pattern. The lower the energy function gets the more stable the network is. On the other side, patterns are stored as the weights between pairs of neurons. By other means when two values are changing with a high correlation, the weights between the neurons corresponding to those values get higher.

The benefit is the learner system that converges the given set of vectors to the stored pattern. In order to learn the patterns, the chaotic dynamics of single neuron of noise chaotic neural is described as follows:

$$x_{ij}(t) = \frac{1}{1 + e^{-y_{jk}(t)/\varepsilon}},$$

$$y_{jk}(t+1) = k y_{jk}(t) + \alpha \left\{ \sum_{i=1, i \neq j}^{N} \sum_{l=1, l \neq k}^{M} w_{jkil} x_{jk}(t) + I_{ij} \right\} \quad (1)$$
$$- z(t)\left(x_{jk}(t) - I_0\right) + n(t),$$

where $z(t+1) = (1 - \beta_1)z(t)$ and $n(t+1) = (1 - \beta_2)n(t)$.

Here, x_{jk} and y_{jk} are outputs and inputs of neuron jk, respectively, and w_{jkil} is the weight of the connection between neurons jk and il. K is the damping factor, I_{ij} is the input bias of neuron ij, and β_1 and β_1 are damping factors of neural self-coupling and stochastic noise. α is a positive scaling factor, ε is steepness parameter of the output function, $n(t)$ is the random injected noise, and I_0 is the initial value which controls the chaotic behavior. The single-neuron dynamics of the noisy chaotic neural network correspond and are controlled by different values of I_0. In our experiments, the chaotic phase can be reached at $I_0 = 0.3$, which has been used to inject chaotic noise into the network.

In the next sections, we consider several dimensionality reduction methods for facial biometric and will compare the resulting biometric verification system performance against other popular approaches.

2.3. Knowledge-Based Methods.

Knowledge-based facial recognition methods are rule-based methods that utilize the knowledge of geometry of human face structure and expected position and symmetry of facial elements (i.e., eyes). To finely adjust the position of each face image of the database, we use the knowledge-based method augmented with the skin tone detection to first identify the face. The knowledge-based methods are relying on the simple set of rules. For example, every face has symmetric features (eyes), and the color of the eyes area is normally darker compared to the other facial areas (i.e., forehead, cheeks). By using these rules, we identify facial areas. The main challenge for this category of methods is to find a proper set of rules. If the rules set are too general, then the false acceptance rate increases dramatically while specific types of rules may result in high false rejection rate due to facial gestures and artifacts.

By using the color tone, we overcame many problems in our application. The color tone is very simple to use while very effective for normalized pictures. There are different approaches to use the color tone. Researchers have proposed to use both RGB and HSV color models to recognize the skin area of the image. We have used the same parameters to detect the face area while a postdetection face was required in some of the images to detect the face area more accurately. Figure 4 shows an example of detection, normalization, and selection of the area of interest. The parameters are set according to the following criteria:

$$0.4 \le r \le 0.6, \quad 0.22 \le g \le 0.33, \quad r > g > (1 - r)/2, \quad (2)$$

$$0 \le H \le 0.2, \quad 0.3 \le S \le 0.7, \quad 0.22 \le V \le 0.8. \quad (3)$$

Since each new image contains a large number of pixels ($256 * 256$ in case of FERET database), we need to remove the redundant or correlated pixels which are our features but will not be important for the final learning pattern. For example, the background of the images in the database should not be considered in the final learning machine. This is illustrated in Figure 5 where the background is a smooth pattern and face recognition phase should ignore that area.

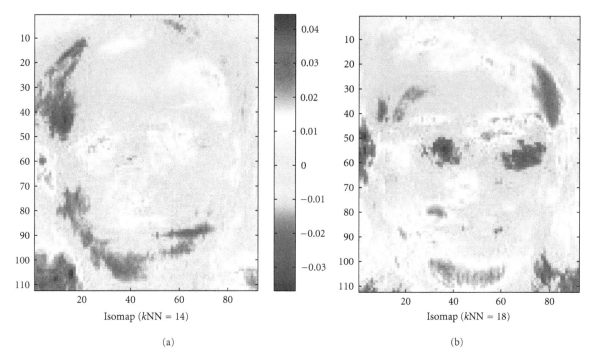

Isomap (kNN = 14)

(a)

Isomap (kNN = 18)

(b)

FIGURE 7: Reconstructed images based on the first two eigenvectors.

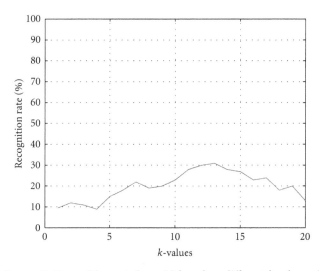

FIGURE 8: Recognition rate (*oy* axis) based on different k-values of isomap (*ox* axis).

We propose to use a specialized subspace clustering method to remove the redundant features and gain a lower-dimensional subspace where the new features show less correlation and are more meaningful and easier to use in the verification process.

2.4. Subspace Clustering Method. Clustering aims at dividing datasets into subsets (clusters), where objects in the same subset are similar to each other with respect to a given similarity measure, whereas objects in different clusters are dissimilar [12]. There are many applications of cluster analysis in biometric, GIS, and oil and gas fields.

When clustering high-dimensional data of biometric features, we face a variety of problems [12]. The presence of irrelevant features or of correlations among subsets of features heavily influences the appearance of clusters in the full-dimensional space. The main challenge for clustering here is that different subsets of features are relevant to different clusters, that is, the objects cluster in subspaces of the data space but the subspaces of the clusters may vary. Additionally, different correlations among the attributes may be relevant for different clusters. This assumption implies that different biometric features or a different correlation of biometric features may be relevant for varying clusters the local feature relevance or local feature correlation.

A common way to overcome problems of high-dimensional data spaces where several features are correlated or only some features are relevant is to perform feature selection before performing any other data mining task. Due to the problem of local feature relevance and local feature correlation, usually no global feature selection can be applied to overcome the challenges of clustering high-dimensional biometric data.

Instead of a global approach to feature selection, we propose to use a local approach accounting for the local feature relevance and/or local feature correlation problems. Since traditional methods, like feature selection, dimensionality reduction, and conventional clustering, do not solve the previously sketched problems, novel methods need to integrate feature analysis into the clustering process more tightly.

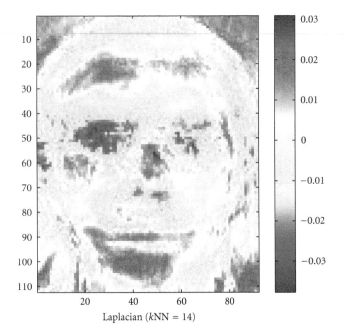

Laplacian (kNN = 14)

(a)

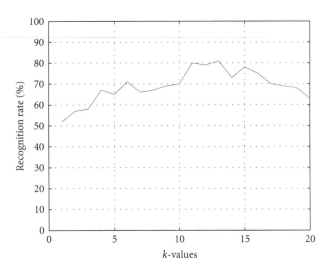

FIGURE 10: Recognition rate (*oy* axis) for different *k*-values of Laplacian (*ox* axis).

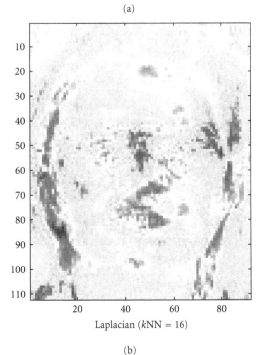

Laplacian (kNN = 16)

(b)

FIGURE 9: Reconstructed images based on the first two eigenvectors.

The main idea of the method is to project d-dimensional vector of biometric feature points in the parameter space represented through a $(d - 1)$-dimensional hyperplane. The algorithm for projecting biometric feature points is adapted from [13]. In order to detect those linear hyperplanes in the data space, the task is to search for points in the parameter space where many sinusoidal curves intersect. Since computing all possibly interesting intersection points is too expensive, we discretize the parameter space by some grid and search for grid cells with which many sinusoidal curves

intersect. For that purpose, for each grid cell the number of intersecting sinusoidal curves is aggregated. Below, this interpretation is discussed in more detail.

Since higher dimensions cannot be depicted easily, we have chosen 3 pixels of the image of a single person to explain the process which forms a 3D vector (see Figure 4). Normally, the intensity value of a pixel in RGB space is a value between 0 and 255. We normalize this value to the range of 0 to 1. Later we incorporate other features and aim to normalize all the vectors to the scale. This preserves the intercorrelation of pixels within a single image. However, we can make a global correlation map by creating vector from the same pixels of different images. The new scheme is shown in Figure 6.

As it has been shown in Figure 5, the first step in processing the input image is to create the input vectors of the subspace clustering method. The vectors are created based on grouping same pixels from all the input images, for example, if we have 100 images, each of which featuring 256 pixels, the output of the grouping phase is 256 vectors of 100 dimensions each. By utilizing such a method, the relation between the points is preserved and they could be grouped as a single class if they show high correspondence (as correlation in PCA). Next, using the parameterization functions, the points are translated into sinusoidal curves. The intersection of the curves would be the passing plane from the points. The plain is considered as a class or cluster.

With the proposed concepts, one can transform the original subspace clustering problem (in data space) into a grid-based clustering problem (in parameter space) [12]. More details on how to apply this method to biometric research domain can be found in [11].

3. Exploring Dimensionality: Reduction

In this section we look at the dimensionality reduction methods to compare their performance against the proposed system.

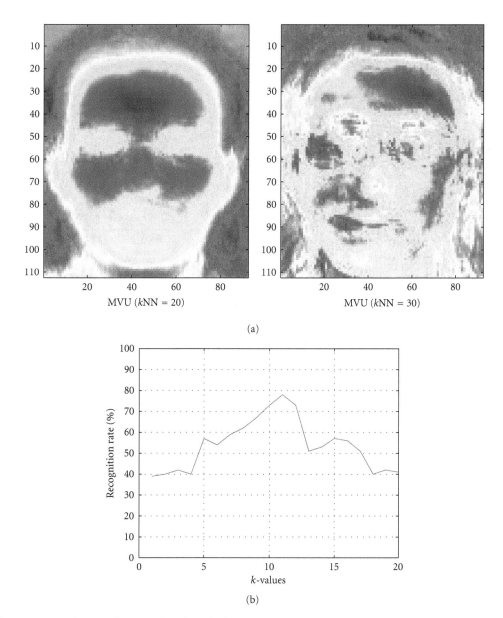

FIGURE 11: (a) Reconstructed images for MVU based on the first two eigenvectors. (b) Recognition rates for different k-values of MVU.

3.1. Isomap. The Isomap algorithm is designed based on the Floyd-Warshall algorithm and classic multidimensional scaling [14]. The Isomap method performs the same while considering the neighbors only. The kernel matrix can be used to show the distance of Isomap. The common form of geodesic distance matrix is as follows:

$$k = \frac{1}{2} \, h D^2 H, \qquad (4)$$

where D^2 is the square of the geodesic distance matrix and H is matrix:

$$H = I_n - \frac{1}{n} e_N e_N^T. \qquad (5)$$

In order to choose best k nearest neighbors (kNN) for the Isomap method we have tried different kNN values for the pixels of the original space. Based on these values we have reconstructed the images based on the first two eigenvectors of the highest eigenvalues as it can be seen in Figure 7.

Our next task was to choose the proper number of eigenvectors for the recognition purpose. Experimentally, we found out that for the first 30 eigenvectors (sorted based on the corresponding eigenvalues) the correlation between the values is low, which makes these eigenvectors highly useful in the recognition phase. The recognition rate of Isomap for different k-values is shown in the following chart.

We can see that the best recognition rate is recorded for kNN values in the range from 12 to 14 and is below 40%.

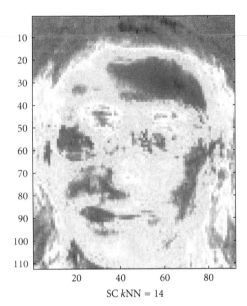

SC kNN = 14

FIGURE 12: Reconstructed image based on the first two eigenvectors for SC.

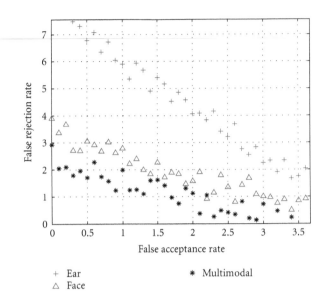

+ Ear   * Multimodal
△ Face

FIGURE 14: FAR-FRR graphs for multimodal biometric system.

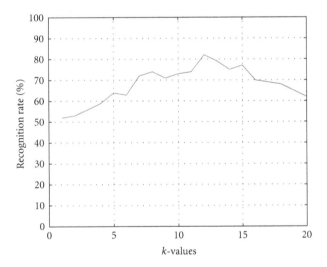

FIGURE 13: Recognition rate for different k-values for the proposed subspace clustering method.

This is clearly not an acceptable result for any security system. Thus, we move to examine another method.

3.2. Laplacian Eigenmaps. The Laplacian eigenmaps method is based on using spectral approach to reduce dimensionality [15]. The Laplacian eigenmaps method also assumes that important data is located on a lower-dimensional manifold in the high dimension space. The Laplacian eigenmaps method also utilizes the k nearest neighbor method. However, instead of creating the weight matrix, in the Laplacian Eigenmaps method a graph is produced where each two vertices are connected if they are considered as neighbors. The graph is considered as a lower-dimensional manifold in the original high-dimensional space.

Similar to Isomap, in order to choose best k nearest neighbors for the Laplacian method, we have tried different k-NN values for the pixels of the original space (Figure 9). Based on these values, we have reconstructed the images based on the first two eigenvectors of the highest eigenvalues as it can be seen in Figure 8.

The recognition rate of the Laplacian for different k-values is shown in the following chart in Figure 10.

We can note recognition significantly higher than in the Isomap method and the range of values where it reaches its maximum potential of 80% is for k values between 12 and 16.

3.3. Maximum Variance Unfolding. The final alternative to the subspace clustering method is maximum variance unfolding (MVU). MVU maps the data of high-dimensional space into a lower-dimensional space, preserving the distances between neighbor points [16]. MVU has to create the neighborhood graph G first. In G each data point is connected to its k nearest neighbors. MVU tries to maximize the square Euclidean distances between all of the points or solves an optimization problem.

Using a singular value decomposition and by solving K of the SDP, we can obtain the low-dimensional data representation Y.

The recognition rate of MVU for different k-values is shown in Figure 11. The method outperforms Isomap but has a higher volatility than Laplacian method, ranging from 38% to 78% recognition rate with the best rates achieved around $k = 11$ values. It is a close contender to Laplacian but cannot outperform it.

As it can be seen above, the results are reduced dimensions (the unnecessary details of each image have been removed). This makes the learning system able to process the data with less effort and the recognition rate gets higher due to the simpler nature of the system.

3.4. Subspace Clustering Method Performance. Here, we provide the comparison of our proposed subspace clustering (SC) method for dimensionality reduction against previously described Isomap, Laplacian, and LLE methods. The LLE method is not suitable for biometric security application due to highly inconsistent performance. The recognition rate of Isomap is not high enough to make the method useful in any commercial application. The results of the Laplacian method (the best method so far among all compared for the given database FERET) are thus the best so far. Now let us look at the performance of the proposed subspace clustering method. Figure 12 shows the resulted reconstructed image based on subspace clustering with kNN value of 14. Figure 13 presents recognition rates obtained for different *k*-values. The range of values with high recognition rate is from 10 to 16, and the recognition rates are higher than those of Laplacian or MVU method. It significantly outperforms the Isomap method as well. Figure 14 shows overall performance of resulting multi-modal system for both face and ear biometrics. As it can be seen, it outperforms single biometric system in FAR/FRR rates.

4. Conclusions

In this paper, we argued that the chaotic neural network approach for learning biometric patterns is a powerful tool to improve recognition rate of biometric system. We have discussed a biometric system based on a recently devised approach for feature dimension reduction on an example of face recognition system. We compared and contrasted the proposed methodology against other dimensionality reduction methods such as isomap, Laplacian Eigenmap, and MVU. The experimental results show a better accuracy rate for the biometric system tested on FERET facial database among all tested methods. Further improvement of recognition can be obtained by combining facial image biometrics with other biometric traits such as ear biometric.

Acknowledgments

The authors would like to acknowledge support from National Sciences and Engineering Research Council of Canada, and University of Calgary, Canada, for partial support of this project. They are also grateful for valuable comments from reviewers and for assistance with paper revisions from Advances in Artificial Intelligence Journal Editorial members and staff.

References

[1] S. T. Roweis and L. K. Saul, "Nonlinear dimensionality reduction by locally linear embedding," *Science*, vol. 290, no. 5500, pp. 2323–2326, 2000.

[2] Y. Gao and M. K. H. Leung, "Face recognition using line edge map," *IEEE Transactions on Pattern Analysis and Machine Intelligence*, vol. 24, no. 6, pp. 764–779, 2002.

[3] L. Wiskott, J.-M. Fellous, N. Krüger, and C. D. Von Malsburg, "Face recognition by elastic bunch graph matching," *IEEE Transactions on Pattern Analysis and Machine Intelligence*, vol. 19, no. 7, pp. 775–779, 1997.

[4] P. J. Phillips, "Support vector machines applied to face recognition," in *Proceedings of Advances in Neural Information Processing Systems*, vol. 11, pp. 113–123, 1998.

[5] M. S. Bartlett, J. R. Movellan, and T. J. Sejnowski, "Face recognition by independent component analysis," *IEEE Transactions on Neural Networks*, vol. 13, no. 6, pp. 1450–1464, 2002.

[6] P. N. Belhumeur, J. P. Hespanha, and D. J. Kriegman, "Eigenfaces vs. fisherfaces: recognition using class specific linear projection," *IEEE Transactions on Pattern Analysis and Machine Intelligence*, vol. 19, no. 7, pp. 711–720, 1997.

[7] K. I. Kim, K. Jung, and H. J. Kim, "Face recognition using kernel principal component analysis," *IEEE Signal Processing Letters*, vol. 9, no. 2, pp. 40–42, 2002.

[8] G. Baudat and F. Anouar, "Generalized discriminant analysis using a kernel approach," *Neural Computation*, vol. 12, no. 10, pp. 2385–2404, 2000.

[9] S. Z. Li and J. Lu, "Face recognition using the nearest feature line method," *IEEE Transactions on Neural Networks*, vol. 10, no. 2, pp. 439–443, 1999.

[10] P. P. Paul, M. M. Monwar, M. L. Gavrilova, and P. S. P. Wang, "Rotation invariant multiview face detection using skin color regressive model and support vector regression," *International Journal of Pattern Recognition and Artificial Intelligence*, vol. 24, no. 8, pp. 1261–1280, 2010.

[11] M. L. Gavrilova and K. Ahmadian, "Dealing with biometric multi-dimensionality through chaotic neural network methodology," *International Journal of Information Technology and Management*, vol. 11, no. 1-2, pp. 18–34, 2012.

[12] H.-P. Kriegel, P. Kröger, and A. Zimek, "Clustering high-dimensional data: a survey on subspace clustering, pattern-based clustering, and correlation clustering," *ACM Transactions on Knowledge Discovery from Data*, vol. 3, no. 1, pp. 1–58, 2009.

[13] E. Achtert, C. Böhm, J. David, P. Kröger, and A. Zimek, "Robust clustering in arbitrarily oriented subspaces," in *Proceedings of the 8th SIAM International Conference on Data Mining (SDM '08)*, pp. 763–774, Atlanta, Ga, USA, 2008.

[14] W. N. Anderson Jr. and T. D. Morley, "Eigenvalues of the Laplacian of a graph," *Linear and Multilinear Algebra*, vol. 18, pp. 141–145, 1985.

[15] M. Belkin and P. Niyogi, "Laplacian eigenmaps and spectral techniques for embedding and clustering," in *Proceedings of Advances in Neural Information Processing Systems*, vol. 14, pp. 1–17, 2002.

[16] K. Q. Weinberger and L. K. Saul, "Unsupervised learning of image manifolds by semidefinite programming," *International Journal of Computer Vision*, vol. 70, no. 1, pp. 77–90, 2006.

3

Development of Robots with Soft Sensor Flesh for Achieving Close Interaction Behavior

Tomoaki Yoshikai, Marika Hayashi, Yui Ishizaka, Hiroko Fukushima, Asuka Kadowaki, Takashi Sagisaka, Kazuya Kobayashi, Iori Kumagai, and Masayuki Inaba

Department of Mechano-Informatics, The University of Tokyo, 7-3-1 Hongo, Bunkyo-ku, Tokyo 113-8656, Japan

Correspondence should be addressed to Tomoaki Yoshikai, yoshikai@jsk.t.u-tokyo.ac.jp

Academic Editor: Michele Folgheraiter

In order to achieve robots' working around humans, safe contacts against objects, humans, and environments with broad area of their body should be allowed. Furthermore, it is desirable to actively use those contacts for achieving tasks. Considering that, many practical applications will be realized by whole-body close interaction of many contacts with others. Therefore, robots are strongly expected to achieve whole-body interaction behavior with objects around them. Recently, it becomes possible to construct whole-body tactile sensor network by the advancement of research for tactile sensing system. Using such tactile sensors, some research groups have developed robots with whole-body tactile sensing exterior. However, their basic strategy is making a distributed 1-axis tactile sensor network covered with soft thin material. Those are not sufficient for achieving close interaction and detecting complicated contact changes. Therefore, we propose "Soft Sensor Flesh." Basic idea of "Soft Sensor Flesh" is constructing robots' exterior with soft and thick foam with many sensor elements including multiaxis tactile sensors. In this paper, a constructing method for the robot systems with such soft sensor flesh is argued. Also, we develop some prototypes of soft sensor flesh and verify the feasibility of the proposed idea by actual behavior experiments.

1. Introduction

In order to achieve robots working around humans, it is indispensable for such robots to have ability to contact safely against objects, humans, and environments with broad area of their body.

Many practical applications, such as nursing care or carrying a number of stuffs using whole upper body, include whole-body close interaction with humans or objects. Robots around humans should utilize soft contacts actively as humans or other animals do.

Historically, robotics research for interacting with objects or humans started from strict modeling of the contacts by limiting the contact points only at their end effectors. Of course, this methodology achieve a certain result. But, it is difficult to achieves whole-body interaction with objects or humans like other animals or humans by an extension of this methodology. As the development of tactile sensing system

proceeds [1, 2], it becomes possible to construct whole-body tactile sensor network for robots. Using such tactile sensors, some research groups have developed robots with whole-body tactile sensing exterior [3–8]. Although there are some differences on how to achieve distributed tactile sensor exterior among them, their basic strategy is that they distribute many small 1-axis force/pressure sensors which detect normal direction force, and they are covered with thin soft material, which can be said as "skin." However, various types of contacts, not limited to just a push, can be occurred during whole-body close interaction. For detecting such complicated contacts, multiaxis force or deformation sensing of the exterior is necessary. From that point of view, Iwata et al. proposed a whole-body tactile sensor cover which detects both position and multiaxis force vector applied on the sensor cover [9]. However, the module of their sensor cover which can detect both force position and vector is relatively large, and local multiaxis deformation of the soft exterior cannot be detected by their method. Also, for constructing soft tactile sensor exterior with detecting ability for local multiaxis deformation, sensor element itself should be soft and small. Although there are some studies about multiaxis tactile sensors embedded inside soft materials [10–12], they are in the developmental stage and it is difficult to use them for constructing whole-body tactile sensor exterior.

In this paper, we propose "Soft Sensor Flesh," a new construction method for whole-body tactile sensor system. Human body have thick flesh structure embedded with many sensor elements in different depths, not the thin skin with distributed sensors. Basic idea of "Soft Sensor Flesh" resembles such human structure, that is, constructing robots' exterior with soft and thick foam, inside which many tactile sensor elements including multiaxis deformation detectable sensors are embedded. For achieving this goal, not only the combination of existing sensors, but also new soft tactile sensors are necessary. Therefore, we also propose some soft tactile sensors as core functionality of "Soft Sensor Flesh".

In the following sections, a constructing method for the robot systems with such soft sensor flesh is argued from both hardware and software aspects. Also, we develop some prototypes and verify the feasibility of the proposed ideas by actual behavior experiments. This paper is organized as follows: requirements for achieving soft sensor flesh is argued in Section 2. Sections 3 and 4 are basics of the soft sensor flesh. In Section 3, basic structure and construction method for soft sensor flesh is proposed, and the experimental results from the first generation of our soft sensor flesh is discussed. In Section 4, computer simulation model for soft sensor flesh is described. Next, Sections 5 and 6 propose improved soft sensor flesh: construction method for soft sensor flesh with integral molded sensors is proposed in Section 5, and new soft multiaxis deformation sensor is proposed in Section 6. Then, Sections 7 and 8 argue other possibilities for soft sensor flesh. In Section 7, soft sensor flesh for self-protective behaviors is argued. In Section 8, additional soft tactile sensors which compensate the contact sensing ability of the basic soft sensor flesh is proposed. Lastly, this paper is concluded in Section 9.

2. Close Interaction Behavior by Robots with Soft Sensor Flesh

By having soft contacts with humans or objects and detecting those contact states at the same time without any limitation of touched place, robots can conduct close interaction behavior safely. Humans and animals can propagate force effectively to other objects with the broad region of their body by closely interacting with those objects. Implementing such close interaction behavior for robots opens a gate to develop many practical applications: nursing care robots which hold up patients, robots carrying large stuffs during move, or shopping assistant robots holding some packages under its arm, and so forth. On the other hand, soft physical interaction can make a great influence on human's mind. For constructing good communication, robots are expected to give humans more cuddles. Studying such robots is one way to

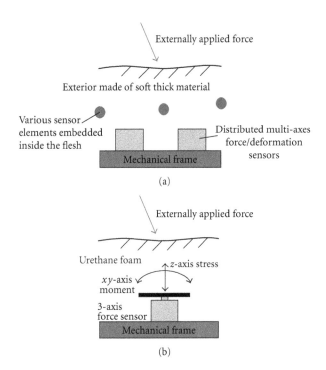

FIGURE 1: Basic idea of "Soft Sensor Flesh". (a) basic structure of soft sensor flesh, (b) 1st prototype of soft sensor flesh.

achieve partner robots necessary in aging society with fewer children, such as baby sitting robots or elderly care robots.

In order to construct robots which can achieve such close interaction behavior, at least following requirements should be met.

(i) Whole-body region is covered by soft exterior like humans or animals for being touched anywhere on the body.

(ii) Tactile sensors detecting various contact states on real time are distributed all over the body.

(iii) Multiaxis force/deformation sensing is done for detecting contact state changes caused by the change of applied force even when the touched places do not change so much during close contact states.

Considering those points, hardware and software system of the "Soft Sensor Flesh" is constructed. In the following sections, basic idea and the application of the robots with soft sensor flesh is argued. Firstly, basic idea of "Soft Sensor Flesh" and its construction method is proposed in Section 3.

3. Basic Structure of "Soft Sensor Flesh"

The basic idea of "Soft Sensor Flesh" is shown in Figure 1(a). Mechanical frame of the robot is covered with soft thick material, and multiaxis force/deformation sensor is embedded deeply inside the exterior. Also, other various sensors are molded and placed in the middle depth of the exterior. Figure 1(b) shows the schematic of our first prototype of the soft sensor flesh. Here, commercially available 3-axis force/torque sensor is fixed to the mechanical frame of the

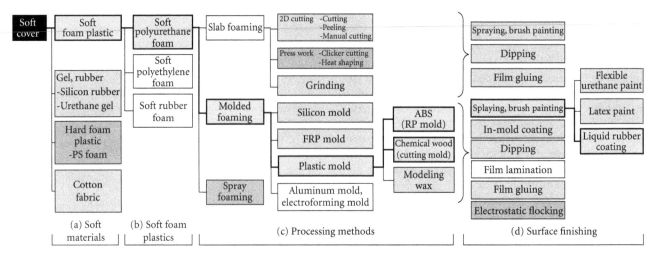

FIGURE 2: Possible soft materials and processing methods for soft sensor flesh.

robot, and the externally applied force including shear component is propagated through thick layer of urethane foam. Selection of the soft thick material is one important point for constructing soft sensor flesh. The material of the exterior should be easily customizable for studying many variations of the construction method of soft sensor flesh. Also, it should be light enough for covering whole-body region of the robot. Considering those requirements, we have tested many materials (Figure 2). In Figure 2, blue boxes indicate conclusive methods. Green boxes indicate methods which we have tested ever. The gray boxes indicate methods which we have not tested. Lastly, the white boxes indicate methods which we have determined that test production is impossible.

Among possible soft materials shown in Figure 2 ((a) Soft Materials), we selected foam plastic. Compositive materials used for animatronic works such as rubber (exterior) and soft foam (interior) were ignored in this research, because they require technical manual skill for creating robot exterior by ourselves. Also, we have made prototypes of costume for robots with cotton and stretchable fabric before. But, these choices are rejected because of the difficulty in making a precise copy of 3D CAD model. Specific gravity of silicone rubber (Shin-Etsu Chemical Co., Ltd.) and urethane gel (Exseal Corporation) is higher (about 1.0) than that of foam plastic (about 0.05–0.1). Degrees of heat conductivity of silicone rubber and urethane gel are higher (about 0.2–0.4 W/mK) than that of foam plastic (about 0.02–0.07 W/mK). In order to construct whole-body exterior with enough thickness to embed various types of tactile sensors inside, both weight and heat problem should be considered. Here, we place much value on reducing total weight. Thus, we decided to use soft foam plastic with concern to heat problem. Next, among soft foam plastics ((b) soft foam plastics), representative examples of soft foam plastics are made of polyurethane, polyethylene, and rubber. Polyethylene foam and rubber foam are produced by kneading base compound and bloating agent and then heating them, which are relatively difficult to produce experimentally. Some kinds of soft polyurethane foam can be molded by simply mixing base compound and curing

agent at room temperature. Also cure time is not long (several minutes). Therefore we decided to use soft polyurethane foam. For processing methods ((c) processing methods), molding method is adopted. In order to give form to soft polyurethane foam, there are three methods. First method is cutting, grinding, and press work of slab foam, second method is molding, and third method is spray foaming. Spray foaming does not require time-consuming measuring and mixing process. However, commercially available spray foaming polyurethane foam is not suitable for our application in hardness and shape forming. Soft polyurethane foam deteriorates due to ultraviolet rays, mechanical friction, and heat. Deteriorated foam turns yellow then crumbs. This crumbing problem was observed more often on slab foam than on molded foam, which has skin layer on the surface. In consequence, we employed molding method. Next, finishing surface of the exterior ((d) surface finishing) should be considered for avoiding significant deterioration of the surface. In-mold coating and film laminating have fine texture and durability capacity. But, these methods require precise temperature and pressure management and expensive mold. Thus, we employed painting method, especially liquid rubber for coating, taking care of surface appearance and odor. Both molded foam and paint film contract with curing. Therefore it is necessary to design molds larger in advance. We measured its shrink ratio (about 1.5%) experimentally. Lastly, molded foam is covered by stretchable cloth for achieving comfortable contacts against humans.

In Figure 3, our first prototype of a humanoid robot with soft sensor flesh is shown. This robot is named "macra" [13], and "macra" is a small humanoid which has soft urethane foam exterior and embedded 3-axis force/torque sensors. The height is about 700 mm, and the weight is about 7.5 kg. Its internal mechanical frame has 22 DOFs. Some parts of the internal frame and circuit boards for driving actuators are built using HOAP-1 manufactured by Fujitsu Automation Ltd. [14]. As embedded tactile sensors, 49 small 3-axis force/torque sensors (PFS, manufactured by Nitta corporation) are used. Since they are embedded in

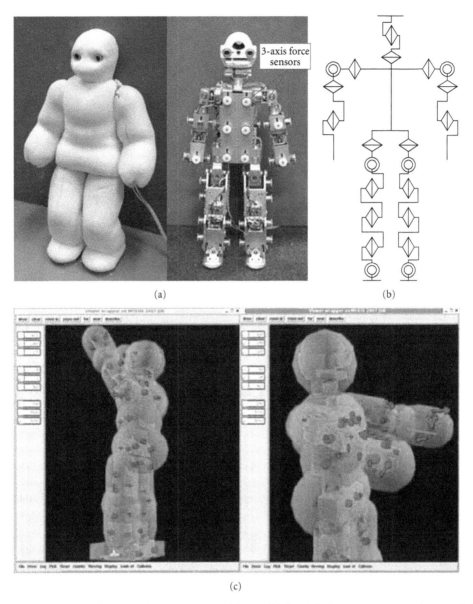

(a)

(b)

(c)

FIGURE 3: "macra": a humanoid with soft sensor flesh. (a) Photos of "macra," left: whole-body image covered with soft flesh, right: internal mechanical frame. (b) An arrangement of DOFs. (c) 3-axis force sensor outputs drawn on robot's geometrical model.

the soft urethane foam and can detect three-dimensional force directions, deformation forces applied to the soft exterior can be calculated by the interpolation of the distributed force sensors. Therefore whole-body contacts of macra can be detected as a bundle of the flow of the applied forces. Figure 3(c) shows some examples of macra's sensing abilities. The sensor output vectors are illustrated as red arrows from corresponding sensors in the robot's geometrical model, and 3D force directions can be seen.

In Figure 4, outputs of one 3-axis force/torque sensor during close interaction behavior are shown. On Figure 4(a) the output of a 3-axis force/torque sensor which is located on front body of the robot is shown. It shows that there is enough difference from each other to be detected separately while a human touches in a various manner. Figure 4(b)

shows an application case. Softness of the exterior enables the robot to hold a bundle of objects. Soft exterior deforms and fits the objects. If a person tries to take the objects away from the robot, output of the sensor at right forearm in x-y direction changes. In this case, the person pulled the bundle of objects up and down (Figure 4(b)).

In Figures 5 and 6, tactile sensor output changes during close interaction behavior are drawn on a geometrical model of the robot. In the geometrical model, 3D force vector is expressed as white arrows. In Figure 5, it is confirmed that a human applies not only pushing force, but also shear force to the robot's torso. Also, Figure 6 shows sensor output changes during self-collision.

In this section, basic structure of "Soft Sensor Flesh" is proposed and the idea is confirmed by the developed first

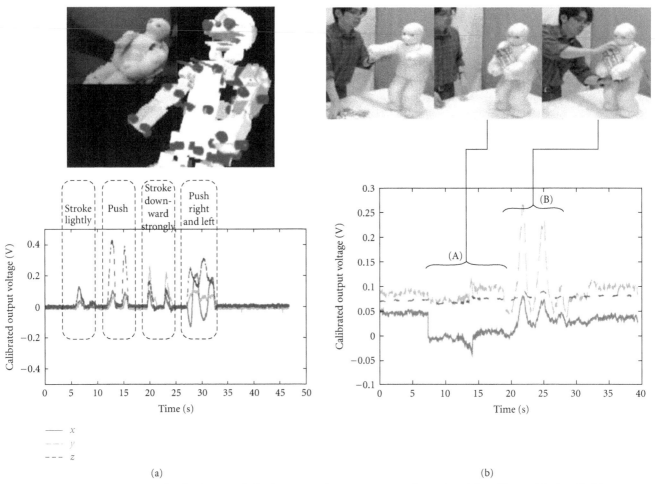

(a)   (b)

FIGURE 4: Output example of soft sensor flesh of macra: various contacts on a front chest (a); pulling grabbed stuffs (b).

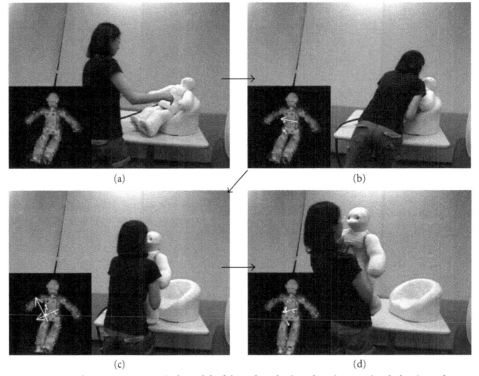

(a)   (b)

(c)   (d)

FIGURE 5: Tactile sensor outputs drawn on geometrical model of the robot during close interaction behavior: a human holds up macra.

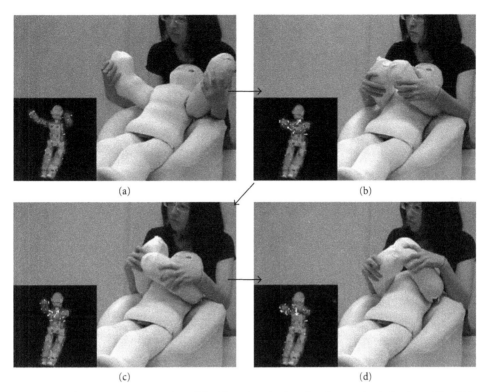

FIGURE 6: Tactile sensor outputs drawn on geometrical model of the robot during close interaction behavior: self-collision occurred between both arms.

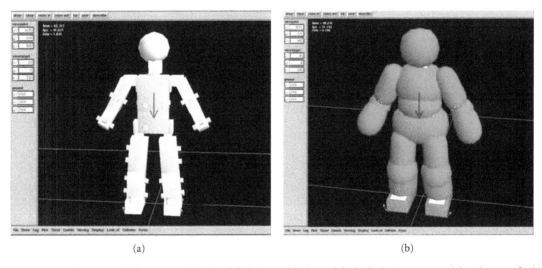

FIGURE 7: Simulation model for macra ((a) simplified internal link model; (b) link structure model with outer flesh).

prototype. In the next section, how to emulate the tactile sensor outputs of this soft sensor flesh in computer simulation is argued.

4. Computer Simulation Model of Soft Sensor Flesh

In order to test various behaviors, acquiring behaviors by evolutionary methods such as GA (genetic algorithm) is one good way. In this section, implementation of a computer

simulation model of soft sensor flesh for acquiring whole-body contact behavior using GA is described [15]. Here, robot programming environment EusDyna [16], which integrates robot motion programming environment and dynamics simulator, is used. In Figure 7, approximate model for macra in EusDyna is shown. In the simplified link model at Figure 7(a), yellow boxes attached to the links indicate 3-axis force/torque sensors. Red arrow and orange arrows show the direction of gravity and contact forces between soles and ground. Figure 7(b) shows a model with flesh. Each flesh

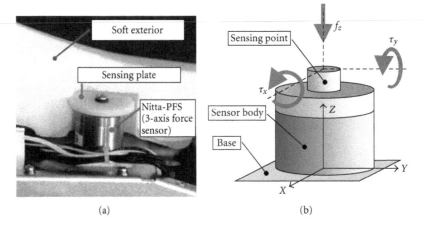

FIGURE 8: Tactile sensor used in macra ((a) implementation on the robot; (b) sensor schematic).

models are approximately constructed by combining spheres, rectangular solids, and capsules (cylindrical structures of half spheres at both ends) and attached to corresponding links. The weights of those flesh models are decided by the actual measurement of the macra's flesh parts. To express flesh viscosity and elasticity, those flesh models are allowed to intersect with each other to some extent.

Since all sensing points are embedded in the soft flesh, it is not enough to simulate tactile sensing ability with dynamics models alone. In order to emulate sensor outputs in a real environment, flesh and sensor properties actually used in macra should be considered in the simulation model. In Figure 8, tactile sensor used in macra is shown. As shown in Figure 8(a), 3-axis force/torque sensors (PFS) are fixed to the internal frame. A sensing plate is used for broadening sensing area. Figure 8(b) shows the schematic of the sensor. This 3-axis force/torque sensor detects τ_x, τ_y (torques against horizontal axes), and f_z (perpendicular force against the plane at which the sensor is fixed). Here, only f_z is considered for modeling this sensor to simplify the model. From the dynamics simulator, contact forces at fixed contact points on the surface of soft exterior are given. To emulate actual sensor outputs, those contact forces should be converted to the outputs of the distributed 3-axis force sensors. Sensor and flesh properties are modeled for conversion.

As a sensor property, force-voltage characteristics are modeled as a linear function. When they are expressed as in (1), whereas kgf/V is gain, bs kgf is offset, and ns kgf is noise, the first two parameters are decided by actually measuring the macra's force sensor with a 1-axis digital force gauge (IMADA DPX-50T). From temporal data recorded on input force and output voltage, parameters that give the least square errors are chosen. Also, Gaussian random number is introduced as a noise model since the sensor noise is not negligible. The amount of noise ns is calculated as a standard variation of 125 samples of sensor output voltage under no load. Because of individual sensor differences, parameters are calculated for each of the 49 sensors used for macra.

$$\text{force} = \text{as} \times \text{voltage} + \text{bs} + \text{ns}. \quad (1)$$

As a flesh property, force propagation of the soft flesh is modeled. Especially, spatial decay is examined here. In order to collect sufficient data, we use a test piece for soft sensor flesh, that has uniform thickness and 1 embedded 3-axis force sensor. The proportional relationship between load F_{in} and transferred force F_{out} is assumed, where F_{in} is the z-axis component of force applied by vertical pressing on the surface, and F_{out} is the z-axis component of force detected by the 3-axis force sensor (see schematic model in Figure 9(a)). The proportional coefficient is expressed as force transmission rate G. The force transmission rate G decays as the distance expands between the contact point of the test piece and the center of 3-axis force sensor. In this case, G is modeled by a 2-dimensional Gaussian of horizontal distance R and vertical distance T. To collect data, three types of flesh with different thicknesses (T is 2, 30, and 60 mm) are prepared, and G is calculated at different horizontal distances. Figure 9(b) shows the distribution of the collected data, where the horizontal axis is horizontal distance R mm, and the vertical axis is force transmission rate G kgf/kgf. In the graph, each line expresses the fitted 2-dimensional Gaussian model from collected data. As a result, (2) is calculated as the force transmission decay model.

$$G(R, T) = 0.887 \cdot \exp\left(-0.0034 \cdot R^2 - 0.00193 \cdot T^2\right). \quad (2)$$

Using this simulation model for soft sensor flesh, we have developed a system for acquiring rolling-over motion based on tactile sensor information. For acquiring sensor-based behavior that closely interacts with the environment, behavior system with tactile sensor information feed-back for the current motion is necessary. An artificial neural network connecting sensor values and joint angle commands achieves such behavior system, and optimized parameters of the neural network for rolling-over motion are acquired using a GA. In behavior acquisition process, evaluation of each trial is repeated in the above simulation environment until fitness improving is converged. The acquired neural network is tested by using macra in a real environment.

In Figure 10, schematic image of the constructed system is shown. While behavior is being acquired, calculation

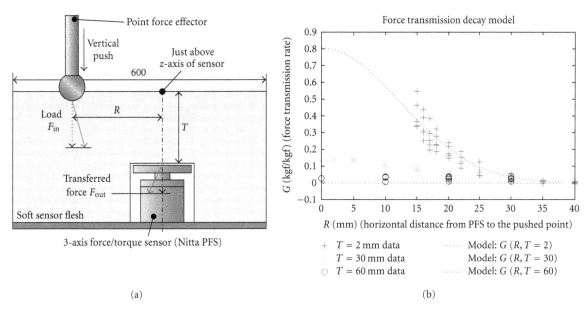

(a)   (b)

FIGURE 9: (a) Schematic image of test piece for measuring spatial decay. (b) Distribution of the measured data for investigating force transmission decay model for soft flesh.

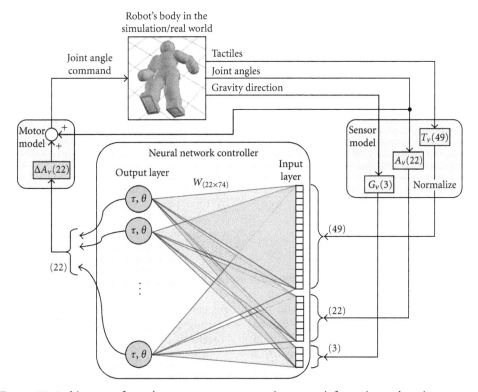

FIGURE 10: Architecture of agent's nervous system connecting sensor information and motion outputs.

is done in the simulation environment. After behavior is acquired, the actual robot body receives joint angle commands from "Motor model" and sends sensor information to "Sensor model." From the real or virtual robot's body, three types of sensor information are sent to "Sensor model" in Figure 10. In "Sensor model", each sensor value is normalized from 0 to 1. As a result, T_v (normalized tactile vector: 49

dimensions, force toward normal direction, that is, z-axis for the sensor), A_v (normalized angle vector: 22 dimensions), and G_v (normalized gravity direction vector: 3 dimensions) are obtained. Normalized signals are aligned and a 74-dimensional sensor vector is input to the neural network controller. Output of the neural network controller is a 22-dimensional vector δA_v, relative changes against the current angle vector. In "Motor model", these changes (values from 0 to 1) are converted to an adequate range from −5 to 5, and added to current angle vector A_v. The updated angle vector is then sent to the robot's body as a joint angle command. Thus, the nervous system having sensory feedbacks to joint angle commands is constructed. Basically, for correctly feeding back sensor inputs, update cycle for the robot's body system should be shorter than that for the nervous system. In this study, update cycle for the simulation world is 25 ms, and that for the nervous system is 50 ms.

In the behavior acquisition phase, a real-coded genetic algorithm is used to search for optimized parameters. However, there is a problem that behavior acquisition phase takes too long because each gene evaluation takes some seconds to minutes in the dynamics simulation environment, and total evaluation time becomes some days. In order to reduce behavior acquisition time, parallel GA system conducted in the PC cluster environment is used here.

During acquisition phase, rolling-over motion is evaluated as follows (see (3)). In the equation, score_j is the score for the jth trail during N times trails in one evaluation. G_x is x-axis components of the direction of gravity at the torso link (the front face of the torso is positive at the x-axis of torso link coordinates). g is the gravity acceleration. Therefore, the score is higher when macra lies on its stomach as soon as possible as a result of the rolling-over motion after starting the behavior from lying on its back. How soon macra turns from the state on its back to the state on its stomach is the indication for the achievement of rolling-over motion in this experiment. Fitness for one evaluation is calculated by the average of the N trials in the evaluation.

$$\text{score}_j = \int_0^T \frac{G_x}{g} dt,$$

$$\text{Fitness} = \sum_{j=1}^N \frac{\text{score}_j}{N}. \tag{3}$$

Figure 11 shows fitness transition during the behavior acquisition phase. The horizontal axis is the generation in GA, and the vertical axis is the fitness. The red solid line is the best fitness in each generation, and the blue dashed line is the average fitness in each generation. Evolution stops after 189 generations, and the best gene in the 189th generation is called the acquired gene. Rolling-over motion is tested using actual macra in the real environment by decoding this acquired gene. Acquired rolling-over motion is shown in Figure 12. Figure 12(a) shows the motion in the simulation environment, and the right shows the real environment. In this experiment, rolling-over motion takes 10 s.

Soft sensor flesh used in Sections 3 and 4 is our first prototype. In the next two sections, improved soft sensor flesh is proposed. Firstly, soft sensor flesh embedded with both 3-axis force/torque sensors and integral molded sensors are presented in Section 5.

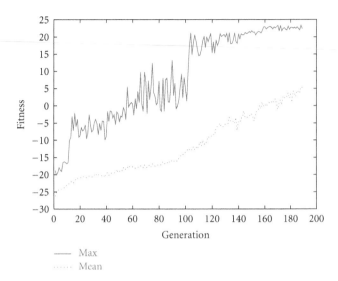

FIGURE 11: Fitness transition through evolution.

5. Soft Sensor Flesh with Integral Molded Sensors

Since soft thick exterior has enough room to embed various sensor elements in the middle of the exterior, sensors can be arranged at intended depth in the flesh as described in the basic idea of soft sensor flesh. For embedding sensor elements, we developed integral molding method for various types of sensors [17]. Required position accuracy for the sensor layout is about the same as the size of sensors and its cost is required to be low since implementation to the whole-body size flesh is considered. As one method that meets these requirements, we propose the method which is shown in Figure 13. At first, embedded sensors are glued at the tip of magnet type attachment (Figure 13(a)). After these attachments are set inside the mold by magnetic attraction, urethane foam is molded (Figure 13(b)). Sensor attachments can be removed easily after completion of the integral molding while sensors are left inside the foam. By adjusting the height of the attachment, intended depth inside flesh can be achieved. Thus integral molded sensors in soft flesh are constructed. In Figure 14, actual molding process for creating the sensor embedded torso flesh for a humanoid "macra" is shown.

Although other methods can be considered for realizing integral molding, each methods have difficulties compared with the proposed method.

(i) If sensors are inserted by cutting foam after the foam are made, precise arrangement of the slits is relatively difficult.

(ii) If sensors are molded after creating the sensor arrangement surface and placing the sensors on it by adding sensor locating mold, glued surfaces become hard. Also, increased number of necessary molds makes the cost higher.

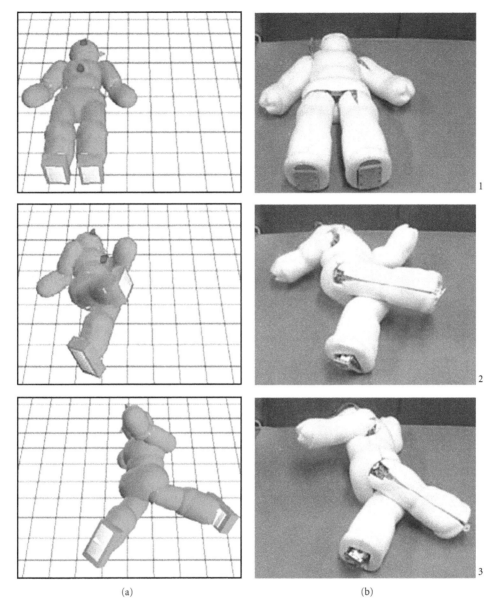

(a)   (b)

FIGURE 12: Acquired rolling-over motion ((a) in simulation environment. (b) in real environment, (1) $t = 0.0$ s, (2) $t = 1.6$ s, and (3) $t = 10.0$ s).

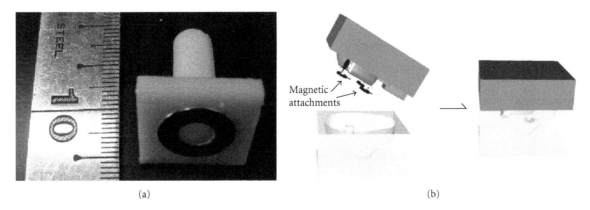

(a)   (b)

FIGURE 13: Integral molding methods for sensors. (a) A photo of magnetic attachment, (b) A method to mold sensors inside foam.

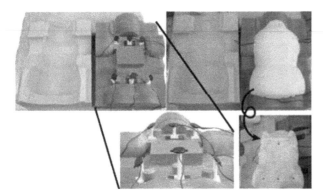

FIGURE 14: Molding process of the sensor embedded torso flesh for a humanoid.

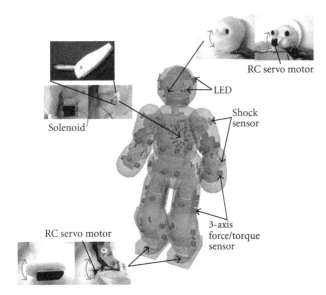

FIGURE 15: Implemented functional elements embedded in soft sensor flesh.

(iii) In the industrially used methods, there are the ones that metal parts and resin parts are molded integrally. However, there is no appropriate method for embedding sensors completely inside the foam.

By the proposed methods, we have developed second prototype of soft sensor flesh for a humanoid "macra" (Figure 15). As complementary sensors used with distributed 3-axis force/torque sensors, shock sensors (PKS1-4A-1, manufactured by Murata Manufacturing Co., Ltd.) are embedded in the flesh. Also, thick flesh can contain many other functional elements other than sensors. As is shown in Figure 15, following elements are embedded: RC servo motors for driving flesh locally, LEDs for displaying some internal states, and solenoids that expresses heart beat which can be felt during interactions in a very close distance.

For confirming sensing ability of the implemented humanoid sensor flesh system, sensor outputs were recorded while a human is holding macra up and then hugged it softly and patted it (Figure 16). In the right column of Figure 16, sensor outputs are drawn on the robot's geometrical model:

outputs for 3-axis force/torque sensors are drawn as red thick arrows, and the ones for shock sensors are drawn as white circles. Here, centers of each white circle are located at the place where each shock sensors are embedded, and the radius for the circles is proportional to the strength calculated from the shock and frequency of the patting action. In the middle row of Figure 16, the person grabbed the robot at the side of its torso and held the robot up. There is a big red arrow in the right column of Figure 16. In this phase, outputs for 3-axis force/torque sensors at the side of its torso became high. Then the person patted the robot. The patting frequency was about 5-6 Hz. In the bottom row of Figure 16, white circles which correspond to shock sensors are big. Outputs for 3-axis force/torque sensors are small since the human hugged "macra" lightly.

In this section, functional elements are embedded in a soft flesh, and sensing and expressing abilities of a robot are improved. However, if the elements inside a flesh is rigid, softness for the exterior can be ruined. In the next section, we propose new soft multiaxis deformation sensor for solving this problem.

6. Improved Soft Sensor Flesh with Soft Multiaxis Deformation Sensors

Even if the robot's exterior is softly made and exterior itself is suit to close contacts with humans, tactile impression can be ruined by the embedded rigid and hard tactile sensing devices. So far, there are many studies about developing soft tactile sensors [10–12]. However, these sensors are still in the developmental stage, and it is not easy to introduce those elements into our robot system. Therefore, we have developed the soft 3D deformable sensing device [18] for giving multiaxis distributed tactile sensation to our robot.

The developed sensor is shown in Figure 17(a). The basic principle of deformation sensing for this sensor is illustrated in Figure 17(b). Sensing part for infrared rays ("Light-receiving box") is molded in the soft urethane cube, and the 3D deformation of the urethane body can be speculated from the changing value of the received infrared ray at the sensing part (influence from outer environment for infrared rays can be reduced by embedding this sensor into thick foam, a "flesh").

In Figure 17, arrows from "Light-receiving box" indicate normal directions for each light-receiving elements. By adopting the method to convert the deformation to the received light strength, the problem of the drift of the sensor output caused by heat, which is a big problem for capacitance-type force sensors that we used in our first prototypes, is solved. The arrangement of the light-receiving elements is very important for distinguishing multiaxis deformation. In some arrangements, received light patterns for different simulations can become almost the same. In our sensor prototype, we assume that these sensor elements are covered by soft thick exterior. Under this assumption, local deformation is not large enough to have almost same value between two different stimulus when the light-receiving elements are attached to the plane of some polygon which

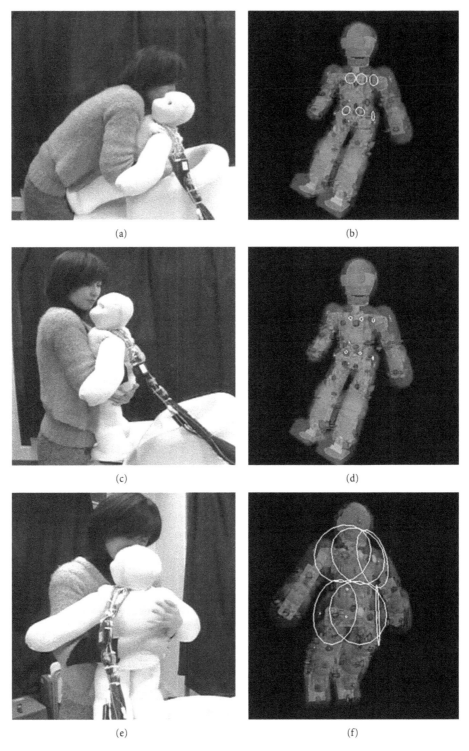

FIGURE 16: Actual sensor results when a human hug the robot softly and pat it.

is referred to "Light-receiving box" in Figure 17 (it is an inclined cubic shape in this case).

In Figure 18, schematics of the internal structure of the developed sensor is shown. Developed sensing element is molded to $20 \times 20 \times 20$ mm cubic shape. Here, cubic shape is adopted for preventing displacement between the urethane exterior and the attached sensor elements. The size of the sensor can be smaller by selecting the mechanically small lightreceiving device (in this implementation, photo-transistor). As shown in Figure 18, 3 infrared LEDs are placed at the bottom of the sensor for ensuring the enough amount of the received light. For speculating 3D deformation of

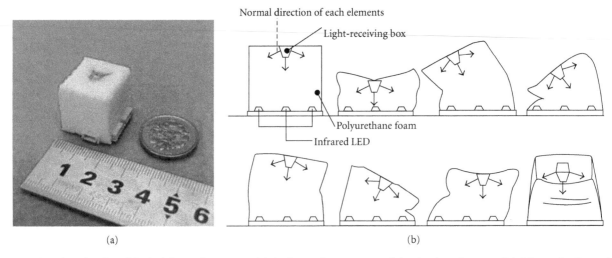

FIGURE 17: Developed soft multiaxis deformation sensor. (a) A photo of a prototype of the developed sensor. (b) Schematics for multiaxis deformation of the developed sensor.

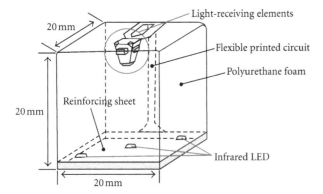

FIGURE 18: Schematics of soft tactile sensor for multiaxis deformation sense.

the sensor unit, light-receiving devices should be arranged as they are mounted on the surfaces facing each other. It is easy to make such structure when those devices is arranged at the top of the sensing element. The circuit board including the light-receiving part is made by FPC. After the light-receiving part is glued to the small cubic-shaped plastic box and the circuit board is fixed to the mold, the urethane sensor cube is molded by integral molding method.

The example of this sensor output is shown in Figure 19. Here, this output is corresponding to the one when the plate put on the sensor is rotated from 0 to 40 deg by 5 deg interval toward direction "A" in the top view of Figure 19. The horizontal axis of the graph expresses the rotated degree in deg, and the vertical axis expresses the output AD value (ADC has 10-bit value and FS is 1024). In the graph, 5 lines corresponds to the sensor outputs for each light-receiving devices (4 devices on the lateral face and 1 device on the bottom face). From the graph, output of the inclined side, that is the receiving device "A", output the discriminable level compared with other 3 receiving devices that are located on the lateral face of the light-receiving cube. Although the

sensor output from bottom device is relatively high against the output of "A", it is not the problem since the bottom output is usually used independently from other 4 devices for deciding the vertical displacement of the light-receiving cube. We confirm similar results when rotating toward other directions. However, they are not shown here because of the space limitation. In the graph, it is confirmed that there is a little hysteresis for this sensor. It is mainly due to the physical characteristics of urethane foam. Although there are some materials which have less hysteresis for molding sensor elements, soft and light property of urethane foam is considered to be more important factor than other property in this paper for achieving whole-body enclosing type soft thick sensor exterior for robots.

Sensitivity and force ranges of this sensor unit can be adjusted to some extent by changing the property of the urethane foam. In our developed prototype, it can detect the applied force from 0 to about 1.4 kgf linearly, and around 1.5 kgf the sensor output reached almost the maximum value.

In Figure 20, a prototype of the sensor flesh is shown. Developed sensor cubes are embedded in the 30 mm thick urethane foam. Here, 9 sensor elements are arranged in about 10 cm × 10 cm area. In Figure 20(b), sensor output is drawn on the geometrical model. 3D deformation is expressed as the incline of the bar arranged at each sensor cube model, and the magnitude for each light-receiving device is expressed as the radius of the drawn circle. As you can see from Figure 20, pinching the sensor flesh prototype makes the 3D deformation of the sensors. Since this sensor is assumed to be embedded in the thick foam and used in the sensor distribution density like this prototype, influence of the leak infrared rays from the adjacent sensor elements can be almost ignored.

As it stands now, accuracy of this sensor is not so high, because assembling and molding process is totally hand-crafted. But the important thing is that discrimination of the natural human-like contact states, not only pushing, but also

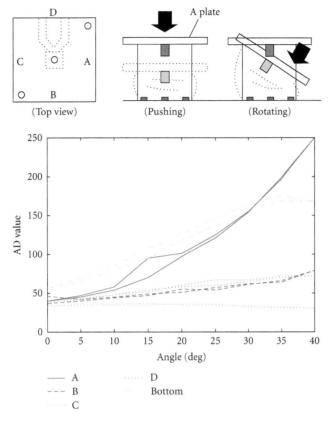

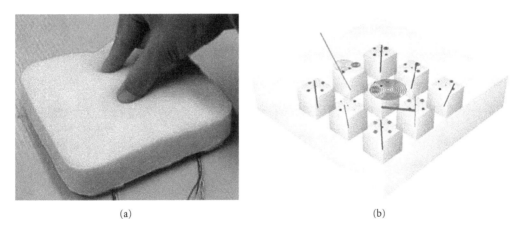

FIGURE 19: Sensor output of the Developed sensor (when rotating toward direction "A").

FIGURE 20: Pinching a prototype of sensor flesh with Two Fingers.

contacts with 3D deformation, such as pinching or twisting, can be possible by this kind of simple structure. Also, easiness to realize the distributed tactile sensors for the actual robot is another key issue. Therefore, each 3D deformable sensor has a microprocessor for A/D conversion, and it can send a signal through SMBus Protocol.

Using this soft 3D deformable sensor elements, we have developed "macket" (Figure 21), a second prototype of our humanoid robot with soft sensor flesh [19]. Figure 21(a) shows the appearance of macket with sensor flesh and bone structure. In Figure 21(b), arrangement of the degrees of freedom is shown. Also, specification of macket is shown in the Table 1, and the part of locomotion performance of the macket is shown in Figure 22.

In Figure 23, an arrangement for the sensor elements and the actual situations of the human touch are shown. In the current setup, macket has 48 soft 3D deformable sensor elements inside of the thick urethane foam exterior. In the left of the figure, small blue boxes indicate each sensor element. Those elements are mainly arranged at both arms, torso, and head. Sensors for legs are planed to be added in the future. In the right of Figure 23, lower images are corresponded

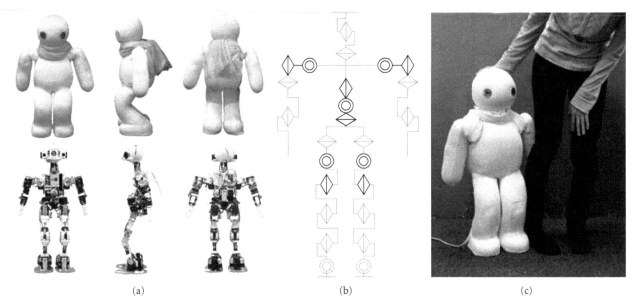

(a)   (b)   (c)

FIGURE 21: "macket:" a humanoid with improved soft sensor flesh. (a) Photos for the robot and its internal frame, (b) D.O.F arrangement of the robot. (c) Size comparison with human.

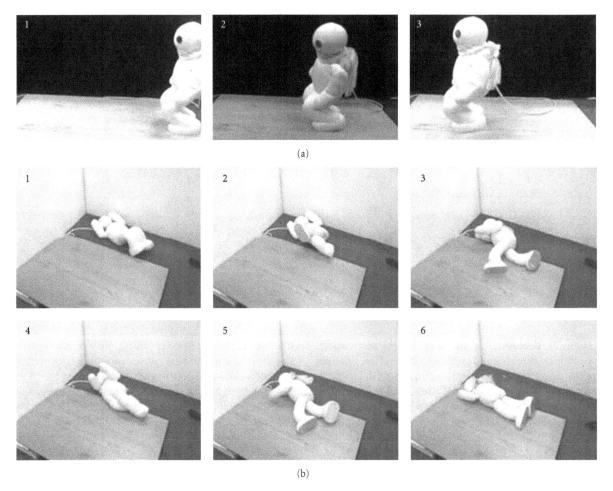

(a)

(b)

FIGURE 22: Locomotion performance of macket. (a) Dynamic walking. (b) Rolling-over motion.

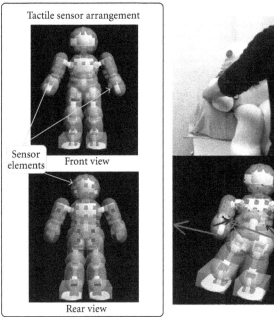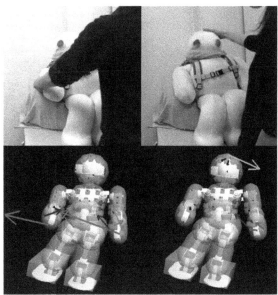

FIGURE 23: Soft deformable sensor outputs of macket, drawn on the geometrical model.

TABLE 1: Specifications of macket's skeleton.

Total DOF	26
Height	800 mm
Weight	5.6 kg (not including soft cover)
Actuator	RX-64 (maximum hold torque 64 kgf·cm) (ROBOTIS Co.)
	RX-28 (maximum hold torque 28 kgf·cm) (ROBOTIS Co.)
Sensor	FSRs for tactile and ZMP sensor (Interlink Co.), potentiometers for dislocation sensor (ALPS Electric Co.), 3D Motion Sensor MDP-A-3U9S-DK (NEC/TOKIN Co.), two cameras, two microphones, and 3D deformation sensor (explained in Section 3)
Electric interface	RS-485 (actuators, sensors), USB (sensors)
Human interface	Two cameras, two microphones, and speaker

to the upper photos. For each situation, 3D deformation is calculated by comparing facing pairs of light-receiving devices in each sensor element, and the result is drawn on the robot's geometrical model as an arrow. For the robot with distributed tactile sensors, information processing which eliminates undesirable tactile signals generated by self interferences is very important. Those self-interferences can be eliminated by constructing sensor signal output table relating to the robot's joint angles. This method is originally proposed by Hoshino et al. for their sensor suit [3], and this method can be extended for multiaxis force distribution.

Recently, soft 3D deformable sensor elements developed by us are commercially available as ShokacCube CL manufactured by Touchence Inc., based on the license agreement between University of Tokyo and Touchence Inc. Using them, we have applied our soft sensor flesh to life-sized humanoid robot HRP-2 [20, 21]. Figure 24 shows an appearance of HRP2 with soft sensor flesh. Inside the soft sensor flesh of HRP2, there are 347 elements whole around the body. In Figure 25(b), 3D deformation vectors around front chest and right forearm regions are drawn as arrows on the geometrical model of the robot.

Our research on soft sensor flesh begins from developing prototype soft sensor flesh for achieving close safe interaction behavior between robot and human. However, such soft exterior can work to protect the robot itself. From such point of view, new structure of soft sensor flesh for self-protective behavior is proposed in the next section.

7. Soft Sensor Flesh for Self-Protective Behaviors

Soft thick exterior is not only for close interaction with humans and objects. In some case, it works for saving themselves from physical and direct impact. From this viewpoint, we develop new design of soft sensor flesh: multilayered soft thick exterior [22]. Marshmal is a robot with this new type of soft sensor flesh (Figure 26).

New soft thick flesh contains particularly flexible parts (on elbows and knees), high elasticity parts (hands and toes, which contact with the environment firstly in an accident), and shock-absorbing gel parts (inner flesh, and around precision machinery). Finally, they are wrapped by very thin film and stretchable cloth cover in whole-body surface to protect all flesh structure against wearing. It is hard to mold small

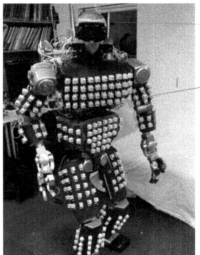
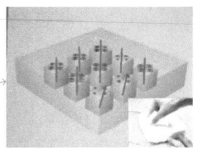

Soft 3D deformable sensor

FIGURE 24: Life-sized humanoid HRP-2 with soft sensor flesh.

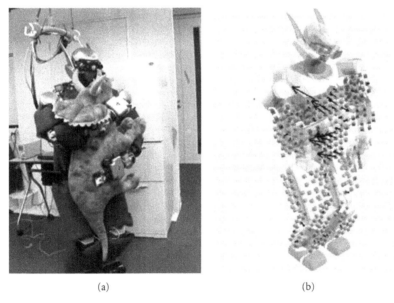

(a)   (b)

FIGURE 25: Deformation vector is acquired during hugging a soft toy.

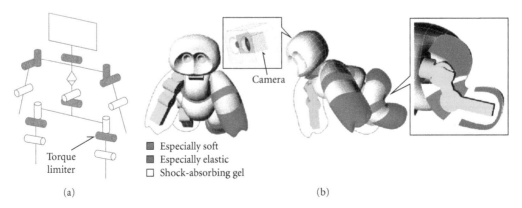

Camera

■ Especially soft
■ Especially elastic
□ Shock-absorbing gel

Torque
limiter

(a)   (b)

FIGURE 26: Structure of inner robot frame and multilayered flesh for Marshmal.

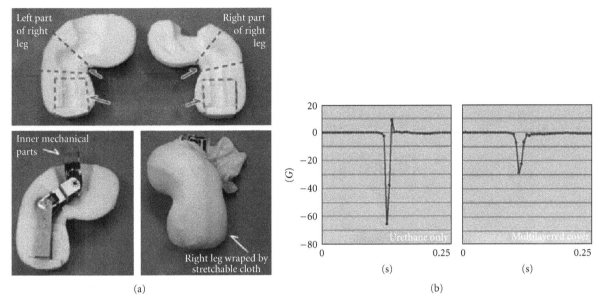

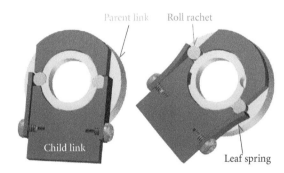

FIGURE 27: Trial pieces and a preliminary experiment for self-protective soft sensor flesh. (a) Trial piece of multilayered flesh exterior for right leg. (b) Preliminary experiment results for shock absorbing using the trial piece.

flesh part with accuracy, therefore softness quality of some parts like around eyes and neckline which are not necessary for self-protection for some accidents is unwarranted. Unlike macra and macket, mold die for Marshmal is made of nylon-resinous molding dies, which is manufactured by rapid prototyping method. This new mold die has only 3 mm thickness and is very light. Easy handling and opening arbitrary injection ports over the surface enable multilayered molding.

In Figure 27(a), trial pieces for Marshmal's right leg are shown. These pieces are foamed by urethane parts as main material, and include urethane sponge parts and shock-absorbing gel parts (shown in the top row of Figure 27(a)). Additionally, they are wrapped with soft and stretchable cloth layer, which helps very well in self-protective flesh surface against being deteriorated or worn down. In Figure 27(b), z-axis acceleration in fall down experiment using this test piece for right leg with an uniform urethane and multilayered materials is shown. These trial pieces fell from height of 300 mm with 2.5 kg weight to the popular carpet. The greatest value of fall down impact decreases remarkably, and impact time simultaneously increases by using multilayered flesh cover with the shock-absorbing gel material. With this experiment, we have confirmed a usability of multilayered flesh exterior with the special gel from the point of view of self-protection against fall down impact.

At the same time, we have developed a protection mechanism set directly in robot's multijointed structure, since soft cover can only absorb the shock to the body but not extinguish the load itself. Shock resistive mechanism, such as a torque limiter structure on rotational joints, must be introduced to protect the robot against failure by the load. So far, we have developed small torque limiter using a ratchet method for preventing from damage during interaction with humans [19, 23]. We improved our previous torque limiter for absorbing falling down shock. The size of our new

FIGURE 28: implementation of torque limiter; left: normal position, right: dislocated.

torque limiter is 37 mm diameter and up to 20 mm height. In Figure 28, the structure of the developed torque limiter is shown. The two ratchet balls are each held down by the leaf springs, and easy adjustment of yield torque is available by modifying the number of leaf springs. Only when torque acts to the joint, small rolls come off, so that parent link and child link slip relatively: this is a joint dislocation. In addition to that, a potentiometer board is built into every dislocatable structure, so that measurement of dislocation angle and auto recovery are available.

In Figures 29 and 30, falling down experiment from the ordinary desk is shown. In this experiment, the height of the desk is 750 mm. When the robot detects falling down event from the change of sitting attitude angle of the pelvis, it shifts to the contact posture in preparation of falling down contact and makes all servos off. The contact pose is not to place both arms but to land by the abdominal flesh. After landing on the ground, the robot checks which joints dislocated in whole body, and recovers all dislocated joints. In Figure 30(b) shows the change of all dislocatable angles throughout falling

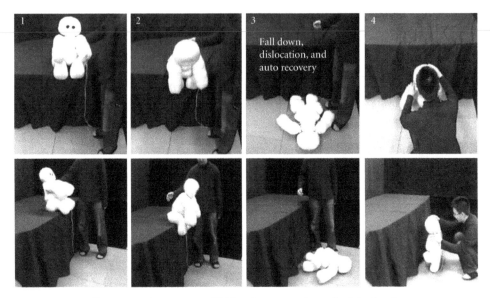

FIGURE 29: Appearance of falling down experiment by Marshmal.

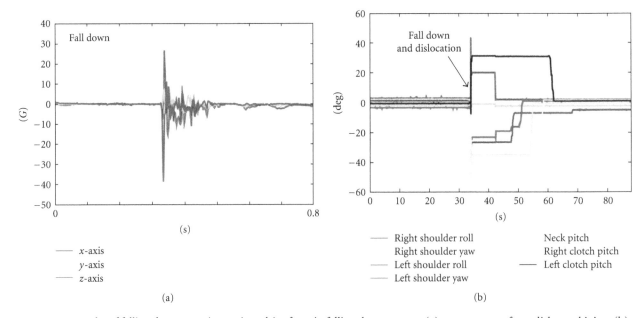

FIGURE 30: Results of falling down experiment: impulsive force in falling down contact (a); autorecovery from dislocated joints (b).

down accident. This robot has eight dislocatable joints, and in this experiment seven joints are exposed to overload stress. As shown in the graph, dislocation recovery is executed in all seven dislocated joints. Figure 30(a) shows the impulsive force in this experiment. Robot has suffered a very large impact, even though shock-absorbing flesh works very well, and motor joints are well protected. This may indicate the limit of fixed and passive flesh structures. For improving shock absorbing function of the soft sensor flesh, some types of active control of the flesh are necessary.

In this section, combined system of soft sensor flesh and joint dislocation mechanism for absorbing falling down shock is argued. It is one challenge for adding new features to soft sensor flesh from hardware aspect. In the next section,

other challenges from sensing aspects are explained. New additional soft tactile sensors which improve contact sensing ability of soft sensor flesh are proposed.

8. Additional Soft Tactile Sensors Which Improves Contact Sensing Ability

For improving tactile sensing ability of soft sensor flesh, we also develop some other types of additional sensor elements. For keeping softness of the exterior, those sensors should also be soft. In this section, two different type soft sensor elements are explained: one is a stretchable knit sensor [24], and the other is a 4-axis soft deformable sensor [25].

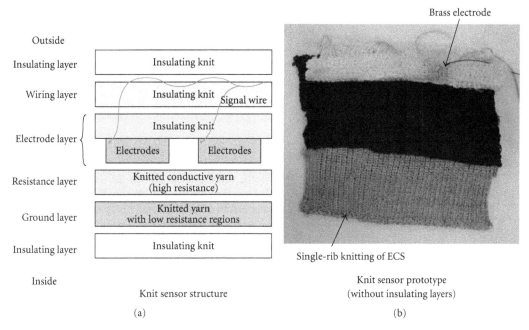

FIGURE 31: Developed knit sensor: a schematic of the sensor structure (a), and a photo of a prototype (b).

8.1. Soft Sensor Flesh with Stretchable Knit Sensor. One of the most difficult part of the body for acquiring tactile information is joint region. Since the degree of the change for joint region is large, soft and stretchable tactile sensor element is necessary for covering joint region. Proposed soft sensor flesh itself also has this problem. For solving this problem, additional stretchable sensing element is developed for detecting tactile sensor change around joint region.

So far, there are some studies for constructing soft and stretchable sensing structure. For example, Hoshi and Shinoda have developed a touch-area-sensitive tactile sensing element [11], where stretchable conductive fabrics are sandwiched by two compressive insulators having different softness. Although their sensing element has softness and stretchable properties, those parameters largely depend on the mechanical properties of the compressive insulators, and they do not discuss the feasibility for their sensor element to implement it as a humanoid's exterior. Also, Tada et al. have developed flexible and stretchable tactile sensor element based on static electricity phenomenon [26]. Although their sensing element is made of conductive silicone rubber and it can be stretched until 300% of the original length, their sensor can detect only touching and releasing events, not the pressure. Nagakubo et al. have developed wire-saving stretchable tactile sensing element [6] using EIT (electrical impedance tomography) technique based on inverse problem theory. In their method, pressure distribution can be calculated by measuring potential differences of the electrodes which is arranged around the boundary of the measuring region. They have tested 150% stretchable conductive knitted fabrics which are made by spraying water-based carbonic paint over cotton knit. However, such complicated structure can limit the stretching property, and the cost for making whole-body enclosing type exterior is not so easy.

Therefore, we adopt Hoshino et al.'s method for constructing our stretchable sensor element, and extend their method for making it more stretchable and getting the analog continuous pressure value at each sensing points by using pressure sensitive knitted electro-conductive yarn. Figure 31 shows the sensor structure (a) and a test piece of the sensor element (b).

As shown in Figure 31, there are six layers in the developed sensor element and each layer is manufactured as follows.

(1) Outer and inner insulating layers: these layers are made for protecting the internal layers and knitted by insulating yarn using single-rib knitting method.

(2) Wiring layer: soft thin coated copper wires are embroidered on a insulating structure knitted by single-rib knitting method. For keeping the stretchability of the knit structure, wires are sewed with a half-back stitch.

(3) Electrode layer: in this layer electrodes connected with signal wires from wiring layer are attached on the insulating knit. For electrodes, small brass circular plates (diameter 8 mm, thickness 0.4 mm) are used, and the terminals of the signal wires are soldered to the electrodes.

(4) Resistance layer: high resistant conductive strings are knitted by single-rib knitting method. For making a pressure sensitive structure whose resistance uniformly changes in proportion to the contact force, this layer should be knitted only with the high resistant conductive strings. Although the strings used here requires trained skill to knit them, easier method

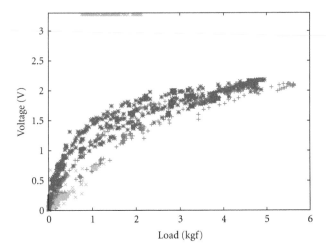

FIGURE 32: Load-Voltage properties for analog knit sensor (red "+": not stretched, green "×": filling 200% stretched, blue "∗": wrap 150% stretched).

like double knitting of these strings and normal insulator strings deteriorates the pressure sensitiveness remarkably.

(5) Ground layer: this layer is connected with the signal ground.

Next, relationship between the applied force and output voltage is examined. In Figure 32, output voltages for developed knit sensor are shown. In this experiment, applied force is increased at about 4 kgf/sec via flat circular metal parts having 16 mm diameter. In Figure 32 horizontal axis indicates the applied force in kgf while vertical axis expresses the output voltage in V. There are 3 different stretching conditions plotted in the graphs. Those are no stretching condition and stretching conditions toward two directions. For knitted fabrics, those two directions are defined as wrap direction and filing direction. In the single-rib knitting method, stretching degree toward filling direction is much larger than the one toward wrap direction. In Figure 32, the red "+" signs express no stretching condition while green "×" signs and blue signs "∗" indicate stretching condition toward filling direction and the one toward wrap direction, respectively. The maximum stretching length is 200% toward filling direction while the one toward wrap direction is 150%.

Although the output voltage changes nonlinearly as an applied force increases, it is confirmed that the knit sensor can output continuous analog value in all measured conditions from the graph. Also, the load-voltage properties are affected by how long and which direction the sensor element is stretched. When it is stretched toward filling direction, output voltages are smaller than the ones for nonstretched condition. This can be due to the different density changes of the resistance layer and ground layer. Since the size of the string for ground layer is smaller than that for the resistance layer, ground layer becomes more sparse than resistance

layer. As a result, resistance around contact region becomes larger compared with the no-stretched condition, and output voltages become smaller in such situation as described above. On the other hand, sensor output voltages become a little bit larger than no-stretched condition when it is stretched toward wrap direction. This can be also due to the different density changes for the resistance layer and ground layer. Ground layer becomes dense when it is stretched toward wrap direction. As a result, resistance around contact region becomes smaller compared with the no-stretched condition, and output voltages become larger. Also, it is confirmed that the sensor output becomes easier to get maximized when the applied force is larger than about 1 kgf in the filling stretched conditions. This is partly because the fabrics both in resistance layer and ground layer tangle each other when they are pressed strongly.

Using developed analog knit sensor, sensor outputs while human touches the sensor in a various way is examined here (Figure 33). In this experiment, knit sensor is not stretched and fixed on a table. As shown in Figure 33, temporal sensor output patterns differ from each other, and at least the contact state examined here can be discriminated from the shapes of the sensor outputs. For example, the difference between "push softly" and "push strongly" can be recognized clearly. Also, developed sensor can respond against relatively weak contacts like "stroke" and "tickle." Furthermore, it can sense impulsive pattern like "pat." Using proposed method, cardigan type knit sensor exterior that covers soft sensor flesh is developed (Figure 34). The developed cardigan knit sensor is created for macket. In Figure 34, (a) shows the developed cardigan knit sensor while (b) shows how the sensor is implemented on the humanoid. Here, processing boards for this sensor are put in a backpack. For this knit sensor, the inner insulator layer is omitted since macket has already soft urethane exterior. Here in this case, the cardigan knit sensor is expected to work as add-on type functional exterior. Without this knit sensor, macket cannot detect weak contacts with its own tactile sensor flesh. The developed cardigan knit sensor has 75 electrodes. Electrodes at the front body and back body are arranged uniformly as a whole. For both arms, electrodes are arranged mainly around shoulders, elbows, and wrists since these parts are expected to be touched by humans frequently during the interaction. In the current situation, sensor calibration is manually done by checking load-voltage properties for each sensor electrode.

In Figure 35, some of the example reactive behaviors based on the sensation of the knit sensor are shown. In the graphs of each figure, only data from electrodes which output values beyond a threshold voltage are drawn. In Figure 35(a), electrodes for left elbow (Electrodes 33 and 34) detect "soft push" while an electrode for right elbow (Electrode 69) detects "strong push." But, reaction behavior against the "soft push" for left arm (watching left arm) is generated since the soft push is detected earlier than the strong push.

On the other hand, "stroke," defined as weaker outputs than "soft push", is detected for left arm's electrodes (Electrodes 24, 25, and 26) in Figure 35(b). After detecting the stroke, nodding, a reactive action against "stroke" in this situation, is generated as shown in the photo.

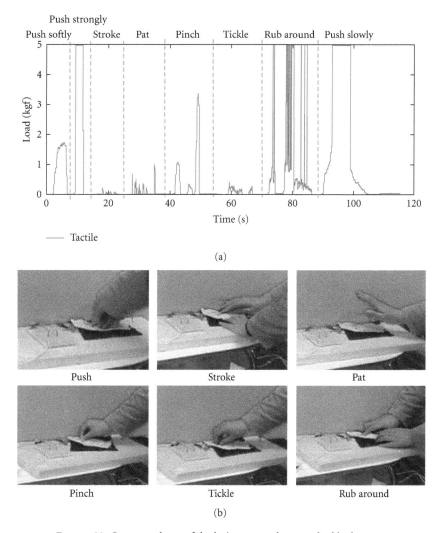

(a)

Push

Stroke

Pat

Pinch

Tickle

Rub around

(b)

FIGURE 33: Output voltage of the knit sensor when touched by human.

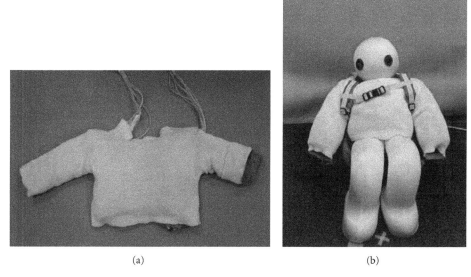

(a)

(b)

FIGURE 34: Cardigan-type knit sensor for a humanoid.

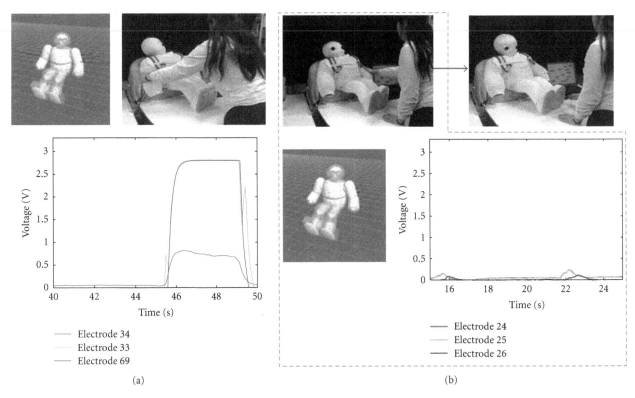

FIGURE 35: Reaction against soft push (a); reaction against stroke (b).

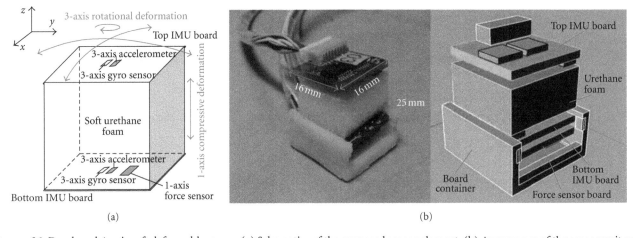

FIGURE 36: Developed 4-axis soft deformable sensor. (a) Schematics of the proposed sensor element. (b) Appearance of the sensor unit prototype.

8.2. 4-Axis Soft Deformable Sensor for Detecting Twisting Deformation. With the soft 3D deformable sensor element we have developed, twisting deformation cannot be detected by one sensor unit. In some parts of the body, detection of the twisting deformation of the sensor exterior can be used as some social signal from a person that the robot communicates with.

Therefore we propose a new design of soft deformable sensor. Figure 36(a) shows the basic structure of the newly designed sensor, "4-axis soft deformable sensor." This sensor consists of two basic elements: a pair of IMUs (Inertia Measurement Unit) and 1 force sensor. On both of a top and

bottom IMU board, one 3-axis MEMS accelerometer and one 3-axis gyro-sensor are implemented. By sandwiching a soft urethane foam with two IMU boards, soft 3-axis rotational deformation of this sensor unit can be detected from the output differences between two IMUs. Also, 1-axis compressive deformation is detected from the 1-axis MEMS force sensor arranged at the bottom. In total, this sensor can detect 4-axis soft deformation. Especially, by detecting the 3-axis rotational deformation from the differential output between two IMUs, sensor changes due to the externally applied force to the internal frame, or the subtle vibration of the actuator can be canceled. This leads to a robust sensing

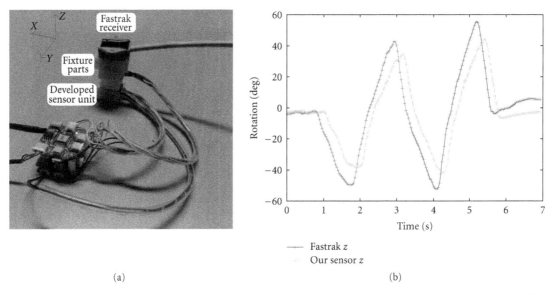

(a)   (b)

FIGURE 37: Evaluation experiment for developed sensor element: experimental setups (a) and observed rotation around z-axis for the developed sensor prototype (green line) and Fastrak (red line).

of the soft deformation of the sensor unit. By the proposed sensor design, detection of twisting sensation by one sensor unit is possible by estimating rotational deformation from 3-axis acceleration and 3-axis angular velocity.

For online estimation of 3D orientation from both top and bottom IMU boards, a method using extended kalman filter [27] or a method using complementary filter [28] can be applied. Here, quaternion for 3D orientation of the sensor unit is estimated using extended kalman filter. In our sensor design, drifting problem of the estimated result can be solved. Since two IMU boards are connected with elastic urethane foam and the relative position is getting back to the original position without any external force, estimated quaternion is reset to the original posture when no external force is monitored.

In Figure 36(b), developed prototype of 4-axis soft deformable sensor is shown. The external dimensions of this sensor prototype is 16 mm × 16 mm × 25 mm. Its weight is 6.7 g. For this prototype, we developed common IMU boards for estimating 3D rotation of top and bottom plane of the sensor unit. Although IMU boards developed here are rigid PCB, softness of the sensor unit is not ruined since sandwiched urethane foam has enough thickness. For detecting normal direction force, we developed another circuit board and arrange it under the bottom IMU board. Motion of the bottom IMU board and attached force sensor board is constrained only to the normal direction by plastic board container. For urethane foam, we use commercially available semirigid polyurethane foam called EMT (density is 60 ± 5 cm^3, elasticity is less than 30%. Hardness is less than 14.71 kPa), manufactured by Inoac corporation.

Evaluation experiment for investigating twisting sensation ability of developed 4-axis soft deformation sensor is done. Figure 37(a) shows experimental setups. In the experiment, we use magnetic 3D motion tracking sensor, Fastrak

manufactured by Polhemus, for evaluating our sensor prototype. Since Fastrak has 0.8 mm of position accuracy and 0.15 deg rotational accuracy, it can be used as a true value of 3D rotation for our sensor prototype. Upper IMU board is connected with a receiver of Fastrak while bottom surface of the sensor prototype is fixed to a desk. Rotation against z-axis of the coordinate system in Figure 37 is measured at 30 Hz. During the measurement, the sensor prototype is kept still for about 3 seconds. This is because average values of initial 100 samples are used as offsets of gyro sensors. This process is an only necessary calibration for 3-axis rotational deformation. This calibration process is largely simplified compared with the previous 3-axis soft deformation sensor.

Measurement result for z-axis rotation is shown in Figure 37(b). In Figure 37, horizontal axis indicates time in seconds while vertical axis expresses rotation in degree. Red solid line expresses the output from Fastrak while green dashed line expresses the estimated output of the developed sensor prototype. Although overall behavior of the developed sensor prototype is similar to the one of Fastrak, the output of the sensor prototype has 200 ms delay and about 10 to 15 degree estimation error in maximum. When rotational changes from 0 to peak value is compared, the output of the sensor prototype is about ±24%.

For testing feasibility of the developed sensor, simple soft sensor flesh which contains 4-axis soft deformation sensor is developed for a small humanoid robot NAO, manufactured by Aldebaran. In Figure 38, developed sensor flesh and its geometrical model are shown. In Figure 38(a), inside of the exterior is shown. This prototype exterior consists of two urethane parts and two 4-axis deformation sensors. Two deformation sensors are arranged at each side of the torso. In Figure 38(b), NAO with developed soft sensor flesh is shown. Also, geometrical model for NAO with this sensor flesh is shown. This model is used for behavior generation and

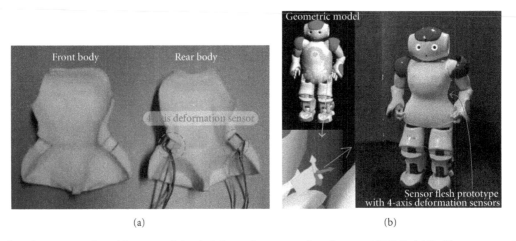

(a)   (b)

FIGURE 38: Developed sensor exterior with proposed 4-axis deformation sensors for a humanoid NAO. (a) Inside structure of the developed exterior. (b) NAO with developed soft sensor flesh.

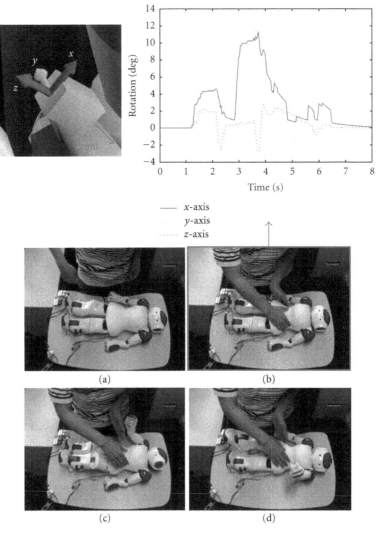

FIGURE 39: Reactive behavior based on tactile sensation; the rotation of the sensor at right side of NAO torso.

online sensor view in the experiment. At the bottom left of Figure 38(b), magnified image of the sensor model is shown. This sensor model shows the 3D rotational deformation by the orientation of the three perpendicular arrows, and magnitude of normal direction force is shown by the length of the pink arrows and color of the sensor box.

Reactive behavior against tactile sensation of the side of the trunk is implemented for an experiment. NAO starts wriggling only when both outputs of the sensor show the deformation toward front inside of the body: that is, if the sensor outputs for an x-axis of the sensor local coordinates go beyond a positive threshold by human inputs, predefined motion sequence is replayed by the robot. Result of this experiment is shown in Figure 39. As you can see from the photos, it succeeded in reacting human's contacts on its side of the torso. Detailed outputs of the embedded deformation sensor on the right side of the torso are shown in upper part of Figure 39. In the graph, horizontal axis indicates time in seconds while vertical axis expresses rotation in degree. Three lines corresponded to each axis of the sensor local coordinates are drawn at the left of the graph. In the graph, rotations for both x-axis and y-axis show positive values. Here, positive rotation around x-axis expresses forward deformation of the flesh while positive rotation around y-axis indicates deformation toward inside of the body. This means that human touch was correctly measured in this experiment.

9. Conclusion

In order to achieve close interaction behavior of robots against humans, objects, and environments, the idea of "Soft Sensor Flesh" is proposed. Unlike other ordinary artificial skin with distributed tactile sensor network, soft sensor flesh consists of soft and thick foam and many tactile sensor elements embedded inside the foam including multiaxis deformation detectable sensors. In this paper, several types of prototype of soft sensor flesh are shown, and multiple humanoid robots with those soft sensor flesh are developed. Furthermore, feasibility of the soft sensor flesh is confirmed through both actual behavior experiments and computer simulation.

One of the important challenges for the next step is the information processing of the enormous amount of tactile sensor information, which is now being worked on by the authors [29]. Also, using developed robots with soft sensor flesh for concrete targets, such as nursing care task, is another important challenge. Knowledge accumulated by using soft sensor flesh for various practical tasks will accelerate the study for improving soft sensor flesh itself.

References

[1] V. J. Lumelsky, M. S. Shur, and S. Wagner, "Sensitive skin," *IEEE Sensors Journal*, vol. 1, no. 1, pp. 41–51, 2001.

[2] R. S. Dahiya, G. Metta, M. Valle, and G. Sandini, "Tactile sensing-from humans to humanoids," *IEEE Transactions on Robotics*, vol. 26, no. 1, pp. 1–20, 2010.

[3] Y. Hoshino, M. Inaba, and H. Inoue, "Model and processing of whole-body tactile sensor suit for human-robot contact interaction," in *Proceedings of the IEEE International Conference on Robotics and Automation*, pp. 2281–2286, May 1998.

[4] N. Mitsunaga, T. Miyashita, H. Ishiguro, K. Kogure, and N. Hagita, "Robovie-IV: a communication robot interacting with people daily in an office," in *Proceedings of the International Conference on Intelligent Robots and Systems (IEEE/RSJ '06)*, pp. 5066–5072, October 2006.

[5] T. Minato, Y. Yoshikawa, T. Noda, S. Ikemoto, H. Ishiguro, and M. Asada, "CB2: a child robot with biomimetic body for cognitive developmental robotics," in *Proceedings of the 7th IEEE-RAS International Conference on Humanoid Robots (HUMANOIDS '07)*, pp. 557–562, December 2007.

[6] A. Nagakubo, H. Alirezaei, and Y. Kuniyoshi, "A deformable and deformation sensitive tactile distribution sensor," in *Proceedings of the IEEE International Conference on Robotics and Biomimetics (ROBIO '07)*, pp. 1301–1308, December 2007.

[7] T. Mukai, M. Onishi, T. Odashima, S. Hirano, and Z. Luo, "Development of the tactile sensor system of a human-interactive robot "RI-MAN"," *IEEE Transactions on Robotics*, vol. 24, no. 2, pp. 505–512, 2008.

[8] T. Mukai, S. Hirano, M. Yoshida, H. Nakashima, G. Shijie, and Y. Hayakawa, "Whole-body contact manipulation using tactile information for the nursing-care assistant robot riba," in *Proceedings of IEEE International Conference on Intelligent Robots and Systems*, pp. 2445–2451, 2011.

[9] H. Iwata and S. Sugano, "Whole-body covering tactile interface for human robot coordination," in *Proceedings of the IEEE International Conference on Robotics and Automation*, pp. 3818–3824, May 2002.

[10] S. Saga, H. Kajimoto, and S. Tachi, "High-resolution tactile sensor using the deformation of a reflection image," *Sensor Review*, vol. 27, no. 1, pp. 35–42, 2007.

[11] T. Hoshi and H. Shinoda, "Robot skin based on touch-area-sensitive tactile element," in *Proceedings of the IEEE International Conference on Robotics and Automation (ICRA '06)*, pp. 3463–3468, May 2006.

[12] S. Kiyota and H. Shinoda, "Cubic stress tensor sensor for robot skins," in *Proceedings of the Annual International Conference on Instrumentation, Control and Information Technology (SICE '08)*, pp. 910–914, August 2008.

[13] M. Hayashi, T. Sagisaka, Y. Ishizaka, T. Yoshikai, and M. Inaba, "Development of functional whole-body flesh with distributed three-axis force sensors to enable close interaction by humanoids," in *Proceedings of the IEEE/RSJ International Conference on Intelligent Robots and Systems (IROS '07)*, pp. 3610–3615, November 2007.

[14] Y. Murase, Y. Yasukawa, K. SAKAI, and M. Ueki, "Design of a compact humanoid robot as a platform," in *Proceedings of the 19th Annual Conference of the Robotics Society of Japan*, pp. 789–790, 2001.

[15] T. Yoshikai, T. Sagisaka, M. Hayashi, and M. Inaba, "Acquisition and realization of a rolling-over motion for a humanoid with soft sensor flesh," *Journal of Robotics and Mechatronics*, vol. 20, no. 2, pp. 241–249, 2008.

[16] T. Ogura, K. Okada, and M. Inaba, "Realization of dynamics simulator embedded robot brain for humanoid robots," in *Proceedings of the IEEE International Conference on Robotics and Automation (ICRA '07)*, pp. 2175–2180, April 2007.

[17] M. Hayashi, Y. Ishizaka, T. Yoshikai, and M. Inaba, "Development of whole body multisensory soft flesh with vibrotactile and deep pressure sense for humanoid close interaction," in *Proceedings of the IEEE International Conference on Multisensor Fusion and Integration for Intelligent Systems (MFI '08)*, pp. 665–670, August 2008.

[18] A. Kadowaki, T. Yoshikai, M. Hayashi, and M. Inaba, "Development of soft sensor exterior embedded with multi-axis

deformable tactile sensor system," in *Proceedings of the 18th IEEE International Symposium on Robot and Human Interactive (RO-MAN '09)*, pp. 1093–1098, October 2009.

[19] T. Yoshikai, M. Hayashi, A. Kadowaki, T. Goto, and M. Inaba, "Design and development of a humanoid with soft 3D-deformable sensor flesh and automatic recoverable mechanical overload protection mechanism," in *Proceedings of the IEEE/RSJ International Conference on Intelligent Robots and Systems (IROS '09)*, pp. 4977–4983, October 2009.

[20] K. Kaneko, F. Kanehiro, S. Kajita et al., "Humanoid robot HRP-2," in *Proceedings of the IEEE International Conference on Robotics and Automation*, pp. 1083–1090, May 2004.

[21] I. Kumagai, K. Kobayashi, S. Nozawa et al., "Development of a full body multi-axis soft tactile sensor suit for life sized humanoid robot and an algorithm to detect contact states," in *Proceedings of International Conference on Humanoid Robots (IEEE/RSJ '12)*, 2012.

[22] K. Kobayashi, T. Yoshikai, and M. Inaba, "Development of humanoid with distributed soft flesh and shock-resistive joint mechanism for self-protective behaviors in impact from falling down," in *Proceedings of IEEE International Conference on Robotics and Biomimetics (ROBIO '11)*, pp. 2390–2396, 2011.

[23] T. Yoshikai, M. Inaba, M. Hayashi, and R. Ueda, "A fall down resistant humanoid robot with soft cover and automatically recoverable mechanical overload protection," in *Proceedings of the 12th International Conference on Climbing and Walking Robots and the Support Technologies for Mobile Machines*, pp. 1225–1232, 2008.

[24] T. Yoshikai, H. Fukushima, M. Hayashi, and M. Inaba, "Development of soft stretchable knit sensor for humanoids' whole-body tactile sensibility," in *Proceedings of the 9th IEEE-RAS International Conference on Humanoid Robots (HUMANOIDS '09)*, pp. 624–631, December 2009.

[25] T. Yoshikai, M. Hayashi, A. Kadowaki, T. Goto, and M. Inaba, "Design and development of a humanoid with soft 3D-deformable sensor flesh and automatic recoverable mechanical overload protection mechanism," in *Proceedings of the IEEE/RSJ International Conference on Intelligent Robots and Systems (IROS '09)*, pp. 4977–4983, October 2009.

[26] Y. Tada, M. Inoue, T. Kawasaki, Y. Kawahito, H. Ishiguro, and K. Suganuma, "A flexible and stretchable tactile sensor utilizing static electricity," in *Proceedings of the IEEE/RSJ International Conference on Intelligent Robots and Systems (IROS '07)*, pp. 684–689, November 2007.

[27] E. J. Lefferts, F. L. Markley, and M. D. Shuster, "Kalman filtering for spacecraft attitude estimation," *Journal of Guidance, Control, and Dynamics*, vol. 5, no. 5, pp. 417–429, 1982.

[28] R. Mahony, T. Hamel, and J. M. Pflimlin, "Complementary filter design on the special orthogonal group SO_3," in *Proceedings of the 44th IEEE Conference on Decision and Control, and the European Control Conference (CDC-ECC '05)*, pp. 1477–1484, December 2005.

[29] T. Yoshikai, K. Kobayashi, and M. Inaba, "Spatial and temporal coarse to fine structuring method of distributed tactile sensors based on changing velocity of the sensation," in *Proceedings of IEEE International Conference on Robotics and Biomimetics (ROBIO '11)*, pp. 1427–1432, 2011.

4

Artificial Neural Network-Based Fault Distance Locator for Double-Circuit Transmission Lines

Anamika Jain

Department of Electrical Engineering, National Institute of Technology, Raipur 492010, India

Correspondence should be addressed to Anamika Jain; anamikajugnu4@gmail.com

Academic Editor: Jun He

This paper analyses two different approaches of fault distance location in a double circuit transmission lines, using artificial neural networks. The single and modular artificial neural networks were developed for determining the fault distance location under varying types of faults in both the circuits. The proposed method uses the voltages and currents signals available at only the local end of the line. The model of the example power system is developed using Matlab/Simulink software. Effects of variations in power system parameters, for example, fault inception angle, CT saturation, source strength, its X/R ratios, fault resistance, fault type and distance to fault have been investigated extensively on the performance of the neural network based protection scheme (for all ten faults in both the circuits). Additionally, the effects of network changes: namely, double circuit operation and single circuit operation, have also been considered. Thus, the present work considers the entire range of possible operating conditions, which has not been reported earlier. The comparative results of single and modular neural network indicate that the modular approach gives correct fault location with better accuracy. It is adaptive to variation in power system parameters, network changes and works successfully under a variety of operating conditions.

1. Introduction

Protection of double-circuit transmission lines poses additional problems due to zero sequence mutual coupling between faulted and healthy circuits during earth faults [1]. The nature of mutual coupling is highly variable; and it is affected by network changes such as switching in/out of one of the parallel lines, thus causing underreach/overreach of conventional distance relaying [2]. Artificial neural network has emerged as a relaying tool for protection of power system equipments [3]. ANN has pattern recognition, classification, generalization, and fault tolerance capability. ANN has been widely used for developing protective relaying schemes for transmission lines protection. Most of the research on ANN-based protection schemes has been carried out for single-circuit transmission lines [4–16].

An adaptive distance protection of double-circuit line using zero sequence thevenin equivalent impedance and compensation factor for mutual coupling to increase the reach and selectivity of relay has been developed in [2]. Fault classification using ANN for one circuit of parallel double-circuit line has been reported in [17]. A neural network based protection technique for combined 275 kV/400 kV double-circuit transmission lines has been proposed in [18]. The fundamental components of voltages and currents are used as input to neural network for a particular type of fault (single-line to ground) distance location and zone of fault estimation. A novel fault classification technique of double-circuit lines based on a combined unsupervised/supervised neural network has been presented in [19]. It considers only A1G, B2G, A1B1G, and A1C2 faults and other types of faults have not been considered. Cascade correlation algorithm-based ANN is used for fault location and fault resistance determination [20]. Kohonen network is used to improve the accuracy of distance relay for single-line to ground fault on one circuit of double-circuit lines [21]; faults on circuit 2 line have not been considered. The Clarke Concordia transformation, eigenvalue approach, and NN are used to locate the fault of double-circuit line [22]. Adaptive distance relaying scheme for high-resistance faults on two terminal

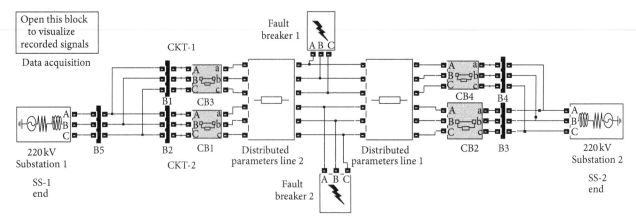

FIGURE 1: Power system model simulated using Matlab software.

parallel transmission lines using radial basis functions neural network has been reported [23]. It uses changes in active and reactive power flow and resistance as input to RBFNN, and reactance is the output. Only single-line to ground faults was considered in this work.

The work presented in this paper deals with fault distance location using artificial neural network for all the 10 types of faults in a double-circuit transmission lines. Throughout the study a 220 kV double end fed double-circuit transmission line of 100 km length has been chosen as a representative system. The work reports the results of extensive "offline" studies using the Matlab and its associated toolboxes: Simulink, SimPowerSystems and Neural Network Toolbox [24]. The neural networks based protection scheme have been developed for double-circuit transmission line using fundamental components of three-phase voltages and currents in each circuit. The following two ANN architectures were explored for this task:

  (i) single neural network for all the 10 type of faults in both the circuits;

  (ii) modular neural network for each type of faults (consisting four ANN modules).

All the 10 types of shunt faults (3 phase to ground faults, 3 phase to phase faults, 3 double phase to ground faults, and 1 three-phase fault) on each circuit have been investigated with variation in power system parameters, namely, fault inception angle (Φ_i in °), source strengths at either end (GVA) and its X/R ratio, fault resistance (R_f in Ω), and distance to fault (L_f in km). Additionally, the effects of CT saturation and network changes, for example, double-circuit operation and single-circuit operation with other circuit switched out and grounded at both ends, have also been considered. This encompasses practically the entire range of possible operating conditions and faults which have not been reported in previous works.

2. Power System Network Simulation

A 220 kV double-circuit transmission line of line length 100 km which is fed from sources at each end is simulated

TABLE 1: Double circuit transmission line parameters.

Parameters	Set value
Positive sequence resistance R_1, Ω/km	0.01809
Zero sequence resistance R_0, Ω/km	0.2188
Zero sequence mutual resistance R_{0m}, Ω/km	0.20052
Positive sequence inductance L_1, H/km	0.00092974
Zero sequence inductance L_0, H/km	0.0032829
Zero sequence mutual inductance L_{0m}, H/km	0.0020802
Positive sequence capacitance C_1, F/km	$1.2571e - 008$
Zero sequence capacitance C_0, F/km	$7.8555e - 009$
Zero sequence mutual capacitance C_{0m}, F/km	$-2.0444e - 009$

using Matlab/Simulink and SimPowerSystems toolbox. The Power system model simulated is shown in Figure 1. The internal impedance of two sources on two sides of the line at SS-1 end and SS-2 end is $45\angle82°$ and $79.5\angle85°$, respectively. The transmission line is simulated using distributed parameter line model using power line parameter of SimPowerSystems toolbox of Matlab software. The effect of mutual coupling between the two circuits and various types of faults with different system conditions and parameters is considered. Double-circuit transmission line parameters are given in Table 1.

3. Single Artificial Neural Network-Based Fault Distance Locator

A single artificial neural network for fault distance location (FDL) of all the ten types of faults in both the circuit under varying power system operating conditions has been developed. The block diagram of the proposed single ANN-based FDL approach is shown in Figure 2.

The implementation procedures for designing the neural network for fault distance location estimation are as follows.

Step 1. Obtain input data and target data from the simulation.

Step 2. Assemble and preprocess the training data for single and modular ANN-based FDL.

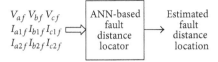

FIGURE 2: Block diagram of single ANN-based fault distance locator.

Step 3. Create the network architecture and train the network until conditions of network setting parameters are reached.

Step 4. Test and performance analysis.

Step 5. Stored the trained network. Steps 1–5 are offline processes. Next, the network is ready to test with the new input, which is an online process.

Step 6. The new input is preprocessed before presented to the trained single and modular ANN-based FDL.

3.1. Selection of Network Inputs and Outputs. One factor in determining the right size and architecture for the neural network is the number of inputs and outputs that it must have. The lower the number of inputs, the smaller the network can be. However, sufficient input data to characterize the problem must be ensured. The signals recorded at one end of the line only are used. The inputs to conventional distance relays are mainly the voltages and currents. Hence the network inputs chosen here are the magnitudes of the fundamental components (50 Hz) of three-phase voltages and three-phase currents of each circuit, that is, six currents measured at the relay location. As the basic task of fault location is to determine the distance to the fault, fault distance location, in km (L_f) with regard to the total length of the line, is the only output provided by the fault location network. Thus, the inputs X and the outputs Y for the fault location network are given by:

$$X = \left[V_{af}, V_{bf}, V_{cf}, I_{a1f}, I_{b1f}, I_{c1f}, I_{a2f}, I_{b2f}, I_{c2f}\right],$$
$$Y = \left[L_f\right]. \tag{1}$$

3.2. Fault Patterns Generation and Preprocessing. To train the network, a suitable number of representative examples of the relevant phenomenon must be selected, so that the network can learn the fundamental characteristics of the problem. The steps involved in fault pattern generation and preprocessing are depicted in Figure 3. Three-phase voltages and three-phase current signals of both the circuits obtained through Matlab simulation are sampled at a sampling frequency of 1 kHz and further processed by simple second-order low-pass Butterworth filter with cut off frequency of 400 Hz. Then one full cycle discrete fourier transform is used to calculate the fundamental component of three-phase voltages and currents of both circuits which are used as input to the ANN. It should be mentioned that the input signals have to be normalized in order to reach the ANN input level (±1). The routine "premnx" of the neural network toolbox of

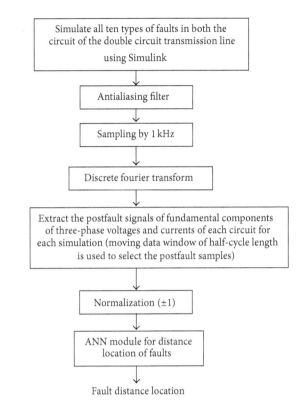

FIGURE 3: Proposed methodology of ANN-based fault distance location.

Matlab is used to normalize the input signals. For training pattern or input matrix formation, the postfault samples (ten number) of fundamental components of three-phase voltages and currents of each circuit are extracted. For this a moving data window of half-cycle length (which consists of 10 samples) is used to select the postfault data after one cycle from the inception of fault as an input to the artificial neural network. Using Simulink and SimPowerSystem toolbox of Matlab all the ten types of faults at different fault locations between 0 and 100% of line length and fault inception angles 0 and 90° have been simulated as shown in Table 2. The total number of ground faults simulated is 12*10*2*3 = 720 and phase faults 8*10*2 = 160; thus total fault cases are 880, and from each fault cases 10 number of postfault samples have been extracted, also 35 no fault samples are taken to form the training data set for neural network. Thus the total number of patterns generated for training is 8800 + 35 = 8835. Training matrices were built in such a way that the network trained produces an output corresponding to the fault distance location. The proposed methodology of fault distance location using ANN is depicted in Figure 3.

3.3. ANN Architecture. Once it was decided how many input and output the network should have, the number of layers and the number of neurons per layer were considered. The major issue in the design of ANN architecture is to ensure that when choosing the number of hidden layers and number of neurons in the hidden layers, its attribute for generalization is well maintained. In this respect, since there

TABLE 2: Training patterns generation for single and modular ANN-based FDL.

Parameter	Set value
Fault type	LG: A1N, A2N, B1N, B2N, C1N, and C2N
	LL: A1B1, A2B2, B1C1, B2C2, A1C1, and A2C2
	LLG: A1B1N, A2B2N, B1C1N, B2C2N, A1C1N, and A2C2N
	LLL: A1B1C1, A2B2C2
Fault location (L_f in KM)	1, 10, 20, 30, . . ., 80, and 90 KM
Fault inception angle (Φ_i)	0° and 90°
Fault resistance (R_f)	0, 50 and 100 Ω
Prefault power flow angle (δ_s)	45°

TABLE 3: Comparison of ANN models for FDL.

S. number	Number of hidden neurons	Number of epochs	Mean square error
1	10	300	0.0116445
2	15	300	0.0067783
3	20	300	0.0021979
4	25	300	0.000853473
5	30	300	0.000645901
6	35	300	0.000557819
7	40	300	0.000466127

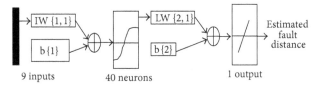

FIGURE 4: Architecture of single ANN-based fault distance locator.

is no parametric/theoretic guidance available, the design has to be based on a heuristic approach. The ANN architecture, including the number of inputs to the network and the number of neurons in hidden layers, is determined empirically by experimenting with various network configurations. Through a series of trials and modifications of the ANN architecture, the best performance is achieved by using a three-layer neural network with 9 inputs, 1 output, and the optimal number of neurons in the hidden layer was found to be 40 (as per comparison of different ANN models shown in Table 3). The architecture of single ANN-based fault locator (9-40-1) is shown in Figure 4 [25–28].

The final determination of the neural network requires the relevant transfer functions in the hidden and output layers to be established. Activation function of the hidden layer is hyperbolic tangent sigmoid function. Neurons with sigmoid function produce real-valued outputs that give the ANN ability to construct complicated decision boundaries in an n-dimensional feature space. This is important because the smoothness of the generalization function produced by the neurons, and hence its classification ability, is directly dependent on the nature of the decision boundaries. Purely linear transfer function (purelin) has been used in the output layer as the output is fault distance location which varies between 0 and 100 KM linearly.

3.4. Training Process. Various learning techniques were applied to the different network architectures, and it was concluded that the most suitable training method for the architecture selected was based on the Levenberg-Marquardt (LM) technique, as it gives fastest convergence [29]. The

single ANN-based FDL was trained by LM training algorithm. This learning strategy converges quickly, and the mean squared error (mse) decreases in 300 epochs to $4.66127e - 04$ in around 15 minutes computation time on a PC (P4, 2.66 GHz, and 2 GB RAM). The single ANN-based FDL requires large training sets (all types of faults in both circuit with varying fault parameters) and long training time. Also the network complexity is higher, and it has slower learning capability. However, once the network is trained sufficiently with large training data set, the network gives the correct output when subjected to fault situations. The test results of single and modular ANN-based FDL are discussed in Section 5.

4. Modular Artificial Neural Network-Based Fault Distance Locator

The single ANN-based FDL has the disadvantages of complexity, large training sets, long training time, and slow learning capability. Thus, it was decided to develop a modular neural network for each type of faults. In this approach any task is divided into number of possible subtasks where each one is accomplished by an individual neural network. Finally, all network outputs are integrated to achieve the overall task. Obviously the approach has the advantages of simplicity, higher accuracy, less training sets and training time, easier interpretation, model complexity reduction, and better learning capability.

In modular approach, on the occurrence of a fault, the fault detection/classification unit [25–28, 30] activates the modular ANN-based fault distance locator unit. Four different ANN-based fault detector and classifier modules have been developed according to type of fault, that is, LG, LL, LLG, and LLL as shown in Figure 5. The output of ANN-based fault detector and classifier modules are

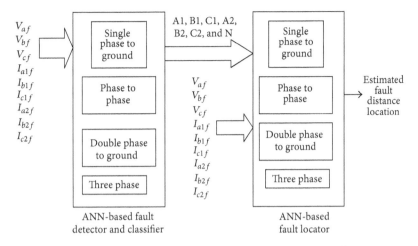

FIGURE 5: Block diagram of modular ANN-based fault distance locator.

TABLE 4: Architecture of modular ANN-based fault distance locator.

S. No.	Modular ANN-based fault distance locators	Architecture	Mean square error (MSE)
1	Phase to ground	9-30-7	$5.02509e - 04$
2	Phase to phase	9-30-7	$2.0906e - 04$
3	Double phase to ground	9-20-7	$2.7078e - 04$
4	Three phase	9-5-7	$8.52572e - 005$

total seven: three-phases of each circuit A1, B1, C1, A2, C2, and N neutral to determine whether fault involves ground or not. Based on the fault type which occurs on the system, output should be 0 or 1 in corresponding phase(s) and neutral. Fault detection/classification unit detects and identifies the type of fault and thus activates the particular type of fault locator to estimate the fault distance location. The inputs and output of modular ANN-based FDL are the same as selected for single ANN-based FDL approach, that is, total (9) inputs and one (1) output. The procedure of development of the architecture of modular ANN-based FDL is same as that is single ANN-based FDL. The block diagram of the proposed modular ANN-based FDL approach is shown in Figure 5. The fault location unit comprises of four feed forward neural networks, one network each for the four categories of fault (LG, LL, LLG, and LLL). The final architectures of modular ANN-based FDLs are shown in Table 4.

5. Comparison of Test Results of Single and Modular ANN-Based Fault Distance Locator

After training, single and modular ANN-based FDLs were extensively tested using independent data sets consisting of fault samples never used previously in training. The network was tested by presenting fault patterns with varying fault type, distance locations (L_f = 0–95 km), fault inception angles (Φ_i = 0–360°), and fault resistance (R_f = 0–100 Ω). Additionally, the effect of change in source strength at end, CT saturation, prefault power flow angle, fault resistance, and single-circuit operation is also studied. The test results

of single and modular ANN-based FDLs under different fault conditions are depicted in Table 5. At various locations different types of faults were tested to find out the maximum deviation of the estimated distance L_e measured from the relay location and the actual fault location L_f. Then the resulting estimated error "e" is expressed as a percentage of total line length L as

$$e = \frac{L_f - L_e}{L_f} \times 100\%. \tag{2}$$

It can be seen from the test results in Table 5, that the % error in locating the fault using single ANN-based FDL is within −1.973% to 7.162%, and that of modular ANN-based FDL lies between −1.362% and 1.201%. Thus, modular ANN-based FDL determines the fault distance location more accurately than the single ANN-based FDL. Some of the simulation results under different fault situations with varying power system parameters are discussed below. The extreme fault cases near to the source end (1 km) and at far end of the line (90 km) were also investigated.

5.1. Phase to Phase Fault with Varying Source Strength. During training, the strengths of both the sending and receiving end sources (GVA and X_s/R_s ratio) were taken as 1.25 GVA its X_s/R_s ratio is 10, and it is tested by varying the strengths of either end. To check the performance of the proposed techniques, the test conditions simulated is "A2C2" fault at 18 km from "SS-1" end. Fault has occurred at 65 ms (Φ_i = 90°), δ_s = 45°; source at SS-1 end has strength of 1.25 GVA, and its X_s/R_s ratio is 10; source at SS-2 end has strength of

TABLE 5: Test results of single and modular ANN-based fault distance locator.

Fault type	Fault inception angle Φ_i (°)	Fault resistance R_f (Ω)	Fault location L_f (km)	Output of single ANN-based FDL L_e (km)	Output of modular ANN-based FDL L_e (km)	% Error of single ANN-based FDL $e = ((L_f - L_e)/L_f) \times 100\%$	% Error of modular ANN-based FDL $e = ((L_f - L_e)/L_f) \times 100\%$
A1N	45	80	67	64.470	66.95	2.53	0.05
A2N	90	90	77	76.447	57.111	0.553	−0.111
B1N	135	0	5	4.9724	4.8895	0.0276	0.1105
B2N	270	80	89	88.624	88.681	0.376	0.319
C1N	360	95	95	92.405	94.604	2.595	0.396
C2N	180	70	38	35.449	38.385	2.551	−0.385
A1B1	270	—	83	83.020	83.25	−0.02	−0.25
A2B2	0	—	15	15.066	15.009	−0.066	−0.009
B1C1	0	—	76	75.049	75.894	0.951	0.106
B2C2	135	—	90	89.490	89.977	0.51	0.023
C1A1	90	—	22	22.144	22.134	−0.144	−0.134
C2A2	225	—	59	58.762	58.984	0.238	0.016
A1B1N	135	30	85	82.955	83.799	2.045	1.201
A2B2N	45	60	57	56.459	56.047	0.541	0.953
B1C1N	225	100	88	88.246	88.1006	−0.246	−0.1006
B2C2N	270	80	89	88.632	90.133	0.368	−1.133
C1A1N	225	30	58	50.838	57.047	7.162	0.953
C2A2N	90	40	24	20.105	25.362	3.895	−1.362
A1B1C1	225	—	33	33.757	32.952	−0.757	0.048
A2B2C2	360	—	85	86.973	85.136	−1.973	−0.136

0.25 GVA, and its X_s/R_s ratio is 5. During any fault situation in any one circuit of the double-circuit line which is fed from sources at both the ends as shown in Figure 6, remote end source also feed current to the fault point. This remote end infeed is not measurable at the relay location which causes the conventional relays to mal-operate.

Test results of single and modular ANN-based FDL for a phase to phase fault in circuit 2 with variation in source strength are shown in Figures 7(a) and 7(b), respectively. The neural network is trained to show the output as 100 km for no fault situations or fault outside the zone of protection. For faults within its zone of protection, it will show the estimated fault distance location. The output of single and modular ANN-based FDLs during prefault or steady-state conditions is around 110 km, as the networks are trained with a target location 110 km which is outside the line segment as shown in Figures 7(a) and 7(b), respectively. After the inception of the fault the algorithm takes one cycle to get the correct estimate of the fault distance location. The output of single and modular ANN-based FDLs at 98 ms is 18.5849 km and 18.1617 km as against 18 km, respectively. This shows that the modular ANN-based FDL has more accuracy in fault distance estimation as compared to single ANN-based FDL; however, the operating time of both the algorithms is more than one cycle time.

The reason behind the statement "operating time is after one cycle" is that one full cycle DFT is used to estimate the fundamental components of three-phase currents and

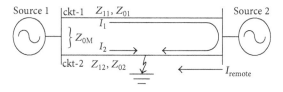

FIGURE 6: Single-line diagram of a three-phase double-circuit line connected with source at each end under fault condition.

voltages which is further given to ANN for fault distance location estimation. The estimation of fundamental components by DFT is being done continuously, thus immediately after the fault occurrence there is increase in the estimate of fundamental components of corresponding phase currents involved in the fault loop and decrease in estimate of fundamental components of corresponding phase voltages. ANN-based FDLs detects these changes (decrease) in fundamental components of voltages and (increase) currents, and its output decreases from the 110 km to the desired value after one-cycle time when the correct estimates of voltage and current are obtained (after one cycle from the inception of fault because of 1-cycle DFT).

5.2. Double Phase to Ground Fault with High Fault Resistance. When fault occurs with high fault resistance, the conventional

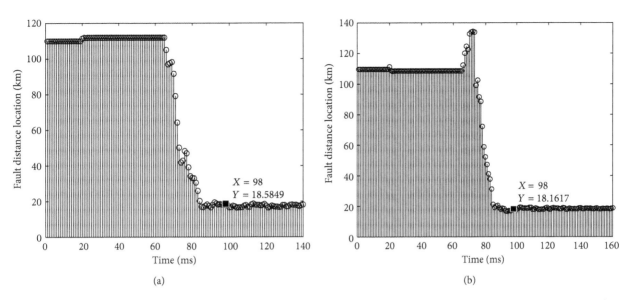

FIGURE 7: Test results of single and modular ANN-based FDL for "A2C2" fault in ckt-2 at $\Phi_i = 90°$ (inception time 65 ms) at 18 km, $\delta_s = 45°$, SS-1 end source strength =1.25 GVA, $X_s/R_s = 10$, and SS-2 end source strength = 0.25 GVA, $X_s/R_s = 5$, respectively.

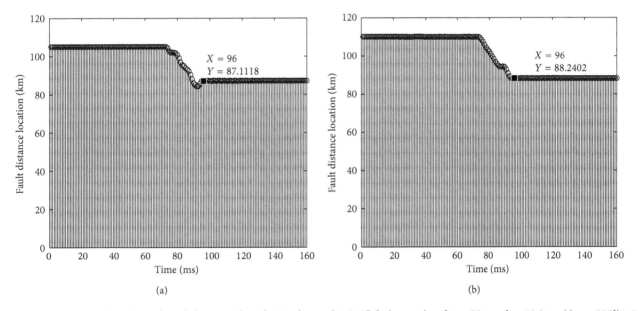

FIGURE 8: Test results of single and modular ANN-based FDL during "B1C1G" fault at 88 km from SS-1 end at 72.5 ms ($\Phi_i = 225°$) with $R_f = 100\,\Omega$, $\delta_s = 45°$, respectively.

distance relays under reach due to conversion of the fault resistance into effective fault impedance. To study the effect of high fault resistance a double phase to ground fault has been simulated with high fault resistance. Test conditions were "B1C1G" fault at 88 km from "SS-1" end with $R_f = 100\,\Omega$ and occurred at 72.5 ms with $\Phi_i = 225°$. Test results of single and modular ANN-based FDLs under this condition are shown in Figures 8(a) and 8(b). After one cycle from the inception of fault (72.5 ms), that is, 92.5 ms, the fundamental components of three-phase voltages and currents in both circuit are estimated correctly by DFT, thereafter the ANN-based algorithm gives correct result. As shown in Figures 8(a) and 8(b) at 96 ms, the outputs of single and modular

ANN-based FDL are 87.11 km and 88.2402 km, respectively, as against the set value of 88 km.

5.3. Three-Phase Close in Fault. When fault occurs very near to the source end where the relays are installed, it is called as a close in fault. A three-phase close in fault is simulated in ckt-2 of the selected power system model at 1 km from SS-1 end. Test conditions were "A2B2C2" fault at 1 km from "SS-1" end with $R_f = 0\,\Omega$ and occurred at 77.5 ms with $\Phi_i = 225°$. Test results of single and modular ANN-based FDLs under this condition are shown in Figures 9(a) and 9(b), respectively. From the Figure 9(a), it can be seen that

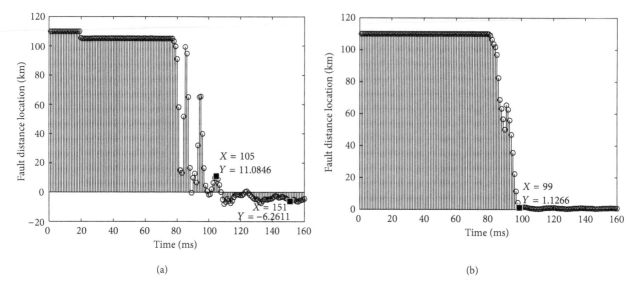

(a)

(b)

FIGURE 9: Test result of single and modular ANN-based FDL during "A2B2C2" fault at 1 km from source "SS-1" at $\Phi_i = 315°$ (fault inception time 77.5 ms) and $\delta_s = 45°$, respectively.

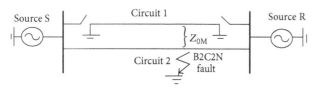

FIGURE 10: Double-circuit line with ckt-1 out of service, opened and grounded, and fault in ckt-2.

the single ANN-based FDL output fluctuates between 11.0846 km and −6.2611 km and finally settles at the later value as against the set value of 1 km. The output is negative for most of time; this is because the transfer function in the output layer is pure linear. Thus it is concluded that single ANN-based FDL is not able to locate the close in fault.

On the other hand the output of the modular ANN-based FDL after one cycle from the inception of fault (77.5 ms), that is, at 99 ms, is 1.1266 km instead of 1 km actual fault location as shown in Figure 9(b). Further the output is almost constant around 1 km. Thus it is clear that modular ANN-based FDL can precisely locate the close in three-phase fault also.

5.4. Single-Circuit Operation. The conventional distance relays overreach when both circuits are in service and underreach if one of the circuits is out of service and earthed at either ends [19]. The performance of single and modular ANN-based FDLs during fault in ckt-2 when ckt-1 is out of service and grounded is investigated as shown in Figure 10. For example, ckt-1 opened and grounded and double phase to ground fault in ckt-2, that is, "B2C2N" fault at 60 km from SS-1 end at 40 ms ($\Phi_i = 0°$) with $R_f = 50\,\Omega$, $\delta_s = 45°$ are examined.

Test results of single and modular ANN-based FDL are shown in Figures 11(a) and 11(b). The output of the single and modular ANN-based fault locators is 60.0222 km and

60.012 km at 63 ms, that is, after one cycle from the inception of fault as shown in Figures 11(a) and 11(b), respectively. This shows that the networks respond correctly and accurately when the double-circuit line is operated as a single-circuit line and there is fault in the healthy circuit. It can be concluded that ANN-based FDLs are adaptive to network changes, namely, double-circuit and single-circuit operation modes.

5.5. Single Phase to Ground Fault with CT Saturation. The test results of single and modular ANN-based FDL with CT saturation taken into account are shown in Figures 12(a) and 12(b), respectively. The test condition is single phase to ground fault applied on C1 phase of ckt-1, that is, "C1N fault at 60 ms ($\Phi_i = 0°$) at 90 km from "SS-1" end with $R_f = 0\,\Omega$ and $\delta_s = 45°$. It is observed from Figure 12(a) that the estimated fault distance by single ANN-based FDL during the same fault conditions with CT saturation taken into account has some variations. During prefault condition, the output is around 110 km, that is, out of the protected zone. At 86 ms output shows 90.6503 km as against the set value of 90 km. However, the estimated fault distance by modular ANN-based FDL at 86 ms is 89.8859 km as against 90 km actual fault distance as shown in Figure 12(b). This shows that the modular ANN-based FDL has more accuracy in fault distance estimation as compared to single ANN-based FDL.

6. Comparison with the Existing Schemes

The proposed modular ANN-based FDLs scheme is compared with the some of the reported works employing ANN. The proposed modular ANN-based fault locator scheme is developed for all the ten types of faults in both the circuits with wider range of fault resistance, fault inception angle, and source strengths variations which had been used for training pattern generation shown in Table 2. Once the network is trained its structural parameters are fixed

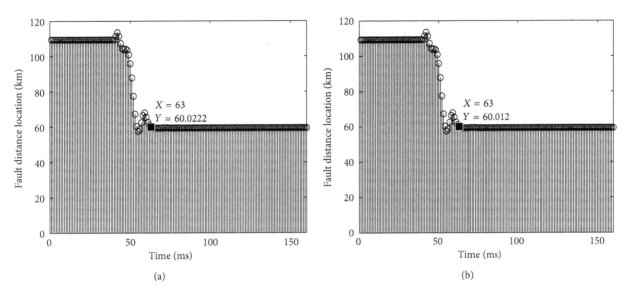

(a)

(b)

FIGURE 11: Test result of single and modular ANN-based FDL during "B2C2N" fault at 60 km from SS-1 end at 40 ms ($\Phi_i = 0°$) with $R_f = 50\,\Omega$, $\delta_s = 45°$, respectively.

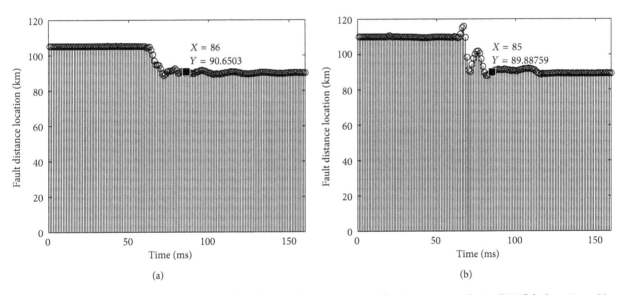

(a)

(b)

FIGURE 12: Test results of single and modular ANN-based FDL *with CT saturation* taken into account during "C1N" fault at 60 ms ($\Phi_i = 0°$) at 90 km from "SS-1" end with $R_f = 0\,\Omega$ and $\delta_s = 45°$, respectively.

(i.e., number. of layers, neurons, weight, bias, etc.). Further it is tested for different fault situation that has been not used during training of the network. The effects of remote source infeed, zero sequence mutual coupling, CT saturation, and network changes, for example, single-circuit operation, have also been considered without training the network again. The salient features of some of the existing ANN-based fault location schemes and the proposed scheme is presented in Table 6. Accuracy of the algorithm are lies between −1.362% and 1.201% as shown in Table 5 is which is quite good when compared to existing schemes. Response time of the proposed scheme for detection of the fault and distance location estimation is 1 cycle from the inception of fault which is comparable to the conventional distance relay.

7. Conclusions

Single and modular neural network modules were developed for determining the fault distance location in double-circuit transmission lines. The test results of single and modular ANN-based FDLs have been shown under variety of the fault situations, namely, LG faults (A1N, A2N, B1N, B2N, C1N, and C2N), LL faults (A1B1, A2B2, B1C1, B2C2, C1A1, and C2A2), LLG faults (A1B1N, A2B2N, B1C1N, B2C2N, C1A1N, and C2A1N), and LLL faults (A1B1C1 and A2B2C2). Also, variations in the power system parameters, namely, fault locations (0–95%), fault resistances (0–100 Ω), fault inception angles (0–360°), source strengths, CT saturation, and network changes, for example, single-circuit operation, have

TABLE 6: Comparison of neural network-based fault location schemes.

Schemes suggested by authors	Fault locator inputs	Line configuration	Fault resistance R_f range (Ω)	Fault inception angle Φ_i (°)	Other factors considered	Response time and accuracy
Mahanty and Gupta [13]	Samples of 3-phase V and I	Single-circuit line for LG and LL faults only	0–200	0–90°	Other types of faults and wide variation in inception angle not considered.	Response time not indicated and error is 6%.
Mazon et al. [9]	Samples of 50 Hz components of 3-phase voltages and currents of each circuits	Double-circuit line for LG faults only	0–20	—	Other types of faults and variation in inception angle not considered.	Response time not indicated and error is 0.19%.
Bhalja and Maheshwari [23]	Δp, δq, and resistance	Double-circuit line for LG faults only	0–200	—	Mutual coupling, remote source infeed.	Not indicated.
Singular distance locator (by Jain et al.) [25]	Samples of 50 Hz components of 3-phase voltages and currents of each circuits	Double-circuit line for all 10 types of faults in both the circuits (total 20 types of faults)	0–100	0–360°	Mutual coupling, remote source infeed, and all 10 types of faults in each circuit.	1-cycle time from inception of faults and % error is from −7% to +1.97%.
Proposed scheme (modular distance locator)	Samples of 50 Hz components of 3-phase voltages and currents of each circuits	Double-circuit line for all 10 types of faults in both the circuits (total 20 types of faults)	0–100	0–360°	Mutual coupling, remote source infeed, all 10 types of faults in each circuit, source strength variation, CT saturation, and single-circuit operation.	1-cycle time from inception of faults and % error is from −1.362% to +1.201%.

been considered. The comparison of the test results of single and modular approach shows that the modular approach is more accurate. The modular ANN-based FDLs test results are very encouraging and confirm the suitability of the technique for protection of double-circuit transmission line. The ANN-based fault locators calculates the fault distance up to 0–90% of the line length with high accuracy and enhances the performance of distance relaying scheme by increasing its reach setting. The proposed technique can be applied as an alternative protection scheme or a supplement to existing schemes.

References

[1] M. Agrasar, F. Uriondo, and J. R. Hernández, "Evaluation of uncertainties in double line distance relaying. A global sight," *IEEE Transactions on Power Delivery*, vol. 13, no. 4, pp. 1033–1039, 1998.

[2] A. G. Jongepier and L. van der Sluis, "Adaptive distance protection of a double-circuit line," *IEEE Transactions on Power Delivery*, vol. 9, no. 3, pp. 1289–1297, 1994.

[3] V. S. S. Vankayala and N. D. Rao, "Artificial neural networks and their applications to power systems—a bibliographical survey," *Electric Power Systems Research*, vol. 28, no. 1, pp. 67–79, 1993.

[4] S. A. Khaparde, N. Warke, and S. H. Agarwal, "An adaptive approach in distance protection using an artificial neural network," *Electric Power Systems Research*, vol. 37, no. 1, pp. 39–44, 1996.

[5] D. V. Coury and D. C. Jorge, "Artificial neural network approach to distance protection of transmission lines," *IEEE Transactions on Power Delivery*, vol. 13, no. 1, pp. 102–108, 1998.

[6] M. Sanaye-Pasand and O. P. Malik, "High speed transmission system directional protection using an Elman network," *IEEE Transactions on Power Delivery*, vol. 13, no. 4, pp. 1040–1045, 1998.

[7] M. Sanaye-Pasand and H. Khorashadi-Zadeh, "Transmission line fault detection & phase selection using ANN," in *Proceedings of the International Conference on Power Systems Transients (IPST'03)*, pp. 1–5, New Orleans, La, USA, 2003.

[8] M. Sanaye-Pasand and H. Khorashadi-Zadeh, "An extended ANN-based high speed accurate distance protection algorithm," *International Journal of Electrical Power and Energy Systems*, vol. 28, no. 6, pp. 387–395, 2006.

[9] A. J. Mazon, I. Zamora, J. F. Miñambres, M. A. Zorrozua, J. J. Barandiaran, and K. Sagastabeitia, "New approach to fault location in two-terminal transmission lines using artificial neural networks," *Electric Power Systems Research*, vol. 56, no. 3, pp. 261–266, 2000.

[10] R. Venkatesan and B. Balamurugan, "A real-time hardware fault detector using an artificial neural network for distance protection," *IEEE Transactions on Power Delivery*, vol. 16, no. 1, pp. 75–82, 2001.

[11] P. K. Dash, A. K. Pradhan, and G. Panda, "Application of minimal radial basis function neural network to distance protection," *IEEE Transactions on Power Delivery*, vol. 16, no. 1, pp. 68–74, 2001.

[12] W. M. Lin, C. D. Yang, J. H. Lin, and M. T. Tsay, "A fault classification method by RBF neural network with OLS learning procedure," *IEEE Transactions on Power Delivery*, vol. 16, no. 4, pp. 473–477, 2001.

[13] R. N. Mahanty and P. B. D. Gupta, "Application of RBF neural network to fault classification and location in transmission lines," *IEE Proceedings: Generation, Transmission and Distribution*, vol. 151, no. 2, pp. 201–212, 2004.

[14] T. Bouthiba, "Fault location in EHV transmission lines using artificial neural networks," *International Journal of Applied Mathematics and Computer Science*, vol. 14, no. 1, pp. 69–78, 2004.

[15] S. R. Samantaray, P. K. Dash, and G. Panda, "Fault classification and location using HS-transform and radial basis function neural network," *Electric Power Systems Research*, vol. 76, no. 9-10, pp. 897–905, 2006.

[16] H. Wang and W. W. L. Keerthipala, "Fuzzy-neuro approach to fault classification for transmission line protection," *IEEE Transactions on Power Delivery*, vol. 13, no. 4, pp. 1093–1104, 1998.

[17] T. Dalstein and B. Kulicke, "Neural network approach to fault classification for high speed protective relaying," *IEEE Transactions on Power Delivery*, vol. 10, no. 2, pp. 1002–1011, 1995.

[18] Q. Y. Xuan, R. K. Aggarwal, A. T. Johns, R. W. Dunn, and A. Bennett, "A neural network based protection technique for combined 275 kV/400 kV double circuit transmission lines," *Neurocomputing*, vol. 23, no. 1–3, pp. 59–70, 1998.

[19] R. K. Aggarwal, Q. Y. Xuan, R. W. Dunn, A. T. Johns, and A. Bennett, "A novel fault classification technique for double-circuit lines based on a combined unsupervised/supervised neural network," *IEEE Transactions on Power Delivery*, vol. 14, no. 4, pp. 1250–1256, 1999.

[20] G. K. Purushothama, A. U. Narendranath, D. Thukaram, and K. Parthasarathy, "ANN applications in fault locators," *International Journal of Electrical Power and Energy Systems*, vol. 23, no. 6, pp. 491–506, 2001.

[21] S. Skok, A. Marusic, S. Tesnjak, and L. Pevik, "Double-circuit line adaptive protection based on Kohonen neural network considering different operation and switching modes," in *Proceedings of the Power Engineering 2002 Large Engineering Systems Conference on LESCOPE*, vol. 2, pp. 153–157, 2002.

[22] L. S. Martins, J. F. Martins, V. F. Pires, and C. M. Alegria, "A neural space vector fault location for parallel double-circuit distribution lines," *International Journal of Electrical Power and Energy Systems*, vol. 27, no. 3, pp. 225–231, 2005.

[23] B. R. Bhalja and R. P. Maheshwari, "High-resistance faults on two terminal parallel transmission line: analysis, simulation studies, and an adaptive distance relaying scheme," *IEEE Transactions on Power Delivery*, vol. 22, no. 2, pp. 801–812, 2007.

[24] H. Demuth, M. Beale, and M. Hagan, *Neural Network Toolbox User's Guide, Revised for Version 6.0.4*, MathWorks, Natick, Mass, USA, 2010.

[25] A. Jain, A. S. Thoke, and R. N. Patel, "Double circuit transmission line fault distance location using artificial neural network," in *Proceedings of the World Congress on Nature and Biologically Inspired Computing (NABIC'09)*, pp. 13–18, Coimbatore, India, December 2009.

[26] A. Jain, A. S. Thoke, E. Koley, and R. N. Patel, "Double phase to ground fault classification and fault distance location of double circuit transmission lines using ANN," in *Proceedings of the 18th IEEE Bangalore Section Annual Symposium on Emerging Needs of Computing, Communication, Signals and Power*, paper no. ENCCSP-177, August 2009.

[27] A. Jain, A. S. Thoke, E. Koley, and R. N. Patel, "Fault classification and fault distance location of double circuit transmission

lines for phase to phase faults using only one terminal data," in *Proceedings of the International Conference on Power Systems (ICPS'09)*, paper no. 41, pp. 1–6, Kharagpur, India, December 2009.

[28] A. Jain, A. S. Thoke, and R. N. Patel, "Symmetrical fault detection, classification and distance location of double circuit transmission line using ANN," *CSVTU Research Journal*. In press.

[29] M. T. Hagan and M. B. Menhaj, "Training feedforward networks with the Marquardt algorithm," *IEEE Transactions on Neural Networks*, vol. 5, no. 6, pp. 989–993, 1994.

[30] A. Jain, A. S. Thoke, P. K. Modi, and R. N. Patel, "Classification and location of single line to ground faults in double circuit transmission lines using artificial neural networks," *International Journal of Power and Energy Conversion*, vol. 2, no. 2, pp. 109–225, 2010.

5

A Hybrid Reasoning Model for "Whole and Part" Cardinal Direction Relations

Ah-Lian Kor[1] and Brandon Bennett[2]

[1] *Arts Environment and Technology Faculty, Leeds Metropolitan University, Headingley Campus, Leeds LS6 3QS, UK*
[2] *School of Computing, University of Leeds, Leeds LS2 9JT, UK*

Correspondence should be addressed to Ah-Lian Kor; a.kor@leedsmet.ac.uk

Academic Editor: Ian Mitchell

We have shown how the nine *tiles* in the projection-based model for cardinal directions can be partitioned into sets based on horizontal and vertical constraints (called *Horizontal and Vertical Constraints Model*) in our previous papers (Kor and Bennett, 2003 and 2010). In order to come up with an expressive hybrid model for direction relations between two-dimensional single-piece regions (without holes), we integrate the well-known RCC-8 model with the above-mentioned model. From this expressive hybrid model, we derive 8 basic binary relations and 13 feasible as well as jointly exhaustive relations for the x- and y-directions, respectively. Based on these basic binary relations, we derive two separate 8×8 composition tables for both the expressive and weak direction relations. We introduce a formula that can be used for the computation of the composition of expressive and weak direction relations between "whole or part" regions. Lastly, we also show how the expressive hybrid model can be used to make several existential inferences that are not possible for existing models.

1. Introduction

Relative positions of regions in large-scale spaces, and particularly in the geographic domain, are often described by relations referring to cardinal directions. These relations specify the direction from one region to another in terms of the familiar compass bearings: north, south, east, and west. The intermediate directions northwest, northeast, southwest, and southeast are also often used. Some models for reasoning with cardinal directions are the cone-shaped [1, 2], projection-based models (ibid), and direction matrix [3–5].

Papadias and Theodoridis [6] describe topological and direction relations between regions using their minimum bounding rectangles (MBRs). However, the language used is not expressive enough to describe direction relations. Additionally, the MBR technique yields erroneous outcome when involving regions that are not rectangular in shape [4] Some work has been done on hybrid direction models. Escrig and Toledo [7] and Clementini et al. [8] integrated qualitative

orientation and distance to obtain positional information. Isli [9] combined Frank's [1, 2] cardinal direction relations model and Freksa's [10] orientation model to facilitate a more expressive reasoning mechanism. Sharma and Flewelling [11] infer spatial relations from integrated topological and cardinal direction relations. Liu and colleagues [12] have developed reasoning algorithms which combine RCC-8 [13] for topological relations (discussed in Section 4) and the cardinal direction calculus (CDC [3–5], discussed in Section 2) for direction relations. Li and colleagues' work [14, 15] focuses on the development and evaluation of an efficient reasoning mechanism for RCC-8 and RA (Rectangle Algebra, and further explanation can be found in [16, 17]) which is employed to solve the satisfiability problem of these two joint constraint networks.

Typically, composition tables are used to infer spatial relations between objects. They have been employed to make different inferences about cardinal directions relations [3, 19–24]. One of the advantages of composition tables is that they

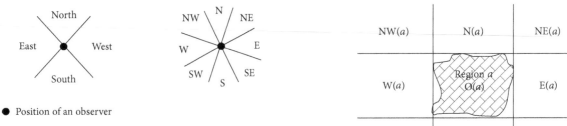

FIGURE 1: Cone-shaped direction model with 4 or 8 partitions (ibid).

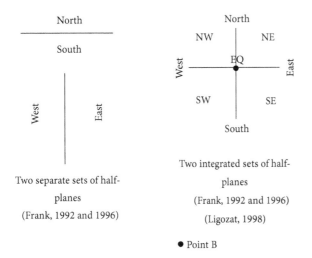

Two separate sets of half-planes

(Frank, 1992 and 1996)

Two integrated sets of half-planes

(Frank, 1992 and 1996)

(Ligozat, 1998)

● Point B

FIGURE 2: Cardinal directions defined by half-planes.

FIGURE 3: Cardinal directions defined by tiles for extended objects [1, 2].

can lead to tractable computation of inferences [25]. In this paper, we have developed an expressive hybrid model for direction relations. We will describe the binary relations in the model and define *"whole and part"* relations. Based on this model, we derive two 8 × 8 composition tables for *expressive and weak* direction relations. This is followed by introducing a formula which could be used to compute both *expressive and weak* direction relations for *"whole and part"* regions. Finally, we will demonstrate how the model could be used to make several types of existential inferences.

2. Cardinal Direction Models

Frank [1, 2] defines cardinal directions as cones which are related to the angular direction between an observer's position (in the form of a point) and a destination point. The cone-shaped cardinal direction model could have 4, 8, or more partitions (look at Figure 1).

Frank defines the four major cardinal directions (north, south, east, and west) as pair-wise opposites and half planes. When the two sets of half planes are combined, it yields four intermediate cardinal directions (northeast, northwest, southeast, and southwest) which are depicted in Figure 2. Ligozat [21] applies the model to points in a two-dimensional space. Thus, the referent object, *Point B*, will be given the four major directions. However, the relations between two objects will be denoted by one of the following basic relations: N, S, E, W, NE, NW, SE, SW, or EQ.

Frank [1, 2] extends the half-planes to tiles for regions (as shown in Figure 3). In this projection-based model, the plane of an arbitrary single-piece region *a* is partitioned into nine *tiles*, North-West, NW(*a*); North, N(*a*); North-East, NE(*a*); South-West, SW(*a*); South, S(*a*); South-East, SE(*a*); West, W(*a*); Neutral Zone, O(*a*); East, E(*a*). According to Frank, the O tile is considered a neutral zone, because in this tile, the relative cardinal direction between two regions cannot be determined due to their proximity.

Frank compares and contrasts reasoning with the cone-shaped and the projection-based models for cardinal directions. The reasoning capability for both the systems is limited and weak though they do not differ substantially in their reasoning outcomes. In order to create a more expressive reasoning model, Isli [26] integrates the Frank's cone-shaped and projection-based models to facilitate reasoning about relative position of points of the 2-dimensional space. This hybrid model is well suited for applications of large-scale high-level vision, such as, for example, satellite-like surveillance of a geographic area.

The cardinal direction calculus (CDC) [3–5] is a very expressive qualitative calculus for directional information of extended objects. A direction relation matrix (DRM) in (1) is used to represent direction relations between connected plane regions. Liu and colleagues [27, 28] have shown that consistency checking of complete networks of basic CDC constraints is tractable, while reasoning with the CDC in general is NP hard. However, if some constraints are unspecified, then consistency checking of incomplete networks of basic CDC constraints is intractable.

The cardinal direction of a target object (region *b*) to a referent object (region *a*) as shown in Figure 4 is described by recording those tiles covered by the target object. According to Goyal and Egenhofer [4], a 3 × 3 matrix is employed to register the intersections between the target object and the tiles of the referent object (see (1)). The elements in the direction-relation matrix correspond to the tiles of the referent object, region *a* (in Figure 4).

In (1), the symbol Ø represents empty tile while ¬Ø represents nonempty tile. These are used to describe cardinal directions at a coarse granularity level. In Figure 4, region *b* occupies the N, NW, and E tiles of region *a*. Thus, these three

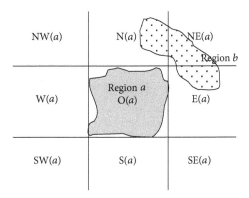

FIGURE 4: Nine tiles with regions a (as the referent object) and b (as the target object) [4, 5].

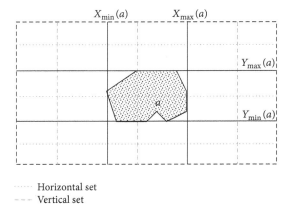

.... Horizontal set

- - - Vertical set

FIGURE 5: Horizontal and vertical sets of *tiles* for a.

tiles are considered nonempty while the rest are considered empty (as shown in (1)).

Goyal and Egenhofer [5] extend the direction relation matrix, so that it will be more expressive. Instead of using the empty and nonempty notations, it registers how much (in terms of proportion) the target region occupies each tile (see (2)). The expressive direction relation matrix in (2) has 6 elements of zero and three nonzero elements which sum up to 1.0. If the matrix has only one nonzero element then it is known as a *single element direction relation matrix* while a matrix with more than one nonzero element is called a *multielement direction relation matrix* (ibid).

Coarse direction relation matrix [4]:

$$\text{dir}_{RR}(a,b) = \begin{pmatrix} \text{NW}(a) \cap b & \text{N}(a) \cap b & \text{NE}(a) \cap b \\ \text{W}(a) \cap b & \text{O}(a) \cap b & \text{E}(a) \cap b \\ \text{SW}(a) \cap b & \text{S}(a) \cap b & \text{SE}(a) \cap b \end{pmatrix},$$

(1)

$$\text{dir}_{RR}(a,b) = \begin{pmatrix} \emptyset & \neg\emptyset & \neg\emptyset \\ \emptyset & \emptyset & \neg\emptyset \\ \emptyset & \emptyset & \emptyset \end{pmatrix}.$$

Expressive direction relation matrix [5]:

$\text{dir}_{RR}(a,b)$

$$= \begin{pmatrix} \dfrac{\text{area}(\text{NW}(a) \cap b)}{\text{area of } b} & \dfrac{\text{area}(\text{N}(a) \cap b)}{\text{area of } b} & \dfrac{\text{area}(\text{NE}(a) \cap b)}{\text{area of } b} \\ \dfrac{\text{area}(\text{W}(a) \cap b)}{\text{area of } b} & \dfrac{\text{area}(\text{O}(a) \cap b)}{\text{area of } b} & \dfrac{\text{area}(\text{E}(a) \cap b)}{\text{area of } b} \\ \dfrac{\text{area}(\text{SW}(a) \cap b)}{\text{area of } b} & \dfrac{\text{area}(\text{S}(a) \cap b)}{\text{area of } b} & \dfrac{\text{area}(\text{SE}(a) \cap b)}{\text{area of } b} \end{pmatrix},$$

$$\text{dir}_{RR}(a,b) = \begin{pmatrix} 0 & 0.05 & 0.45 \\ 0 & 0 & 0.50 \\ 0 & 0 & 0 \end{pmatrix}.$$

(2)

3. Horizontal and Vertical Constraints Model

Every region has a minimal bounding box with specific minimum and maximum x (and y) values. The boundaries of the minimal bounding box of a region a are depicted in Figure 5. The set of boundaries of the minimal bounding box for region a could be represented as $\{X_{\min}(a), X_{\max}(a), Y_{\min}(a), Y_{\max}(a)\}$, and these values will be employed to define each tile.

The definition of the nine tiles in terms of the boundaries of the minimal bounding box is listed as below. Note, in this paper, all the tiles are regarded as mutually exclusive. Thus neighboring tiles cannot share common boundaries:

(i) $\text{N}(a) \equiv \{\langle x, y\rangle \mid X_{\min}(a) \le x < X_{\max}(a) \wedge y \ge Y_{\max}(a)\}$,

(ii) $\text{NE}(a) \equiv \{\langle x, y\rangle \mid x \ge X_{\max}(a) \wedge y \ge Y_{\max}(a)\}$,

(iii) $\text{NW}(a) \equiv \{\langle x, y\rangle \mid x < X_{\min}(a) \wedge y \ge Y_{\max}(a)\}$,

(iv) $\text{S}(a) \equiv \{\langle x, y\rangle \mid X_{\min}(a) \le x < X_{\max}(a) \wedge y < Y_{\min}(a)\}$,

(v) $\text{SE}(a) \equiv \{\langle x, y\rangle \mid x \ge X_{\max}(a) \wedge y < Y_{\min}(a)\}$,

(vi) $\text{SW}(a) \equiv \{\langle x, y\rangle \mid x < X_{\min}(a) \wedge y < Y_{\min}(a)\}$,

(vii) $\text{E}(a) \equiv \{\langle x, y\rangle \mid x \ge X_{\max}(a) \wedge Y_{\min}(a) \le y < Y_{\max}(a)\}$,

(viii) $\text{W}(a) \equiv \{\langle x, y\rangle \mid x < X_{\min}(a) \wedge Y_{\min}(a) \le y < Y_{\max}(a)\}$,

(ix) $\text{O}(a) \equiv \{\langle x, y\rangle \mid X_{\min}(a) \le x < X_{\max}(a) \wedge Y_{\min}(a) \le y < Y_{\max}(a)\}$.

In our previous papers [29, 30], we have shown how to partition the nine *tiles* (in Figure 5) into sets based on horizontal and vertical constraints called the *Horizontal and Vertical Constraints Model*. However, in this paper, we shall rename the sets for easy comprehension purposes. The following are the definitions of the partitioned regions.

(i) WeakNorth(a) is the region that covers the *tiles* NW(a), N(a), and NE(a). WeakNorth(a) $\equiv$ NW(a) $\cup$ N(a) $\cup$ NE(a).

(ii) Horizontal(a) is the region that covers the *tiles* W(a), O(a), and E(a). Horizontal(a) $\equiv$ W(a) $\cup$ O(a) $\cup$ E(a).

(iii) WeakSouth(a) is the region that covers the *tiles* SW(a), S(a), and SE(a). WeakSouth(a) $\equiv$ SW(a) $\cup$ S(a) $\cup$ SE(a).

(iv) WeakWest(a) is the region that covers the *tiles* SW(a), W(a), and NW(a). WeakWest(a) $\equiv$ SW(a) $\cup$ W(a) $\cup$ NW(a).

(v) Vertical(a) is the region that covers the *tiles* S(a), O(a), and N(a). Vertical(a) $\equiv$ S(a) $\cup$ O(a) $\cup$ N(a).

(vi) WeakEast(a) is the region that covers the *tiles* SE(a), E(a), and NE(a). WeakEast(a) $\equiv$ SE(a) $\cup$ E(a) $\cup$ NE(a).

4. RCC Model

RCC stands for region connection calculus [13, 18, 31]. It is a first-order theory employed for qualitative spatial representation as well as reasoning and is based on Clarke's logic of connection [32, 33]. The connection predicate, C(a, b), which means "*region a is connected with region b*", is the only primitive predicate for RCC. This dyadic relation is both reflexive and symmetric and holds whenever regions a and b are "*connected*." The two main axioms expressing reflexivity and symmetry [18] are as follows:

$$\forall_a [C(a,a)] \quad \text{(reflexive)}$$
$$\forall_a \forall_b [C(a,b) \longrightarrow C(b,a)] \quad \text{(symmetric)}. \tag{3}$$

Based on this primitive, a basic set of dyadic relations are defined as shown in Table 1.

The relations P, PP, TPP, and NTPP are nonsymmetrical and will have their respective inverses (Pi, PPi, TPPi, and NTPPi). Of all the listed relations, only 8 relations in the following set {DC, EC, PO, EQ, TPP, NTPP, TPPi, NTPPi} are provably jointly exhaustive and pairwise disjoint (JEPD—which means any two regions are related by exactly one of these eight relations [34, 35]). Randell and colleagues [13] refer this set of relations as RCC-8, and they are depicted in Figure 6.

5. Expressive Hybrid Model

In our expressive hybrid model, we have combined our *Horizontal and Vertical Constraints Model* [29, 30] and RCC-8 [13].

5.1. Definitions.
If there is a referent region a and another arbitrary region b, the possible basic binary relations between them can be defined as below.

In terms of weak relations,

(i) *WeakNorth(b,a)*: $b \subseteq$ WeakNorth(a),

(ii) *Horizontal(b,a)*: $b \subseteq$ Horizontal(a),

(iii) *WeakSouth(b,a)*: $b \subseteq$ WeakSouth(a),

(iv) *WeakEast(b,a)*: $b \subseteq$ WeakEast(a),

(v) *Vertical(b,a)*: $b \subseteq$ Vertical(a),

(vi) *WeakWest(b,a)*: $b \subseteq$ WeakWest(a).

In terms of RCC-8 relations,

(i) DCy(a,b): y-dimension of a is disconnected from y-dimension of b,

(ii) EQy(a,b): y-dimension of a is identical with y-dimension of b,

(iii) POy(a,b): y-dimension of a partially overlaps y-dimension of b,

(iv) ECy(a,b): y-dimension of a is externally connected to y-dimension of b,

(v) TPPy(a,b): y-dimension of a is a tangential proper part of y-dimension of b,

(vi) NTPPy(a,b): y-dimension of a is a nontangential proper part of y-dimension of b,

(vii) TPPiy(a,b): y-dimension of b is a tangential proper part of y-dimension of a,

(viii) NTPPiy(a,b): y-dimension of b is a non-tangential proper part of y-dimension of a,

(ix) DCx(a,b): x-dimension of a is disconnected from x-dimension of b,

(x) EQx(a,b): x-dimension of a is identical with x-dimension of b,

(xi) POx(a,b): x-dimension of a partially overlaps x-dimension of b,

(xii) ECx(a,b): x-dimension of a is externally connected to x-dimension of b,

(xiii) TPPx(a,b): x-dimension of a is a tangential proper part of x-dimension of b,

(xiv) NTPPx(a,b): x-dimension of a is a non-tangential proper part of x-dimension of b,

(xv) TPPix(a,b): x-dimension of b is a tangential proper part of x-dimension of a,

(xvi) NTPPix(a,b): x-dimension of b is a non-tangential proper part of x-dimension of a.

5.2. Basic Binary Relations of the Hybrid Model.
In this section, we shall demonstrate how we come up with all possible binary direction relations for the hybrid model. All the possible basic binary relations for each horizontal set are shown in Figure 7. The notations that will be used in this section are as follows.

(i) RELy(b,Z) is any basic binary relation between b and the horizontally partitioned region, Z.

(ii) RELx(b,Z) is any basic binary relation between b and the vertically partitioned region, Z.

Based on Figure 7, the total number of possible binary relations for the hybrid model in the y-direction is $[(2 + 4 + 2) + (2 \times 4) + (2 \times 2) + (4 \times 2) + (2 \times 4 \times 2)]$ which equals 44 cases. However, due to the single-piece condition, the following rules apply.

Rule 1. $\neg(b \subseteq \text{WeakNorth}(a) \land b \subseteq \text{WeakSouth}(a))$.

Rule 2. Assume U to be {WeakNorth(a), Horizontal(a), WeakSouth(a)}.

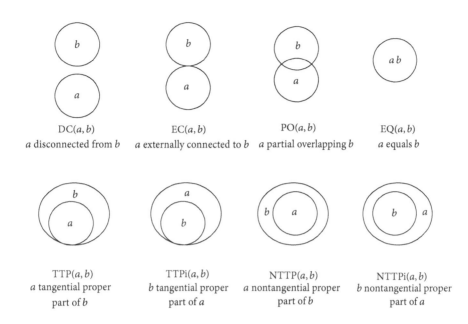

FIGURE 6: 8 basic JEPD RCC binary relations [13].

TABLE 1: Spatial relations defined in terms of $C(a, b)$ [18].

Relations	Semantics	Definition
$DC(a, b)$	a is disconnected from b	$\neg\, C(a, b)$
$P(a, b)$	a is part of b	$\forall_e [C(e, a) \rightarrow C(e, b)]$
$PP(a, b)$	a is a proper part of b	$P(a, b) \wedge \neg\, P(b, a)$
$EQ(a, b)$	a is identical with b	$P(a, b) \wedge P(b, a)$
$O(a, b)$	a overlaps b	$\exists_e [P(e, a) \wedge P(e, b)]$
$DR(a, b)$	a is discrete from b	$\neg\, O(a, b)$
$PO(a, b)$	a partially overlaps b	$O(a, b) \wedge \neg\, P(a, b) \wedge \neg\, P(b, a)$
$EC(a, b)$	a is externally connected to b	$C(a, b) \wedge \neg\, O(a, b)$
$TPP(a, b)$	a is a tangential proper part of b	$PP(a, b) \wedge \exists_e [EC(e, a) \wedge EC(e, b)]$
$NTPP(a, b)$	a is a nontangential proper part of b	$PP(a, b) \wedge \neg\, \exists_e [EC(e, a) \wedge EC(e, b)]$

If $NTPP y(b, R)$ where $R \in U$ then $\neg(NTPP y(b, R) \wedge$ REL$y(b, S))$,

where $S \in U - R$, or $\neg(NTPP y(b, R) \wedge$ REL$y(b, S) \wedge$ REL$y(b, T))$,

where $T \in U - S$.

Rule 3. Assume U to be {WeakNorth(a), WeakSouth(a)}.
If $(TPP y(b,$Horizontal$(a)) \wedge EC y(b, R))$, where $R \in U$,
then $\neg(TPP y(b,$Horizontal$) \wedge EC y(b, R) \wedge$ REL$y(b, S))$,
where $S \in U - R$.

Based on the rules above, the total number of feasible binary relations for single-piece regions in the y-direction is (44-4-23-4) which equals 13 cases. The thirteen feasible and jointly exhaustive binary relations for the hybrid model are depicted in Figure 8. This means that, in the hybrid model, the number of jointly exhaustive binary relations (in both the x-

and y-directions) that hold between two single-piece regions will be 13 × 13. This concurs with the 13 × 13 basic relations in the *Rectangle Algebra Model* [16, 17].

6. Combined Mereological, Topological, and Cardinal Direction Relations

Mereology (from the Greek μερος, "part") is the theory of parthood relations: of the relations of part to whole and the relations, of part to part within a whole [36]. In this section, we shall make two distinctions: "*whole and part*" cardinal directions, as well as "*weak and expressive*" relations. We shall rewrite the notations used in our previous paper [29]. $P_R(b,a)$ means that only part of the destination extended region, b, is in tile $R(a)$. The direction relation $A_R(b, a)$ means that whole destination extended region, b, is in the tile R(a). As

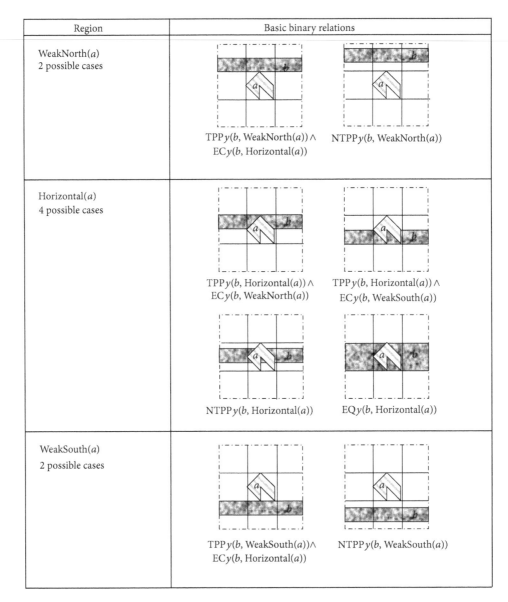

Region	Basic binary relations
WeakNorth(a) 2 possible cases	TPPy(b, WeakNorth(a)) ∧ ECy(b, Horizontal(a)) NTPPy(b, WeakNorth(a))
Horizontal(a) 4 possible cases	TPPy(b, Horizontal(a)) ∧ ECy(b, WeakNorth(a)) TPPy(b, Horizontal(a)) ∧ ECy(b, WeakSouth(a)) NTPPy(b, Horizontal(a)) EQy(b, Horizontal(a))
WeakSouth(a) 2 possible cases	TPPy(b, WeakSouth(a)) ∧ ECy(b, Horizontal(a)) NTPPy(b, WeakSouth(a))

FIGURE 7: Possible basic binary relations for each horizontally partitioned region (note: it will be similar for vertically partitioned region).

an example, when b is completely in the South-East tile of a, this direction relation can be represented as shown below:

$$A_{SE}(b, a) = \neg P_N(b, a) \wedge \neg P_{NE}(b, a) \wedge \neg P_{NW}(b, a)$$
$$\wedge \neg P_S(b, a) \wedge P_{SE}(b, a) \wedge \neg P_{SW}(b, a) \qquad (4)$$
$$\wedge \neg P_W(b, a) \wedge \neg P_E(b, a) \wedge \neg P_O(b, a).$$

The *"whole and weak"* direction relations are defined in terms of horizontal and vertical sets:

(i) $A_N(b, a) \equiv$ WeakNorth(b, a) ∧ Vertical(b, a),

(ii) $A_{NE}(b, a) \equiv$ WeakNorth(b, a) ∧ WeakEast(b, a),

(iii) $A_{NW}(b, a) \equiv$ WeakNorth(b, a) ∧ WeakWest(b, a),

(iv) $A_S(b, a) \equiv$ WeakSouth(b, a) ∧ Vertical(b, a),

(v) $A_{SE}(b, a) \equiv$ WeakSouth(b, a) ∧ WeakEast(b, a),

(vi) $A_{SW}(b, a) \equiv$ WeakSouth(b, a) ∧ WeakWest(b, a),

(vii) $A_E(b, a) \equiv$ Horizontal(b, a) ∧ WeakEast(b, a),

(viii) $A_W(b, a) \equiv$ Horizontal(b, a) ∧ WeakWest(b, a),

(ix) $A_O(b, a) \equiv$ Horizontal(b, a) ∧ Vertical(b, a).

The *"whole and expressive"* direction relations are defined in terms of expressive horizontal and vertical sets. A general form of such direction relation can be represented as follows:

$$^{REL y(b, H(a))} \left[A_R(b, a) \right]_{REL x(b, V(a))}$$
$$\equiv REL y(b, H(a)) \wedge REL x(b, V(a)), \qquad (5)$$

where H(a) and V(a) are horizontally and vertically partitioned regions for a, respectively, where $b \subseteq R(a)$ and R(a) ⊆ (H(a) ∩ V(a)).

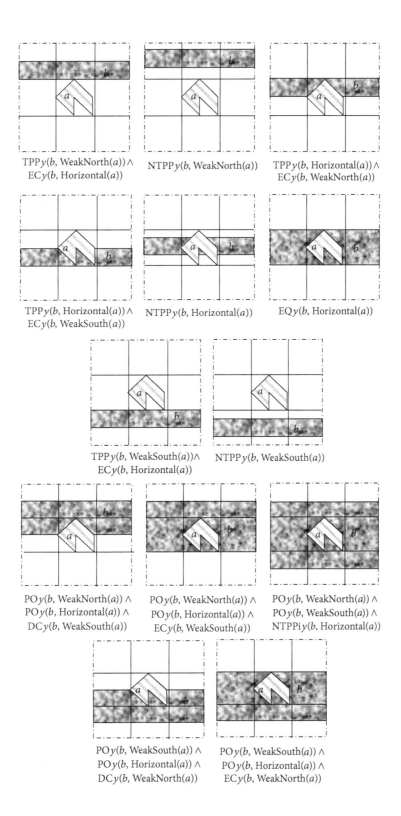

FIGURE 8: Thirteen feasible and jointly exhaustive binary relations in the y-direction for the hybrid model (note: this will be similar for x-direction for the model).

7. Composition Table

Composition is a common inference mechanism for a wide range of relations and has been exploited for automated reasoning. It has been employed for reasoning about temporal descriptions of events based on intervals [37], topological relations [5, 38–42], direction relations [1, 24, 29, 30], and combined topological relations with cardinal direction relations [19]. To reiterate, one of the main advantages of using composition tables is that they can lead to tractable computation of significant classes of inference [25].

Given the relation between a and b and the relation between b and c, a composition table allows for concluding the relation between a and c. Bennett [41] defines the concept of the composition of two binary relations as follows.

> Given a theory Θ which is used to define a set β of mutually exhaustive and pairwise disjoint dyadic relations (i.e., a basis set), the composition, Comp(R_1, R_2), of two relations R_1 and R_2 which are taken from ß is defined to be the disjunction of all relations R_3 in ß, such that, for arbitrary constants a, b, and c, the formula $R_1(a,b) \wedge R_2(b,c) \wedge R_3(a,c)$ is consistent with Θ.

7.1. Composition of Regions with Parts. In our previous paper [29], the method for computing the composition of cardinal direction relations for part regions is not robust enough, because it does not hold for all cases. In order to address this problem, we introduce a formula (obtained through case analyses) for computing the composition of cardinal direction relations. The basis of the formula is to consider the direction relation between a and each individual part of b followed by the direction relation between each individual part of b and c.

Assume that the region covers one or more *tiles* of region a while region c covers one or more *tiles* of b. The direction relation between a and b is $R(b,a)$ while the direction relation between b and c is $S(c,b)$. The composition of direction relations could be written as follows:

$$R(b,a) \wedge S(c,b). \tag{6}$$

Firstly, establish the direction relation between a and each individual part of b:

$$R(b,a) \wedge S(c,b)$$

$$\equiv [R_1(b_1,a) \wedge R_2(b_2,a) \cdots \wedge R_k(b_k,a)] \tag{7}$$

$$\wedge [S(c,b)],$$

where $1 \le k \le 9$.

Consider the direction relation of each individual part of b and c. Equation (7) becomes

$$[[R_1(b_1,a) \wedge S_{11}(c_1,b_1)] \vee [R_1(b_1,a) \wedge S_{12}(c_2,b_1)] \cdots$$

$$\vee [R_1(b_1,a) \wedge S_{1m}(c_{1m},b_1)]]$$

$$\wedge [[R_2(b_2,a) \wedge S_{21}(c_1,b_2)] \vee [R_2(b_2,a) \wedge S_{22}(c_2,b_2)] \cdots$$

$$\vee [R_2(b_2,a) \wedge S_{2m}(c_{2m},b_2)]]$$

$$\wedge \cdots [[R_k(b_k,a) \wedge S_{k1}(c_1,b_k)] \vee [R_k(b_k,a) \wedge S_{k2}(c_2,b_k)] \cdots$$

$$\vee [R_k(b_k,a) \wedge S_{km}(c_{km},b_k)]], \tag{8}$$

where $1 \le k, \ m \le 9$.

7.2. Composition of Weak Direction Relations. Firstly, we shall demonstrate how to apply the formula for the composition of weak direction relations followed by more expressive direction relations.

Type 1. $A_R(b,a) \wedge A_R(c,b)$.
   Find the composition of $A_O(b,a) \wedge A_{SW}(c,b)$.
   Use (8) with $k = 1$ and $m = 1$:

$$R_1(b_1,a) \wedge S_{11}(c_1,b_1)$$

$$\equiv A_O(b,a) \wedge A_{SW}(c,b)$$

$$\equiv [\text{Horizontal}(b,a) \wedge \text{Vertical}(b,a)]$$

$$\wedge [\text{WeakSouth}(c,b) \wedge \text{WeakWest}(c,b)] \tag{9}$$

$$\equiv [\text{Horizontal}(b,a) \wedge \text{WeakSouth}(c,b)]$$

$$\wedge [\text{Vertical}(b,a) \wedge \text{WeakWest}(c,b)].$$

The outcome of the composition is

$$[\text{Horizontal}(c,a) \vee \text{WeakSouth}(c,a)]$$

$$\wedge [\text{Vertical}(c,a) \vee \text{WeakWest}(c,a)]. \tag{10}$$

This means that the region $c \subseteq O(a) \vee W(a) \vee S(a) \vee SW(a)$.

Type 2. $A_R(b,a) \wedge P_R(c,b)$.
   Find the composition of $A_E(b,a) \wedge [P_{NW}(c,b) \wedge P_N(c,b)]$.
   Use (8) with $k = 1$, and $1 \le m \le 2$:

$$[[R_1(b_1,a) \wedge S_{11}(c_1,b_1)] \vee [R_1(b_1,a) \wedge S_{12}(c_2,b_1)]]$$

$$\equiv [[A_E(b,a) \wedge A_{NW}(c_1,b)] \vee [A_E(b,a) \wedge A_N(c_2,b)]]$$

$$\equiv [[\text{Horizontal}(b,a) \wedge \text{WeakEast}(b,a)]$$

$$\wedge [\text{WeakNorth}(c_1,b) \wedge \text{WeakWest}(c_1,b)]]$$

$$\vee [[\text{Horizontal}(b,a) \wedge \text{WeakEast}(b,a)]$$

$$\wedge \left[\text{WeakNorth}\,(c_2, b) \wedge \text{Vertical}\,(c_2, b) \right]]$$

$$\equiv \left[\left[\text{Horizontal}\,(b, a) \wedge \text{WeakNorth}\,(c_1, b) \right] \right.$$

$$\wedge \left[\text{WeakEast}\,(b, a) \wedge \text{WeakWest}\,(c_1, b) \right]]$$

$$\vee \left[\left[\text{Horizontal}\,(b, a) \wedge \text{WeakNorth}\,(c_2, b) \right] \right.$$

$$\wedge \left[\text{WeakEast}\,(b, a) \wedge \text{Vertical}\,(c_2, b) \right]] .$$

$$(11)$$

The outcome of the composition is

$$\left[\left[\text{Horizontal}\,(c_1, a) \vee \text{WeakNorth}\,(c_1, a) \right] \right.$$

$$\wedge \left[\text{WeakEast}\,(c_1, a) \vee \text{Vertical}\,(c_1, a) \vee \text{WeakWest}\,(c_1, a) \right]]$$

$$\vee \left[\left[\text{Horizontal}\,(c_2, a) \vee \text{WeakNorth}\,(c_2, a) \right] \right.$$

$$\wedge \left[\text{WeakEast}\,(c_2, a) \right]] .$$

$$(12)$$

Viewing the fact that $c_1 \subset c$ and $c_2 \subset c$, the above outcome can be written as

$$\left[\left[\text{Horizontal}\,(c, a) \vee \text{WeakNorth}\,(c, a) \right] \right.$$

$$\wedge \left[\text{WeakEast}\,(c, a) \vee \text{Vertical}\,(c, a) \vee \text{WeakWest}\,(c, a) \right]] .$$

$$(13)$$

This means that the region $c \subseteq \text{E}(a) \vee \text{O}(a) \vee \text{W}(a) \vee \text{NE}(a) \vee \text{N}(a) \vee \text{NW}(a)$.

Type 3. $P_R(b, a) \wedge A_R(c, b)$.

Find the composition of $[P_O(b_1, a) \wedge P_N(b_2, a)] \wedge A_{\text{NE}}(c, b)$. Establish the relationship between c and each individual part of b. In this case, $A_{\text{NE}}(c, b)$, $P_{\text{NE}}(c, b_1)$ and $P_{\text{NE}}(c, b_2)$ holds (this is not necessarily true for all cases).

Use (8) with $1 \leq k \leq 2$ and $m = 1$.

$$\left[\left[P_{R1}\,(b_1, a) \right] \wedge \left[P_{R11}\,(c_1, b_1) \right] \right]$$

$$\wedge \left[\left[P_{R2}\,(b_2, a) \right] \wedge \left[P_{R21}\,(c_1, b_2) \right] \right]$$

$$\equiv \left[\left[P_O\,(b_1, a) \right] \wedge \left[P_{\text{NE}}\,(c, b) \right] \right]$$

$$\wedge \left[\left[P_N\,(b_2, a) \right] \wedge \left[P_{\text{NE}}\,(c, b) \right] \right] .$$

$$(14)$$

Therefore, the above composition can be rewritten as

$$\left[\left[P_O\,(b_1, a) \right] \wedge \left[P_{\text{NE}}\,(c, b_1) \right] \right] \wedge \left[\left[P_N\,(b_2, a) \right] \wedge \left[P_{\text{NE}}\,(c, b_2) \right] \right]$$

$$\equiv \left[\left[\text{Horizontal}\,(b_1, a) \wedge \text{Vertical}\,(b_1, a) \right] \right.$$

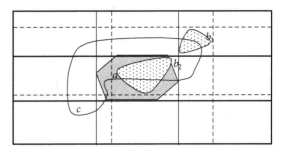

—— Boundaries of minimal bounding box for region a
--- Boundaries of minimal bounding box for region b

FIGURE 9: An example.

$$\wedge \left[\text{WeakNorth}\,(c, b_1) \wedge \text{WeakEast}\,(c, b_1) \right] \right]$$

$$\wedge \left[\left[\text{WeakNorth}\,(b_2, a) \wedge \text{Vertical}\,(b_2, a) \right] \right.$$

$$\wedge \left[\text{WeakNorth}\,(c, b_2) \wedge \text{WeakEast}\,(c, b_2) \right] \right]$$

$$\equiv \left[\left[\text{Horizontal}\,(b_1, a) \wedge \text{WeakNorth}\,(c, b_1) \right] \right.$$

$$\wedge \left[\text{Vertical}\,(b_1, a) \wedge \text{WeakEast}\,(c, b_1) \right] \right]$$

$$\wedge \left[\left[\text{WeakNorth}\,(b_2, a) \wedge \text{WeakNorth}\,(c, b_2) \right] \right.$$

$$\wedge \left[\text{Vertical}\,(b_2, a) \wedge \text{WeakEast}\,(c, b_2) \right] \right] .$$

$$(15)$$

The outcome of the composition is

$$\left[\left[\text{Horizontal}\,(c, a) \vee \text{WeakNorth}\,(c, a) \right] \right.$$

$$\wedge \left[\text{WeakEast}\,(c, a) \vee \text{Vertical}\,(c, a) \right]]$$

$$\wedge \left[\left[\text{NTPP}_y\,(c, \text{WeakNorth}\,(a)) \right] \right.$$

$$\wedge \left[\text{WeakEast}\,(c, a) \vee \text{Vertical}\,(c, a) \right] \right]$$

$$= \left[\left[\text{NTPP}_y\,(c, \text{WeakNorth}\,(a)) \right] \right.$$

$$\wedge \left[\text{WeakEast}\,(c, a) \vee \text{Vertical}\,(c, a) \right] \right] .$$

$$(16)$$

This means that the $Y_{\min}(c)$ of the minimal bounding box for region c is greater than $Y_{\max}(a)$ of the minimal bounding box for region a and $c \subseteq \text{NE}(a) \vee \text{N}(a)$.

Type 4. $P_R(b, a) \wedge P_R(c, b)$.

Find the composition of

$$\left[P_O(b_1, a) \wedge P_{\text{NE}}\,(b_2, a) \right] \wedge \left[P_O(c, b) \wedge P_W\,(c, b) \wedge P_{\text{SW}}\,(c, b) \right] .$$

$$(17)$$

Figure 9 has been drawn for this example. Establish the direction relation between each individual part of b and c.

Use (8) with $1 \leq k \leq 2$; the value of m_1 for b_1 is $1 \leq m_1 \leq 4$, while the value m_2 for b_2 is $1 \leq m_2 \leq 7$:

$$[[P_{R1}(b_1, a) \wedge P_{R11}(c_1, b_1)] \vee [P_{R1}(b_1, a) \wedge P_{R12}(c_2, b_1)]$$
$$\vee [P_{R1}(b_1, a) \wedge P_{R13}(c_3, b_1)]$$
$$\vee [P_{R1}(b_1, a) \wedge P_{R14}(c_4, b_1)]]$$
$$\wedge [[P_{R2}(b_2, a) \wedge P_{R21}(c_1, b_2)] \vee [P_{R2}(b_2, a) \wedge P_{R22}(c_2, b_2)]$$
$$\vee [P_{R2}(b_2, a) \wedge P_{R25}(c_5, b_2)] \vee [P_{R2}(b_2, a) \wedge P_{R26}(c_6, b_2)]$$
$$\vee [P_{R2}(b_2, a) \wedge P_{R27}(c_7, b_2)]]$$
$$\equiv [[P_O(b_1, a) \wedge P_S(c_1, b_1)] \vee [P_O(b_1, a) \wedge P_{SW}(c_2, b_1)]$$
$$\vee [P_O(b_1, a) \wedge P_W(c_3, b_1)]$$
$$\vee [P_O(b_1, a) \wedge P_O(c_4, b_1)]]$$
$$\wedge [[P_{NE}(b_2, a) \wedge P_{NE}(c_1, b_2)]$$
$$\vee [P_{NE}(b_2, a) \wedge P_N(c_2, b_2)]$$
$$\vee [P_{NE}(b_2, a) \wedge P_{NW}(c_3, b_2)]$$
$$\vee [P_{NE}(b_2, a) \wedge P_E(c_4, b_2)]$$
$$\vee [P_{NE}(b_2, a) \wedge P_O(c_5, b_2)]$$
$$\vee [P_{NE}(b_2, a) \wedge P_W(c_6, b_2)]$$
$$\vee [P_{NE}(b_2, a) \wedge P_{SW}(c_7, b_2)]].$$

(18)

In part (1) of the above composition, $c_1, c_2, c_3, c_4 \subset c$. To simplify the composition, we consider the combined horizontal and vertical sets of all the parts of c. Thus, we have the following:

$$[\text{WeakNorth}(b_1, a) \wedge \text{WeakEast}(b_1, a)]$$
$$\wedge [[\text{Horizontal}(c, b_1) \vee \text{WeakSouth}(c, b_1)]$$
$$\wedge [\text{Vertical}(c, b_1) \vee \text{WeakWest}(c, b_1)]]$$
$$\equiv [[\text{WeakNorth}(b_1, a)]$$
$$\wedge [\text{Horizontal}(c, b_1) \vee \text{WeakSouth}(c, b_1)]]$$
$$\wedge [[\text{WeakEast}(b_1, a)]$$
$$\wedge [\text{Vertical}(c, b_1) \vee \text{WeakWest}(c, b_1)]]$$
$$= [\text{WeakNorth}(c, a) \vee \text{Horizontal}(c, a)$$
$$\vee \text{WeakSouth}(c, a)]$$
$$\wedge [\text{WeakEast}(c, a) \vee \text{Vertical}(c, a) \vee \text{WeakWest}(c, a)].$$

(19)

In part (2) of the above composition, $c_1, c_2, c_3, c_4, c_5, c_6, c_7 \subset c$. The simplified version of the composition is as follows:

$$[\text{Horizontal}(b_2, a) \wedge \text{Vertical}(b_2, a)]$$
$$\wedge [[\text{WeakNorth}(c, b_2) \vee \text{Horizontal}(c, b_2)$$
$$\vee \text{WeakSouth}(c, b_2)]$$
$$\wedge [\text{WeakEast}(c, b_2) \vee \text{Vertical}(c, b_2)$$
$$\vee \text{WeakWest}(c, b_2)]]$$
$$\equiv [[\text{Horizontal}(b_2, a)]$$
$$\wedge [\text{WeakNorth}(c, b_2) \vee \text{Horizontal}(c, b_2)$$
$$\vee \text{WeakSouth}(c, b_2)]]$$

(20)

$$\wedge [[\text{Vertical}(b_2, a)]$$
$$\wedge [\text{WeakEast}(c, b_2) \vee \text{Vertical}(c, b_2)$$
$$\vee \text{WeakWest}(c, b_2)]]$$
$$= [[\text{WeakNorth}(c, a) \vee \text{Horizontal}(c, a)$$
$$\vee \text{WeakSouth}(c, a)]]$$
$$\wedge [\text{WeakEast}(c, a) \vee \text{Vertical}(c, a)$$
$$\vee \text{WeakWest}(c, a)]].$$

The final outcome of the composition is part (1) $\wedge$ part (2) is equivalent to

$$[\text{WeakNorth}(c, a) \vee \text{Horizontal}(c, a) \vee \text{WeakSouth}(c, a)]$$
$$\wedge [\text{WeakEast}(c, a) \vee \text{Vertical}(c, a) \vee \text{WeakWest}(c, a)].$$

(21)

This means that the region $c \subseteq U$ which is the union of all the 9 *tiles* of region a. However, based on Figure 9, region $c \not\subseteq$ SW(a).

7.3. Composition of Expressive Direction Relations. We shall use the following notations to represent the 13 binary y-direction relations:

(i) REL1$y(b, a)$-NTPP$y(b, \text{WeakNorth}(a))$,

(ii) REL2$y(b, a)$-TPP$y(b, \text{WeakNorth}(a))$ $\wedge$ EC$y(b, \text{Horizontal}(a))$,

(iii) REL3$y(b, a)$-TPP$y(b, \text{Horizontal}(a))$ $\wedge$ EC$y(b, \text{WeakNorth}(a))$,

(iv) REL4$y(b, a)$-TPP$y(b, \text{Horizontal}(a))$ $\wedge$ EC$y(b, \text{WeakSouth}(a))$,

(v) REL5$y(b, a)$-NTPP$y(b, \text{Horizontal}(a))$,

(vi) REL6$y(b, a)$-EQ$y(b, \text{Horizontal}(a))$,

(vii) REL7$y(b, a)$-NTPP$y(b, \text{WeakSouth}(a))$,

(viii) REL8$y(b, a)$-TPP$y(b, \text{WeakSouth}(a))$ $\wedge$ EC$y(b, \text{Horizontal}(a))$,

(ix) $\text{REL9}\,y\,(b,a)\text{-PO}\,y\,(b,\text{WeakNorth}(a))$
$\wedge \text{PO}\,y\,(b,\text{Horizontal}(a)) \wedge$
$\text{DC}\,y\,(b,\text{WeakSouth}(a)),$

(x) $\text{REL10}\,y\,(b,a)\text{-PO}\,y\,(b,\text{WeakNorth}(a))$
$\wedge \text{PO}\,y\,(b,\text{Horizontal}(a)) \wedge$
$\text{EC}\,y\,(b,\text{WeakSouth}(a)),$

(xi) $\text{REL11}\,y\,(b,a)\text{-PO}\,y\,(b,\text{WeakNorth}(a))$
$\wedge \text{PO}\,y\,(b,\text{WeakSouth}(a)) \wedge$
$\text{NTPPi}\,y\,(b,\text{Horizontal}(a)),$

(xii) $\text{REL12}\,y\,(b,a)\text{-PO}\,y\,(b,\text{WeakSouth}(a))$
$\wedge \text{PO}\,y\,(b,\text{Horizontal}(a)) \wedge$
$\text{DC}\,y\,(b,\text{WeakNorth}(a)),$

(xiii) $\text{REL13}\,y\,(b,a)\text{-PO}\,y\,(b,\text{WeakSouth}(a))$
$\wedge \text{PO}\,y\,(b,\text{Horizontal}(a)) \wedge$
$\text{EC}\,y\,(b,\text{WeakNorth}(a)).$

Similar notations will be used to represent the 13 binary x-direction relations (*WeakNorth* is replaced by *WeakEast*, *Horizontal* with *Vertical*, and *WeakSouth* by *WeakWest*).

Example 1. Find the composition of the following:

$$\left[\left[{}^{\text{REL3}\,y(b_1,a)}\left[P_O\,(b_1,a)\right]_{\text{REL3}x(b_1,a)}\right]\right.$$

$$\wedge\left[{}^{\text{REL2}\,y(b_2,a)}\left[P_{NE}\,(b_2,a)\right]_{\text{REL2}x(b_2,a)}\right]\right] \tag{22}$$

$$\wedge\left[{}^{\text{REL1}\,y(c,b)}\left[A_N\,(c,b)\right]_{\text{REL5}x(c,b)}\right].$$

Establish the direction relation between c and each individual part of b. Use (8), with $1 \le k \le 2$ and $1 \le m_1 \le 2$, and $1 \le m_2 \le 2$:

$$\left[\left[P_{R1}\,(b_1,a)\right] \wedge \left[P_{R11}\,(c_1,b_1) \vee P_{R12}\,(c_2,b_1)\right]\right]$$
$$\wedge \left[\left[P_{R2}\,(b_2,a)\right] \wedge \left[P_{R21}\,(c_1,b_2) \vee P_{R22}\,(c_2,b_2)\right]\right]. \tag{23}$$

Use (5), and the above composition can be rewritten in the following expressive form:

$$\left[\left[\text{REL3}\,y\,(b_1,a) \wedge \text{REL3}x\,(b_1,a)\right]\right]$$

$$\wedge\left[\left[\text{REL1}\,y\,(c_1,b_1) \wedge \text{REL3}x\,(c_1,b_1)\right]\right.$$

$$\left.\vee\left[\text{REL1}\,y\,(c_2,b_1) \wedge \text{REL2}x\,(c_2,b_1)\right]\right]$$

$$\wedge\left[\left[\text{REL2}\,y\,(b_2,a) \wedge \text{REL2}x\,(b_2,a)\right]\right]$$

$$\wedge\left[\left[\text{REL1}\,y\,(c_1,b_2) \wedge \text{REL8}x\,(c_1,b_2)\right]\right.$$

$$\left.\vee\left[\text{REL1}\,y\,(c_2,b_2) \wedge \text{REL4}x\,(c_2,b_2)\right]\right]$$

$$\equiv\left[\text{REL3}\,y\,(b_1,a) \wedge \left[\text{REL1}\,y\,(c_1,b_1) \vee \text{REL1}\,y\,(c_2,b_1)\right]\right]$$

$$\wedge\left[\text{REL3}x\,(b_1,a) \wedge \left[\text{REL3}x\,(c_1,b_1) \vee \text{REL2}x\,(c_2,b_1)\right]\right]$$

$$\wedge\left[\text{REL2}\,y\,(b_2,a) \wedge \left[\text{REL1}\,y\,(c_1,b_2) \vee \text{REL1}\,y\,(c_2,b_2)\right]\right]$$

$$\wedge\left[\text{REL2}x\,(b_2,a) \wedge \left[\text{REL8}x\,(c_1,b_2) \vee \text{REL4}x\,(c_2,b_2)\right]\right]. \tag{24}$$

Use Tables 2 and 3, and $c_1 \subset c$ and $c_2 \subset c$. Thus, the outcome of the composition can be written as follows:

$$\text{REL1}\,y\,(c,a) \wedge \left[\text{REL2}x\,(c,a) \vee \text{REL3}x\,(c,a)\right] \wedge \text{REL1}\,y\,(c,a)$$

$$\wedge\left[\text{REL2}x\,(c,a) \vee \text{REL3}x\,(c,a)\right.$$

$$\left.\vee\;\text{REL6}x\,(c,a) \vee \text{REL13}x\,(c,a)\right]$$

$$=\text{REL1}\,y\,(c,a) \wedge \left[\text{REL2}x\,(c,a) \vee \text{REL3}x\,(c,a)\right]. \tag{25}$$

The outcome of the composition is:

$$\text{NTPP}\,y\,(c,\text{WeakNorth}\,(a))$$

$$\wedge\left[\text{TPP}x\,(c,\text{WeakEast}\,(a)) \wedge \text{EC}\,y\,(c,\text{Horizontal}\,(a))\right. \tag{26}$$

$$\left.\vee\text{TPP}x\,(c,\text{Vertical}\,(a)) \wedge \text{EC}\,y\,(c,\text{Horizontal}\,(a))\right].$$

Example 2. This example is similar to the fourth example in the previous section of this paper.
Find the composition of

$$\left[P_O\,(b_1,a) \wedge P_{NE}\,(b_2,a)\right]$$
$$\wedge\left[P_O\,(c,b) \wedge P_W\,(c,b) \wedge P_{SW}\,(c,b)\right]. \tag{27}$$

Establish the direction relation between c and each individual part of b. Use (8), with $1 \le k \le 2$ and $1 \le m_1 \le 4$, and $1 \le m_2 \le 7$.

The composition in expressive form will be as follows.

For part b_1,

$$\left[\left[\text{REL2}\,y\,(b_1,a) \wedge \text{REL2}x\,(b_1,a)\right]\right]$$

$$\wedge\left[\left[\text{REL4}\,y\,(c_1,b_1) \wedge \text{REL4}x\,(c_1,b_1)\right]\right.$$

$$\vee\left[\text{REL8}\,y\,(c_2,b_1) \wedge \text{REL4}x\,(c_2,b_1)\right] \tag{28}$$

$$\vee\left[\text{REL4}\,y\,(c_3,b_1) \wedge \text{REL8}x\,(c_3,b_1)\right]$$

$$\left.\vee\left[\text{REL8}\,y\,(c_4,b_1) \wedge \text{REL8}x\,(c_4,b_1)\right]\right].$$

The regions $c_1, c_2, c_3, c_4 \subset c$; the above composition can be written as follows:

$$\left[\text{REL2}\,y\,(b_1,a)\right.$$

$$\wedge\left[\text{REL4}\,y\,(c,b_1) \vee \text{REL8}\,y\,(c,b_1)\right.$$

$$\left.\left.\vee\;\text{REL4}\,y\,(c,b_1) \vee \text{REL8}\,y\,(c,b_1)\right]\right]$$

$$\wedge\left[\text{REL2}x\,(b_1,a)\right.$$

$$\wedge\left[\text{REL4}x\,(c,b_1) \vee \text{REL4}x\,(c,b_1)\right.$$

$$\left.\left.\vee\;\text{REL8}x\,(c,b_1) \vee \text{REL8}x\,(c,b_1)\right]\right] \tag{29a}$$

$$=\left[\text{REL2}\,y\,(c,a) \vee \text{REL3}\,y\,(c,a)\right.$$

$$\left.\vee\;\text{REL6}\,y\,(c,a) \vee \text{REL13}\,y\,(c,a)\right]$$

$$\wedge\left[\text{REL2}x\,(c,a) \vee \text{REL3}x\,(c,a)\right.$$

$$\left.\vee\;\text{REL6}x\,(c,a) \vee \text{REL13}x\,(c,a)\right].$$

TABLE 2: (a) Composition of binary relations in the y-direction for the hybrid model (composed relations of {WN} and {WN,H}). (b) Composition of binary relations in the y-direction for the hybrid model (composed relations of {H} and {WN,H}). (c) Composition of binary relations in the y-direction for the hybrid model (composed relations of {S} and {WN,H}). (d) Composition of binary relations in the y-direction for the hybrid model (composed relations of {WN,H,S} and {WS}).

(a)

Composed relations of {WN} and {WN,H}	WN(c,b)		H(c,b)			
	NTPPy(c,WN(b))	TPPy(c,WN(b)) ∧ECy(c,H(b))	TPPy(c,H(b)) ∧ECy(c,WN(b))	TPPy(c,H(b)) ∧ECy(c,WS(b))	NTPPy(c,H(b))	EQy(c,H(b))
NTPPy(b,WN(a))	NTPPy(c,WN(a))	NTPPy(c,WN(a))	NTPPy(c,WN(a))	NTPPy(c,WN(a))	NTPPy(c,WN(a))	NTPPy(c,WN(c))
TPPy(b,WN(a)) ∧ECy(b,H(a)) WN(b,a)	NTPPy(c,WN(a))	NTPPy(c,WN(a))	NTPPy(c,WN(a))	**TPPy(c,WN(a)) TPPy(c,WN(a)) ∧ECy(c,H(a))**	NTPPy(c,WN(a)) NTPPy(c,WN(a))	**TPPy(c,WN(a)) ∧ECy(c,H(a))**
WN(b,a)	**NTPPy(c,WN(a))**				**WN(c,a)**	

Note: the data in bold are results of the composition of relations.

(b)

Composed relations of {H} and {WN,H}	WN(c,b)		H(c,b)			
	NTPPy(c,WN(b))	TPPy(c,WN(b)) ∧ECy(c,H(b))	TPPy(c,H(b)) ∧ECy(c,WN(b))	TPPy(c,H(b)) ∧ECy(c,WS(b))	NTPPy(c,H(b))	EQy(c,H(b))
TPPy(b,H(a)) ∧ECy(b,WN(a))	**NTPPy(c,WN(a))**	**TPPy(c,H(a)) ∧ECy(c,H(a))**	**NTPPy(c,H(a))**	NTPPy(c,H(a))	NTPPy(c,H(b))	**TPPy(c,H(a)) ∧ECy(c,WN(a))**
H(b,a)	[NTPPy(c,H(a))]∨ [TPPy(c,H(a)) ∧ECy(c,WN(a))]∨ [POy(c,WN(a)) ∧POy(c,H(a)) ∧DCy(c,WS(a))]	[NTPPy(c,H(a))]∨ [PPy(c,H(a)) ∧ECy(c,WN(a))]∨ [POy(c,WN(a)) ∧POy(c,H(a)) ∧DCy(c,WS(a))]	NTPPy(c,H(a))	TPPy(c,H(a)) ∧ECy(c,WN(a))	NTPPy(c,H(a))	TPPy(c,H(a)) ∧ECy(c,WN(a))
TPPy(b,H(a)) ∧ECy(b,WS(a))	[NTPPy(c,H(a))]∨ [TPPy(c,H(a)) ∧ECy(c,WN(a))]∨ [POy(c,WN(a)) ∧POy(c,H(a)) ∧DCy(c,WS(a))]	[NTPPy(c,H(a))]∨ [TPPy(c,H(a)) ∧ECy(c,WN(a))]∨ [POy(c,WN(a)) ∧POy(c,H(a)) ∧DCy(c,WS(a))]	TPPy(c,H(a)) ∧ECy(c,WN(a))	NTPPy(c,H(a))	NTPPy(c,H(a))	TPPy(c,H(a)) ∧ECy(c,WS(a))
NTPPy(b,H(a))	**NTPPy(c,WN(a))**	**NTPPy(c,H(a))**	NTPPy(c,H(a))	NTPPy(c,H(a))	NTPPy(c,H(a))	NTPPy(c,H(a))
EQy(b,H(a))	**NTPPy(c,WN(a))**	**TPPy(c,WN(a)) ∧ECy(c,H(a))**	TPPy(c,H(a)) ∧ECy(c,WS(a))	TPPy(c,H(a)) ∧ECy(c,WS(a))	NTPPy(c,H(a))	EQy(c,H(a))

(b) Continued.

Composed relations of {H} and {WN,H}	WN(*c*,*b*)		H(*c*,*b*)			
	NTPP*y*(*c*,WN(*b*))	TPP*y*(*c*,WN(*b*)) ∧ EC*y*(*c*,H(*b*))	TPP*y*(*c*,H(*b*)) ∧ EC*y*(*c*,WN(*b*))	TPP*y*(*c*,H(*b*)) ∧ EC*y*(*c*,WS(*b*))	NTPP*y*(*c*,H(*b*))	EQ*y*(*c*,H(*b*))
H(*b*,*a*)	**WN(*c*,*a*) ∨ H(*c*,*a*)**		**H(*c*,*a*)**			

Note: the data in bold are the results of the composition of relations.

(c)

Composed relations of {S} and {WN,H}		WN(*c*,*b*)		H(*c*,*b*)			
		NTPP*y*(*c*,WN(*b*))	TPP*y*(*c*,WN(*b*)) ∧ EC*y*(*c*,H(*b*))	TPP*y*(*c*,H(*b*)) ∧ EC*y*(*c*,WN(*b*))	TPP*y*(*c*,H(*b*)) ∧ EC*y*(*c*,WS(*b*))	NTPP*y*(*c*,H(*b*))	EQ*y*(*c*,H(*b*))
S(*b*,*a*)	NTPP*y*(*b*,WS(*a*))	**U-13 relations**	**[NTPP*y*(*c*,WS(*a*))] ∨ [TPP*y*(*c*,WS(*a*)) ∧ EC*y*(*c*,H(*a*))] ∨ [PO*y*(*c*,WS(*a*)) ∧ PO*y*(*c*,H(*a*)) ∧ DC*y*(*c*,WN(*a*))] ∨ [PO*y*(*c*,WS(*a*)) ∧ PO*y*(*c*,H(*a*)) ∧ EC*y*(*c*,WN(*a*))] ∨ [PO*y*(*c*,WS(*a*)) ∧ PO*y*(*c*,WN(*a*)) ∧ NTPPi*y*(*c*,H(*a*))]**	**NTPP*y*(*c*,WS(*a*))**	**NTPP*y*(*c*,WS(*a*))**	**NTPP*y*(*c*,WS(*a*))**	**NTPP*y*(*c*,WS(*a*))**
	TPP*y*(*b*,WS(*a*)) ∧ EC*y*(*b*,H(*a*))	**[NTPP*y*(*c*,H(*a*))] ∨ [TPP*y*(*c*,H(*a*)) ∧ EC*y*(*c*,WN(*a*))] ∨ [TPP*y*(*c*,WN(*a*)) ∧ EC*y*(*c*,H(*a*))] ∨ [NTPP*y*(*c*,WN(*a*))] ∨ [PO*y*(*c*,WN(*a*)) ∧ PO*y*(*c*,H(*a*)) ∧ DC*y*(*c*,WS(*a*))]**	**[TPP*y*(*c*,H(*a*)) ∧ EC*y*(*c*,WS(*a*))] ∨ [EQ*y*(*c*,H(*a*))] ∨ [PO*y*(*c*,WN(*a*)) ∧ PO*y*(*c*,H(*a*)) ∧ EC*y*(*c*,WS(*a*))]**	**TPP*y*(*c*,WS(*a*)) ∧ EC*y*(*c*,H(*a*))**	**NTPP*y*(*c*,WS(*a*))**	**NTPP*y*(*c*,WS(*a*))**	**TPP*y*(*c*,WS(*a*)) ∧ EC*y*(*c*,H(*a*))**
	S(*b*,*a*)	**WN(*c*,*a*) ∨ H(*c*,*a*) ∨ WS(*c*,*a*)**		**WS(*c*,*a*)**			

Note: the data in bold are the results of the composition of relations.

(d)

Composed relations of {WN,H,S} and {WS}		WS(c,b)	
	NTPP*y*(*b*,WN(*a*))	NTPP*y*(*c*,WS(*b*))	TPP*y*(*c*,WS(*b*)) ∧ EC*y*(*c*,H(*b*))
WN(*b*,*a*)	TPP*y*(*b*,WN(*a*)) ∧ EC*y*(*b*,H(*a*))	**U-13 relations**	**[NTPP*y*(*c*,WN(*a*))] ∨ [TPP*y*(*c*,WN(*a*)) ∧ EC*y*(*c*,H(*a*))] ∨ [PO*y*(*c*,WN(*a*)) ∧ PO*y*(*c*,H(*a*)) ∧ DC*y*(*c*,WS(*a*))] ∨ [PO*y*(*c*,WN(*a*)) ∧ PO*y*(*c*,H(*a*)) ∧ EC*y*(*c*,WS(*a*))] ∨ [PO*y*(*c*,WN(*a*)) ∧ PO*y*(*c*,WS(*a*)) ∧ NTPPi*y*(*c*,H(*a*))]**

(d) Continued.

| Composed relations of {WN,H,S} and {WS} | WS(c,b) | |
WN(b,a)	WN(c,a) ∨ H(c,a) ∨ WS(c,a)	
WN(b,a) TPPγ(b,H(a)) ∧ ECγ(b,WN(a))	**TPPγ(c,H(a)) ∧ ECγ(c,WN(a))**	[NTPPγ(c,H(a))] ∨ [TPPγ(c,H(a)) ∧ ECγ(c,WS(a))] ∨ [TPPγ(c,WS(a)) ∧ ECγ(c,H(a))] ∨ [NTPPγ(c,WS(a))] ∨ [POγ(c,WS(a)) ∧ POγ(c,H(a)) ∧ DCγ(c,WN(a))]
H(b,a) TPPγ(b,H(a)) ∧ ECγ(b,WS(a))	**TPPγ(c,H(a)) ∧ ECγ(c,WN(a))**	**NTPPγ(c,WS(a))**
NTPPγ(b,H(a))	[NTPPγ(c,H(a))] ∨ [TPPγ(c,H(a)) ∧ ECγ(c,WS(a))] ∨ [TPPγ(c,WS(a)) ∧ ECγ(c,H(a))] ∨ [NTPPγ(c,WS(a))] ∨ [POγ(c,WS(a)) ∧ POγ(c,H(a)) ∧ DCγ(c,WN(a))] **NTPPγ(c,WS(a))**	[NTPPγ(c,H(a))] ∨ [TPPγ(c,H(a)) ∧ ECγ(c,WS(a))] ∨ [TPPγ(c,H(a)) ∧ ECγ(c,H(a))] ∨ [POγ(c,WS(a)) ∧ POγ(c,H(a)) ∧ DCγ(c,WN(a))] **TPPγ(c,WS(a)) ∧ ECγ(c,H(a))**
EQγ(b,H(a)) H(b,a)	**H(c,a) ∨ WS(c,a)**	
S(b,a) NTPPγ(b,WS(a)) TPPγ(b,WS(a)) ∧ ECγ(b,H(a)) S(b,a)	**NTPPγ(c,WS(a))** **NTPPγ(c,WS(a))** **NTPPγ(c,WS(a))**	**NTPPγ(c,WS(a))** **NTPPγ(c,WS(a))**

Note: the data in bold are the results of the composition of relations.

TABLE 3: (a) Composition of binary relations in the x-direction for the hybrid model (composed relations of {WE} and {WE,V,WW}). (b) Composition of binary relations in the x-direction for the hybrid model (part 1: composed relations of {V} and {WE,V,WW}). (c) Composition of binary relations in the x-direction for the hybrid model (part 2: composed relations of {V} and {WE,V,WW}). (d) Composition of binary relations in the x-direction for the hybrid model (part 2: composed relations of {WW} and {WE,V,WW}).

(a)

Composed relations of {WE} and {WE,V,WW}		WE(*c*,*b*)		V(*c*,*b*)				WW(*c*,*b*)	
		NTPP*x*(*c*,WE(*b*))	TPP*x*(*c*,WE(*b*)) ∧ EC*x*(*c*,V(*b*))	TPP*x*(*c*,V(*b*)) ∧ EC*x*(*c*,WE(*b*))	TPP*x*(*c*,V(*b*)) ∧ EC*x*(*c*,WW(*b*))	NTPP*x*(*c*,V(*b*))	EQ*x*(*c*,V(*b*))	NTPP*x*(*c*,WW(*b*))	TPP*x*(*c*,WW(*b*)) ∧ EC*x*(*c*,V(*b*))
WE(*b*,*a*)	NTPP*x*(*b*,WE(*a*))	**NTPP*x*(*c*,WE(*a*))**	**NTPP*x*(*c*,WE(*a*))**	**NTPP*x*(*c*,WE(*a*))**	**NTPP*x*(*c*,WE(*a*))**	**NTPP*x*(*c*,WE(*a*))**	**NTPP*x*(*c*,WE(*a*))**	**U-13 relations**	**[NTPP*x*(*c*,WE(*a*))] ∨ [TPP*x*(*c*,WE(*a*)) ∧ EC*x*(*c*,V(*a*))] ∨ [PO*x*(*c*,WE(*a*)) ∧ PO*x*(*c*,V(*a*)) ∧ DC*y*(*c*,WW(*a*))] ∨ [PO*x*(*c*,WE(*a*)) ∧ PO*x*(*c*,V(*a*)) ∧ EC*x*(*c*,WW(*a*))] ∨ [PO*x*(*c*,WE(*a*)) ∧ PO*x*(*c*,WW(*a*)) ∧ NTPPi*x*(*c*,V(*a*))]**
	TPP*x*(*b*,WE(*a*)) ∧ EC*x*(*b*,V(*a*))	**NTPP*x*(*c*,WE(*a*))**	**NTPP*x*(*c*,WE(*a*))**	**NTPP*x*(*c*,WE(*a*))**	**TPP*x*(*c*,WE(*a*)) ∧ EC*x*(*c*,V(*a*))**	**NTPP*x*(*c*,WE(*a*))**	**TPP*x*(*c*,WE(*a*)) ∧ EC*x*(*c*,V(*a*))**	**[NTPP*x*(*c*,V(*a*))] ∨ [TPP*x*(*c*,V(*a*)) ∧ EC*x*(*c*,WW(*a*))] ∨ [TPP*x*(*c*,WW(*a*)) ∧ EC*x*(*c*,V(*a*))] ∨ [NTPP*x*(*c*,WW(*a*))] ∨ [PO*x*(*c*,WW(*a*)) ∧ PO*x*(*c*,V(*a*)) ∧ DC*y*(*c*,WE(*a*))]**	**[TPP*x*(*c*,V(*a*)) ∧ EC*x*(*c*,WE(*a*))] ∨ [EQ*x*(*c*,V(*a*))] ∨ [PO*x*(*c*,WW(*a*)) ∧ PO*x*(*c*,V(*a*)) ∧ EC*x*(*c*,WE(*a*))]**
	WE(*b*,*a*)	**NTPP*x*(*c*,WE(*a*))**		**WE(*c*,*a*)**				**WE(*c*,*a*) ∨ V(*c*,*a*) ∨ WW(*c*,*a*)**	

Note: the data in bold are the results of the composition of relations.

(b)

Part 1 of composed relations of {V} and {WE,V,WW}		WE(*c*,*b*)		V(*c*,*b*)				WW(*c*,*b*)	
		NTPP*x*(*c*,WE(*b*))	TPP*x*(*c*,WE(*b*)) ∧ EC*x*(*c*,V(*b*))	TPP*x*(*c*,V(*b*)) ∧ EC*x*(*c*,WE(*b*))	TPP*x*(*c*,V(*b*)) ∧ EC*x*(*c*,WW(*b*))	NTPP*x*(*c*,V(*b*))	EQ*x*(*c*,V(*b*))	NTPP*x*(*c*,WW(*b*))	TPP*x*(*c*,WW(*b*)) ∧ EC*x*(*c*,V(*b*))
V(*b*,*a*)	TPP*x*(*b*,V(*a*)) ∧ EC*x*(*b*,WE(*a*))	**NTPP*x*(*c*,WE(*a*))**	**TPP*x*(*c*,WE(*a*)) ∧ EC*x*(*c*,V(*a*))**	**TPP*x*(*c*,V(*a*)) ∧ EC*x*(*c*,WE(*a*))**	**NTPP*x*(*c*,V(*a*))**	**NTPP*x*(*c*,V(*a*))**	**TPP*x*(*c*,V(*a*)) ∧ EC*x*(*c*,WE(*a*))**	**[NTPP*x*(*c*,V(*a*))] ∨ [TPP*x*(*c*,V(*a*)) ∧ EC*x*(*c*,WW(*a*))] ∨ [TPP*x*(*c*,WW(*a*)) ∧ EC*x*(*c*,V(*a*))] ∨ [NTPP*x*(*c*,WW(*a*))] ∨ [PO*x*(*c*,WW(*a*)) ∧ PO*x*(*c*,V(*a*)) ∧ DC*y*(*c*,WE(*a*))]**	**[NTPP*x*(*c*,V(*a*))] ∨ [TPP*x*(*c*,V(*a*)) ∧ EC*x*(*c*,WW(*a*))] ∨ [PO*x*(*c*,WW(*a*)) ∧ PO*x*(*c*,V(*a*)) ∧ DC*y*(*c*,WE(*a*))]**

(b) Continued.

Part 1 of composed relations of {V} and {WE,V,WW}	WE(c,b)		V(c,b)					WW(c,b)	
	NTPPx(c,WE(b))	TPPx(c,WE(b)) ∧ ECx(c,V(b))	TPPx(c,V(b)) ∧ ECx(c,WE(b))	NTPPx(c,V(b))	TPPx(c,V(b)) ∧ ECx(c,WW(b))	NTPPx(c,V(b))	EQx(c,V(b))	NTPPx(c,WW(b))	TPPx(c,WW(b)) ∧ ECx(c,V(b))
V(b,a) TPPx(b,V(a)) ∧ ECx(b,WW(a))	[NTPPx(c,V(a))] ∨ [TPPx(c,V(a)) ∧ ECx(c,WE(a))] ∨ [TPPx(c,WE(a)) ∧ ECx(c,V(a))] ∨ [NTPPx(c,WE(a))] ∨ [POx(c,WE(a)) ∧ POx(c,V(a)) ∧ DCy(c,WW(a))]	[NTPPx(c,V(a))] ∨ [TPPx(c,V(a)) ∧ ECx(c,WE(a))] ∨ [POx(c,WE(a)) ∧ POx(c,V(a)) ∧ DCy(c,WW(a))]	NTPPx(c,V(a))	NTPPx(c,V(a))	**TPPx(c,V(a)) ∧ ECx(c,WE(a))**	NTPPx(c,V(a))	**TPPx(c,V(a)) ∧ ECx(c,WE(a))**	**NTPPx(c,WW(a))**	**TPPx(c,WW(a)) ∧ ECx(c,V(a))**

(c)

Note: the data in bold are the results of the composition of relations.

Part 2 of composed relations of {V} and {WE,V,WW}	WE(c,b)		V(c,b)					WW(c,b)	
	NTPPx(c,WE(b))	TPPx(c,WE(b)) ∧ ECx(c,V(b))	TPPx(c,V(b)) ∧ ECx(c,WE(b))	NTPPx(c,V(b))	TPPx(c,V(b)) ∧ ECx(c,WW(b))	NTPPx(c,V(b))	EQx(c,V(b))	NTPPx(c,WW(b))	TPPx(c,WW(b)) ∧ ECx(c,V(b))
V(b,a) NTPPx(b,V(a))	[NTPPx(c,V(a))] ∨ [TPPx(c,V(a)) ∧ ECx(c,WE(a))] ∨ [TPPx(c,WE(a)) ∧ ECx(c,V(a))] ∨ [NTPPx(c,WE(a))] ∨ [POx(c,WE(a)) ∧ POx(c,V(a)) ∧ DCy(c,WW(a))]	[NTPPx(c,V(a))] ∨ [TPPx(c,V(a)) ∧ ECx(c,WE(a))] ∨ [POx(c,WE(a)) ∧ POx(c,V(a)) ∧ DCy(c,WW(a))]	NTPPx(c,V(a))	**NTPPx(c,V(a))**	**NTPPx(c,V(a))**	**NTPPx(c,V(a))**	**NTPPx(c,V(a))**	[NTPPx(c,V(a))] ∨ [TPPx(c,V(a)) ∧ ECx(c,WW(a))] ∨ [TPPx(c,WW(a)) ∧ ECx(c,V(a))] ∨ [POx(c,WW(a)) ∧ POx(c,V(a)) ∧ DCy(c,WE(a))]	[NTPPx(c,V(a))] ∨ [TPPx(c,V(a)) ∧ ECx(c,WW(a))] ∨ [POx(c,WW(a)) ∧ POx(c,V(a)) ∧ DCy(c,WE(a))]
EQx(b,V(a))	NTPPx(c,WE(a))	**TPPx(c,WE(a)) ∧ ECx(c,V(a))**	**TPPx(c,V(a)) ∧ ECx(c,WE(a))**	**NTPPx(c,V(a))**	**TPPx(c,V(a)) ∧ ECx(c,WW(a))**	**NTPPx(c,V(a))**	**EQx(c,V(a))**	**NTPPx(c,WW(a))**	**TPPx(c,WW(a)) ∧ ECx(c,V(a))**

(c) Continued.

Part 2 of composed relations of {V} and {WE,V,WW}	WE(c,b)			V(c,b)			WW(c,b)	
	NTPPx(c,WE(b))	TPPx(c,WE(b))∧ ECx(c,V(b))	TPPx(c,V(b))∧ ECx(c,WE(b))	NTPPx(c,V(b))	EQx(c,V(b))	TPPx(c,V(b))∧ ECx(c,WW(b))	NTPPx(c,WW(b))	TPPx(c,WW(b))∧ ECx(c,V(b))
V(b,a)	**WE(c,a) ∨ V(c,a)**			**V(c,a)**			**V(c,a) ∨ WW(c,a)**	

Note: the data in bold are the results of the composition of relations.

(d)

Composed relations of {WW} and {WE,V,WW}	WE(c,b)			V(c,b)			WW(c,b)	
	NTPPx(c,WE(b))	TPPx(c,WE(b))∧ ECx(c,V(b))	TPPx(c,V(b))∧ ECx(c,WE(b))	NTPPx(c,V(b))	EQx(c,V(b))	TPPx(c,V(b))∧ ECx(c,WW(b))	NTPPx(c,WW(b))	TPPx(c,WW(b))∧ ECx(c,V(b))
NTPPx(b,WW(a))	U-13 relations	[NTPPx(c,WW(a))] ∨ [TPPx(c,WW(a)) ∧ECx(c,V(a))] ∨ [POx(c,WW(a)) ∧ POx(c,V(a)) ∧ DCy(c,WE(a))] ∨ [POx(c,WW(a)) ∧ POx(c,V(a)) ∧ ECx(c,WE(a))] ∨ [POx(c,WW(a)) ∧ POx(c,WE(a)) ∧ NTPPix(c,V(a))]	**NTPPx(c, WW(a))**	**NTPPx(c, WW(a))**	**NTPPx(c, WW(a))**		**NTPPx(c, WW(a))**	**NTPPx(c, WW(a))**
WW(b,a)	TPPx(b,WW(a)) ∧ ECx(b,V(a))	[NTPPx(c,V(a))] ∨ [TPPx(c,V(a)) ∧ ECx(c,WE(a))] ∨ [NTPPx(c,WE(a))] ∨ [POx(c,WE(a)) ∧ POx(c,V(a)) ∧ DCy(c,WW(a))]	[TPPx(c,V(a)) ∧ ECx(c,WW(a))] ∨ [EQx(c,V(a))] ∨ [POx(c,WE(a)) ∧ POx(c,V(a)) ∧ ECx(c,WW(a))]	TPPx(c,WW(a)) ∧ECx(c,V(a))	**NTPPx(c, WW(a))**	**NTPPx(c, WW(a))**	TPPx(c,WW(a)) ∧ ECx(c,V(a))	**NTPPx(c, WW(a))**
WW(b,a)	**WE(c,a) ∨ V(c,a) ∨ WW(c,a)**			**WW(c,a)**			**NTPPx(c,WW(a))**	

Note: the data in bold are the results of the composition of relations.

For part b_2

$$[[\text{REL3}y\,(b_2, a) \wedge \text{REL3}x\,(b_2, a)]]$$

$$\wedge\,[[\text{REL8}y\,(c_1, b_2) \wedge \text{REL7}x\,(c_1, b_2)]$$

$$\vee\,[\text{REL6}y\,(c_2, b_2) \wedge \text{REL8}x\,(c_2, b_2)]$$

$$\vee\,[\text{REL2}y\,(c_3, b_2) \wedge \text{REL8}x\,(c_3, b_2)]$$

$$\vee\,[\text{REL2}y\,(c_4, b_2) \wedge \text{REL6}x\,(c_4, b_2)]$$

$$\vee\,[\text{REL3}y\,(c_5, b_2) \wedge \text{REL6}x\,(c_5, b_2)]$$

$$\vee\,[\text{REL3}y\,(c_6, b_2) \wedge \text{REL2}x\,(c_6, b_2)]$$

$$\vee\,[\text{REL2}y\,(c_7, b_2) \wedge \text{REL2}x\,(c_7, b_2)]]$$

$$=\,\,[[\text{REL2}y\,(c, a) \vee \text{REL3}y\,(c, a)$$

$$\vee\,\text{REL5}y\,(c, a) \vee \text{REL12}y\,(c, a)]$$

$$\wedge\,[\text{REL2}x\,(c, a) \vee \text{REL3}x\,(c, a)$$

$$\vee\,\text{REL4}x\,(c, a) \vee \text{REL5}x\,(c, a)$$

$$\vee\text{REL7}x\,(c, a) \vee \text{REL8}x\,(c, a) \vee \text{REL12}x\,(c, a)]]\,. \tag{29b}$$

The final outcome of the composition is the composition of part b_1 (29a) $\wedge$ part b_2 (29b).

Apply Rule 3 from the earlier part of the paper, and we will get the following:

$$[[\text{REL2}y\,(c, a) \vee \text{REL3}y\,(c, a)$$

$$\vee\,\text{REL6}y\,(c, a) \vee \text{REL13}y\,(c, a)]$$

$$\wedge\,[\text{REL2}y\,(c, a) \vee \text{REL3}y\,(c, a) \vee \text{REL12}y\,(c, a)]$$

$$\wedge\,[\text{REL2}x\,(c, a) \vee \text{REL3}x\,(c, a) \tag{30}$$

$$\vee\,\text{REL4}x\,(c, a) \vee \text{REL8}x\,(c, a) \vee \text{REL12}x\,(c, a)]$$

$$\wedge\,[\text{REL2}x\,(c, a) \vee \text{REL3}x\,(c, a)$$

$$\vee\,\text{REL6}x\,(c, a) \vee \text{REL13}x\,(c, a)]]\,.$$

We collapse some of the disjunction of relations:

$$\text{REL6}y\,(c, a) \vee \text{REL13}y\,(c, a) = \text{REL13}y\,(c, a)$$

$$\text{REL4}x\,(c, a) \vee \text{REL8}x\,(c, a) \vee \text{REL12}x\,(c, a) = \text{REL12}y\,(c, a)$$

$$\text{REL6}x\,(c, a) \vee \text{REL13}x\,(c, a) = \text{REL13}x\,(c, a)\,. \tag{31}$$

Equation (30) becomes

$$[\text{REL2}y\,(c, a) \vee \text{REL3}y\,(c, a) \vee \text{REL13}y\,(c, a)]$$

$$\wedge\,[\text{REL2}y\,(c, a) \vee \text{REL3}y\,(c, a) \vee \text{REL12}y\,(c, a)] \tag{32}$$

$$\wedge\,[\text{REL2}x\,(c, a) \vee \text{REL3}x\,(c, a) \vee \text{REL12}x\,(c, a)]$$

$$\wedge\,[\text{REL2}x\,(c, a) \vee \text{REL3}x\,(c, a) \vee \text{REL13}x\,(c, a)]\,.$$

Region c is single piece. Therefore, (32) becomes

$$[\text{PO}y\,(c, \text{WeakNorth}\,(a)) \wedge \text{PO}y\,(c, \text{WeakSouth}\,(a))$$

$$\wedge\,\text{NTPP}iy\,(c, \text{Horizontal}\,(a))] \tag{33}$$

$$\wedge\,[\text{PO}x\,(c, \text{WeakEast}\,(a)) \wedge \text{PO}x\,(c, \text{WeakWest}\,(a))$$

$$\wedge\,\text{NTPP}ix\,(c, \text{Vertical}\,(a))]\,. \tag{34}$$

This means that the region $c \subseteq U$ which is the union of all the 9 *tiles* of region a. As mentioned earlier, based on Figure 9, region $c \not\subset \text{SW}(a)$. Thus, the outcome of the composition for weak relations (in the previous section) yields the same result as this composition. However, the computation for the latter is more tedious and complex when involving regions with many parts.

8. Existential Inference

The composition table in Table 2 is the result of transitive inferences made about regions a and c, given the hybrid cardinal direction relations for regions a and b as well as regions b and c. In the context of this paper, an existential inference is the inference made about the spatial relation between a and b, given the relations between c and a or/and the given relations between c and b. We shall demonstrate how our expressive hybrid cardinal direction model could be used to make several existential inferences which are not possible in existing models.

Example 3 (Find $R(b, a)$ such that $c \subset \text{WeakNorth}(b)$ and $c \subset \text{WeakNorth}(a)$). To answer this query, we must first specify the expressive relation between a and c.

There are two possible relations: $\text{TPP}y(c, \text{WeakNorth}(a))$ or *WeakNorth(c,a)*. If it is the former then composition is *WeakNorth(b,a)* $\wedge$ *WeakNorth(c,b)* which means $R(b,a)$ is *WeakNorth(b,a)*. If it is the latter, there are several combinations:

    (i) WeakNorth$(b, a) \wedge$ Horizontal(c, b)

    (ii) WeakNorth$(b, a) \wedge$ WeakSouth(c, b)

    (iii) Horizontal$(b, a) \wedge$ WeakNorth(c, b)

    (iv) WeakSouth$(b, a) \wedge$ WeakNorth(c, b).

This means $R(b, a)$ are Horizontal*(b,a)* or WeakSouth*(b,a)* when $c \subset \text{WeakNorth}(b)$ and $c \subset \text{WeakNorth}(a)$.

Example 4 (Find $R(b,a)$ and $S(c,b)$ such that $T(a,c)$ is $\neg[\text{TPP}y(c, \text{Horizontal}(a)) \wedge \text{EC}y(c, \text{WeakSouth}(a))]$). Based on Table 2, 9 different compositions will yield the following outcome:
$\text{TPP}y(c, \text{Horizontal}(a)) \wedge \text{EC}y(c, \text{WeakSouth}(a))$
The set of possible compositions, Q, is:
$\{\text{REL1}y(b, a) \wedge \text{REL7}y(c, b), \text{REL2}y(b, a) \wedge \text{REL7}y(c, b),$
$\text{REL3}y(b, a) \wedge \text{REL7}y(c, b), \text{REL3}y(b, a) \wedge \text{REL8}y(c, b),$
$\text{REL5}y(b, a) \wedge \text{REL7}y(c, b), \text{REL5}y(b, a) \wedge \text{REL8}y(c, b),$
$\text{REL6}y(b, a) \wedge \text{REL4}y(c, b), \text{REL7}y(b, a) \wedge \text{REL1}y(c, b),$
$\text{REL8}y(b, a) \wedge \text{REL12}(c, b)\}$.

If U equals 8×8 basic binary direction relations, then the set of all possible ordered pairs of R and S which satisfy the above query will be $U - Q$.

Example 5 (Find $R(b,a)$ and $S(c,b)$ such that $T(a,c)$ is POy(*c*,WeakSouth(*a*)) $\wedge$ POy(*c*,Horizontal(*a*)) $\wedge$ ECy(*c*, WeakNorth(*a*))). Based on Table 2, we have 4 pairs of R and S which satisfy T. They are: REL1y(*b,a*) $\wedge$ REL7y(*c,b*), REL2y(*b,a*) $\wedge$ REL8y(*c,b*), REL7y(*b,a*) $\wedge$ REL1y(*c,b*), REL7$y(b,a)$ $\wedge$ REL2$y(c,b)$.

9. Conclusion

In this paper, we have shown how topological and direction relations can be integrated to produce a more expressive hybrid model for cardinal directions. The composition table derived from this model could be used to infer both *weak and expressive* direction relations between regions. We have also introduced and demonstrated how to use a formula to compute the composition of weak or expressive relations between "*whole and part*" regions. We have also demonstrated how the composition table with expressive direction relations could be used to make several difficult existential inferences.

References

[1] A. U. Frank, "Qualitative spatial reasoning with cardinal directions," *Journal of Visual Languages and Computing*, vol. 3, pp. 343–371, 1992.

[2] A. U. Frank, "Qualitative spatial reasoning: cardinal directions as an example," *International Journal of Geographic Information Systems*, vol. 10, no. 3, pp. 269–290, 1996.

[3] R. K. Goyal, *Similarity assessment for cardinal directions between extended spatial objects [Ph.D. thesis]*, University of Maine, 2000.

[4] R. Goyal and M. Egenhofer, "Consistent queries over cardinal directions across different levels of detail," in *Proceedings of the 11th International Workshop on Database and Expert Systems Applications, Greenwich, UK, 2000*, A. M. Tjoa, R. Wagner, and A. Al-Zobaidie, Eds., pp. 876–880, IEEE Computer Society, September 2000.

[5] R. Goyal and M. Egenhofer, "Similarity of cardinal directions," in *Proceedings of the 7th International Symposium on Spatial and Temporal Databases*, C. Jensen, M. Schneider, B. Seeger, and V. Tsotras, Eds., vol. 2121 of *Lecture Notes in Computer Science*, pp. 36–55, Springer, Berlin, Germany, 2001.

[6] D. Papadias and Y. Theodoridis, "Spatial relations, minimum bounding rectangles, and spatial data structures," Tech. Rep. KDBSLAB-TR-94-04, University of California, Berkeley, Calif, USA, 1994.

[7] M. T. Escrig and F. Toledo, "A framework based on CLP extended with CHRS for reasoning with qualitative orientation and positional information," *Journal of Visual Languages & Computing*, vol. 9, no. 1, pp. 81–101, 1998.

[8] E. Clementini, P. Di Felice, and D. Hernández, "Qualitative representation and positional information," *Artificial Intelligence*, vol. 95, pp. 315–356, 1997.

[9] A. Isli, "Combining cardinal direction relations and relative relations in QSR," in *Proceedings of the 8th International Symposium on Artificial Intelligence and Mathematics (AI&M)*, Fort Lauderdale, Fla, USA, January 2004.

[10] C. C. Freksa, "Using orientation information for qualitative spatial reasoning," in *Proceedings of GIS—From Space to Territory: Theories and Methods of Spatio-Temporal Reasoning*, A. U. Frank, I. Campari, and U. Formentini, Eds., Springer, Berlin, Germany, 1992.

[11] J. Sharma and D. Flewelling, "Inferences from combined knowledge about topology and directions," in *Proceedings of the 4th International Symposium on Advances in Spatial Databses*, pp. 271–291, Portland, Me, USA, 1995.

[12] W. M. Liu, S. J. Li, and J. Renz, "Combining RCC-8 with qualitative direction calculi: algorithms and complexity," in *Proceedings of the 21st International Joint Conference on Artificial Intelligence (IJCAI'09)*, pp. 854–859, Pasadena, Calif, USA, July 2009.

[13] D. Randell, Z. Cui, and A. G. Cohn, "A spatial logic based on regions and connection," in *Proceedings of the 3rd International Conference on Knowledge Representation and Reasoning*, 1992.

[14] S. J. Li, "Combining topological and directional information for spatial reasoning," in *Proceedings of the 20th International Joint Conference on Artifical Intelligence (IJCAI'07)*, pp. 435–440, 2007.

[15] S. J. Li and A. G. Cohn, "Reasoning with topological and directional spatial information," *Computational Intelligence*, vol. 28, no. 4, pp. 579–616, 2012.

[16] P. Balbiani, J. Condotta, and L. F. A. del Cerro, "A Model for reasoning about bidimensional temporal relations," in *Proceedings of the 6th International Conference on Knowledge Representation and Reasoning*, 1998.

[17] P. Balbiani, J. Condotta, and L. F. del Cerro, "A new tractable subclass of the rectangle algebra," in *Proceedings of the 16th International Joint Conference on Artifical Intelligence (IJCAI'99)*, vol. 1, pp. 442–447, 1999.

[18] A. G. Cohn, B. Bennett, J. Gooday, and N. M. Gotts, "Qualitative spatial representation and reasoning with the region connection calculus," *GeoInformatica*, vol. 1, no. 3, pp. 275–316, 1997.

[19] J. Sharma, *Integrated spatial reasoning in geographic information systems: combining topology and direction [Ph.D. thesis]*, University of Maine, 1993, http://www.library.umaine.edu/theses/pdf/Sharma.pdf.

[20] D. Papadias, M. J. Egenhofer, and J. Sharma, "Hierarchical reasoning about direction relations," in *Proceedings of the 4th ACM workshop on Advances on Advances in Geographic Information Systems (GIS'96)*, ACM-GIS, Rockville, Md, USA, November 1996.

[21] G. Ligozat, "Reasoning about cardinal directions," *Journal of Visual Languages and Computing*, vol. 9, pp. 23–44, 1998.

[22] M. T. Escrig and F. Toledo, *Qualitative Spatial Reasoning: Theory and Practice: Application to Robot Navigation*, IOS Press, Amsterdam, The Netherlands, 1998.

[23] S. Skiadopoulos and M. Koubarakis, "Composing cardinal direction relations," in *Proceedings of the SSTD-01*, Redondo Beach, Calif, USA, July 2001.

[24] S. Skiadopoulos and M. Koubarakis, "Composing cardinal direction relations," *Artificial Intelligence*, vol. 152, no. 2, pp. 143–171, 2004.

[25] B. Bennett, A. Isli, and A. G. Cohn, "When does a composition table provide a complete and tractable proof procedure for a relational constraint language?" in *Proceedings of the IJCAI-97 Workshop on Spatial and Temporal Reasoning*, Nagoya, Japan, 1997.

[26] A. Isli, "Integrating existing cone-shaped and projection-based cardinal direction relations and a TCSP-like decidable generalisation," CoRR cs.AI/0311051, 2003.

[27] W. M. Liu, X. T. Zhang, S. J. Li, and M. S. Ying, "Reasoning about cardinal directions between extended objects," *Artificial Intelligence*, vol. 174, pp. 951–983, 2011.

[28] W. M. Liu and S. J. Li, "Reasoning about cardinal directions between extended objects: the NP-hardness result," *Artificial Intelligence*, vol. 175, no. 18, pp. 2155–2169, 2011.

[29] A.L. Kor and B. Bennett, "Composition for cardinal directions by decomposing horizontal and vertical constraints," in *Proceedings of the AAAI 2003 Spring Symposium*, D. Dicheva and D. Dochev, Eds., Stanford University, Stanford, Calif, USA, March 2003.

[30] A. L. Kor and B. Bennett, "Reasoning mechanism for cardinal direction relations," in *AIMSA 2010*, D. Dicheva and D. Dochev, Eds., vol. 6304 of *Lecture Notes in Artificial Intelligence (LNAI)*, pp. 32–41, Springer, 2010.

[31] A. G. Cohn, B. Bennett, J. Gooday, and N. Gotts, "Representing and reasoning with qualitative spatial relations about regions," in *Temporal and Spatial Reasoning*, O. Stock, Ed., Kluwer, New York, NY, USA, 1997.

[32] B. L. Clarke, "Calculus of individuals based on connection," *Notre Dame Journal of Formal Logic*, vol. 23, no. 3, pp. 204–218, 1981.

[33] B. L. Clarke, "Individuals and points," *Notre Dame Journal of Formal Logic*, vol. 26, no. 1, pp. 61–75, 1985.

[34] B. Bennett, A. Isli, and A. G. Cohn, "A system handling RCC-8 queries on 2D regions representable in the closure algebra of half-planes ?" in *Proceedings of the 11th International Conference on Industrial and Engineering Applications of Artificial Intelligence and Expert Systems (IEA/AIE'98)*, pp. 281–290, Springer, 1998.

[35] F. Wolter and M. Zakharyaschev, "Spatio-temporal representation and reasoning based on RCC-8," in *Proceedings of the 7th Conference on Principles of Knowledge Representation and Reasoning (KR'00)*, 2000, http://citeseerx.ist.psu.edu/viewdoc/summary?doi=10.1.1.33.4558.

[36] A. C. Varchi, "Parts, wholes, and part-whole relations: the prospects of mereotopology," *Data And Knowledge Engineering*, vol. 20, pp. 259–286, 1996.

[37] J. F. Allen, "Maintaining knowledge about temporal intervals," *Communications of the ACM*, vol. 26, no. 11, pp. 832–843, 1983.

[38] M. Egenhofer, "Reasoning about binary topological relations," in *Proceedings of the 2nd Symposium on Large Spatial Databases (SSD'91)*, O. Gunther and H. J. Schek, Eds., vol. 525, pp. 143–160, Lecture Notes in Computer Science, Zurich, Switzerland, 1991.

[39] M. Egenhofer, "Deriving the composition of binary topological relations," *Journal of Visual Languages and Computing*, vol. 5, no. 2, pp. 133–149, 1994.

[40] Z. Cui, A. G. Cohn, and D. A. Randell, "Qualitative simulation absed on logical formalism of space and time," in *Proceedings of the AAAI'92*, pp. 679–684, AAAI Press, Menlo Park, Calif, USA, 1992.

[41] B. Bennett, "Some observations and puzzles about composing spatial and temporal relations," in *Proceedings of the 11th European Conference on Artificial Intelligence, Workshop on Spatial and Temporal Reasoning (ECAI)*, Amsterdam, The Netherlands, August 1994.

[42] G. Ligozat, "Simple models for simple calculi," in *COSIT'99*, C. Freksa and D. M. Mark, Eds., vol. 1661 of *Lecture Notes in Computer Science*, pp. 173–188, Springer, Berlin, Germany, 1999.

6

Crowd Evacuation for Indoor Public Spaces Using Coulomb's Law

Pejman Kamkarian[1] and Henry Hexmoor[2]

[1] *Electrical and Computer Engineering Department, Southern Illinois University, Carbondale, IL 62901, USA*
[2] *Department of Computer Science, Southern Illinois University, Carbondale, IL 62901, USA*

Correspondence should be addressed to Pejman Kamkarian, pejman@siu.edu

Academic Editor: Thomas Mandl

This paper focuses on designing a tool for guiding a group of people out of a public building when they are faced with dangerous situations that require immediate evacuation. Despite architectural attempts to produce safe floor plans and exit door placements, people will still commit to fatal route decisions. Since they have access to global views, we believe supervisory people in the control room can use our simulation tools to determine the best courses of action for people. Accordingly, supervisors can guide people to safety. In this paper, we combine Coulomb's electrical law, graph theory, and convex and centroid concepts to demonstrate a computer-generated evacuation scenario that divides the environment into different safe boundaries around the locations of each exit door in order to guide people through exit doors safely and in the most expedient time frame. Our mechanism continually updates the safe boundaries at each moment based on the latest location of individuals who are present inside the environment. Guiding people toward exit doors depends on the momentary situations in the environment, which in turn rely on the specifications of each exit door. Our mechanism rapidly adapts to changes in the environment in terms of moving agents and changes in the environmental layout that might be caused by explosions or falling walls.

1. Introduction

The gathering of a group of people at the same location and time is called a crowd. People who form the crowd often share a common activity. In order to study crowd evacuation, we need to have clear understanding of all their relevant attributes. Determining crowd dynamics based on their psychological identifications is one of the many ways that is broadly explored by previous researches. Crowd dispersion is unpredictable. There are many studies conducted that explore crowd behavior from different perspectives. One of the major crowd behaviors with psychological underpinnings is identified as *deindividuation*, which is the situation where antinormative individual behavior is exhibited in groups in which individuals are not seen as separate individuals. Simply put, deindividuation is blending in a group such that the individual decision making ceases to be observed separately. *Submergence* is largely acknowledged as the root of contemporary theories of deindividuation, [1]. Numerous studies have explored relationships between deindividuation and behavioral changes [1–6]. It is important to understand how individuals conceive themselves in the crowd since once being a member of a crowd they no longer act independently but behave in concert with others. There is a distinction between public self-awareness, which has to do with the individual's concerns about how others evaluate them and private self-awareness, which approximates to the concept of objective self-awareness and has to do with monitoring the extent to which ones behavior matches ones internal standards [7–9]. It is generally assumed that when an emergency occurs, occupants panic and exit by the nearest doors. According to Canada's NRC scientist Guylene Proulx, the activities and the interactions among the occupants in a building before the occurrence of an emergency are relevant to understand the notion of panic and may not lead to hysterical or irrational behaviors as stated in the definition and supported by some authors. In contrary, people behave in a rational way. For example, people who come together will also tend to leave together. Therefore, family members will try to be together before making the decision to exit [10–12]. Some people, depending on their role (e.g.,: owner, employees etc.) may decide first to leave the building, but at some points, go back trying to retrieve items left behind, such as documents, money, people in danger, and so forth. The irrationality of their actions is often evident in a retrospective view. However, at the time of the action, it was conceived to be perfectly rational. Evacuees are assumed to be rational, so after realizing that they need to escape, they should make decisions leading them to exit as fast as possible [13]. Environments in an emergency situation are dynamic. Since in such situations the evacuees do not have enough time to become familiar with the new environment, plans should be made quickly. According to the information gathered, people have to select the exit that can guarantee them the greatest opportunity to escape from the threat as fast as possible to decide which persons can be helpful to fulfill that goal, [14]. Exit selection has a great influence in the outcome of an evacuation. How people choose exits is a complex process. Generally, they make their decision based on their familiarity with the exit and its visibility, [15]. Among methods for exit selection are cellular automata models. A few (e.g., [16, 17]) consider the variety in the environment (i.e., exit width and obstacles) to have an impact in the exit dynamics of evacuees. According to personality trait theory [10, 11, 18–20], these models demonstrate the influence of evacuees' personalities (i.e., shy, aggressive, collaborative) in the outcome of evacuation. A shy person would rarely take decisions but he would act as a "follower," an aggressive person would exhibit "selfish behavior," and a collaborative person would try to cooperate with others to come out with a suitable solution for all Agent-based models [21]. In these models, evacuees act as "rational" agents whose objectives are to find the best set of actions that will maximize their profit toward the exit doors relying on the partners that will guarantee them to reach safe places in a minimum of time. Finally, the choice of an exit will depend on the interaction between evacuees and their environment. An evacuee will preselect a route based on his knowledge of the environment, and that initial route may change depending on his estimation of queuing time, traveling time to that particular exit, and sometimes because of group decisions [22]. An evacuation crowd consists of individuals that interact with each other [11]. Occupants have to escape from the danger as quickly as possible, and by doing so they may have to collaborate with others. Evacuees are assumed to be rational. They pursue their own interest [23]. An evacuee will tend to cooperate with another one if he estimates that he can have a good payoff (maximum chance of being safe), or in contrary, will avoid cooperating or associating with another one if his safety is decreased. They might have to be collaborative with others or try to develop skills (e.g., exploring and visual memory). The urgency theory is used to explain some behaviors of occupants, for instance blockage at exit doors, stampede, or trampling [24]. Three factors are essential to understand the concept of urgency [25]

(1) the nature of the emergency,

(2) the consequence of not exiting quickly,

(3) the time available to exit.

For example, a seriously injured person will try to reach a group to get him out as fast as possible, so that he can receive medical attention. At that time, his level of urgency is higher than a person who is safe [26]. Regardless of crowd specifications, we need to consider a model for the study crowds. Understanding human crowds by previous modeling is conducted in computer graphics, robotics, traffic engineering, and social sciences. A survey of recent research can be found in [27]. By and large, simulations of crowds are either macroscopic by modeling environmental parameters that affect a group of agents simultaneously, or microscopic by modeling interaction rules for each agent. A mesolevel modeling is offered in [28, 29], where movement fields are composed of external inputs that influence agents combined by their own local reasoning. Inclusion of diverse agents and their diverse capacities provides a diverse set of reactions in the environment. For example, [30] proposed an approach based on the motion dynamics whereas [31, 32] report on investigations of psychological nature. The work in [33] presented an approach based on the sociological factors, while [34–36], approaches are based on cognitive and behavioral models. The model in [37] is based on the situation-guided control, however, [38], used a particle-based system to simulate human behaviors. Each agent is regarded as a particle, augmented with a state and a feedback function to control its behavior and all agents' behaviors that constituted the whole system performance. The work in [39–41] focused on emergency evacuation conditions of a crowd and abstracted the model by observing real crowds in his work. Helbing's group adopted a particle system to study the crowd behavior in emergency situations based on social psychology and dynamics [42]. Adriana et al., [43] extended the idea with additional aspects of individual characteristics and relational behaviors to clarify evacuation. In order to accurately replicate evacuation strategies in a crowd, we need a model, which is able to accurately reflect the crowd behavior especially in emergency situations. As an earlier method to prediction emergency movement, which was developed based on fire emergency egress, BFIRES-II is paintable, [44]. ASET [45] and EVACNET+ [46] are other methods that presented as the earliest methods. Because of its importance, evacuation modeling is subject to introduced increasingly by different researchers. [47], indicated, such methods are increasingly growing based on a comparison of his past and present surveys, [48]. In terms of highlighting advantages and disadvantages of different evacuation methods, researchers started to study on them [49]. In this paper, we demonstrate a strategy to repeatedly divide the environment to distinctly safe boundaries around each exit door. Boundaries are subject to change based on the location of each agent at any moment using a crowd evacuation model. In order to develop our strategy, we will not to only focus on crowd specifications and movements of individuals, but also the physical specifications of the environment. In order to make more accurate decisions for controlling the crowd, we use sensors and detectors to identify and locate individuals and exit door locations on a continual basis. These data will be useful for timely decision making processes. Having such a strategy is useful in terms of helping the supervisory security agents in the control room to guide people through each exit door in the shortest possible times, while reducing mistakes during events that the evacuation environment is obscured from full view. This will be the case when there are explosions, smoke, or other hazards blocking visibility of security personnel. We will focus on the relationships between locations of exit doors and agent movements in the environment to develop our strategy accordingly. Pedestrian motion can produce a *social force*, [50] that exerts an invisible force of repulsion upon nearby fellow pedestrians. This is very similar to our charged particle model of human movement force. While Helbing's model of force accounts for force as a result of directions of force, ours is omnidirectional [50].

2. Related Work

Anyone living in a populated, gregarious world has experienced the effects of crowds. Crowds exert an invisible force on individuals. Directly, movements of an individual's crowd neighbors will physically propel the individual in the direction of crowd's general moving trajectory. Indirectly, in order to maintain personal space, the person will experience social forces to accommodate for the crowd movement [51].

Derived from safety concerns in indoor spaces, there is a force to evacuate that people toward exit openings. This has best been modeled in terms of a game among members of a crowd [52]. Game theoretic modeling and analysis as well as an extensively validated fire evacuation simulator are reported from a Finish research center [52]. There have been attempts to learn human movement from animal behaviors. Argentine ants have been studied as test organisms to explore their natural evacuation processes in response to fire. It was observed that any movement in response to citronella does not necessarily follow a simple set of rules. As citronella was repellent to ants, they showed negative taxis, moving away from the stimulus towards the exit. This is similar to what one can expect when a crowd of people is running away from a source of danger (e.g., a fire) towards a safe place [53]. This demonstrated how such empirical data from non-human organisms such as ants can overcome the shortage of human panic data for model calibration and validation, something which has intrigued researchers for decades. Experiments with ants were used to model the consideration of both attractive and repulsive forces under panic condition to maintain the coherence of collective dynamics. Ant models are in the class of microscopic models where individual behaviors are modeled. However, people are not like homogeneous, interchangeable, nonrational, noncognitive entities. We must incorporate human factors into microscopic models in [54]. Navigation fields were introduced in order to direct virtual crowds using goal-directed navigation functions. Macroscopic behavior is generated by microscopic modeling methods [29].

A force-enabled version of the floor field pedestrian is presented in [54], where a building is treated as an information system through which people move. Using Henein's model through communication agents update and maintain multiple perspectives of their environment.

Recently, there has been an increasing interest in pedestrian traffic [55]. For instance, a method for determining density using Voronoi cells is found in [56]. A Survey of mathematical modeling techniques for traffic flow and crowd models are also available [57]. Common methodological approaches for crowd evacuation are reviewed in [58]. Macroscopic models are computationally less expensive because they consider fewer detailed interactions among people and with their environment. Instead, mathematical models are used to describe crowd movements as liquid flows [59–61].

3. The Main Attributes for the Environment

Generally, based on its usage, each environment will consist of many different groups of objects; such as obstacles (i.e., a row of chairs or trash cans), the agents, and the exit doors. Agents can be any type of living beings, such as pets or humans. In this paper, we assume only human agents in the environment. The two most important attributes in the environment for us are the agents (i.e., simulating individuals) and exit doors (i.e., evacuations points). These attributes affect each other and are used to determine safe boundaries. In this paper, we considered each environment generally having one or more convex zones corresponding to the map. Each of the convex zones is composed of a collection of α zones, which are the spheres belonging to each exit doors, with β zones and θ angles for each. Each convex zone must have at least a single exit door inside. If there were no exit doors available for a convex zone, we have to merge it with its adjacent convex zone, which has at least one exit door.

4. The Main Attributes for Exit Doors

We considered two general attributes for each exit door that are zones and boundaries. We assumed three different zones for each exit door. The first zone is the area nearest to the exit door we call α zone, determined by each exit door's width. Figure 1 shows two exit doors of different width and their proportionally sized α zones. This zone is always the same in size and never changes during the movement of each agent. The only way that α zone could change would be if it is completely blocked or the door width was partially blocked (for instance, by some obstacle that might be a fallen agent, or debris in the environment). In such cases, due to the change in width of the exit door, the α zone will change. Each environment may contain several α zones, one for each exit door.

The second zone is called β zone (see Figure 1). β is the area that is bound by the walls and each contains a single α zone. Areas between several α zones are divided into the same number of β zones. The third attribute is the θ angle, which is the largest angle that contains a corresponding β zone within each quadrant. Boundaries separate β zones. The θ angle varies based on the locations of agents in

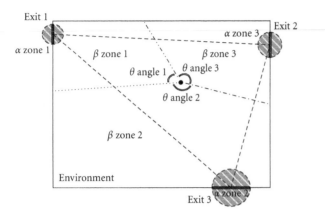

FIGURE 1: The α and β zones and θ angels related to exit door 1 and 2.

each moment. For example, the angle can be reduced if the number of people around a certain exit door increases. Figure 1 shows an environment consisting of three exit doors with corresponding zones and angles.

5. A Synopsis of Electrostatic Fields

5.1. Charge. A property of matter that prepares an object so as to participate in electrical forces is called *charge*. This is so it can be distinguished from the common usage of this term, which is used indiscriminately for anything electrical. There are three different statuses of charge available that are negative, positive, and no charge. Two or more objects which have a same type of charge will exert a force of repulsion on each other when they are relatively close.

A charged particle has a corresponding force-per-charge-of-would-be-victim vector to at each point in the region of space around it. *A vector field* is the infinite set of force-per-charge-of-would-be-victim vectors. All charged particles in the region of space with the force-per-charge-of-would-be-victim vector field will have a force exerted upon them by the force-per-charge-of-would-be-victim field. The force-per-charge-of-would-be-victim field is also called the *electric field*. The charged particle forming the electric field is the *source charge*. Two objects that have excess opposite charges, one positively charged and the other negatively charged, attract each other when they are relatively near each other. The so-called source charge creates an electric field which exerts a force on the so called victim charge. For this paper, we primarily focus on net effects that each charged particle exerts a force on other charged particles. This is at the core of Coulomb's Law. The force is called the Coulomb force; that is, the electrostatic force. The charge is one of source or victim that establishes a perspective. By analogy, this is similar to identifying an object whose motion or equilibrium is explored using Newton's second Law of motion as shown by (1):

$$F = ma. \tag{1}$$

The Coulomb's Law can apply completely in case of having only two charges in our environment without need

to considering electric fields affects, while in case of having more than two charges in our environment, we have to consider about to applying the electric fields as well. In the environment, each single charge is affected by all other charges. Since forces from all other charges on a specific charge are linear, we can apply superposition on each particular charge. Based on superposition, if we assume charge C_1 with the vector electric field E_1 and charge C_2 with vector electric field E_2, the resulting equivalent vector electric field E_3 between vector electric field E_1 and E_2 would be the vector sum of E_1 and E_2 as it shown by (2) [62]:

$$\vec{E_3} = \vec{E_1} + \vec{E_2} \tag{2}$$

Because two different types of charge cancel each other, for simplicity and also to discuss the total amount of charge of an object, we label them using negative "−" and positive "+" signs. There are other kinds of naming different charges. For instance, Benjamin Franklin defined the label "A" as the negative charge and "B" as the positive charge. If an object does not have any charge, or in the other hand if there is an equivalent amount of both types of charges available for an object, it is referred to as electrically neutral.

5.2. Coulomb's Law. Coulomb's Law is a physics law that expresses the electrostatic interaction among the charged objects. It remained for French physicist Charles Augustin de Coulomb in 1783 and electromagnetism theory developed based on its concepts. Henry Cavendish discovered, but not published, the relation between the distance and charge prior to Coulomb's work. Also, the relation of the electric force with distance had been proposed previously by Joseph Priestley [63].

Coulomb's law indicates the magnitude of the electrostatics force of interaction that is available between two point charges is directly proportional to the scalar multiplication of the magnitudes of charges and inversely proportional to the square of the distances between them.

The scalar form of Coulomb's Law indicates an expression for the magnitude and sign of the electrostatic force between two idealized point charges, with a small size compared to their separation. For instance, if we assumed having two point charges q_1 and q_2, the force F acting simultaneously among them is given by the following equation:

$$F = k_e \frac{|q_1| \times |q_2|}{r^2}, \tag{3}$$

where r the separation is distance and k_e is proportionality constant. The signs of the charges indicate the type of force between them. In other words, repulsive behavior indicates having a positive force and attractive behavior shows having a negative force between the charges.

Based on the vector form, the force in the equation represents a vector force that is acting on either point charge, so directed as to push it away from the other point charge. The right side of the equation requires a coefficient multiplier for a unit vector pointing in one of two opposite directions.

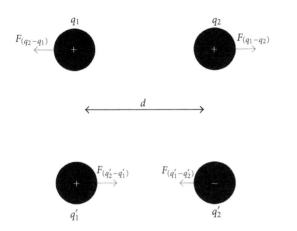

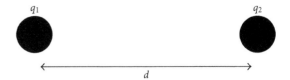

FIGURE 3: Two charges q_1 and q_2 which are placed at the distance of d.

FIGURE 2: Charges with a same signs repel each other and charges with a different signs will attract each other.

For example, from q_1 to q_2 if the force is acting on q_2; the charges may have either sign and the sign of their product determines the ultimate direction of that force. The force of pushing/pulling away the charges from/towards each other (based on their signs) is directly proportional to the product of the charges and inversely proportional to the square of the distance between them. The square of the distance shows force field due to an isolated point charge is uniform in all directions and is weakened with distance as much as the area of a sphere centered on the point charge expands with its radius. The law of superposition allows this law to be extended to include any number of point charges, to derive the force on any one point charge by a vector addition of these individual forces acting alone on that point charge. The resulting vector located as parallel to the electric field vector at that point, with that point charge removed. Coulomb's Law can also be interpreted in terms of atomic units with the force expressed in Hartrees per Bohr radius, the charge in terms of the elementary charge, and the distances in terms of the Bohr radius.

As it shown by Figure 2, and (4), when the charges have the same signs, they will repel each other while when they have a different signs, they should attract each other:

$$\left| \overrightarrow{F_{q_2-q_1}} \right| = \left| \overrightarrow{F_{q_1-q_2}} \right| = k \frac{|q_1 \times q_2|}{d^2}. \tag{4}$$

Coulomb's Law in equation form is exact for point particles as well as for spherically symmetric charge distributions such as uniform balls of charge as long as one uses the center-to-center distance. A particle which has a certain amount, say, 5 Coulombs of the negative kind of charge is said to have a charge of -5 Coulombs and one with 5 Coulombs of the positive kind of charge is said to have a charge of $+5$ Coulombs. Plus and minus signs designating the kind of charge has the usual arithmetic meaning when the charges enter into equations. Figure 3 shows two charges q_1 and q_2 which are located at the distance d.

The arithmetic interpretation of the kind of charge in the vector form of Coulomb's Law provides that equation to

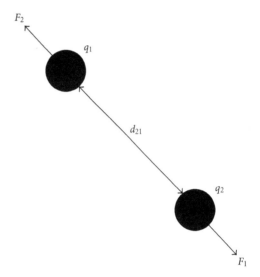

FIGURE 4: The graphical representation of the Coulomb's Law having two charges.

give the correct direction of the force for a combination of different charges.

Assuming having two charges q_1 and q_2. We use the Figure 4 representation of Coulomb's Law for charges and forces among them graphically when $q_1 \times q_2 > 0$. The vector F_1 shows the force experienced by the charge q_2 and the vector F_2 represents the force experienced by the charge q_1. The vector d_{12} is also the displacement vector between two charges (q_1 and q_2). The magnitudes if the vectors F_1 and F_2 will always equal.

As an example, we will explain the equilibrium for charges between three charges. We assume that there are three fixed charged objects collinear on a straight line as it shown by Figure 1. We also assumed the charges on the objects are q_1 and q_2 and they also have the same sign or type of charge. The d_{13} indicates the distance between object 1 and object 3. We assumed that the positions of object 1 and object 3 are kept fixed. This is shown by the Figure 5.

In order to achieve equilibrium between charges, the total amount of forces between each adjacent pairs of charges must be the same. The following equation shows the concept to exist for the middle, charged object:

$$F_{21} = F_{23}, \tag{5}$$

d_{13} represents the distance between object 1 and object 3 as shown in:

$$d_{12} + d_{23} = d_{13}. \tag{6}$$

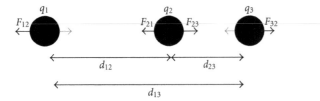

FIGURE 5: Darker arrows are electrostatic forces and lighter arrows are reaction based on the Newton 3rd Law.

Based on Newton's 3rd Law, the forces between each pair of adjacent charges must be the same. The following equation (7) show equilibrium forces between the pair of q_1 and q_2 and between pair of q_2 and q_3, respectively,

$$F_{12} = F_{23},$$
$$F_{21} = F_{32}. \tag{7}$$

Our goal is to find the distances between objects. To find the needed values, we use (5) and (6). The result of applying Coulomb's Law to (5) is shown by (8a):

$$k\frac{q_1 \times q_2}{d_{12}^2} = k\frac{q_2 \times q_3}{d_{23}^2}. \tag{8a}$$

After applying the algebra rules, (8a) becomes as (8b):

$$q_1 d_{23}^2 - q_3 d_{12}^2 = 0. \tag{8b}$$

Based on (6) we can write the following equation (9):

$$d_{23} = d_{13} - d_{12}. \tag{9}$$

Substituting (9) into (8b) and sorting with respect to d_{12}, which is our unknown value, we get the following equation (10):

$$d_{12}^2(q_1 - q_3) - d_{12}2q_1d_{13} + q_1d_{13}^2 = 0. \tag{10}$$

The following equation (11) is a standard quadratic equation for (10), which is written in a general format:

$$x^2a + xb + c = 0. \tag{11}$$

By solving (11), we will get two values for d_{12} and d_{23} distances. The solution correct from the physics point of view is the first one. The second would put the charge q_2 to the right of charge q_3. It causes the electrostatic forces resulting from interaction with q_1 and q_2 would be acting in one direction to the right side and the net force could never be equal to zero consequently.

6. Different Combinations of Exit Doors

As a matter of standard, each building should have at least one exit door located at a place that is visible to the public. In case of a single exit door in the environment, the only way to evacuate people will be to guide them to the exit door and through it and hence there is only one α zone and the rest of the environment belongs to one β zone. There will be no θ angle, which means that there are no safe boundaries available. Our solution is applicable only if we have more than two exit doors at each convex zone. If there are two or more exit doors, there will be a corresponding number of α zones, β zones, and θ angles, respectively.

7. Application of Customized Coulomb's Law

In this section, we demonstrate and apply the customized Coulomb's Law to exit doors based on the current locations of the agent sets of each moment. We divided the process of dividing the environment and decision making of each boundary into four different phases: initialization, which is the process of determining locations and status for each exit door to form the initial safety boundaries, detection of boundaries, gathering data from sensors, which is sensing and detecting the locations of agents and also their physical specifications and movements by cameras and detectors to send them to the processing unit, and updating the boundaries and decision making which is updating and redrawing the safe boundaries based on the latest information gathered and sent by the detector devices that are installed in the environment. Each phase consists of many other substeps. We use different techniques for each phase. The phases and relative steps are described next.

7.1. Phase (1) Initialization. This phase starts by detecting the location of each exit door and also measures the width of each exit door. We consider each exit door as a sphere with the diameter equal to the exit door width. We assume an abstract line drawn from each sphere's center point to other sphere center points in such a manner as to form the largest enclosing polyhedral configuration. This configuration must meet each sphere only once. Because the goal of this step is to only determine the initial values and measures of locations and specifications for each exit door in the environment, to calculate and draw the initiate safe boundaries, we consider our environment to be empty; that is, devoid of agents.

7.1.1. Initializing the Exit Doors. At this level, all exit doors located inside the environment will have been detected possibly using a raster map. We need to have two different measures for each. The width and the central point of each exit door, which is placed on the central straight line that connects two edges of exit doors. This can be done by the cameras and detectors that are installed in the environment. We may use some techniques to increase the speed of detecting and measuring locations of exit doors such as using a wire frame viewing of the environment.

7.1.2. Determining the Sphere of Charges. We assumed that each exit door behaves as a sphere of charge with the diameter equal of the width called α zone. The α zone may be considered to have a simple 2D circular shape or a complete 3D sphere. In this paper, we considered the α zones as a complete 3D shape. The amount of charge for each α zone is equal to relevant exit door charge. If an exit door blocked for any reason during monitoring the environment, we must consider its sphere and hence its charge considered to be 0.

7.1.3. Determining Zones.
At this level, we divide our environment into different convex zones. To do this, we use convexity concepts and rules that have previously been used in the neural networks. On the other hand, the environment must be divided into convex shapes such that each default line must meet the edges of the shape only two times. Each convex area must has at least a simple exit door inside; otherwise, we have to join this zone with the adjacent convex zone which has at least a single exit door.

7.1.4. Determining the Exit Doors Boundary.
This point consists of determining the largest simple nondirected cycle graph of length m where m is total number of exit doors located in each zone. This graph has m vertices and m edges. Every vertex has degree of 2. We label this graph C_m. For example, in case of 5 exit doors among the convex zone, the largest simple, nondirected cycle graph has the length equal to 5 and also we have 5 different pairs of adjacent charges.

7.1.5. Determining the Amount of Charge for Each Exit Door.
We considered each exit door as a sphere with the diameter equal to the width of each exit door. Based on the metric measurement, the amount of positive charge for each exit door is given by the following equation:

$$Q_{ED_i} = \lceil W_{ED_i} \times 100 \rceil, \tag{12}$$

where Q_{ED_i} is the charge of ith exit door, and W_{ED_i} is the width of ith exit door. For instance, in case of an exit door with the width of 1 meter, the charge of the mentioned exit door would be 100.

7.2. Phase (2) Detection of Boundaries.
At this phase, the process will determine the initial boundaries for each exit door using the initial values gathered in the previous phase. To determine the initial boundaries, this phase will find the point which is located on the line that connects the centers of each pair of exit doors (as charges). The location of this point obtained by considering the width of each exit door, then drawing a virtual vertical page crossing that point. This phase bisects the intersectional boundaries between different vertical pages to reach β zones.

7.2.1. Calculating the Charge for Each Adjacent Pair of Exit Doors.
At this step, we will calculate the amount of charge between each adjacent pair of exit doors. To do this, we assumed a straight line between each pair of adjacent exit doors. We also assume that the locations of all exit doors are fixed and that the charges for each exit door are positive. We will put a positive charge on the straight line between each adjacent exit doors. The amount of the positive charge is given by the following equation:

$$Q_t = \left| \frac{Q_{ED_i} + Q_{ED_j}}{2} \right|, \tag{13}$$

where Q_t is the amount of charge between two charges Q_{ED_i} and Q_{ED_j} where located at the adjacent pair on the mentioned straight line. The assumed that the positive charge we used between each pairs is the average value for them, using this strategy guarantees that the positive charge will stay somewhere between two fixed charges and not beyond them.

7.2.2. Determining Equilibrium Point.
At this step, the process will find the equilibrium location for each positive charge that is placed on the straight line between each pair of positive charges. All exit doors as positive charges are fixed. The positive charge will locate on the straight line and closer to the smaller positive charge. Since the two charges around the positive charge are positive, they will push the positive charge away from themselves. In such a case, the positive charge will stay closer to the smaller positive charge because the grater positive charge has a larger exert force than the smaller one. The equations demonstrated in the three electric charges in equilibrium are used to determine the location of the mentioned positive charges.

7.2.3. Finding the Centroid Point for Each Shape.
At this step, the process finds that the geometric center (i.e., centroid point) for each shape that contain related exit doors. The center of mass, or centroid of a 2D shape, is the intersection point of all straight lines that divide the shape into two areas with equal moment about the line. The centroid point is the arithmetic mean of all intersection points. The next step is to draw a line from that location to all positive charges and continue that line until it reaches an environment. This line separates the environment into two different areas such that each of them belongs to a different exit door.

7.2.4. Determining and Binding β Zones.
Each exit door has a θ angle that belongs to it, which is drawn from the centroid point to the equilibrium points of the straight lines crossing from the relative adjacent charges. At the next point, we bind the largest θ angle which includes only a single exit door as the β zone of the relative exit door. The process continues until all β zones are specified for each exit door.

7.3. Phase (3) Data Gathering and Analysis.
There should be several sensors, cameras, and detectors installed at different locations in the environment in order to be able to determine the location of each exit door and especially the location of the agent set at each moment. These facilities estimate the status of each exit door in each instant in terms of evacuation ability rate. These devices will send pertinent data for agents in terms of their size and an estimate of their movement speeds to the central unit in order to classify analyzes and makes decisions. This phase generally gathers and analyzes the data obtained by different sensors and detectors installed inside the environment.

7.3.1. Determining the Agent Locations.
The crowd is dynamic and is constantly changing locations. The rate of movement is more unpredictable when agents are faced with

an emergency situation. The process at this step will be to detect each individual position in the environment. One way to determine the positions is by using a grid. In order to make decision about the boundaries in real time, the sensors should be fast enough to determine individual locations and to send them to the central processing unit for analysis.

7.3.2. Determining Each Agent's Charge. The sensors and detectors should be able to determine the specifications of each individual such as body size and movement rate. For instance, based on the agent movement rate, the detector might determine the health status of each individual. Having these measures we are able to assign an accurate value as a charge to each agent. At this step, the process will determine the amount of charge for each individual located in the environment based on physical specifications. Each general convex zone consists of a collection of distinct α zones, β zones, and θ angle belonging to it. Each β zone has its distinct α zone and θ angle belonging to it. Furthermore, α and β zones and θ angles are non-overlapping among zones and angles as shown in:

$$Z_i = \left\{ Z_{\beta_1}, Z_{\beta_2}, \ldots, Z_{\beta_i} \right\},$$
$$Z_{\beta_i} = Z_{\alpha_i} \cup Z_{\beta_i} \cup \hat{\theta}_i. \tag{14}$$

Here Z is the general convex zone, Z_{α_i} is the ith α zone of ith zone and Z_{β_i} is the ith β zone of ith zone and $\hat{\theta}_i$ is ith θ angle, respectively. The environment may consist of a number of general convex zones inside. Each general convex zone must consist of at least a single exit door. In case of having a convex area without an exit door, we will join it to with its neighboring zone that contains at least a single exit door. The relations are shown by the following equation:

$$\text{Env} = \{Z_1, Z_{12}, Z_3, \ldots, Z_n\}, \tag{15}$$

Env indicates that there is a collection of convex zones available in the environment. Each zone has its own set of agents. Each agent may have a different situation in terms of the physical status. A sample set of agent set in a sample general convex zone is shown by the following equation:

$$Z_i = \left\{ \text{Ag}_1, \text{Ag}_2, \text{Ag}_3, \ldots, \text{Ag}_m \right\}. \tag{16}$$

Here Z_i is the ith zone and Ag_m is the mth agent that belongs to ith zone.

Of all the agents available in each general convex zone, each β zone and hence exit door depend on their situations and locations support a number of them shown by the following equation:

$$Z_{\beta_i} = \left\{ \text{Ag}_1, \text{Ag}_2, \text{Ag}_3, \ldots, \text{Ag}_n \right\}, \tag{17}$$

where Z_{β_i} indicates the ith β zone. We assumed that each agent has a negative charge based on the specifications that he/her possesses. The key features that we considered in this paper were age, sex, and health status. The amount of charge for each agent is given by the following equation:

$$Q_{\text{Ag}_i} = A_i \times G_i \times \text{HS}_i < 0, \tag{18}$$

where Q_{Ag_i} is the amount of negative charge for the ith agent, A_i is the age of the ith agent, and the HS_i is the health status for the ith agent. Because all given values of the equation are negative, the final result of Q_{Ag_i} is always smaller than zero. In case that there are no agents in any β zones, the total amount of charge for the mentioned zone will be considered to be 0. In order for having agents, the amount of charge in the β zone is relative to the amount of charge for the number of agents s and it is always smaller than 0. However (19) shows the amount of charge for β zones in different situations depending on the number of agents available in them:

$$Q_{Z_i} = \begin{cases} 0 & \text{if } Z_i = \varnothing \\ \sum\limits_{k=1}^{p} Q_{\text{Ag}_k} < 0 & \text{otherwise,} \end{cases} \tag{19}$$

where Q_{Ag_k} is the amount of negative charge for the kth agent. One of key features related to the physical specification of agents that we considered in this paper is the age of each individual. The ranges of ages are varied from a place to another place and it depends on the usage of the environment and determination is based on the average age of the majority of people in the environment. We consider the normal value to be −1 and in order for having a reasonable result; we have to bind this value to the majority of people with the same range of age. For example, the usage of values in a kindergarten is different from a conference room because in a kindergarten the majority of people are children so we may bind the normal value to the group of ages below than 10 years old whereas in a conference room, because the average range of age is between 20 and 40, we need to bind the normal value to this group of age.

In our case study, we focused on a night club station, which consists of adult people as the majority range of ages inside, so we have to bind the normal values (*of* −1) to the ages that are placed between 10 and 40 years old. Based on the ages of agents in the environment, we used Table 1 to assign values to calculate the charges of each agent.

The other key feature in terms of calculation of agent charges is the gender of individuals. The values that may be used for each gender are different from situation to situation. In this paper, we assumed the default value, (*of* −1) for the males. In case of having only one gender in our environment, we have to consider default value for it. The amount of charge related to the gender of each agent is shown by the following Table 2.

The third physical key feature that we considered in this paper is the health status. The health status may vary from a place to place and it depends on the environment usage and is determined based on the health status of majority of the people are the environment. In this paper, we considered having only two options: Healthy and Disable. In some places, like hospitals or elder houses, there should be other options available in order to have a better estimate of the charges for each agent. The amount of charge related to the health status of each agent is shown by the following Table 3.

We have to pick a suitable value from each of the tables for each agent based on his/her physical specifications in order to be able to determine their amount of charge.

TABLE 1: The amount of charge related to the age for the mth agent that belongs to ith zone.

Age	A_i
<10	−3
≥10 and <40	−1
≥40 and <60	−2
≥60	−3

TABLE 2: The amount of charge related to the gender for the mth agent that belongs to ith zone.

Gender	S_i
Male	−1
Female	−1.5

TABLE 3: The amount of charge related to the health status for the mth agent that belongs to ith zone.

Health status	HS_i
Healthy	−1
Disable	−2

TABLE 4: The safety rates for exit doors based on their situation at moment t.

Safety rate for exit doors	
Status	Rate
Still open and ready to use	−1
Not stable	−1.5
Partial blocked	−2

Apart from the physical specifications of each agent, focusing on the status of each exit doors is essential. We determine the amount of charge for each single exit door based on its situation at each time instant.

Different situations for the status of each exit door may vary based on other options that are related to the usage of the environment, as well as the location of each exit door. We always used the default rate for the best situation of exit door when it is usable, reliable and can evacuate people to its full capacity. In this paper, we used Table 4 to determine the safety rate for each exit door based on the status of it. We assumed the following values for each group of safety rates for exit doors.

To obtain the new values for charges of exit doors, we have to consider previous amount of charge for each exit door, and the latest safety status of each. The total amount of positive charge is shown by the following equation:

$$Q_{\mathrm{ED}_i} = \left| \frac{Q'_{\mathrm{ED}_i}}{\mathrm{SR}_{\mathrm{ED}_i}} \right|, \qquad (20)$$

where Q_{ED_i} is the total positive charge of the ith exit door, Q_{ED_i} is the initial charge of the same exit door, and $\mathrm{SR}_{\mathrm{ED}_i}$ is the safety rate for the ith exit door. If the exit door completely

is blocked or not usable, we have to consider its charge as 0 as shown in:

$$Q_{\mathrm{ED}_i} = 0. \qquad (21)$$

The cameras and detectors will determine the safety rates of each exit door and send their status to the processing unit. In such situations, we have to remove the exit door from our environment and reassign its zone to the other ones that are still usable. The exit door will not be considered in forming the largest nondirected simple graph.

7.3.3. Determining the New Charge for Each Exit Door. After all agent's amount of charge is determined, at this step the process will calculate the new amount of positive charges for each exit doors based on the results obtained at the previous step. In order to determine the new value of each exit door charges, we need to consider all agents that are belong to that exit door at the moment. The new amount of charge for each exit door is shown by the following equation:

$$Q'_{\mathrm{ED}_i} = \left| Q_{Z_i} + Q_{\mathrm{ED}_i} \right|, \qquad (22)$$

where Q'_{ED_i} is the new positive charge for ith exit door, Q_{Z_i} is the initial positive amount of charge for the ith zone which belongs to the ith exit door, and Q_{ED_i} is the previous positive amount of charge for the ith exit door. The key feature of calculating the new charges for each exit door is based on (19) which is to expand the zone of those exit doors that have the smaller number of people inside and they are also are usable and stable. For example, assume having an exit door with 10 people in its zone and the adjacent exit door with the smaller width with only 3 people in its zone. Equation (19) will expand the area of the exit door with the smaller number of people. For the next round of processing, we might consider many of the people that belong to the bigger exit door for the smaller one.

7.3.4. Determining the New Status for Each Exit Door. Regardless of the already mentioned features, there are many other features that may exist in the environment that should be mentioned while determining each zones and boundaries. Determining exit door status is necessary, especially in emergency situations. In the case of blocked exit doors for such reasons as smashed walls or people who block the exit door by pushing or shoving each other, the reliability of the exit door can be significantly decreased. In such cases, the amount of positive charge of exit door will reduce if its reliability decreases. We called the reliability factor for each exit door as safety rate of that exit door. At the initialization phase, the safety rate for each exit door that is ready to use is set to +1. This rate will change based on the new environmental information gathered by sensors based on each exit door status. The safety rate is shown by the following equation:

$$\mathrm{SR}_{\mathrm{Ed}_i} = \left| \mathrm{SR}_{(\mathrm{ED}_i)_{t-1}} \times \mathrm{SR}_{(\mathrm{ED}_i)_t} \right|, \qquad (23)$$

where $\mathrm{SR}_{(\mathrm{ED}_i)_t}$ is the safety rate for the ith exit door at the moment t.

TABLE 5: The α zones and the amount of charges for each exit doors based on their width.

No.	Exit doors Width (m)	Charge
1	1	100
2	2	200
3	1	100
4	1	100

7.4. Phase (4) Decision Making and Updating the Boundaries. To make the decision and updating the safe boundaries for each of the general convex zones, having the values described in the previous third phases is essential. Based on the new values for each β zones in each moment, the value of charges for each exit door, and hence the safe boundaries of the general convex zones will change. The process of determining the boundaries for each exit door should continue updating by gathering new data from different installed sensors at each moment. Having a reliable and real-time hardware in order to detect and determine the different physical status of the exit doors, people status, and locations is essential in forming the safe boundaries in a reasonable time. The process refreshes the results all the time to redirect to the second phase after reaching and completion of the third phase.

Having the safe boundaries, which is the result of the 4th phase, helps people to make a better decision. This produces lower risk and hence better results in terms of evacuating people out of danger in emergency situations.

8. Case Study

In this section, we apply the optimized Coulomb's Law to a sample environment and compare the results as a step towards validation of our model. We selected the Station nightclub environment. On Thursday, February 20, 2003, at The Station nightclub located at 211 Cowesett Avenue in West Warwick, Rhode Island a fire accident occurred, which was the fourth deadliest nightclub fire in American history. More than 100 people lost their lives because of it. The tour manager of the evening's headlining band used a pyrotechnics during the show that was the main reason of firing. In the beginning, the fire ignited flammable sound insulation foam in the walls and then it spreads on ceilings surrounding the stage. Initially, there were about 132 people inside before the fire incident. Some of them were injured and about 32 escaped uninjured. Based on the what cameras and sensors were installed inside the environment recorded, growing billowing smoke and blocked one of exit doors quickly made escape impossible because of limiting the vision site. In our approach, we will first divide the area to convex zones and then we form the bidirectional cycle crossing all exit doors and based on the centroid location of the formed shape, we form the α zones, β zones, and θ angles. Based on some assumptions about the percentage of people who were spread in the environment and their physical specifications, we form the new zones. To apply the strategy,

we consider only the map of empty building at first step to form the zones and then regarding the crowd distribution, we form the new safe boundaries. Figure 6 shows a general view of the building shown in Figure 6.

In order to increase the speed of processing and also to simplify the map, we consider the wire frame view for it. Showing the map in frame view also helps to distinguish between objects and people easier. Figure 7 shows the frame view of Figure 6.

At this level, because of determining the initial safe boundaries, we only focus on exit doors. In order to apply our strategy, at the first step we have to determine the exact locations of each exit door and also the width of each. This task would be done by using a raster technology and will perform and send to the processing unit by detectors and cameras that are installed in the environment. We also need to determine the general convex zones as well. Based on the environment map, we have generally two convex zones as shown by:

$$Z = \{Z_1, Z_2\}. \tag{24}$$

The first general convex zone consists of four exit doors and the second zone consists of a single exit door as it shown by:

$$Z_1 = \{ED_1, ED_2, ED_3, ED_4\},$$
$$Z_2 = \{ED_5\}. \tag{25}$$

Because we have more than one exit door in the first zone, there are α zones, β zones and θ angles for each exit door. Whereas the second zone only has a single α zone related to its exit door. There is no β zone and no θ angle exists for the second zone because it consists of only a single exit door and hence all area of the second zone belongs to its only exit door (ED_5).

We use the metric measurement in our paper and, therefore, of five exit doors available in the environment, the width of exit doors 1, 3, 4, and 5 all equal 1 meter, and exit door 2 is equal to 2 meters. Based on the width of each exit door, we are able to calculate the α zones and the charge of each one as they are shown in Table 5.

We consider each α zone related to each exit door as a sphere of charge which has a center equal the central width location of each exit door. Figure 8 shows the result of dividing the area into convex zones and α zone related to each exit door.

Because the second zone does not have any β zones and θ angles, we only focus on the first zone. We have four exit doors in this zone hence the largest simple non directed cycle graph has the length of 4. To form the mentioned graph, we need to connect the central points of each exit doors together through straight lines. This diagram must meet each exit door only once. Figure 9 shows the largest simple nondirected cycle graph of length 4 crossing all exit doors in the first convex zone.

At the next step, we need to find the centroid point of the 2D shape formed by the mentioned graph. We also need

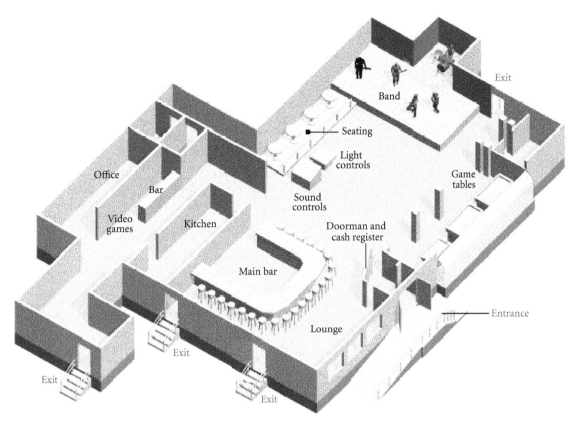

FIGURE 6: General view of the environment.

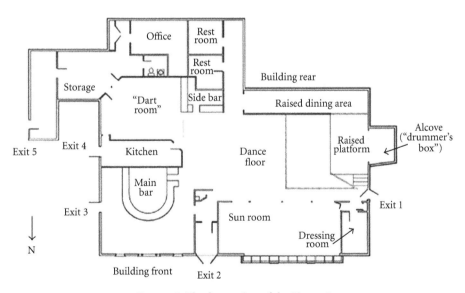

FIGURE 7: The frame view of the Figure 6.

to find the equilibrium points between each adjacent pairs of charges. To do this, we need to have the values of the adjacent pairs of charges. Based on our strategy, we assumed all exit doors have the positive charges and also they are fixed in their places. To find the equilibrium location, we use a positive charge that its amount is equal the average of the adjacent pairs of charges. The mentioned positive charge is placed on the straight line between the pairs of charges, and it is closer

to the smaller charge. In case of having the same amount of charges, the positive charge will locate in the middle of pairs of charges. To form β zones and θ angles, we have to connect from the centroid point to each equilibrium point and continue the line to the environment. Figure 10 shows the centroid location of the 2D shape for the mentioned graph, the equilibrium locations, the β zones, and θ angles related to the exit doors of the first zone.

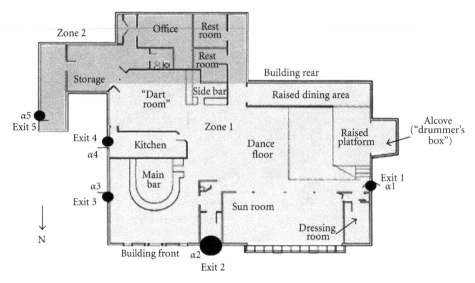

FIGURE 8: Convex zones of the area and α zones for each exit door.

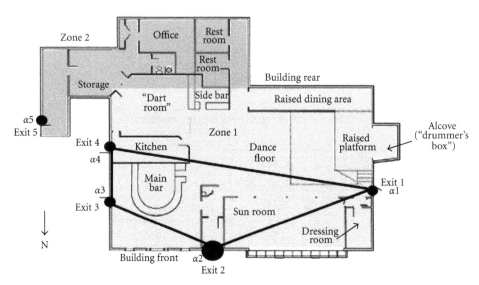

FIGURE 9: The largest simple non directed cycle graph of length 4 crossing exit doors in the first convex zone.

Figure 10 shows all areas needed for the first zone when there is no any individual available in the environment. At this step, we will calculate the charges of the agents are available in the environment and will update the safe boundaries based on their distribution in the environment. The process of gathering information about the physical specifications of the agents and their locations is done by sensors and detectors that are installed in the environment. This data will then be processed by our method. Of 230 people that we assumed are available in the environment, we consider 200 people are located in the first zone and 30 people are places in the second zone. We also assumed that in each area, half of the people are male and the other half are female. We considered that all people in our environment have normal health status. We consider in each zone, the ages range is between 20 and 40 years old. We assumed that all exit doors are open all the time and safe to use with their full

evacuation capacity which means no blocking will happen in the environment during the experiment. We apply our strategy in two different modes. When the distribution is the same and when it is not. Equation (26) shows the collections of the agents in each zones:

$$Z_1 = \left\{ Ag_1, Ag_2, Ag_3, \ldots, Ag_{200} \right\},$$
$$Z_2 = \left\{ Ag_1, Ag_2, Ag_3, \ldots, Ag_{30} \right\}. \tag{26}$$

8.1. Mode 1: Equal Crowd Distribution. Based on our assumption for the first mode, there are 100 males and 100 females available in the first zone. All of them have normal health statuses and are between 20 and 40 years old. We also assumed that their gender percentage for each β zone is the same as 50 percent. Hence, for each β zone in the general convex zone, we have 25 people consisting of 50 percent male

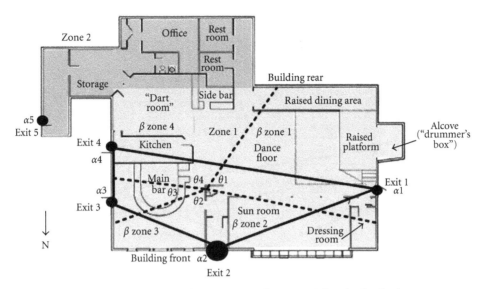

FIGURE 10: The centroid, Equilibrium points, β zones and θ angles for the first zone.

TABLE 6: β zones, initial α zones charges and new α zones charges.

β zone	Initial α zone	New α zone
1	100	75
2	200	175
3	100	75
4	100	75

TABLE 7: The percentages of the people who occupy each β zone.

β zone	Percent %
1	60
2	10
3	20
4	10

(13 people) and 50 percent female (12 people). Table 6 shows the β zones, initial α zone charges, and new α zone charges.

Because we assume the crowd to have the same distribution, we just observed having slight changes for the safe boundaries after applying the charges of agents in each β zone. In this mode, we have four β zones, hence each zone is assumed to support a quarter of the people in it. We also considered having 13 males and 12 females in each β zone. Figure 11 shows the new safe boundaries based on the normal distribution of the crowd in the first general zone.

Considering the mentioned distribution may be useful in many places such as theater saloons or conferences rooms. In such places, because of the kind of usage of environment, the distribution of the crowd is equal for all areas inside, whereas in many other places, such as night clubs or hallways, because the crowd distribution is always subject to significant changes, we need to consider a more accurate and realistic pattern in our environment. In the following mode 2, we will consider having a random crowd distribution based on the different locations that are available in the environment.

8.2. Mode 2: Random Crowd Distribution. In this mode, we consider a rational pattern of crowd distribution based on the usage of the environment and also the different locations available in the general convex zone. We divide and name each β zone into the following groups.

In the first β zone, we have the highest concentration of the crowd available because of its usage. It consists of a

Raised Platform and a Dance Floor. These areas have the most attractive options that can potentially cause the present people to gather in them. The second β zone consists of a Dressing Room and a Sun Room, so we will consider having the least percentage of people in these areas. The third β zone consists of a Bar that may have a number of people between the largest and the smallest area in terms of the percentage of people. The fourth β zone consists of a Kitchen, a Dart Room, and a Side Bar that have the least number of people in it. Of 100 percent of people (200 people) in the first general zone, based on the mentioned locations in each zone, we assumed that we have 60 percent of them in the first β zone (120 People), consisting of 50 percent males (60 people) and 50 percent female (60 people), 10 percent in the second β zone (20 people) consisting of 60 percent male (12 people) and 40 percent female (8 people), 20 percent in the third β zone (40 people) consisting of 70 percent male (28 people) and 30 percent female (12 people), and 10 percent in the fourth zone (20 people) consisting of 40 percent male (8 people) and 60 percent female (12 people). Tables 7 and 8 show the percentages and the number of people consisting of males and females in each β zone.

In this case, because of having a different distribution in each area, the α zones shows bigger differences than their previous values and hence we have different safe boundaries compared to the first mode. The number of people that each exit door supports is varied based on the area occupied by each. In some cases, because of changing the safe boundaries,

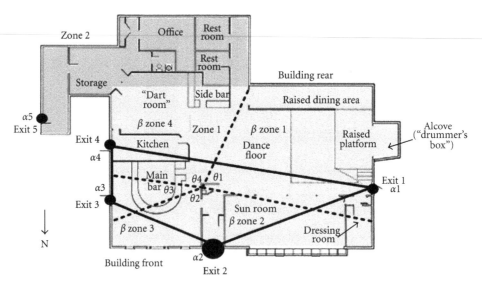

FIGURE 11: New safe boundaries based on the normal crowd distribution.

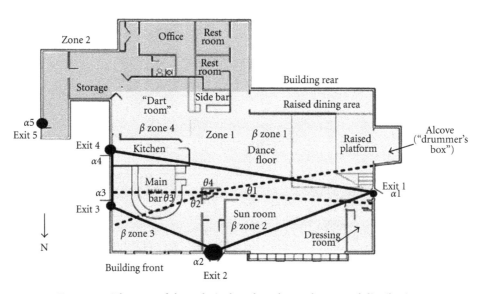

FIGURE 12: The new safe boundaries based on the random crowd distribution.

some people may belong to a new exit door which means in order to have a safe evacuation they have to be guided through the new exit door that they belong to. Table 9 shows the β zones with old α zone charges and new α zone charges.

Based on the mentioned values shown in Table 9, we redraw and form the new safe boundaries based on the new values of charges for exit doors. Figure 12 shows the new safe boundaries based on the random crowd distribution after applying the agent charges in each β zone.

We assumed that all exit doors are stable and reliable during experiments. There are two general reasons that can affect an exit door's status, such as explosions or falling objects around them or fallen or collapsing people around them. In the real word, in order to have better decisions about forming safe boundaries, considering the status of the exit doors is essential. If for any reason an exit door is blocked completely or it is not reliable anymore in terms

of evacuating the crowd, our strategy is not applicable. In such cases, the amount of charge for exit doors will be 0 and it will not conform to the largest simple nondirected graph anymore.

9. Conclusion

This paper explored a powerful mechanism for guiding crowds out of danger using Coulomb's Law, graph theory, and convex and centroid concepts in order to form safe and reliable boundaries around each exit door. The output of our tool for supervising people is rapid identification of exit doors for groups of people fleeing danger. Use of this mechanism can quickly decrease errors committed by exiting individuals. The technology for how the supervisory people in the control room will use our model to guide people is beyond the scope of this article. Detecting people

TABLE 8: The percentage and the number of people for each β zone based on the random distribution assumption.

β Zone 1		β Zone 2		β Zone 3		β Zone 4	
Male %	Female %	Male %	Female %	Male %	Female %	Male %	Female %
50	50	60	40	70	30	40	60
Total							
60	60	12	8	28	12	8	12

TABLE 9: The β zones with the old α zones and new α zones after applying the new random crowd distribution.

β zone	Initial α zone	New α zone
1	100	20
2	200	180
3	100	60
4	100	80

automatically is not trivial and remains to be explored in future studies. To be effective, the detectors and sensors should also be able to determine the specifications of each individual such as body size and movement rate. These are a few challenges to be addressed in the future. Despite challenges, our methodology yields strategies for guiding people who are trapped in an indoor public space, at dangerous locations, to be most rapidly evacuated.

References

[1] F. J. Cannavale, H. A. Scarr, and A. Pepitone, "Deindividuation in the small group: further evidence," *Journal of Personality and Social Psychology*, vol. 16, no. 1, pp. 141–147, 1970.

[2] J. E. Singer, C. A. Brush, and S. C. Lublin, "Some aspects of deindividuation: identification and conformity," *Journal of Experimental Social Psychology*, vol. 1, no. 4, pp. 356–378, 1965.

[3] P. G. Zimbardo, "The human choice: individuation, reason, and order versus deindividuation, impulse and chaos," in *Proceedings of the Nebraska Symposium on Motivation*, University of Nebraska Press, Lincoln, Neb, USA, 1969.

[4] E. Diener, "Deindividuation, self-awareness, and disinhibition," *Journal of Personality and Social Psychology*, vol. 37, no. 7, pp. 1160–1171, 1979.

[5] K. Gergen, M. Gergen, and W. Barton, "Deviance in the dark," *Psychology Today*, vol. 7, pp. 129–130, 1973.

[6] R. D. Johnson and L. L. Downing, "Deindividuation and valence of cues: effects on prosocial and antisocial behavior," *Journal of Personality and Social Psychology*, vol. 37, no. 9, pp. 1532–1538, 1979.

[7] C. S. Carver and M. F. Scheier, *Attention and Self-Regulation: A Control Theory Approach to Human Behavior*, Springer, New York, NY, USA, 1981.

[8] A. Fenigstein, M. F. Scheier, and A. H. Buss, "Public and private self consciousness: assessment and theory," *Journal of Consulting and Clinical Psychology*, vol. 43, no. 4, pp. 522–527, 1975.

[9] S. Prentice-Dunn and R. W. Rogers, "Deindividuation and the self-regulation of behavior," in *The Psychology of Group Influence*, P. Paulus, Ed., Erlbaum, Hillsdale, NJ, USA, 1989.

[10] G. Proulx, "Building Egress Using Photoluminescent Markings," 2011, Construction Technology Update No. 78, National Research Council of Canada, 2011.

[11] T. Korhonen and S. Hostika, "Modeling social interactions in fire evacuation," in *Proceedings 7th International Conference on Performance-Based Codes and Fire Safety Design Methods*, 2008.

[12] H. B. Sharbini and A. Bade, "Analysis of crowd behaviour theories in panic situation," in *Proceedings of the International Conference on Information and Multimedia Technology (ICIMT '09)*, pp. 371–375, December 2009.

[13] V. K. Singh and A. K. Gupta, "Agent based models of social systems and collective intelligence," in *Proceedings of the International Conference on Intelligent Agent and Multi-Agent Systems (IAMA '09)*, July 2009.

[14] L. E. Aik, "Exit-selection behaviors during a classroom evacuation," *International Journal of Physical Sciences*, vol. 6, no. 13, pp. 3218–3231, 2011.

[15] R. D. Peacock, J. D. Averill, and E. D. Kuligowski, "Stairwell evacuation from buildings: what we know we don't know," NIST Technical Note NIST TN 1624, 2009.

[16] Y. Zhao and S. A. Billings, "Neighborhood detection using mutual information for the identification of cellular automata," *IEEE Transactions on Systems, Man, and Cybernetics, Part B*, vol. 36, no. 2, pp. 473–479, 2006.

[17] C. A. Perez-Delgado and D. Cheung, *Models of Quantum Cellular Automata*, Quantum Physics, 2009.

[18] A. Braun, S. Musse, Oliveira, and E. Bardo, "Modeling Individual behaviors in Crowd simulation," in *Proceedings of the 16th International Conference on Computer Animation and Social Agents*, IEE Computer Society, 2003.

[19] H. Yeh, S. Curtis, S. Patil, J. P. Van den Berg, D. Manocha, and M. C. Lin, "Composite agents," in *Proceedings of the Symposium on Computer Animation*, Eurographics Association, 2008.

[20] S. J. Guy, S. Kim, M. C. Lin, and D. Manocha, "Simulating heterogeneous crowd behaviors using personality trait theory," in *Proceedings of the International Symposium on Computer Animation*, Eurographics Association, 2011.

[21] C. Dogbe, "On the modeling of crowd dynamics by generalized kinetic models," *Journal of Mathematical Analysis and Applications*, vol. 18, supplement 1, pp. 1317–1345, 2008.

[22] X. Zheng, T. Zhong, and M. Liu, "Modeling crowd evacuation of a building based on seven methodological approaches," *Building and Environment*, vol. 44, no. 3, pp. 437–445, 2009.

[23] A. Johansson, D. Helbing, H. Z. Al-Abideen, and S. Al-Bosta, "From crowd dynamics to crowd safety: a video-based analysis," *Advances in Complex Systems*, vol. 11, no. 4, pp. 497–527, 2008.

[24] J. Cole and J. Zhuang, *Decisions in Disaster Recovery Operations: A Game Theoretic Perspective on Organization Perspective*, Berkeley Electronic Press, 2011.

[25] R. D. Peacock, J. D. Averill, and E. D. Kuligowski, "Egress from the World Trade Center Towers on September 11, 2001," in *Fire Technology*, Springer, 2011.

[26] H. C. Huang, S. M. Lo, C. M. Zhao, and P. Wang, "Simulation of occupant exit selection behavior during emergency evacuation using a game theory model," in *Proceedings of the 8th WSEAS International Conference on Automatic Control, Modeling and Simulation*, pp. 207–212, Prague, Czech Republic, 2006.

[27] N. Pelechano, J. M. Allbeck, and N. I. Badler, *Virtual Crowds: Methods, Simulation and Control*, Morgan and Claypool Publishers, 2008.

[28] J. Pan, L. Zhang, M. C. Lin, and D. Manocha, "A hybrid approach for simulating human motion in constrained environments," *Computer Animation and Virtual Worlds*, vol. 21, no. 3-4, pp. 137–149, 2010.

[29] S. Patil, J. Van Den Berg, S. Curtis, M. C. Lin, and D. Manocha, "Directing crowd simulations using navigation fields," *IEEE Transactions on Visualization and Computer Graphics*, vol. 17, no. 2, pp. 244–254, 2011.

[30] D. C. Brogan and J. K. Hodgins, "Group behaviors for systems with significant dynamics," *Autonomous Robots*, vol. 4, no. 1, pp. 137–153, 1997.

[31] T. Sakuma, T. Mukai, and S. Kuriyama, "Psychological model for animating crowded pedestrians," *Computer Animation and Virtual Worlds*, vol. 16, no. 3-4, pp. 343–351, 2005.

[32] N. Pelechano, J. M. Allbeck, and N. I. Badler, "Controlling individual agents in high-density crowd simulation," in *Proceedings of the ACM SIGGRAPH/Eurographics Symposium on Computer Animation*, pp. 99–108, 2007.

[33] S. R. Musse and D. Thalmann, "A model of human crowd behavior: group inter-relationship and collision detection analysis," in *Computer Animation and Simulation*, pp. 39–51, 1997.

[34] W. Shao and D. Terzopoulos, "Autonomous pedestrians," in *Proceedings of the ACM SIGGRAPH/5th Eurographics Symposium on Computer Animation*, pp. 19–28, July 2005.

[35] Q. Yu and D. Terzopoulos, "A decision network framework for the behavioral animation of virtual humans," in *Proceedings of the ACM SIGGRAPH/Eurographics Symposium on Computer Animation*, pp. 119–128, 2007.

[36] S. Paris, J. Pettré, and S. Donikian, "Pedestrian reactive navigation for crowd simulation: a predictive approach," *Computer Graphics Forum*, vol. 26, no. 3, pp. 665–674, 2007.

[37] M. Sung, M. Gleicher, and S. Chenney, "Scalable behaviors for crowd simulation," *Computer Graphics Forum*, vol. 23, no. 3, pp. 519–528, 2004.

[38] E. Bouvier, E. Cohen, and L. Najman, "From crowd simulation to airbag deployment: particle systems, a new paradigm of simulation," *Journal of Electronic Imaging*, vol. 6, no. 1, pp. 94–107, 1997.

[39] G. K. Still, *Crowd dynamics [Ph.D. thesis]*, Warwick University, 2000.

[40] P. A. Thompson and E. W. Marchant, "A computer model for the evacuation of large building populations," *Fire Safety Journal*, vol. 24, no. 2, pp. 131–148, 1995.

[41] S. Bandini, M. L. Federici, and G. Vizzari, "Situated cellular agents approach to crowd modeling and simulation," *Cybernetics and Systems*, vol. 38, no. 7, pp. 729–753, 2007.

[42] D. Helbing, I. Farkas, and T. Vicsek, "Simulating dynamical features of escape panic," *Nature*, vol. 407, no. 6803, pp. 487–490, 2000.

[43] B. Adriana, S. R. Musse, P. L. Luiz, and E. J. De Oliveira, "Bardo: modeling individual behaviors in crowd simulation," in *Proceedings of Computer Animation and Social Agents*, pp. 143–148, 2003.

[44] F. I. Stahl, "BFIRES-II: a behavior based computer simulation of emergency egress during fires," *Fire Technology*, vol. 18, no. 1, pp. 49–65, 1982.

[45] L. Y. Cooper, "A mathematical model for estimating available safe egress time in fires," *Fire and Materials*, vol. 6, no. 3-4, pp. 135–144, 1982.

[46] T. M. Kisko and R. L. Francis, "EVACNET+: a computer program to determine optimal building evacuation plans," *Fire Safety Journal*, vol. 9, no. 2, pp. 211–220, 1985.

[47] S. M. Olenick and D. J. Carpenter, "An updated international survey of computer models for fire and smoke," *Journal of Fire Protection Engineering*, vol. 13, no. 2, pp. 87–110, 2003.

[48] R. Friedman, "An international survey of computer models for fire and smoke," *Journal of Fire Protection Engineering*, vol. 4, no. 3, pp. 81–92, 1992.

[49] J. M. Watts, "Computer models for evacuation analysis," *Fire Safety Journal*, vol. 12, no. 3, pp. 237–245, 1987.

[50] D. Helbing and P. Molnár, "Social force model for pedestrian dynamics," *Physical Review E*, vol. 51, no. 5, pp. 4282–4286, 1995.

[51] P. Gawroński and K. Kułakowski, "Crowd dynamics—being stuck," *Computer Physics Communications*, vol. 182, no. 9, pp. 1924–1927, 2011.

[52] T. Korhonen, S. Heliovaara, S. Hostikkaa, and H. Ehtamo, "Counterflow model for agent-based simulation of crowd dynamics," in *Safety Science*, 2010.

[53] N. Shiwakoti, M. Sarvi, G. Rose, and M. Burd, "Animal dynamics based approach for modeling pedestrian crowd egress under panic conditions," *Transpostation Research B*, vol. 45, no. 9, p. 1433, 2011.

[54] C. M. Henein and T. White, "Microscopic information processing and communication in crowd dynamics," *Physica A*, vol. 389, no. 21, pp. 4636–4653, 2010.

[55] R. D. Peacock, E. D. Kuligowski, and J. D. Averill, *Pedestrian and Evacuation Dynamics*, Springer, 2011.

[56] B. Steffen and A. Seyfried, "Methods for measuring pedestrian density, flow, speed and direction with minimal scatter," *Physica A*, vol. 389, no. 9, pp. 1902–1910, 2010.

[57] N. Bellomo and C. Dogbe, "On the modeling of traffic and crowds: a survey of models, speculations, and perspectives," *SIAM Review*, vol. 53, no. 3, pp. 409–463, 2011.

[58] X. Zheng and Y. Cheng, "Modeling cooperative and competitive behaviors in emergency evacuation: a game-theoretical approach," *Computers & Mathematics with Applications*, vol. 62, no. 12, pp. 4627–4634, 2011.

[59] R. Colombo, P. Goatin, and M. Rosini, "A macroscopic model of pedestrian flows in panic situations," in *Current Advances in Nonlinear Analysis and Related Topics*, Mathematical Sciences and Applications, pp. 43–60, Gakuto, 2010.

[60] C. Dogbe, "On the Cauchy problem for macroscopic model of pedestrian flows," *Journal of Mathematical Analysis and Applications*, vol. 372, no. 1, pp. 77–85, 2010.

[61] Y. Q. Jiang, P. Zhang, S. C. Wong, and R. X. Liu, "A higher-order macroscopic model for pedestrian flows," *Physica A*, vol. 389, no. 21, pp. 4623–4635, 2010.

[62] Z. Markus, *Electromagnetic Field Theory: A Problem Solving Approach*, MIT OpenCourseWare, 2003.

[63] R. S. Elliott, *Electromagnetics: History, Theory, and Applications*, Wiley-IEEE Press, 1999.

7

Ant Colony Optimisation for Backward Production Scheduling

Leandro Pereira dos Santos,[1] **Guilherme Ernani Vieira,**[2, 3, 4]
Higor Vinicius dos R. Leite,[4, 5] **and Maria Teresinha Arns Steiner**[4]

[1] *Instituto Federal do Parana, Assis Chateaubriand, 80230-150 Curitiba, PR, Brazil*
[2] *Petrobras S.A., 41770-395 Salvador, BA, Brazil*
[3] *Doutor Jose Peroba 225, Apartment no. 1103, 41.770-235 Salvador, BA, Brazil*
[4] *Department of Industrial Engineering, Pontifical Catholic University of Parana, 80215-901 Curitiba, PR, Brazil*
[5] *Department of Management, Universidade Tecnológica Federal do Paraná, 80230-901 Curitiba, PR, Brazil*

Correspondence should be addressed to Guilherme Ernani Vieira, g.e.vieira@hotmail.com

Academic Editor: Deacha Puangdownreong

The main objective of a production scheduling system is to assign tasks (orders or jobs) to resources and sequence them as efficiently and economically (optimised) as possible. Achieving this goal is a difficult task in complex environment where capacity is usually limited. In these scenarios, finding an optimal solution—if possible—demands a large amount of computer time. For this reason, in many cases, a good solution that is quickly found is preferred. In such situations, the use of metaheuristics is an appropriate strategy. In these last two decades, some out-of-the-shelf systems have been developed using such techniques. This paper presents and analyses the development of a shop-floor scheduling system that uses ant colony optimisation (ACO) in a backward scheduling problem in a manufacturing scenario with single-stage processing, parallel resources, and flexible routings. This scenario was found in a large food industry where the corresponding author worked as consultant for more than a year. This work demonstrates the applicability of this artificial intelligence technique. In fact, ACO proved to be as efficient as branch-and-bound, however, executing much faster.

1. Production Scheduling Still a Differential for Competitiveness

The globalised world economic scenario makes entrepreneurial competitiveness unavoidable and being competitive has become an indispensable prerequisite to organisations that strive for success. Within this context, manufacturing activities become especially important for they decisively influence performance, directly affecting (and being affected by) forecast, planning, and scheduling decisions.

Shop-floor production scheduling, which within the hierarchical production planning covers disaggregate and detailed decisions in short time frame, consists in allocating activities (production orders or jobs) to resources, by obeying sequencing and setup restrictions, with focus on getting the best possible results from limited available resources, and, at the same time, aiming at reducing production costs and meeting service levels as fast and efficiently as possible. To make all this happen in cases where production and financial resources are limited and restrictions are many, adequate algorithms techniques and intelligence are necessary. Almost four decades ago, Garey et al. [1] classified production scheduling problems as being NP-hard, which in practical ways means that it is very difficult for one to obtain an optimal solution through exact algorithms and also demand unacceptable execution (computer or effort) time. The difficulty in using exact techniques for the solution of these problems leads to the use of approximate methods, known as heuristics or metaheuristics, which try to find good acceptable solutions (not necessarily optimal ones) within reasonable computer time.

In this study, a metaheuristic known as ant colony optimisation (ACO) was applied to a specific production scheduling problem found in productive systems having

(i) one processing stage,

(ii) parallel resources with different production capacities,

(iii) backward scheduling (based on due dates), and,

(iv) products with many possible (flexible) production routings.

This particular type of production scenario was found in a large food industry that makes, among many other different products, chocolate bars and eggs—mostly for Easter festivities—common in many countries worldwide, especially in Latin America.

For this particular company, production needs to make all forecasted orders by a given due data, and since demand is highly seasonal, most of the labor is hired under temporary contracts. One can imagine that better production schedules imply less money in hiring temporary workers. Because Easter is an important date for these chocolate products (retailers must receive products one to two months prior to the Easter festivities), backward scheduling approach is also used in this type of scenario.

From the literature, one can see that the ACO metaheuristic has been applied to solve complex production scheduling. C. J. Liao and C. C. Liao [2], for example, presented an ACO algorithm applied to agile manufacturing. Shyu et al. [3] proposed an application of ACO to a scheduling shop-floor problem with two machines. Rajendran and Ziegler [4] analyzed two ACO scheduling algorithms for flow-shops. Bauer et al. [5] implemented ACO for solving a production-scheduling problem with one machine. Lin et al. [6] conducted a study using ACO for production scheduling and also proposed the inclusion of two new features inspired by real ants. Ying and Lin [7] also used ant colony systems to solve production scheduling problems.

For the evaluation of the implemented ACO algorithm, production schedules are analyzed according to two performance measures:

(a) maximum completion time or makespan (i.e., total time needed to manufacture all production orders), and

(b) computer processing time (effort) for the creation of a production schedule.

To measure the proposed ACO's efficiency, comparisons are made with a similar system implemented using branch-and-bound optimisation. For these comparisons, different scenarios (configurations) of the proposed problem are tested. This paper explains the proposed ACO implemented and all tests and analysis performed.

The paper is organised as follows. Section 2 presents a bird's eye view on the ACO metaheuristic. Section 3 details the manufacturing scenario. Section 4 shows how the ACO software was implemented. Section 5 describes the design of experiments (DOEs) performed, tests, and analysis conducted. Main conclusions and suggestions for future studies are presented in Section 6.

2. ACO Metaheuristic

As a background support to understand how ACO was used, this section briefly shows the use of ACO metaheuristic to the travelling salesman problem (TSP) and also describe the ACO metaheuristic applied to production scheduling.

2.1. ACO Metaheuristic Applied to TSP. In ant colony optimisation, a given number of ants leave their nest to search for food and there are many possible paths an ant can take to get there. During their walk, ants leave pheromone, which is a substance that tells other ants about paths they can take for food.

Each ant will do a certain number of trips from the nest to the source of food and back to the nest. In each of these trips, the ants deposit in the performed path a certain quantity of pheromone. There will be a standard quantity in the case that the path travelled by the ant does not present improvements compared to the best previous track, otherwise, there will be a larger quantity of pheromone, in case the path travelled by the ant is shorter than the previous best path.

Meanwhile, there is a continuously decrease in the existing quantities of pheromone in all paths, due to the pheromone evaporation. Finally, the choice of the paths is based in a probability which depends of the quantity of the pheromone on a given arc and its distance. It is important to emphasize that the smaller the path, the greater will be the concentration of the pheromone, and consequently, the greater will be the probability of being chosen.

TSP consists in a set of localities to be visited, each one only once, by any agent which, after completing a loop (cycle), has to go back to the origin position. The goal of this problem is to find the path tour that forms a tour passing through all cities. An instance of TSP can be represented by the valued graph $G(V, E)$, where V represents the nodes (localities to be visited) and E represents the arcs in the graph, where each arc has a cost given by the distance. This distance is denoted by d_{ij} and indicates the distance between the city i and j, as

$$d_{ij} = \sqrt{\left(X_i - X_j\right)^2 + \left(Y_i - Y_j\right)^2}. \tag{1}$$

We assume that exist m ants in the system and that each ant has the following characteristics.

(i) Chooses the next city to be visited with a probability which depends on the distance and the quantity of pheromone in the arcs which link every two cities.

(ii) In order to force the ants to perform a feasible tour, transfers to cities which have already been visited are discarded until a tour is completed.

(iii) When a loop is completed, each ant deposits a certain quantity of pheromone on the arc (i, j) visited.

Be $\tau_{ij}(t)$ the intensity of pheromone in arc (i, j) in time t. Each ant in time t chooses the next city to which it will go in time $(t + 1)$. Defining one ACO iteration as the n movements realised by m ants in the interval $(t, t+1)$, then the n iterations of each ant form a loop, that is, each ant realises a tour passing by all the cities. On every one, the intensity of the pheromone is updated by

$$\tau_{ij}(t + n) = \rho \tau_{ij}(t) + \Delta \tau_{ij}, \tag{2}$$

where ρ is a coefficient (constant) with (1-ρ) representing the pheromone evaporation between the times t and $(t + n)$ of the arc (i, j) and $\Delta\tau_{ij} = \sum_{k=1}^{m} \Delta\tau_{ij}^{k}$, where $\Delta\tau_{ij}^{k}$ is the quantity of the pheromone deposited in the arc (i, j) by the k-th ant between the times t and $(t + n)$. The coefficient ρ has to be adjusted in a value smaller than "1" in order to avoid unlimited accumulation of pheromone. Normally, the intensity of pheromone in time 0, $\tau_{ij}(0)$, is adjusted as an integer positive constant c.

The rule in order to satisfy the constraint that each ant visits n different cities is to associate to each ant a list, called tabu list, which stores the cities which have already been visited and forbids the ant visit them again before the tour has already been completed. When a tour is completed, the tabu list is used to calculate the present solution of the ant (i.e., the distance travelled in the path). It is defined $tabu_k$ as for the vector which grows dynamically and contains the tabu list of k-th and and $tabu_s$ the s-th city visited by ant k at the present tour.

Defining attractiveness η_{ij} as the quantity $1/d_{ij}$, we determine the probability of transaction of city i to city j by the k-th ant as

$$p_{ij}^{k}(t) = \begin{cases} \dfrac{\left[\tau_{ij}(t)\right]^{\alpha} \cdot \left[\eta_{ij}\right]^{\beta}}{\sum_{k \in \text{Allowed}_k} \left[\tau_{ik}(t)\right]^{\alpha} \cdot \left[\eta_{ik}\right]^{\beta}}, & \text{if } j \in \text{Allowed}_k, \\ 0, & \text{otherwise;} \end{cases}$$

(3)

where $\text{Allowed}_k = \{N - tabu_k\}$, being N the number of cities of the problem and α and β are parameters that control the relative importance of the intensity of the pheromone versus the attractiveness. In this way, the transaction probability is a combination between the attractiveness and the intensity of the pheromone in time t.

According to Dorigo et al. [8], there are many different forms to compute the value of $\Delta\tau_{ij}^{k}(t, t + 1)$. One of them is denominated Ant-cycle which is calculated as

$$\Delta\tau_{ij}^{k}(t) = \begin{cases} \dfrac{Q}{L_k}, & \text{if the } k\text{-th ant goes through arc}(i, j) \\ & \text{in its tour between the times } (t, t + 1), \\ 0, & \text{otherwise,} \end{cases}$$

(4)

where Q is a constant and L_k is the length of the way travelled by the k-th ant.

2.2. ACO Metaheuristic Applied to the Production Scheduling. Based on Dorigo et al. [9], Ventresca and Ombuki [10] and Mazzucco Jr. [11], the representation of the production scheduling problem in the form of ant systems may be built through a disjunctive graph. This graph can be defined as $Q = (V, A, E)$, where V is the set of vertexes of the graph, which corresponds to the set of operations to be scheduled, represented here by O. Two fictional operations, described as "0" and "$N + 1$," are also added to the set V, that is, $V = \{0, O, N + 1\}$, representing the origin (nest) and the destination (food source) nodes.

Group A is a set of arcs connecting consecutive operations from the same job (task, activity, or production

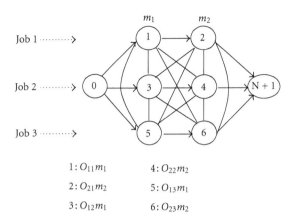

1: $O_{11}m_1$ 4: $O_{22}m_2$

2: $O_{21}m_2$ 5: $O_{13}m_1$

3: $O_{12}m_1$ 6: $O_{23}m_2$

FIGURE 1: Ant system graph for 3 jobs and 2 machines, Dorigo et al. [9].

order), the arcs that connect the operation 0 to the first real operation of each job and the last operation of each one of them to operation $(N + 1)$.

Group E is a set of the edges connecting two operations to be performed by the same resource (in this production scenario, a machine), and it may be expressed as $E = \{\{v, w\}/M_v = M_w\}$.

Each arc has a pair of numbers $\{\tau_{ij}, \eta_{ij}\}$, which are a concentration of pheromone and visibility, respectively. The last one can be considered as the operation processing time at node J.

Figure 1 is a representative ant system graph of a production scheduling problem. In this graph, nodes represent the operations to be performed and each operation corresponds to the processing of a certain quantity of product in a single machine. Each of these operations belongs to a determined job J_1, J_2, and J_3 respectively. In this example, a job can be defined as a production order with a certain quantity of product that must pass through two machines (m_1 and m_2). This way, a job is defined as a set of operations. In the graph, the operations numbered 1, 3, and 5 are executed by the same machine m_1. Likewise, operations 2, 4, and 6 are executed by the same machine m_2 and belong to jobs J_1, J_2, and J_3, respectively. The initial and final operations, labeled "0" and "$N + 1$," are fictional, that is, they are not performed; however, they are required by the metaheuristics. They only exist so that the oriented graph, by being oriented, may have an initial and final operation (nest and food nodes in ACO representation). Since they do not have a processing time, these operations do not affect the production scheduling process.

The nodes numbered from 1 to 6 represent the operations to be scheduled and each operation can be symbolically presented as O_{ijm}, where i: $1, \ldots, N$ represents the operation; j: $1, \ldots, K$ represents the job; m: $1, \ldots, M$ represents the machine. Each operation is indexed according to its position number and the job it belongs to. Node 1, for instance, corresponds to operation O_{11m1}, which means that if an ant passes through this node, the system will schedule the first operation of job 1 to machine 1 (O_{11m1}). Node 2 corresponds to operation O_{21m2}, meaning that operation 2 (second operation) of job 1 can be assigned to machine 2. That happens to all the nodes corresponding to a determined operation, as shown on the right side of the figure.

An orientation set of all the edges transforms the graph in Figure 1 into an oriented graph and represents one of the possible solutions to the modeled problem. In the same way, an orientation set defines a sequence or permutation of the operations processed by each machine in M.

3. The Manufacturing Scenario Considered in this Project

The problem covered in this research consists in optimising production scheduling systems having only one processing stage with parallel resources and flexible routings. In other words, any product has one single operation (or processing stage), which may require one or more resources. Hence, each job J has only one operation $J_j = \{O_{1j}\}$ and the objective is then to schedule a set of S jobs: $S = \{J_1, J_2, \ldots, J_S\}$ within a minimum time-frame (makespan). This scenario was found in a particular food industry where part of this study was accomplished.

The considered productive system is characterised by having parallel resources, that is, an operation can be formed by more than one machine or productive resources (as explained below). Thus, there is a set of M machines available, where $M = \{m_1, m_2, \ldots, m_M\}$. It is worth mentioning such machines can be different in capacity and efficiency and, therefore, the system present different processing capacities for the same product.

Another important characteristic of the considered productive system is that products can have flexible routings, which means that a particular product can have more than one possible process plan. It is assumed in this paper that each job J can be processed by any of the M machines, that is, each job J has a flexible routing. Schematically, $J_1 = \{RF_1\}$, $J_2 = \{RF_2\}$, and $J_S = \{RF_S\}$, where RF_1 is the flexible routing of job 1, RF_2 is the flexible routing of job 2, and $\{RF_S\}$ is the flexible routing of job S. Each flexible routing is formed by a set of similar operations. Schematically, $RF_1 = \{O_{11m1}, O_{11m2}, \ldots, O_{12mM}\}$, $RF_2 = \{O_{12m1}, O_{12m2}, \ldots, O_{12mM}\}$, and $RF_S = \{O_{1Sm1}, O_{1Sm2}, \ldots, O_{1SmM}\}$, where O_{11m1} represents operation 1 of job 1 processed by machine 1, O_{12m1} represents operation 1 of job 2 processed by machine 1, and O_{1Sm1} represents operation 1 of job S processed by machine 1.

The system implemented also uses backward scheduling. Each job J has a due date that must be met. The problem thus consists in scheduling all operations in order to minimise the total time needed for their execution (makespan), bearing in mind the delivery due date of all products. There are also other restrictions in this scenario.

(a) Suppliers lead times: the system should not schedule an order if needed material(s) is (are) not available.

(b) Setup times: this is in fact a setup dependent scheduling algorithm.

The food company studied considers minimizing total production time (makespan) as the main optimisation

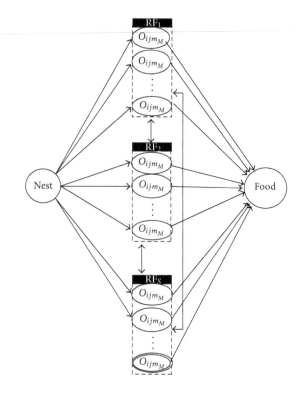

S: Number of jobs to be scheduled

M: Number of machines available

FIGURE 2: ACO graph of a production scheduling problem with one processing stage, parallel resources, and flexible routings.

objective and, therefore, this is the objective function used by the ACO system implemented. This performance measure represents the length (total time) of the production schedule. In other words, it is the ending time of the last job scheduled minus the starting time of the first job scheduled. One can also consider makespan as the ending time of the last operation to be processed minus the starting time of the first machine that begins its operation.

Although minimizing the maximum makespan is the objective of the ACO system developed, this research also considered the total computer time (effort) as a performance measure to evaluate ACO against another optimisation technique: branch-and-bound (BB), which was used in another study and is used in this paper as a benchmark to help us evaluate the efficiency of the proposed ACO.

4. The ACO Production Scheduling Implemented

As previously mentioned, each product process plan (routing) is made of a single operation (monostage). Therefore, one can say that each flexible routing has a set of similar operations and when one of these operations is chosen, the others are discarded.

Under the proposed ACO graph model, each job's flexible routing (RFs) corresponds to a set of nodes (see dashed square lines at Figure 2). In the beginning these are "virtual" models, available for an ant to pass through. Once an ant chooses and passes through a node, it becomes a chosen node, meaning that the operation of this job has been scheduled (all remaining similar possible operations in the RF are discarded).

As previously mentioned, the initial node (nest) and the final node (food) are parts of the ACO graph. These nodes are fictitious, that is, are not actual production scheduling activities, while all other nodes correspond to operations that can be scheduled. The edges correspond to the time or duration of the operation to be scheduled and there are no edges linking operations from the same group (RF), that is, from the same job, considering that they will be eliminated if they are scheduled. There are, however, nonoriented edges that link the operation groups (RF) and indicate that all the jobs need to be scheduled, regardless of the sequencing (see connecting arrows among dashed squares).

Ants leave the "Nest" aiming to find a source of "Food," however, all jobs must be scheduled before the ant gets to the food node (the complete path between nest and food nodes comprises a feasible schedule). In the beginning, the ants find different sources of food, and as the algorithm evolves, the number of food sources converges to the "best food sources."

4.1. Structure of the Implemented Software.
The ACO technique uses the natural behavior of an ant colony, which tries to find the shortest paths between nest and the food through the communication among the agents (ants) using pheromone, a path of "smell for food" for the other ants.

The ACO system has a set of configuration parameters that impact the quality and performance of the algorithm. In this project, six ACO parameters were analysed.

(i) Number of ants (NA): the quantity of ants simultaneously searching for food (each ant will create a possible schedule).

(ii) Number of travels of each ant (NT): it is the number of times that each ant will travel between the nest and the source of food.

(iii) Quantity of initial pheromone (QIP): it is the quantity of pheromone that already exists in all the paths before the ants start their travels.

(iv) Quantity of added pheromone (QAP): it is a quantity of pheromone left by an ant in the path taken between the nest to the food nodes. In this implementation, pheromone is added right after the ant reaches the food node.

(v) Evaporation percentage (EP): it is the quantity of pheromone lost (that evaporates) in each path as time passes.

(vi) Best response valorisation (BRP). The better the solution found by an ant, the more pheromone is added to its path.

The basics of the ACO system implemented are described in Figure 3. It briefly consists of (a) reading the input data; (b) initializing the system, that is, the ants and their respective tabu and feasible nodes' lists; (c) creating the graphs for each ant, with its respective nodes and edges. The stopping criterion is based on the total number of ants and the numbers of travels (from nest to food) each ant must achieve. During the schedule process, each ant goes from node to node, in the ACO graph each ant keeps track of its onw path being created.

The logic of this process lies on the fact that as an ant leaves the nest it starts scheduling production orders until it reaches the food (which means that needed jobs have been scheduled). The scheduling of an order means that a given node was selected and has been included in the ant's path to food.

An ant randomly chooses the next operation (or the next node to go to) based on the operation processing time and on the quantity of pheromone present at edges connecting the node where the ant currently is and the other possible nodes. The more pheromone exists in an arc (edge), the greater the probability for an ant to select it.

When an ant schedules all of its possible operations, it means that it has reached a source of food and one travel is complete. The solution found by each ant is analysed, and depending on the response quality, each ant's path created will get a specific quantity of pheromone, according to previously established quality criteria (the better the schedule the more pheromone are deposited in every arc in the path). Since the probability of selecting a node also depends on quantity of pheromone in the arc, better solutions tend to influence other ants to choose the same path in the future.

When all ants complete the number of needed travels, the scheduling process ends and the best response is presented.

4.2. The ACO System Class Structure.
The ant colony optimisation algorithm was implemented following an object-oriented structure. A total of eight object classes were implemented are briefly explained next and the dependency among these classes are depicted at Figure 4.

(i) ACO_SFS implements setup and configuration procedures, run (execute) commands, evaporation execution, savings, and so forth ("SFS" stands for shop-floor scheduling.)

(ii) Ant_SFS implements: an ant, tabu list procedures, keeps track of edges taken, current node position, calculates probabilities, verifies next possible (feasible) nodes, moves to next node, updates pheromone, and so forth.

(iii) Config_ACO_SFS procedures for the creation and configuration of the ACO.

(iv) Graph_SFS implements the graph where ants will walk through. A graph is basically a list of nodes, a list of edges. In the very beginning, a graph has only two nodes: nest and food.

(v) Edge_SFS an edge is a set of two nodes (begin and end node) and an information about pheromone. Remember that different ants can walk through the same edge and are affected by the same pheromone in the edge.

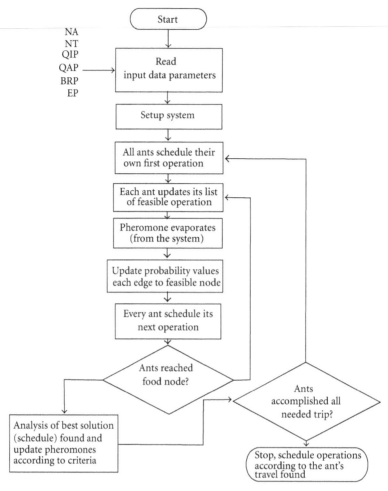

FIGURE 3: ACO software general flowchart.

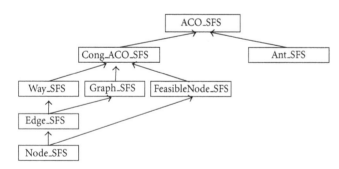

FIGURE 4: Object-oriented ACO classes.

Several other classes were also developed. These classes implemented the production scheduling logic and attributes, such as object classes to model resources, production orders, products, production routings (process plans), calendars, setup matrices, among others (for conciseness reasons, these classes will not be explained.) A screenshot of the system is shown at Figure 5.

5. Experiments Planning and Analysis

Two types of experiments have been made in this project: (a) factorial experiments (2^k) have been used to verify the influence of each ACO configuration parameter in the objective function (makespan + computer time); (b) experiments to verify the ACO efficiency in relation to branch-and-bound have been carried out through an analysis of variance.

5.1. Influence of the ACO Configuration Parameters on Performance. The objective of this first type of analysis is twofold: (a) to understand how the values of the input (or configuration) parameters affect the solution quantity and computer executing time needed; (b) these 2^k factorial experiments will

(vi) Node_SFS a node corresponds to an operation that can be schedule. A production order is basically made of a set of possible operations.

(vii) FeasibleNode_SFS a feasible node is node in the graph were the ant can go to, which means that the ant can "schedule" that operation.

(viii) Way_SFS this class implements the path an ant takes. It is basically a list of edges.

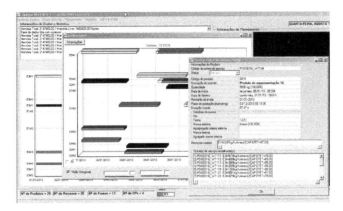

FIGURE 5: A screenshot of the ACO shop-floor scheduling system developed.

TABLE 1: Data for the analysis of the considered 26 factorial experiments.

	Scenarios	1	2	3	4	5	6	7	8	9	10	11	12	13	14	15	16
BRP	Low	5	5	5	5	5	5	5	5	5	5	5	5	5	5	5	5
	High	10	10	10	10	10	10	10	10	10	10	10	10	10	10	10	10
NA	Low	20	20	20	20	10	10	10	10	10	10	10	10	10	10	10	10
	High	50	50	50	50	20	20	20	20	20	20	20	20	20	20	20	20
QIP	Low	1	1	1	1	1	1	1	1	1	1	1	1	1	1	1	1
	High	10	10	10	10	10	10	10	10	10	10	10	10	10	10	10	10
QAP	Low	5	5	5	5	5	5	5	5	5	5	5	5	5	5	5	5
	High	50	50	50	50	50	50	50	50	50	50	50	50	50	50	50	50
NT	Low	60	60	60	60	60	60	60	60	60	60	60	60	60	60	60	60
	High	100	100	100	100	100	100	100	100	100	100	100	100	100	100	100	100
EP	Low	1	1	1	1	1	1	1	1	1	1	1	1	1	1	1	1
	High	5	5	5	5	5	5	5	5	5	5	5	5	5	5	5	5
Number of machines		3	3	3	3	6	6	6	6	10	10	10	10	10	10	10	10
Number of orders		15	20	30	45	15	20	30	45	15	20	30	45	15	20	30	45

also be used to help us identify the best (optimum) values for the ACO system configuration parameters.

In the 2^k factorial analysis performed, two levels for the six parameters (BRP, NA, QIP, QAP, NT, and EP) are considered leading to 64 (2^6) different ACO configuration to be tested. The low and high levels for this analysis are shown on Table 1.

After defining the scope of the 2^k experiments, an analysis of variance (ANOVA) was performed. For this, each one of the 64 configuration scenarios was run sixteen times (sample size was chosen arbitrarily). Table 2 shows the ANOVA experiment results obtained.

By the analysis of Table 2 and based on the theory about ANOVA, one can conclude that the parameters BRP, EP, NT QIP, and QUAP significantly affected the problem results. The only parameter that did not seem to affect performance was the number of ants (NA) always according to a 95% of confidence level. It is possible that the difference between the low and high values for the NA parameter was not enough to cause any significant impact on the system performance and also, possibly the number of travels has hiden some of the effect of this parameter. A detailed analysis is given next.

If the best response valorisation parameter is set too low, the quantity of pheromone deposited in the path will not be sufficient to "make" other ants to follow such path. On the other hand, if BRP is set too high, it forces all ants to follow a single path, prematurely converging to a solution that might be far from a good one.

Parameter EP (evaporation rate) determines the quantity of pheromone lost (that evaporates) in the paths as time passes by. The fact that a higher quantity of substance evaporates within a specific period of time can be important, so that a local minimum solution is not chosen.

Parameter NT (number of travels that each ant must execute) clearly affected the solution quality. As said before, this parameter probably hid the NA effect on performance.

The importance of parameter QIP (quantity of initial pheromone in the system) is noticed when compared to the quantity of pheromone added after a travel is complete. Setting QIP too high and using low QAP may not influence ants to take the best paths. But both parameters significantly affect the response quality.

Finally, as explained previously, parameter NA (number of ants in the system) had no significant influence in the

TABLE 2: ANOVA results for the experiments 2^6.

			ANOVA		
Parameter	SS	DOF	SA	F_o	Ferritic (F_c)
BRP	315.30	1	315.30	96.51	>4
EP	19.74	1	19.74	6.04	>4
NT	72.01	1	72.01	22.04	>4
QIP	35.27	1	35.27	10.79	>4
QAP	17.39	1	17.39	5.32	>4
NA	9.03	1	9.03	2.76	<4
ERROR	186.22	57	3.27		
T	533.96	63			

SS: sum of squares, DOF: degrees of freedom, SA: square average, F_o: F observed.

TABLE 3: Summary of the 2^k experiment results.

Parameter	F_o	F critic	Evaluation
BRP	96.51	4	Significant
EP	6.04	4	Significant
NT	22.04	4	Significant
QIP	10.79	4	Significant
QAP	5.32	4	Significant
NA	2.76	4	Not significant

TABLE 4: Scenarios for the execution of the ACO efficiency tests.

Scenario	Number of possible machines to execute the operation	Number of jobs OPs
1	5	20
2	5	40
3	5	60
4	10	20
5	10	40
6	10	60
7	10	80
8	10	100
9	10	120

quality of the problem responses. This result may also be caused by the fact that in the implemented ACO, the pheromone is only added to the paths after an ant reaches the food node, not during the search. This, however, is closer to the natural behavior of ants, which by carrying food back to their nest, scracth their bellies on the ground, "leaving" the pheromone. One would assume, however, that the number of ants do affect the answer, however, for the two levels considered in this ACO system (20 and 50 ants) and the strong influence of the NT (number of travels), this did not come true. Table 3 brings a summary of this analysis, showing which variables are and are not significant in the proposed experiment 2^k executed.

The main conclusion in the first phase of this study is that most of the configuration parameters considered, which affect directly or indirectly the quantity of pheromone in a path, significantly impact the response quality (except the number of ants, as explained before).

In the next phase, the configuration parameters used for comparative tests are set, according to the methodology proposed by Montgomery and Runger [12], which basically consists in choosing the variable level in which the sum of the response averages is higher. This way, the parameters chosen were

$$BRP = 5; \quad NA = 50; \quad QIP = 10;$$
$$QAP = 50; \quad NT = 100; \quad EP = 5. \tag{5}$$

As previously mentioned, the parameter referring to the number of ants in the system did not seem to be significant for schedule quality (makespan). According to Montgomery and Runger [12], in such cases, a specific parameter level

must be chosen so as to optimise economy, operation or any other strong technical factor when executing the algorithm. This was the only parameter to be changed, by attributing 10 as its value. In so doing, there was a decrease in the computer time required to achieve the response and the maintenance of its quality.

5.2. Analysing the ACO Metaheuristics Efficiency in Comparison to Branch-and-Bound. In order to test the ACO metaheuristics efficiency in production scheduling optimisation (in scenarios similar to the one adopted in this paper), comparative tests of the solution generated by the ACO metaheuristics were made with solutions obtained through the use of a branch-and-bound optimisation method (already implemented by the authors of this article).

For the execution of this second phase of these experiments, a productive system that makes 20 different items was considered. The experiments also considered products with several possible process plans (i.e, routings). These scenarios considered five possible machines for the operations and a total of 20, 40, or 60 jobs. Other six scenarios considered ten possible machines for the operation, and 20 to 120 jobs to be scheduled. This is summarised at Table 4.

Considering a scenario with 5 machines and a particular product A, this product's operation could be done at machine I, II, III, IV, or V. Production capacities in each machine are 5, 6, 7, 8, and 9 units/hour, respectively (so machines

	20 OPs (jobs)		40 OPs (jobs)		60 OPs (jobs)		80 OPs (jobs)		100 OPs (jobs)		120 OPs (jobs)	
	Job	Quant.	Job	Quant.	Job	Quant.	Job	Quant.	Job	Quant.	Job	Quant.
Product A	1	220	21	730	41	110	61	110	81	700	101	700
Product B	2	150	22	560	42	300	62	75	82	530	102	530
Product C	3	450	23	580	43	225	63	225	83	550	103	550
Product D	4	370	24	370	44	740	64	185	84	340	104	340
Product E	5	890	25	960	45	445	65	445	85	930	105	930
Product F	6	450	26	790	46	900	66	225	86	760	106	760
Product G	7	670	27	450	47	335	67	335	87	420	107	420
Product H	8	1.350	28	645	48	675	68	675	88	615	108	615
Product I	9	850	29	375	49	425	69	425	89	345	109	345
Product J	10	760	30	490	50	1.520	70	380	90	460	110	460
Product K	11	490	31	760	51	245	71	245	91	730	111	730
Product L	12	375	32	850	52	750	72	188	92	820	112	820
Product M	13	645	33	1.350	53	323	73	323	93	1.320	113	1.320
Product N	14	450	34	670	54	900	74	225	94	640	114	640
Product O	15	790	35	450	55	395	75	395	95	420	115	420
Product P	16	960	36	890	56	480	76	480	96	860	116	860
Product Q	17	370	37	370	57	740	77	185	97	340	117	340
Product R	18	580	38	450	58	290	78	290	98	420	118	420
Product S	19	560	39	150	59	280	79	280	99	120	119	120
Product T	20	730	40	220	60	365	80	365	100	190	120	190

FIGURE 6: Product quantity in production orders.

are not identical). Considering a scenario with 10 machines, product A could go to machine I, II, III, IV, V, VI, VII, VIII, IX, or X. Production capacities are 5, 6, 7, 8, 9, 10, 11, 12, 13, and 14 units/hour, respectively.

Each of the 9 scenarios has a number of POs (production orders) to be scheduled. Here, each PO corresponds to a Job that comprises a given quantity of a particular product that need to be made. In this part of the paper, it was considered that each scenario would be characterised by having 20, 40, 60, 80, 100, or 120 POs. Figure 6 shows the quantity of each product to be produced in each PO per scenario.

The methodology used for the comparative analysis of the (ACO and BB) techniques was the hypothesis test with two samples, in order to determine the difference between two averages and the difference between two variances.

Table 5 shows the results obtained with the experiments of the previously described scenarios, in which the column named BB brings the results achieved with branch-and-bound and the column named ACO, the results with ACO.

Firstly, an F test was applied to the results of the two response variables studied: objective function (makespan) and computer time (effort). Such test aimed to verify whether the variances between the two techniques were significantly different. After that, a T-test could be applied to verify how significant the difference between the result was, and

TABLE 5: Makespan results and computer time for the studied scenarios.

Scenario	Makespan [hours]		Computer time [s]	
	BB	ACO	BB	ACO
1	14.01	13.29	1	14
2	25.51	26.33	3	56
3	38.24	38.26	14	93
4	10.84	11.30	547	28
5	18.26	19.05	1,298	112
6	24.37	29.20	3,254	186
7	36.41	38.36	8,620	357
8	40.72	43.81	19,865	800
9	56.89	62.39	23,838	2,867

then, to infer about the ACO technique efficiency production scheduling optimisation.

5.2.1. The F-Test for the Response Variables (Prestep). The F-test was executed to verify the difference in variance between the two samples, regarding both makespan and computer time needed to achieve the best results. This is a prestep

TABLE 6: The F test for the makespan variables.

	BB	ACO
Average	29.47	31.33
Variance	219.61	265.60
Observations	9	9
DOF (degrees of freedom)	8	8
F_o	0.83	
$P(F \leq f)$ uni-caudal	0.40	
F critic uni-caudal (F_c)	0.29	

TABLE 7: F test for computer time variances (seconds).

	BB	ACO
Average	6,382	501
Variance	85,393,845	848,108
Observations	9	9
DOF (degrees of freedom)	8	8
F_o	100.69	
$P(F \leq f)$ uni-caudal	0.00	
F critic uni-caudal (F_c)	3.44	

TABLE 8: T test for the makespan analysis.

	BB	ACO
Average	29.47	31.33
Variance	219.61	265.60
Observations	9	9
Hypothesis of mean difference	0	
DOF (degrees of freedom)	16	
Stat t	-0.25	
$P(T \leq t)$ uni-caudal	0.40	
t critic uni-caudal	1.75	
$P(T \leq t)$ bi-caudal	0.80	
t critic bi-caudal	2.12	

TABLE 9: Computer time T test.

	BB	ACO
Average	6,382	501
Variance	85,393,845	848,108
Observations	9	9
Hypothesis of mean difference	0	
DOF (degrees of freedom)	8	
Stat t	1.9	
$P(T \leq t)$ unicaudal	0.047	
t critic unicaudal	1.8	
$P(T \leq t)$ bicaudal	0.094	
t critic bicaudal	2.3	

to define the appropriate test to compare averages (Section 5.2.2). For this test, a package called Data Analysis from Microsoft Excel was employed, more specifically, the F-Test function "two samples for variances," with a significance level $\alpha = 5\%$. Table 6 shows the results obtained.

Since $F_o > F_c$ (0.83 > 0.29), the null hypothesis must not be accepted, once it assumes that the variances of the two samples are equal. Hence, there is statistical evidence that the difference between the variances is significant, which means that, within a 95% confidence level, the variances in makespan obtained with ACO is different from the one obtained using BB. Table 7 presents the F-test result regarding the variance analysis of the computer needed to achieve the results for each technique.

Since $F_o > F_c$ (100.69 > 3.44), the null hypothesis shall not be accepted, once it assumes that the variances of the two samples are equal, that is, there is evidence, again, that the difference between the variances is significant concerning the computer time (effort).

Summing up, F-tests showed that the variance regarding the minimisation of maximum makespan was highly better using BB compared to ACO. However, computer (processing) time variance using ACO was with less than using BB.

5.2.2. T-Test for the Response (Objective) Variables Considered. F-test results for the two response variables showed that for both cases, the variances between the samples are different. That leads to the analysis of the difference between the results averages of the two studied objectives (makespan and computer time) through the use a T-test *employing two samples and presuming different variances.* To do so, the Data Analysis tool from Microsoft Excel was again used, more specifically the *T-test function: two samples presuming different variances, with a significance level $\alpha = 5\%$.* Table 8 presents these results.

Referring to the makespan between the ACO and BB techniques, the null hypothesis must be accepted, once the P-value = 40% is higher than the significance level adopted (5%), that is, the difference between the averages is not significant. This conclusion is interesting because it says that ACO is behaving as well as BB, regarding minimisation of makespan (in this productive scenario and for the ACO and BB softwares implemented).

T-test results regarding the computer time of the two compared techniques are presented in Table 9. So, regarding computer time (effort), the null hypothesis must be rejected, since the P-value (4.7%) is lower than the significance level adopted (5.0%). In other words, there exists significant difference between the averages. By looking at the averages shown on Table 9, one can confirm that ACO runs much faster that BB.

Despite the fact that the makespan was similar using ACO and BB, Ant Colony executed much faster than Branch-and-Bound. Table 10 summarises these results.

The objectives that guided this research were supported by two basic ideas. First, the intention to verify whether the ACO metaheuristics was a feasible technique for solving backward production scheduling optimisation in monostage productive systems, with parallel manufacturing resources, different production capacities, and flexible routings. Second, the study also intended to evaluate the efficiency of ACO compared to the branch-and-bound technique.

TABLE 10: Result summary of the ACO efficiency analysis.

Scenario	Makespan [hours]		Computer time [seconds]	
	BB	ACO	BB	ACO
1	14.01	13.29	1	14
2	25.51	26.33	3	56
3	38.24	38.26	14	93
4	10.84	11.30	547	28
5	18.26	19.05	1298	112
6	24.37	29.20	3254	186
7	36.41	38.36	8620	357
8	40.72	43.81	19865	800
9	56.89	62.39	23838	2867
	F_o	F_c	F_o	F_c
F test	0.83	0.29	100.69	3.44
For the variance:	Statistically different		Statistically different	
	t	α	t	α
T test	40.0%	5.0%	4.7%	5.0%
For the average:	Statistically not different		Statistically different	

By using statistical T-tests and F-tests, the ACO meta-heuristics efficiency was, in fact proved, taking into account the quality of the generated production plan (in terms of makespan) and computer time required for the creation of production schedules.

Although there was no enough statistical difference between BB and ACO regarding makespan, if one assumes that BB gives a good answer, then ACO will perform similarly. In terms of computer time, however, ant colony performed much faster than branch-and-bound. It is important to emphasise that these results were obtained for the type of production scenarios considered.

6. Final Considerations

This paper focused on verifying whether ant colony optimisation could be effectively applied to a production scheduled problem found in some types of food industries operating with backward scheduling and considering monostage productive systems, parallel resources, and flexible routings. This analysis studied the metaheuristics configuration variables regarding their influence on the variations and averages of response variables.

It showed that the ACO configuration parameters (best response valorisation, evaporation, quantity of initial pheromone, quantity of added pheromone, and number of travels) proved to be significant in relation to their influence in the response quality (95% reliability). The only variable among the studied ones that did not prove to be significant was the number of ants in the system.

Besides verifying which system configuration variables affect the algorithm response quality, these experiments also helped to set the ACO configuration variables later used to test the efficiency of the ACO method. Hence, regarding the ACO technique efficiency analysis, quality was measured in terms of makespan and computer time spent to achieve good

responses, while efficiency analysis was done by comparison of ACO results with branch-and-bound optimisation. Regarding makespan, it was not possible to point out any significant difference between the two methods. This led us to conclude that ACO is as efficient as BB in backward production scheduling in monostage problems with routing flexibility.

Regarding computer time, T-tests revealed that the ACO technique runs much faster than branch-and-bound in solving the type of production scenario considered, with large number of resources and jobs (production orders or tasks). One could verify that the time needed to achieve the response increases in higher proportion using branch-and-bound than using the ACO technique. It is important to point out that the conclusions from this study refer strictly to the type of production problems herein covered.

For future studies, some suggestions are

(i) productive systems with more than one processing stage must be considered,

(ii) implementation (and tests) in a forward scheduling environment,

(iii) different ACO implementation characteristics can also be tested, like, for instance, enabling evaporation to occur in each move of the ants and not only when they reach a food source (the same thing for pheromone deposit),

(iv) different metaheuristics configuration (setup) variables could be tested, and

(v) other possible implementations could consider a multiobjective function, with other objectives, such as minimizing lateness, average flow time, setups, and resources' idleness.

References

[1] Garey, MR, and D. S. Johnson, *Computers and Intractability: A Guide to the Theory of NP-Completeness*, W. H. Freeman, 1979.

[2] C. J. Liao and C. C. Liao, "An ant colony optimisation algorithm for scheduling in agile manufacturing," *International Journal of Production Research*, vol. 46, no. 7, pp. 1813–1824, 2008.

[3] S. J. Shyu, B. M. T. Lin, and P. Y. Yin, "Application of ant colony optimization for no-wait flowshop scheduling problem to minimize the total completion time," *Computers and Industrial Engineering*, vol. 47, no. 2-3, pp. 181–193, 2004.

[4] C. Rajendran and H. Ziegler, "Two ant-colony algorithms for minimizing total flowtime in permutation flowshops," *Computers and Industrial Engineering*, vol. 48, no. 4, pp. 789–797, 2005.

[5] A. Bauer, B. Bullnheimer, R. F. Hartl, and C. Strauss, *An Ant Colony Optimizations Approach for the Single Machine Total Tardiness Problem*, Department of Management Science. Universidade de Vienna, Vienna, Austria, 1999.

[6] B. M. T. Lin, C. Y. Lu, S. J. Shyu, and C. Y. Tsai, "Development of new features of ant colony optimization for flowshop scheduling," *International Journal of Production Economics*, vol. 112, no. 2, pp. 742–755, 2008.

[7] K. C. Ying and S. W. Lin, "Multiprocessor task scheduling in multistage hybrid flow-shops: an ant colony system approach," *International Journal of Production Research*, vol. 44, no. 16, pp. 3161–3177, 2006.

[8] M. Dorigo, V. Maniezzo, and A. Colorni, "Positive feedback as a search strategy," Tech. Rep. 91-016, Dipartimento di Elettronica, Politecnico di Milano, Milano, Italy, 1991.

[9] M. Dorigo, V. Maniezzo, and A. Colorni, "Ant system: optimization by a colony of cooperating agents," *IEEE Transactions on Systems, Man, and Cybernetics B*, vol. 26, no. 1, pp. 29–41, 1996.

[10] M. Ventresca and B. Ombuki, "Ant colony optimization for job-shop scheduling problem," Tech. Rep., Department of Computer Science, St. Catharines, Canadá, 2004.

[11] J. Mazzucco Jr., *Uma abordagem híbrida do problema da Programação da produção através dos algoritmos simulated annealing e genético [tese de doutorado (Doutorado Engenharia de Produção, UFSC)]*, Florianópolis, 1999.

[12] D. C. Montgomery and G. C. Runger, *Estatística Aplicada à Engenharia*, LTC, Rio de Janeiro, Brazil, 2004.

8

Efficacious End User Measures—Part 1: Relative Class Size and End User Problem Domains

E. Earl Eiland and Lorie M. Liebrock

Computer Science and Engineering Department, New Mexico Institute of Mining and Technology, 801 Leroy Place, Socorro, NM 87801, USA

Correspondence should be addressed to E. Earl Eiland; eee@nmt.edu

Academic Editor: Konstantinos Lefkimmiatis

Biological and medical endeavors are beginning to realize the benefits of artificial intelligence and machine learning. However, classification, prediction, and diagnostic (CPD) errors can cause significant losses, even loss of life. Hence, end users are best served when they have performance information relevant to their needs, this paper's focus. Relative class size (rCS) is commonly recognized as a confounding factor in CPD evaluation. Unfortunately, rCS-invariant measures are not easily mapped to end user conditions. We determine a cause of rCS invariance, joint probability table (JPT) normalization. JPT normalization means that more end user efficacious measures can be used without sacrificing invariance. An important revelation is that without data normalization, the Matthews correlation coefficient (MCC) and information coefficient (IC) are not relative class size invariants; this is a potential source of confusion, as we found not all reports using MCC or IC normalize their data. We derive MCC rCS-invariant expression. JPT normalization can be extended to allow JPT rCS to be set to any desired value (JPT tuning). This makes sensitivity analysis feasible, a benefit to both applied researchers and practitioners (end users). We apply our findings to two published CPD studies to illustrate how end users benefit.

1. Introduction

Biological compounds and systems can be complex, making them difficult to analyze and challenging to understand. This has slowed applying biological and medical advances in the field. Recently, artificial intelligence and machine learning, being particularly effective classification, prediction and diagnostic (CPD) tools, have sped applied research and product development. CPD can be described as the act of comparing observations to models, then deciding whether or not the observations fit the model. Based on some predetermined criterion or criteria, a decision is made regarding class membership ($x \in A$ or $x \notin A$). In many domains, class affiliation is not the end result, rather it is used to determine subsequent activities. Examples include medical diagnoses, bioinformatics, intrusion detection, information retrieval, and patent classification. The list is virtually endless. Incorrect CPD output can lead to frustration, financial loss, and even death; correct CPD output is important. Hence,

a number of CPD algorithms have been developed and the field continues to be active.

Characterizing CPD effectiveness, then, is necessary. For example, CPD tool developers need to know how their particular modification affects CPD performance, and practitioners want to make informed choices between CPD options before deploying a tool in the field.[1] Jamain and Hand, summarizing their results in a classifier meta-analysis, comment:

> The real question a user generally wants to answer is "which classification methods [are] best for me to use on my problem with my data ..." [1].

This question has not been addressed in studies we have read. Indeed, Jamain and Hand generalize the sentiment of R.P.W Duin's comment regarding comparing automated, heavily parametrized classifiers.

> It is difficult to compare these types of classifiers in a fair and objective way [2].

Seemingly, the research community has viewed the end user's need as too complex to address. Thus, for the most part, researchers have focused on addressing their own needs. End user issues, when discussed, have been constrained to specific problem domains. It might be fair to state that each end user's need is, in some way, unique. However, that does not mean that the apparent complexities faced by end users cannot be identified and managed. Ideally, a means of satisfying end user needs without sacrificing researcher needs will emerge. At a minimum, it should be possible for end users to be enlightened regarding measure suitability (which measures best quantify how a CPD will impact their situation). This paper is a first step in identifying a general structure of CPD problems[2] faced by end users and using that structure to identify CPD evaluation measures and tools relevant to end users. To the extent that research studies present CPD performance information by which end users can estimate impact in their situation, the studies provide improved service to the end user.

Our primary focus is on summary statistics. In the current context, summary statistics are formulae that take measurement suite elements as input[3] and output a single value which represents the target CPD's overall quality. However, because multiple values are condensed into a single value, information is lost. To the extent essential information is retained, the summary statistic can prove useful for CPD evaluation. A key characteristic of summary statistics is that they are not monotonic; they have optima. Useful summary statistic optima indicate overall classifier quality. Ideally, these summary statistics also quantify some aspect of classifier output efficacious to end users. End users can directly use such values to estimate how the CPD will impact their situation.

As presented by Hand [3], measurement theory distinguishes between two entity attribute types: *intrinsic*, those that are part of an entity's definition (e.g., density or mass) and *extrinsic*, those that are expressions of the entity's interaction with the environment (e.g., weight). Attributes such as density and weight can be quantified, so we can also talk about intrinsic and extrinsic measures. When reported in joint probability tables (JPTs), CPD output is partitioned into four distinct categories: T_+, F_+, F_-, and T_-. After any dataset has been tested, the final object count in each category is influenced by the environmental factors rCS and boundary (B). (rCS is the relative sizes of the classes in the test set (rCS = $\overline{Y}/Y$). B is an n element vector that defines a "surface" that encloses one class, for example, "class A." In every case, there will also be an optimum boundary[4] (B^*). All elements outside that surface are in class "$\overline{A}$", rather than class "A." Because T_+, F_+, F_-, and T_- are sensitive to rCS and B, they are extrinsic measures.

1.1. Nomenclature. Although this paper applies well-established stochastic concepts, not all discussions use the same terminology. To avoid confusion, we define our lexicon for quantities measured (each being the size of the defined set):

T_+: correctly identified events in class A, the "class of interest" (if such a class exists);

TABLE 1: Values in the lexicon are often organized into a joint probability table (JPT), such as this.

		Actual target classification		
		A	$\overline{A}$	Totals ↓
Test result	Positive	T_+	F_+	Z
	Negative	F_-	T_-	$\overline{Z}$
	Totals	Y	$\overline{Y}$	N

T_-: correctly identified events of class $\overline{A}$, the other class;

F_+: class $\overline{A}$ events incorrectly flagged as class A;

F_-: class A events incorrectly flagged as class $\overline{A}$;

Z: events flagged as class A;

$\overline{Z}$: events flagged as class $\overline{A}$;

Y: actual class A events in the data set;

$\overline{Y}$: actual class $\overline{A}$ events in the data set;

N: the data set;

These values are often presented in an JPT as in Table 1. When appropriate, these symbols will also be used to represent populations. Context will determine whether a quantity or a population is being referenced.

End users are interested in how a process will function in their environment, so they need measures sensitive to extrinsic factors. From a purely academic perspective, the goal for many researchers is to characterize the CPD process independent of extrinsic factors; thus, they want intrinsic measures. Presumably because of the immediacy of the need, significant progress has been made in identifying and characterizing intrinsic measures.[5] We are interested in extrinsic measures useful for end users; little attention has been paid to their needs.

Because of the disparity between researcher and end user needs, providing for end user needs requires careful consideration. A researcher is interested solely in CPD performance; effects caused by external factors must be accounted for, if not eliminated. In contrast, end users need to incorporate external factors, not compensate for or eliminate them. Thus, in order to have research reports that are readily applicable by end users may require providing values that hold little relevance for researchers. We propose an "end user efficacious" measure suite and a means by which end users can tailor research results to their specific environment.

This study builds on Sokolova et al. and other CPD summary statistic characterization studies [4–14]. A challenge categorical problem evaluators face, when comparing to CPD results reported by others, is adjusting for data set effects. One of the major data set issues is that test sets used may well have different rCSs, with different applicability and/or utility. This can cloud results. As an example, we ran a CPD on two test sets drawn from the same class populations. Since both the class source populations and CPD were the same for each test, one would expect statistically indistinguishable output. However, since JPT categories are extrinsic, the anticipated similarity may be masked. The only difference

TABLE 2: This table shows the total F_+ and F_- for two tests with the same CPD on equally sized data sets (2250 observations), drawn from the same populations. The only difference is the samples have different rCSs. Because the tests were run on data sets with different sized classes, the equivalence of the CPD's effectiveness is not obvious. It would be easy for an observer to erroneously conclude the CPDs were significantly different.

Relative class size	F_+	F_-
1:1	125	250
1:9	25	450

between the test outputs shown in Table 2 is one test set has a relative class size of $9:1$ (rCS = 9) and the other a relative class size of $1:1$ (rCS = 1). The CPD performs equally well in each test; however, rCS introduces a bias in the JPTs that makes the CPD performance equality difficult to recognize. When rCS = 1, there are twice as many F_- observations as F_+. However, when rCS = 9, the ratio between F_- and F_+ goes to $18:1$! Without knowledge of the test sets used, an observer could well conclude that these were two significantly different CPDs, with significantly different applicability and/or efficacy. This is an obvious problem for researchers, thus significant effort has been applied to mitigate it; a selection of rCS invariant measures are available:

(i) the Youden index [15];

(ii) two related measures, diagnostic odds ratio (DOR) [16] and diagnostic power (DP) [17] (DP = $(\sqrt{3}/\pi)\log(\text{DOR})$;

(iii) the Matthews correlation coefficient (MCC) [18];

(iv) the receiver (or relative) operating characteristic[6] area under the curve (AUC) [19, 20];

(v) information theoretic measures such as the information coefficient (IC) [21, 22].

Youden was addressing the rCS's biasing effect in 1950; thus, the problem has been known for well over half a century, yet reports regarding mitigation are still entering the literature [9, 23]. In the works reviewed, consideration of end user problem environment was tightly constrained and the view of the data virtually unrestricted. We invert these criteria; first identifying problem interactions with rCS (a broad view of end user needs), then viewing the data such that it addresses the question posed by Jamain and Hand (a constrained view of the data).

rCS is generally confounding in the research environment; this is presumably also true for some end users. However, for other end users, rCS may be important for their problem. For these end users, basing decisions on rCS invariant measures may be misleading. Hence, we start by asking two questions:

(i) "Is rCS important for all end user CPD problem domains?"

(ii) "If not, what characteristics define when to incorporate rCS?"

Consider relating these two questions to a pair of real-world problems. A less effective CPD used with a rheumatoid arthritis test could lead to either more people than necessary being treated, or fewer. Likewise, a poorly selected intrusion detection boundary could cause an IT system to have excessive errors (false alarms or missed attacks).

In order to consider the two questions posed above, we will use a statistical nomenclature to describe a supervised CPD test bed. Viewed from a statistical perspective, observations on the dataset processed provide estimates of the underlying (class) population probabilities (rCS is the odds expression of that probability). Observations in the test system input are drawn from the specific populations (because the source class populations are known for each observation, a "ground truth" exists). The source population relative class sizes can be represented as a probability, for example, the probability that a randomly selected input will be a member of class A. This is the leading probability (P_{leading}), the probability before the inputs interact with the defined process.[7] In the examples stated, class A members would consist of RA-positive individuals and malicious information system activity. In the field, "ground truth" for any particular individual cannot be known prior to being processed (otherwise there would be no need for evaluation). However, in the test scenario being described, ground truth is known for each test set member. Since the source class is known for each CPD input element, input uncertainty does not affect any individual CPD output.

The balance of this paper is organized as follows. Section 2 considers relative class size. Section 3 describes the research protocol used in this study. Section 4 discusses efficacious measures for end users and considers existing summary statistics. Section 5 considers a cause of rCS invariance in measures and implications thereof. This is followed in Section 6 where we present two examples using the proposed format and tool. The main body of this paper closes with a summary of our findings and presents future work in Section 7. Four appendices with equation derivations and additional JPT normalization details wrap up the paper.

2. Relative Class Size

Abstractly described, test set elements interact with the defined process. This interaction "modifies" the elements (perhaps only by adding a tag indicating strength of the match with a model), leading to a test for class $\overline{A}$ membership. The probability that a randomly selected output will be detected as a member of class $\overline{A}$ is the subsequent probability ($P_{\text{subsequent}}$). $P_{\text{subsequent}}$ describes the state of the data stream after interacting with the defined process and is the combined result of the input mix (quantified as a probability (P_{leading} = Y/N) or an odds ratio (rCS = $\overline{Y}/Y$)) and the defined process. The defined process contributes its own uncertainty (P_{event}) to the observed output. Thus, the test system can be described by the equation $P_{\text{subsequent}} = f(P_{\text{leading}}, P_{\text{event}})$. The CDP test set model is illustrated in Figure 1.

Tying the test set model to the examples, $P_{\text{subsequent}}$ consists of the patient's RA diagnosis and the stream of

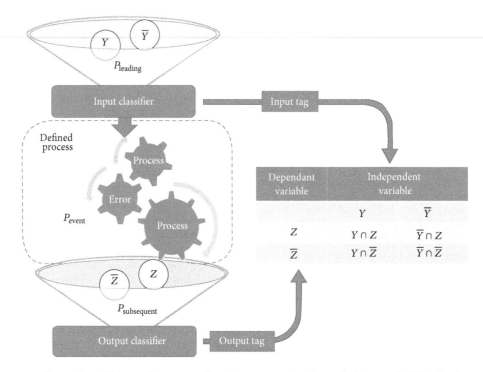

FIGURE 1: The test system "ground truth" inputs have a specific mix, representing the underlying probability for the system (P_{leading}). The test system outputs have a specific mix ($P_{\text{subsequent}}$), representing the interaction of the defined process and the inputs. The defined process contribution to the uncertainty observed in the output is represented by P_{event}. Often, the results are presented in JPTs.

intrusion detector classifications. P_{event} for the RA diagnosis consists of the strength of the match between the compound assayed and RA, test quality and the boundary used to determine class membership (diseased, not diseased). Similarly, P_{event} for the intrusion detection example consists of the appropriateness of the model that represents the malicious activity, the reliability of tags defining the activity, and the algorithm (or perhaps rule set) used to make malicious/non malicious determination.

In the CPD test system described, $\widehat{P}_{\text{leading}}$ is a characteristic of the input test dataset; hence, it is always fixed.[8,9] It is, in fact, related to rCS:

$$\widehat{P}_{\text{leading}} = 1 - \frac{\text{rCS}}{1 + \text{rCS}}. \tag{1}$$

We can now restate the original question within our framework: "are there problem domains where P_{leading} is important rather than confounding?"

One such situation could arise where individual results are significant only to the extent to which they contribute to a cumulative result. Consider setting intrusion detection boundaries. The end user is interested in limiting the impact of intrusions and intrusion prevention. The impact is cumulative, with each evaluation activity contributing. In this case, relative class size (expressed as P_{leading} or rCS) is important. If the end user were to base its boundary on P_{event} by using a rCS invariant measure (a measure that could not reflect the end user's estimate of their attack rate), there would likely be either excessive false alarm processing costs or excessive expenses due to missed attacks. Cases of this type, where

each individual outcome contributes to a cumulative result, require knowledge of both P_{leading} and P_{event}.

Are there conditions in which P_{leading}, rather than being essential, might instead cause errors? We suggest that one such situation is when individual results are important and cumulative results are not. Consider a person tested for rheumatoid arthritis (RA). Depending upon the physician's office ordering the test, the frequency of RA_+s tested could vary considerably.[8] If each office set test boundaries to minimize their respective error rates, there would be a range of test scores that would be classified differently by different offices. Clearly, both diagnoses cannot be correct; a person cannot be simultaneously RA_+ and RA_-. In this case, considering the physician's rCS-based P_{leading} does not minimize the error for the patient.

With regard to rCS, we see that while basic research benefits from rCS invariant measures, these measures are not suitable for all end users; rCS invariance will be confounding for some end users. For these end users, any specific environment can have any of (literally) an infinite number of rCS values. Indeed, an end user's expected rCS can vary over time. Thus, a "one size fits all" solution will not be particularly efficacious. Our goal to provide for end user rCS needs, thus, resolves into two tasks:

(i) identify both rCS-sensitive and rCS-invariant measures that are efficacious for end users;

(ii) identify a means by which end users can tailor reported CPD results to reflect performance for their expected rCS.

3. Research Protocol

Although in many problem domains, populations tend to be normally distributed, this is not universal. In order to avoid limiting the applicability of our results, we use analytic procedures that are insensitive to distribution. To preserve generality, our analysis is strictly nonparametric; medians are used instead of means and quantiles are used instead of standard deviations. We also execute our tests with the Monte Carlo method, a nonparametric analytical tool often used when problem complexity (in our case, potential end user problem complexity) is not amenable to mathematical analysis.

CPD evaluation studies can be partitioned into two groups: those that use "real-world" data and those that use simulated data. Characterizing CPD evaluation measures requires observing how the measures respond as CPD output varies. Real-world data, such as those available in repositories, for example, the UCI Machine Learning Repository, provide the opportunity to test against a wide variety of complex data types [24]. However, observing the effect of incremental changes on real-world data is difficult at best. For our purpose, we use simulated CPD output. Although any distribution could be used, we assert normality when generating datasets. All data sets used in this study were generated such that the classes were normally distributed ($N(\overline{m}, \sigma^2)$; $\overline{m}$ is the distribution mean and σ is the standard deviation). The figures displayed were based on four hundred datasets consisting of two hundred thousand randomly drawn observations from two source populations: positive = $N(1.0, 0.0225)$ and negative = $N(2.0, 0.0625)$. Separate tests were run with datasets having rCSs of

$$2^0{:}1, \quad 2^1{:}1, \quad 2^2{:}1, \dots, \quad 2^{13}{:}1. \tag{2}$$

A total of 5,600 independent data sets were used in this study.

For each summary statistic evaluated, we observed how the reported metric was affected by rCS versus boundary versus metric output. The 3D results are presented as contour plots. Because the measure values are asymptotic to one (thus nonlinear), we use the median of the four hundred runs for each test case; means are not valid for non-linear scales. It is impractical to present confidence intervals on 3D data, but on the 2D graphs in Appendix D, the ninety percent confidence interval (90% CI) is displayed for select test series. To illustrate, the 90% CI is indicated by the vertical lines at each rCS tested in Figure 2; the horizontal line indicates the median.

This protocol provides the flexibility and repeatability necessary for analysis, yet abides by the constraints necessary for analysis of less tractable problem domains with difficult problem environments (e.g., complex CPD input and output distributions).

4. End User Efficacy

End users have two activities: CPD selection and CPD application. Regardless of any end user problem distinctions,

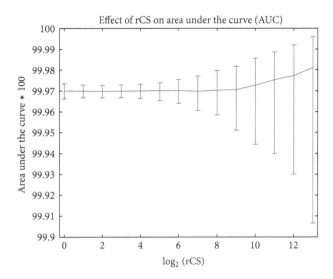

FIGURE 2: The vertical bars in this graph indicate the 90% confidence interval for measurements at each point observed. The horizontal line is the median.

these two activities address common interests:

(i) process application is concerned with the accuracy of the CPD for both possible outcomes:

    (1) "given that the test is positive, to what extent can the result be relied upon?"

    (2) "given that the test is negative, to what extent can the result be relied upon?"

Mathematically, this can be expressed as a conditional probability, or a conditional odds. These values are monotonic, so difficult to use for optimum boundary identification;

(ii) process selection needs to choose the CPD with the best expected accuracy ("given the set of choices for CPD, which CPD will provide the best results and to what extent can its results be relied upon?"). Summary statistic output (based on the two monotonic measures) can inform end users for process selection.

The end user efficacious measures differ for the two rCS problem types; so they are further discussed in the following sections.

4.1. When rCS Is Important. Measure efficacy depends upon whether or not the impact on the end user is cumulative. The two CPD application questions can be expressed mathematically as

(i) "given that the test is positive, to what extent can the result be relied upon?" $\Omega(T_+ \mid Z) = T_+/F_+$;

(ii) "given that the test is negative, to what extent can the result be relied upon?" $\Omega(T_- \mid \overline{Z}) = T_-/F_-$.

Proportions, being asymptotic to one, are not ratio measures [25] and, thus, have limited utility. We use odds ratios instead.

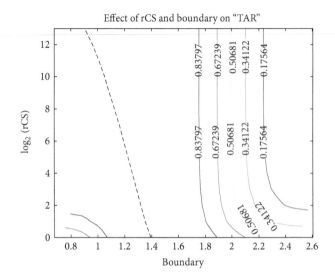

Effect of rCS and boundary on "TAR"

FIGURE 3: Being the sum of the observed correct classifications, TAR is a good measure for evaluating rCS sensitive CPDs. It is significant that the dashed line, indicating the optimum boundary, is not vertical; this shows that TAR is rCS sensitive.

The effect is cumulative (or additive); so the two conditional expressions, instead of being a measure suite, provide ancillary information. For CPD selection, end users will be interested in the proportion of the input stream that can be expected to be correct. Thus, a measure such as the total accuracy rate (TAR)

$$\text{TAR} = \frac{T_+ + T_-}{T_+ + T_- + F_+ + F_-} \qquad (3)$$

represents the per element expected accuracy. TAR, being asymptotic to one, is not a ratio measure; therefore, averaging is not a valid operation. The total accuracy odds ratio (TOR) would be a better choice:

$$\text{TOR} = \frac{T_+ + T_-}{F_+ + F_-}. \qquad (4)$$

Proportions, such as TAR and odds ratios such as TOR, are alternate expressions of the same CPD output. In fact, odds ratios can be transformed into proportions using (1).

Figure 3 shows TAR, as boundary and rCS vary. The TAR contour appears to vary little and be relatively constant over a wide boundary range. The optimum boundary (shown on the graph as the black dashed line) intersects the x-axis at around 1.45 and slopes toward 1.0. Additionally, the contour around the optimum boundary flattens as rCS increases. We can also see the optimum boundary and the reported accuracy rate both change as rCS varies. TAR is sensitive to rCS; thus, it is useful for problem domains where cumulative effects are important.

There are two other commonly seen rCS-sensitive summary statistics: F-score and Matthews correlation coefficient[9] (MCC). Another measure, information coefficient (IC); is becoming more prevalent, so we consider it as well.[10]

4.1.1. F-Score. F-score is the complement of a summary statistic proposed by van Rijsbergen [26]. The measure suite for F-score is recall and precision; van Rijsbergen's measure is based on information retrieval performance criteria put forth by Cleverdon [27]. Cleverdon's criteria address practitioner needs in information retrieval. Recall quantifies a CPD's completeness (the probability that the desired observations in the database are correctly identified). Precision quantifies the probability that undesired observations are mistakenly labeled as desired. For the information retrieval domain, these data[11] seem to be what end users need to know (F-score is now being seen in other problem domains.)

Recall and precision correspond to the conditional probabilities $P(T_+ \mid Y)$ and $P(T_+ \mid Z)$ (also known as "True positive rate" (TPR) and "positive predictive value" (PPV)). In the problem domain within which they were introduced (information retrieval), these measures quantify how well an CPD relates an object to a concept, such as selecting a document based on keywords. F-score is defined as

$$F_\beta = \frac{\left(1 + \beta^2\right)(\text{precision})(\text{recall})}{\left(\beta^2\right)(\text{precision} + \text{recall})}, \qquad (5)$$

where β is the relative weight of precision and recall:

$$\beta = \frac{\text{importance of precision}}{\text{importance of recall}}. \qquad (6)$$

If precision and recall have equal weights, then $F_\beta = F_1$, which is the harmonic mean of precision and recall:

$$F_1 = 2\frac{(\text{precision})(\text{recall})}{\text{precision} + \text{recall}}. \qquad (7)$$

Since precision and recall are conditional probabilities, we can convert the F-score equation into JPT values. After substitution and rearranging terms,

$$F_1 = \frac{T_+}{T_+ + F_+/2 + F_-/2}. \qquad (8)$$

The derivation is provided in Appendix A. Notably, using the harmonic mean results in T_+, F_+ and F_- not being equally weighted in the denominator. While this may be suitable for the information retrieval domain and some others, it is hardly universal.

In contrast to TAR, F-score's rCS sensitivity varies, depending upon the class monitored. The effect can be seen in Figures 4(a) and 4(b). Interestingly, both TAR and F-score are well-accepted measures. This may indicate the existence of another CPD problem structure element. Analysis of this possibility is postponed for later consideration.

4.1.2. Matthews Correlation Coefficient. The Matthews correlation coefficient (MCC) is a more recent measure, introduced by Matthews [18]. MCC is the application of Pearsons correlation coefficient to CPD evaluation. In a subsequent classifier measure survey, Baldi et al. restated the measure in the form commonly seen today [21]:

$$\text{MCC} = \frac{(T_+ * T_-) - (F_+ * F_-)}{\sqrt{Y * \overline{Y} * Z * \overline{Z}}}. \qquad (9)$$

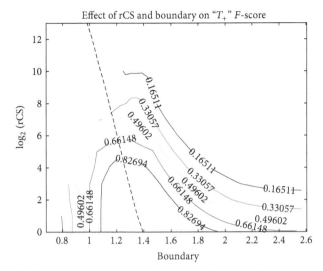

(a) The relatively flat area around the optimum boundary (black dashed line in the graph) with low rCS suggests a low boundary sensitivity. The ridge follows the same optimum boundary as that of the total accuracy rate

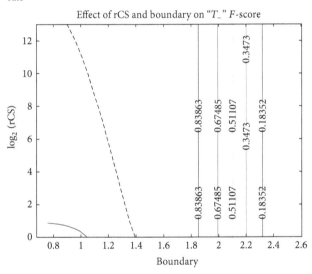

(b) If, instead of selecting T_+, we select T_-, then F-score looks remarkably similar to TAR. Thus, F-score quantifies the categorical process's effect on a specific category

FIGURE 4: These graphs show that F-score, a summary statistic commonly used to compare CPD effectiveness, is rCS-sensitive. This is a desirable characteristic for problem domains such as information retrieval. In addition to rCS sensitivity, F-score is also sensitive to the target class.

Although not mentioned explicitly in Matthews' work, Baldi et al. note that the equation requires normalized distributions:

$$\frac{a - \overline{a}}{\sigma_A}, \quad \text{where } a \in \{A\}, \tag{10}$$

$A = \{a_1, a_2, a_3, \ldots, a_s\}$ is the class of the input dataset and $s = |A|$. $\overline{a}$ is the mean of A. $\overline{A}$ is treated in the same manner. One effect of distribution normalization is class size equalization: rCS = 1 (this is discussed in Section 5). The expressions used

TABLE 3: The expressions in this JPT normalize the category values.

Actual target classification		Y	$\overline{Y}$	
Test result	Positive	T_+/Y	$F_+/\overline{Y}$	
	Negative	F_-/Y	$T_-/\overline{Y}$	
Normalized totals		1	1	2

to generate normalized JPTs are shown in Table 3 the class size equalization is indicated by the ones in the "normalized totals" row. To demonstrate Matthews initial intent to use normalized distributions, we recalculated Matthews et al.'s original results using both actual and normalized JPTs. The values using normalized JPTs matched Matthews results; the values using actual JPT values varied from Matthews reported values by approximately a factor of twenty. Thus, MCC, when introduced, was intended to be calculated on normalized JPTs.

The JPT normalization prerequisite applied by Matthews et al. and noted by Baldi et al. seems to have been lost, although the belief that MCC is rCS-invariant persists [28–34].[12] As a consequence, Baldi et al.'s equation is sometimes applied without first normalizing the JPTs. In two of these reports, Cannon et al. [28] and Mirceva et al. [34] include JPTs. Upon recalculating their results, we determined that the values presented were based on nonnormalized JPTs. In both cases, there were substantial differences between the results on normalized and nonnormalized JPTs. In the Cannon et al. results, the difference affected not only the values, but also the process rankings. Using normalized JPTs, MOLPRINT, the process ranked last, moved into the upper fifty percent of processes tested. Having rankings of processes substantially change due to such changes could result in selection of a suboptimal process for use in real-world settings.

Figure 5 shows how normalization impacts the rCS sensitivity for MCC. Figure 5(a) shows MCC's response when the raw JPT values are used. The peak boundary (indicated on the graph by the dashed line) shifts as rCS varies and the value decreases as rCS increases (indicated by the sloping dashed line that intersects the contours). In contrast, Figure 5(b) shows that with JPT normalization, the peak boundary and calculated optimum MCC value are fixed (indicated by a vertical dashed line and contours that do not intersect the peak boundary). Exactly the same data sets were used for both graphs; the only difference is the presence or absence of JPT normalization.

Comparing MCC results is complicated by the fact that the published reports we surveyed did not identify whether or not the MCC values reported were on normalized JPTs or not. As seen in Figures 5(a) and 5(b), comparing results across tests where rCS is not normalized could lead to errors. Since rCS affects the optimum boundary when raw JPTs are used, a simple correction of reported values by recalculating MCC on normalized JPTs will most probably be for a suboptimal boundary; thus, the corrected MCC value will also be suboptimal.[13] In this section, we characterized MCC using nonnormalized data. Appendix C derives an rCS-invariant MCC expression.

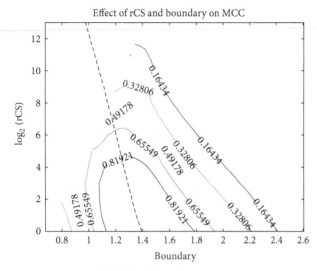

(a) MCC exhibits rCS sensitivity

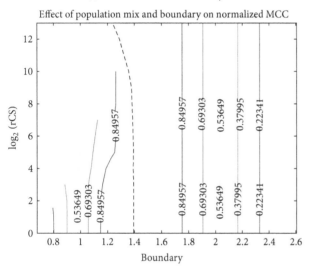

(b) On normalized JPTs, MCC exhibits rCS invariance. The increasing boundary curvature when rCS > 2^6 is a JPT normalization artifact explained in Appendix D

FIGURE 5: If MCC inputs are not normalized, it is rCS-sensitive.

Relative to end user interests, it is unclear what MCC quantifies and under what context the value will be relevant; MCC's end user efficacy is limited to optimum boundary identification.

MCC's complexity makes determining an underlying measure suite difficult. This detail will be addressed in the future.

4.1.3. Mutual Information Coefficient. Rost and Sander introduced an information-theory-based measure into the literature in 1993 [22]. It was subsequently included in a measure comparison by Baldi et al. [21]. Since then, it has gained some traction in biological literature [35–43] and has been seen in network management literature [44]. The measure is sometimes called the information coefficient or mutual information coefficient; we use the acronym IC.

As explained by Baldi et al., IC is the mutual information (I) normalized by the entropy in ground truth (H); I is the mutual information contained in ground truth regarding the test set $S(Y \cup \overline{Y})$ and the CPD prediction of ground truth, as contained in $Z \cup \overline{Z}$:

$$\text{IC} = \frac{I\left(Y \cup \overline{Y}, Z \cup \overline{Z}\right)}{H\left(Y \cup \overline{Y}\right)}. \tag{11}$$

Expressing I and H in terms of JPT categories,

$$\begin{aligned} I\left(Y \cup \overline{Y}, Z \cup \overline{Z}\right) \\ = -H\left(\frac{T_+}{N}, \frac{F_+}{N}, \frac{F_-}{N}, \frac{T_-}{N}\right) \\ - \frac{T_+}{N} \log\left(|Y| * |Z|\right) - \frac{F_+}{N} \log\left(|\overline{Y}| * |Z|\right) \\ - \frac{F_-}{N} \log\left(|Y| * |\overline{Z}|\right) - \frac{T_-}{N} \log\left(|\overline{Y}| * |\overline{Z}|\right), \end{aligned} \tag{12}$$

where

$$\begin{aligned} H\left(\frac{T_+}{N}, \frac{F_+}{N}, \frac{F_-}{N}, \frac{T_-}{N}\right) \\ = -\frac{T_+}{N} \log \frac{T_+}{N} - \frac{F_+}{N} \log \frac{F_+}{N} - \frac{F_-}{N} \log \frac{F_-}{N} - \frac{T_-}{N} \log \frac{T_-}{N}. \end{aligned} \tag{13}$$

Information-theory-based measures are gaining traction in the literature [35–43]. Some of these reports indicate the belief that the measures are rCS-invariant [38, 40, 43]. Solis and Rackovsky [41] note that their particular information theoretic measure may not be rCS-invariant. The belief that information theoretic measures are rCS-invariant comes from the fact that information theory applies to probability density functions, which are always normalized (rCS = 1) [45, 46]. Unless JPTs are normalized prior to use, IC and related measures cannot be guaranteed to be rCS-invariant.

Like other measures, IC compares target CPD output to an CPD using random classification. However, it differs in that IC is based on the entropy existing in the test set and CDP output. If the input and output are the same, then IC = 1; if the output of the process is equivalent to that of random selection, then IC = 0. A side effect of IC's use of logs is increased computational complexity. All of the other measures evaluated have a complexity of $O(N)$, IC is $O(N^2)$. This may limit IC's utility for large data sets. IC's computational complexity did affect our analysis. Had we calculated IC on the two hundred thousand element test sets used for the other measures, it would have taken approximately six months. Consequently, we tested IC on twenty thousand element test sets. In Figure 6, we can see that the peak boundary shifts as rCS increases; thus, IC is not rCS-invariant. As with the other rCS-sensitive measures, JPT normalization can confer rCS invariance.

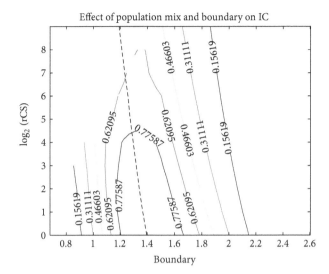

FIGURE 6: The sloped dotted line on the contour graph shows that IC is not rCS-invariant.

4.2. Findings regarding rCS Sensitive Problems

(i) Of the four rCS-sensitive summary statistics reviewed, TAR and F-score appear to be efficacious.

(ii) Because the reaction to rCS of TAR and F-score are opposite, this may indicate the existence of other elements in the CPD problem structure (we will address that in future work.)

(iii) MCC and IC, regardless of their apparent utility for researchers, do not seem to quantify information directly usable by end users.

This section has not covered how end users can take a single reported value and convert it into one applicable to their specific rCS environment. This will be discussed in Section 5.

4.3. When rCS Is Confounding.

When rCS is confounding, in addition to quantifying end user issues, efficacious measures must be rCS-invariant. The following discussion will apply normalized JPT input when necessary.

The CPD application expressions for this problem type are normalized versions of those for rCS-sensitive problems.

"Given that the test is positive, to what extent can the result be relied upon?" Mathematically, this can be expressed as a conditional probability, or a conditional odds on normalized JPTs. For the reason mentioned in Section 4, we use the odds, normalized $\Omega(T_+ \mid Z) = T_+ \overline{Y}/F_+ Y$.

"Given that the test is negative, to what extent can the result be relied upon?" The odds expression for this is normalized $\Omega(T_- \mid \overline{Z}) = T_- Y/F_- \overline{Y}$.

Test selection needs to choose the CPD with the best expected accuracy ("given that a result will be rendered, to what extent can the result be relied upon?"). The two CPD application questions provide operational information, but are also the basis for this noncumulative CPD problem selection decision. As such, they can be considered the measurement suite for the CPD selection decision. The CPD

selection decision requires an end user efficacious summary statistic. The expected prediction accuracy (EPA) is the average of the two odds ratios identified in the previous paragraph. Each CPD event is independent and the conditional values are normalized. The special conditions that dictate applying either the geometrical mean (a compounding effect) or the harmonic mean (unequal set sizes) do not exist; so the arithmetic mean of the conditional odds on normalized JPTs is appropriate:

$$\text{EPA} = \frac{\left(T_+ \overline{Y}\right)/\left(F_+ Y\right) + \left(T_- Y\right)/\left(F_- \overline{Y}\right)}{2}. \tag{14}$$

To our knowledge, this end user summary statistic is not found in the literature. We apply this summary statistic in the meta-analysis in Section 6.

As noted in the introduction, rCS-invariant summary statistics are already in use. We review three commonly seen rCS-invariant summary statistics:

(i) the Youden index [15];

(ii) two related measures: diagnostic odds ratio (DOR) [16] and diagnostic power (DP) [17] (DP = $(\sqrt{3}/\pi)$ log(DOR));

(iii) the receiver (or relative) operating characteristic area under the curve (AUC) [19, 20].

Two other summary statistics, the Matthews correlation coefficient (MCC) [18] and mutual information coefficient (IC) [21] are commonly held to be rCS-invariant, but in fact are not. They were discussed in Section 4.1.

4.3.1. Youden Index.

The Youden index (traditionally represented by J) was proposed in 1950 and is seen in medical diagnostic studies [15]. There are a number of expressions of J. The original is

$$J = \frac{1}{2}\left[\frac{T_+ - F_+}{T_+ + F_+} + \frac{T_- - F_-}{T_- + F_-}\right]. \tag{15}$$

Perhaps a more common representation is

$$J = \text{sensitivity} + \text{specificity} - 1, \tag{16}$$

where

$$\text{sensitivity} = \frac{T_+}{Y}, \qquad \text{specificity} = \frac{T_-}{\overline{Y}}. \tag{17}$$

Further, sensitivity is also known as the *true positive rate* (TPR) and specificity is the complement of the false positive rate; specificity = $1 - \text{FPR} = 1 - (F_+/\overline{Y})$. Hence, an even simpler (thus better, according to the minimum description length principal) definition would be

$$J = \text{TPR} - \text{FPR}. \tag{18}$$

In this form, the Youden index can be taken to be a summary statistic of the measure suite {TPR, FPR}.

J is special in that J = 0 indicates an CPD with an output equal to that of tossing a fair coin. J = 1 with a perfect CPD

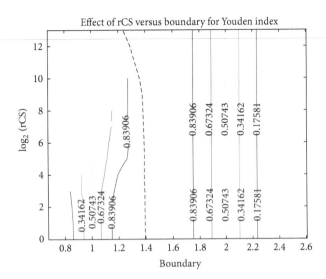

FIGURE 7: The Youden index has a very uniform shape and the optimum boundary lies along the peak of the Youden index ridge. This exhibits the expected rCS invariance.

and $J = -1$ for an CPD that misclassifies everything. As noted in their respective literature bases, J shares a characteristic with AUC, in that it is insensitive to rCS. On our source populations, the optimum boundary is approximately 1.4. This can be seen in Figure 7. There is an issue with end user efficacy, however. J quantifies the spread between the TPR and FPR. This information has little bearing on the "pretest" question posed at the beginning of this section.

4.3.2. Diagnostic Odds Ratio (DOR) and Discriminant Power (DP).

Two related measures are the diagnostic odds ratio (DOR) [16] and discriminant power (DP) [17]. DOR is defined as

$$\text{DOR} = \frac{T_+/F_-}{F_+/T_-}, \qquad (19)$$

where T_+/F_- is *true positive odds* (TPO) and F_+/T_- is *false positive odds* (FPO). After simplification,

$$\text{DOR} = \frac{T_+ T_-}{F_+ F_-}. \qquad (20)$$

Discriminant power is defined as

$$\text{DP} = \frac{\sqrt{3}}{\pi} \left(\log X + \log W \right), \qquad (21)$$

where

$$X = \frac{\text{sensitivity}}{1 - \text{sensitivity}}, \qquad Y = \frac{\text{specificity}}{1 - \text{specificity}}. \qquad (22)$$

Recasting the equation, we get

$$\text{DP} = \frac{\sqrt{3}}{\pi} \log\left(\frac{T_+ T_-}{F_+ F_-} \right). \qquad (23)$$

The derivation is provided in Appendix B. Comparing the two measures, we see that

$$\text{DP} = \frac{\sqrt{3}}{\pi} \log\left(\text{DOR}\right). \qquad (24)$$

DOR and DP are found in medical research. Interestingly, $\text{DP} = -\infty$ and $\text{DOR} = 0$ when either $T_+ = 0$ or $T_- = 0$, both need not equal zero. Similarly, $\text{DP} = \infty$ and $\text{DOR} = \infty$ when either $F_+ = 0$ or $F_- = 0$, both need not equal zero. Hence, an CPD can classify some observations correctly (total Accuracy > 0), yet have $\text{DP} = -\infty$ and $\text{DOR} = 0$. This is counterintuitive, since one would expect $\text{DP} = -\infty$ and $\text{DOR} = 0$ to indicate a totally ineffective CPD and $\text{DP} = \infty$ and $\text{DOR} = \infty$ to indicate a perfect CPD, rather than something in between. Since T_+ and T_- are (statistically) independent,[14] (as are F_+ and F_-), the DP and DOR could, in a probabilistic sense, be interpreted as the odds that, given two random observations, one will be classified T_+ and the other T_- (one will be classified F_+ and the other F_-). While the question seems similar, the fact that the DOR and DP optimum boundaries are different from the other inherently rCS invariant measures tested suggests that the two questions are significantly different. Perhaps this is because the DP and DOR treat the problem as a multiplicative function; we identify the problem as an additive function. This value would seem to be directly relevant in niche CPD scenarios, but not to general CPD problem types.

In medical studies, when the event tested for (T_+) has a low probability, DOR approximates relative risk: the rate at which the event was observed in group A versus the rate observed in group B. This is valuable information. However, when applied in the more general CPD domain, there is a problem. In any specific CPD task, the category of interest may not have a sufficiently low probability T_+; thus, the approximation may not always be acceptably close.

Unfortunately, DOR and DP have a challenging sensitivity to boundary; the optimum boundary is indicated by min(DOR) (or min(DP)). Thus, for any test run, the boundary with the smallest $T_+ T_-$ relative to $F_+ F_-$ gives the best accuracy. Not only is this counterintuitive, but also a potential error source. The problem originates from the fact that the greater the min(DOR) (or min(DP)), the better the results. Thus, if the boundary used to partition the test output is not at min(DOR) (or min(DP)), the results may appear better than they really are.[15] Most observations regarding DOR apply to DP as well. For example, $\text{DP} = 0$ when $T_+ T_- = F_+ F_-$.

One important characteristic of DOR and DP is that they are rCS invariant. An important difference between DOR/DP and the other rCS-invariant measures is that their optimum boundaries, although constant in our tests, are offset from the "minimum error boundary." These effects can be seen in Figure 8.[16] Since DOR and DP are minima, they follow a valley in the contour graph, instead of a ridge, Also contrary to the other measures, DOR decreases when the absolute class size effect becomes noticeable. This means that the contours are closed, instead of open as seen for the other measures. DOR's vertical optimum boundary line and constant value

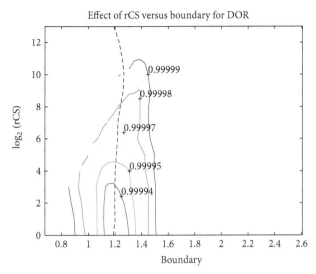

Effect of rCS versus boundary for DOR

(a) Contour graph of rCS versus boundary versus DOR value. Scaling makes the measure seem somewhat rCS sensitive. However, Figure 8(b) shows DOR is actually rCS invariant

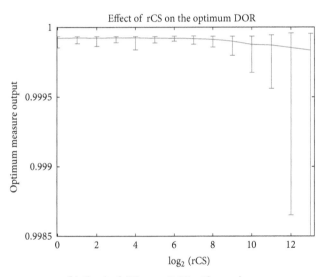

Effect of rCS on the optimum DOR

(b) Graph of rCS versus DOR, with error bars

FIGURE 8: Instead of the optimum value being maxima, like the other measures evaluated, the optimum DOR value is a minimum. Hence, the contours show a valley instead of a ridge. Also contrary to the other measures, DOR decreases when the absolute class size effect becomes noticeable. This means that the contours are closed, instead of open like the others. DOR's vertical optimum boundary line and constant value (seen in Figure 8(b)) indicate that DOR (and hence, DP) is rCS-invariant. DOR/DP optimum boundaries (approx. 1.2) are offset from the optimum boundaries seen in the other rCS-invariant measures (approx. 1.4). DP, the log form of DOR, has the same characteristics as DOR.

(seen in Figure 8(b)) indicate that DOR (and hence, DP) is rCS-invariant. Because of this boundary bias, they may not be useful for selecting boundaries. For example, in our test environment, TAR at the common optimum boundary is 0.994, TAR at DOR optimum boundary is 0.958; the difference is significant at the 95% confidence level.

4.3.3. Receiver Operating Characteristic Area under the Curve (AUC).

ROC has a solid history. Swets campaigned diligently to establish it as the evaluation criterion of choice [20, 47, 48]. The {TPR, FPR} measurement suite is the basis for the AUC summary statistic. The title originates from the fact that it is the area under a "ROC curve," a curve defined by false positive (FPR = $F_+/\overline{Y}$) and true positive (TPR = T_+/Y) rates. These values are calculated from JPTs of CPD output for a number of boundaries across the observed range, then graphed as the ROC curve [19, 49].[17] The literature describes the ROC curve (AUC) as being rCS-invariant as well as boundary-invariant. Because it is boundary-invariant, AUC is a popular tool in our present research environment. However, AUC has been criticized on theoretical terms recently [50, 51].

In contrast to the other summary statistics reviewed, AUC is generally accompanied by the ROC curve (indeed, the ROC curve may be presented without providing AUC). To a person skilled in the art, the ROC curve provides a great deal more information regarding CPD performance than does the single value AUC summary statistic[18] (this is, of course, true for any measure suite, since consolidation of multiple values into a single summary statistic value means that information is lost).

Compared to our end user focused criteria, ROC-AUC, being boundary-invariant, is not useful for boundary identification. Nor is it efficacious for end users.

There are numerous ROC-AUC variants [52, 53]. Vanderlooy and Hüllermeier determined in their comparison, that despite intuitive appeal, none of the variants confer any CPD selection improvement. From the end user perspective, since the underlying measure units remain the same, they all have the same limited efficacy.

Figure 9 shows the optimum boundary versus rCS for the proposed normalized PPV, NPV average and existing summary statistics, normalized MCC, Youden index, and DOR. As can be seen in the figure, DOR peaks at a different boundary than the other rCS-invariant measures tested, and (excepting DOR) the optimum boundary is relatively stable until rCS > 2^6, after which the detected optimum boundary starts dropping rapidly.[19] For our context, a key finding from Figure 9 is that not only does DOR have weak end user efficacy, it also should not be used to identify the optimum boundary.

4.4. Findings regarding rCS-Invariant End User Problems.

For problems requiring rCS invariance, we find that

(i) end users need three values. For CPD selection, the expected total predictive accuracy (a summary statistic) EPA = $((T_+\overline{Y})/(F_+Y) + (T_-Y)/(F_-\overline{Y}))/2$ is important. When the CPD is used in the field, the summary statistic value has no meaning. Instead, end users need the information provided by the two measure suite elements; the positive predictive value odds ratio PPV = $(T_+\overline{Y})/(F_+Y)$ and the negative predictive value odds ratio NPV = $(T_-Y)/(F_-\overline{Y})$.

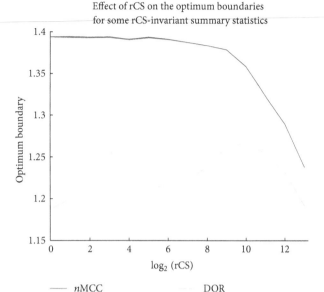

Effect of rCS on the optimum boundaries
for some rCS-invariant summary statistics

— nMCC   DOR
— nTAR   — nT_+ F-score
— J

FIGURE 9: Other than DOR/DP, all of the rCS-invariant measures tested identified the same optimum boundary.

(ii) Although many commonly seen summary statistics can be used to identify the optimum boundary, as seen in this study, not all can (e.g., ROC-AUC and DOR). Figure 9 shows how the optimum boundary identified by DOR differs from that identified by the other summary statistics tested.

(iii) Of the rCS sensitive summary statistics evaluated, only the EPA output answers the end user's CPD selection question. The others may be useful for niche problems, but provide little useful information for the "common" end user.

5. JPT Normalization

In statistical circles, standardizing distributions is a well-established technique. One effect of standardization is that the area under the probability density function (pdf) equals 1. This simplifies pdf analysis, since the area of any segment of the area under the curve can be interpreted as the probability of an event occurring within that segment. Similarly, distribution standardization facilitates pdf comparisons. Since the CPD analysis domain considers processes with overlapping pdfs, it intersects with the pdf comparison domain, but is neither a superset nor a subset.[20] Where appropriate, distribution standardization is a useful tool.

In CPD analysis, distribution standardization takes the form of JPT normalization. Table 4 shows a JPT displaying "raw" data—actual category cardinality. After normalization, the class totals (bottom row in Table 5) are one. Thus, JPT normalization seems to be a cause for rCS-invariance in measures. As such, it provides a benefit to end users

TABLE 4: This JPT holds actual category counts.

Actual target classification		A	$\overline{A}$	
Test result	Positive	T_+	F_+	Z
	Negative	F_-	T_-	$\overline{Z}$
	Total	Y	$\overline{Y}$	N

TABLE 5: The values in this JPT have been normalized. Normalization results in equal class sizes (both total both equal one).

Actual target classification		A	$\overline{A}$	
Test result	Positive	T_+/Y	$F_+/\overline{Y}$	
	Negative	F_-/Y	$T_-/\overline{Y}$	
	Normalized total	1	1	2

with rCS invariant problems: any JPT-based CPD evaluation measure will have rCS invariant output, if the input JPTs are normalized. (Illustrated in Figure 10).

Although any measure can be rCS-invariant when the JPTs are normalized, some measures have emerged which have intrinsic rCS invariance. These inherently rCS invariant measures all have {TPV, FPV} (ratios that normalize the JPTs) as measure suites, thus rather than being counter examples, they provide empirical evidence that JPT normalization is the root cause for rCS invariance in measures; proof is beyond the scope of this paper. An overview of commonly seen rCS invariant measures is provided in Appendix D.

There is also a benefit for end users with rCS-sensitive problems. Statisticians use distribution standardization to mitigate rCS effects; however, the process is reversible. JPTs with rCS = 1 can be "tuned" to any desired rCS simply by multiplying one class by a constant c so that $c\overline{Y}/Y$ equals the desired value.[21] Thus, an end user with an rCS-sensitive problem can adjust reported results to fit their need. JPT tuning also allows end users to execute sensitivity analyses and estimate how the CPD will perform in their environment, over the expected rCS range. These insights are applied to a real-world problem in Section 6; a comparison of two RA diagnostic tests and an intrusion detection problem.

However, the optimum boundary is rCS-dependant; thus, the tool is not complete. To apply to all end users, results for all possible optimum boundaries would need to be provided.[22] This is impractical, if not impossible, for CPD test reports to include. As illustrated in Endnote 15, the tuned JPTs will indicate trends, but cannot be considered definitive. Nonetheless, JPT tuning extends JPT normalization in a way we have not previously seen in the literature and provides end users with a useful capability.

6. Examples

In this section, we use our proposed end user efficacious data analysis on two real-world problems, a meta-analysis[23] comparing two medical diagnostic tests for rheumatoid arthritis (RA) by [54] and data from a cyber security masquerading study by [55].

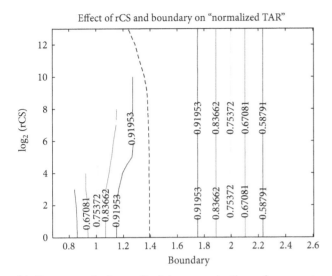

Effect of rCS and boundary on "normalized TAR"

(a) Contour graph of normalized Accuracy rate. The reader may note that, other than the contour values, the graph is almost exactly the same as the Youden index graph

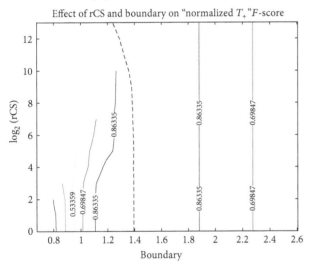

Effect of rCS and boundary on "normalized T_+"F-score

(b) Contour graph of normalized F-score. As with Youden index and normalized accuracy rate, the optimum boundary follows the "minimum error boundary"

FIGURE 10: The normalized accuracy rate and F-score seem to be relatively invariant to rCS. Not only is the value relatively constant, but the boundary stays constant as well.

6.1. A Meta-Analysis of Rheumatoid Arthritis Diagnostic Tests. The meta-analysis is quite thorough and accounts for many potential variations between studies. Three hundred and two relevant studies were found; eighty-six satisfied the rigorous inclusion criteria. The team concludes that one test is better than the other, however, does so without using a summary statistic. Our reanalysis adds the three recommended measures identified in Section 4.3.

The study uses two measures: positive likelihood ratio (LR$_+$) and negative likelihood ratio (LR$_-$). Given a typical test using supervised inputs (where ground truth is known), these two values are efficacious for researchers. They are less

TABLE 6: Rheumatoid arthritis is a disease where both nontreatment and unnecessary treatment have negative consequences. Thus, knowing the overall predictive accuracy rate is useful information for a practitioner. These tables show the summary likelihood ratios originally reported and the corresponding normalized predictive accuracy odds ratios. Although the anti-CCP test is significantly better, its overall accuracy is not as great, nor is the negative predictive value as poor as one might believe, based simply on the likelihood ratio. (the parenthesized range in this and subsequent tables is the 95% confidence interval).

(a)

| Test | Normalized odds ratio measures | |
	LR$_+$	LR$_-$
Anti-CCP	12.46 (9.72–15.98)	0.36 (0.031–0.042)
RF	4.86 (3.95–5.97)	0.38 (0.33–0.44)

(b)

| Test | Normalized odds ratio measures | | |
	PPV	NPV	EPA
Anti-CCP	13.4 (13.0–17.0)	2.88 (2.71–3.0)	8.14 (7.86–10.0)
RF	4.6 (4.25–5.0)	2.74 (2.63–2.87)	3.67 (3.44–3.93)

efficacious where end users have only the CPD output and ground truth is unknown. As we note in Section 4.3, PPV and NPV are more relevant for end users.

On pooled data, the LR$_-$ differences between the tests were statistically insignificant. However, the LR$_+$ results were statistically significant. On the pooled data, the "anti-CCP"[24] positive test results were more frequently correct than the "RF"[25] diagnoses. The authors make one important point regarding rheumatoid arthritis treatment; it is harmful and costly to treat persons with false positive results. Hence, it is important to correctly diagnose negatives as well as positives: total expected predictive accuracy (EPA) is important for rheumatoid arthritis treatment. JPT normalization allows measurement of EPA that is rCS-invariant. Using normalized JPT data,

$$\text{EPA} = \frac{T_+/F_+ + T_-/F_-}{2}. \qquad (25)$$

In our extension to Nishimura et al.'s report, we calculate the normalized EPA, PPV, and NPV on the pooled test data. Table 6 shows the original likelihood ratios reported by Nishimura et al. and EPA (the parenthesized range is the 95% confidence interval.[26]) LR$_-$s and PPV show similar values, but LR$_+$ is about one-sixth of the NPV; end users should be cautious when interpreting likelihood ratios. Comparing EPAs for each test and keeping in mind the end user context requires rCS invariance, the anti-CCP test correct diagnosis rate is a little more than twice the correct diagnoses rate of the RA test. This is true, even though, as can be seen in Table 7, the RF test actually more accurately detects RA's presence.

The authors note that "the better accuracy of anti-CCP antibody was mainly due to its higher specificity." In comparing the JPTs in Table 7, the anti-CCP pooled data

TABLE 7: These normalized JPTs of Nishimura et al.'s [54] pooled anti-CCP and RF test data were generated using their reported sensitivities and specificities. A person without RA is far less likely to be misdiagnosed than one with the disease, when the anti-CCP test is used.

(a)

| | | Actual RA condition | |
		Diseased	Not diseased
Anti-CC test result	Positive	0.67 (0.65–0.68)	0.05 (0.04–0.06)
	Negative	0.33 (0.32–0.35)	0.95 (0.94–0.95)
	Total	1	1

(b)

| | | Actual RA condition | |
		Diseased	Not diseased
RF test result	Positive	0.69 (0.68–0.7)	0.15 (0.14–0.16)
	Negative	0.31 (0.3–0.32)	0.85 (0.84–0.86)
	Total	1	1

TABLE 8: The above two JPTs have been "tuned" to a population where the diseased population is one hundred times the undiseased population. In this environment, the cumulative results will cause the anti-CCP test to appear to outperform the RF test.

(a)

| | | Actual RA condition | |
		Diseased	Not diseased
Anti-CC test result	Positive	67	0.05
	Negative	33	0.95
	Totals	100	1
EPA		670 (850–650)	

(b)

| | | Actual RA condition | |
		Diseased	Not diseased
RF test result	Positive	69	0.15
	Negative	31	0.85
	Totals	100	1
EPA		230 (250–212)	

summary in Table 7 shows that the anti-CCP test is actually less accurate in detecting diseased individuals—and at a statistically significant level (0.67 for anti-CCP is (statistically) significantly worse than the 0.69 reported for RF). We see that the anti-CCP actually detects RA less reliably than the RF test; the improvement is, in fact, entirely due to better specificity (correctly identifying nondiseased). In a case such as this, where each test is more accurate on one class, rather than one test being more accurate on both classes, it may not always be clear if there is any net diagnostic improvement. Normalized total predictive accuracy quantifies net diagnostic improvement in a way that may help clarify these issues.

This RA example is an rCS confounding type problem; in order to mitigate rCS bias, JPT normalization should be applied. We can now apply JPT tuning to illustrate how rCS can skew results; it is possible to estimate the cumulative test results that GPs and RA specialists will actually observe in their respective practices. The method actually "tunes" the JPTs; any desired rCS can be set.[27] A general practitioner may occasionally test for RA. Actual testing rates do not appear to be publicly available; so for computational simplicity, we assume the odds are one to one hundred that someone tested actually has the disease. Because of his/her specialty, a rheumatologist may have a new patient base that is highly skewed toward RA-positive. We assume a one hundred to one ratio. What total accuracy ratios will the two offices observe for the two tests? An JPT tuned to the rheumatologists' patient base is shown in Table 8, an JPT tuned to the GP's patient base is shown in Table 9. The EPA odds ratio observed by the rheumatologist would be anti-CCP: 670, RF: 250; the GP would observe total accuracy ratios of anti-CCP: 144, RF: 131, a statistically insignificant difference. Summary Table 10 shows that practices will have radically different experiences with the two tests, although the anti-CCP test is still best for the patient, regardless of the office.

6.2. A Cyber Security Masquerade Study.

The cyber security problem domain is one where cumulative effects (e.g., processing false alarms (F_+)) are important. Consider an end user desiring to detect masquerading attacks, in which an attacker pretends to be an authorized user in order to gain access to a system. Determining the appropriate boundary for the detector is necessary in order to balance the effects of false alarms and missed attacks. This balance is subject to the relative volume of normal and masquerade system activity; thus, rCS is important; end users will want to incorporate rCS.

Schonlau et al. simulate a masquerade attack by capturing UNIX commands resulting from specific users, then inserting UNIX commands generated by another user into the original command stream. They compare a number of detection algorithms. The best performing was based on data compression. The Bayesian classifier [55] they used did not perform as well. We compare the two algorithms using the seven summary statistics discussed earlier.

Schonlau et al. use ROC curves to compare their various detection algorithms. From a research perspective, this is appropriate, since ROC is invariant to rCS and does not require boundary selection. However, as noted in Section 4.3.3, ROC provides limited information to end users. To illustrate the effect of using an inappropriate measure type, we reanalyze one of the user command streams with both rCS-sensitive and rCS-invariant measures. Table 11 shows the results.

For all seven summary statistics considered, the classifier with the higher value is better. Clearly, regardless of the measure, the compression algorithm outperforms the Bayesian classifier. The summary statistic values and associated optimum thresholds, however, vary widely.

What do we learn about the two classifiers from the measure values? The IC measures information content; MCC measures covariance. Youden index and DOR/DP quantify more esoteric characteristics. All four measure classifier

TABLE 9: The top two JPTs have been "tuned" to a population where the diseased population is one hundredth of the undiseased population. In this environment, the two tests appear statistically indistinguishable.

(a)

		Actual RA condition	
		Diseased	Not diseased
Anti-CCP	Positive	0.67	5
test result	Negative	0.33	95
	Totals	1	100
EPA	144 (136–150)		

(b)

		Actual RA condition	
		Diseased	Not diseased
RF test	Positive	0.69	15
Result	Negative	0.31	85
	Totals	1	100
EPA	137 (131–143)		

TABLE 10: This table shows the total accuracy ratios for RA tested populations of 100 : 1 (the rheumatologist) and 1 : 100 (the general practitioner).

Test	Patient bases (diseased : undiseased)	
	Rheumatologist (100 : 1)	General practitioner (1 : 100)
Anti-CCP	670 (850–650)	144 (136–150)
RF	230 (250–212)	137 (131–143)

performance relative to random selection using a fair coin, an issue particularly relevant to researchers, who generally consider a fair coin to be the most ineffective classifier. ROC-AUC, being rCS- and boundary-invariant, also has attractive characteristics for research. End users, however, are concerned about the net result, not distance from random selection. While each of these five measures quantify a characteristic related to the classifier performance characteristic of interest, none can be transformed into a value useful in the intrusion detection domain.

JPT tuning can help end users make more informed decisions. Schonlau et al.'s test sets consisted of one hundred blocks of concatenated UNIX commands. For "user 24," rCS = 3.7. "In the wild," one would expect rCS to be considerably smaller. For this example, we will assume that the end users expect rCS $\in$ [10 K, 100 K]. For the intrusion detection problem domain, TAR or F-score may provide the most information regarding end result. TAR includes both T_+ and T_-; F-score only includes T_+.[28] An IT system administrator may be most concerned about intrusion risk and detection overhead, thus not so concerned about T_-. If so, then F-score may be most relevant when comparing cyber security tools. Consider the ΩF-score of Schonlau et al.'s raw data in Table 12. The system administrator can tell that when rCS = 3.7, the correctly detected masquerade activity should be almost five times as frequent as errors; this is the system administrators greatest area of concern.

TABLE 11: These tables show the results for the compression-based classifier and the Bayesian classifier. The measures output on different scales and measure different characteristics; they cannot be directly compared. Because these are two different classifiers, the output ranges differ.

(a)

Compression classifier					
rCS-sensitive measures			rCS-invariant measures		
Measure	Value	Boundary	Measure	Value	Boundary
IC	0.528	0.800	Youden	0.791	0.200
TAR	0.930	0.800	DOR	6.78	0.200
MCC	0.786	0.600	ROC-AUC	0.851	NA
T_+ F-score	0.829	0.800			

(b)

Bayesian classifier					
rCS-sensitive measures			rCS-invariant measures		
Measure	Value	Boundary	Measure	Value	Boundary
IC	0.068	188	Youden	0.057	−228
TAR	0.620	638	DOR	0.206	638
MCC	0.053	−228	ROC-AUC	0.505	NA
T_+ F-score	0.543	−387			

TABLE 12: This table shows how JPT tuning can assist end users in estimating how an CPD will work in their environment. An executive looking at TOR will see that there are 25 correct classifications for every incorrect in the expected operating range. The IT system administrator looking at ΩF-score will see that there will be thousands of errors for every correct T_+. Their decisions regarding the usefulness of this CPD may differ.

rCS =	TOR	ΩF-score
1.0	7.8	7.1
3.7	13.3	4.9
1,000	19	0.042
10 K	25	0.0021
100 K	25	0.0004

A corporate executive might be concerned about the effect all four categories could have on the enterprise's performance; thus, TOR would be most relevant. Consider the TOR score of Schonlau et al.'s raw data in Table 12. The executive can tell that when rCS = 3.7, there will be over 13 correctly classified events for every misclassification. Based on these values, both persons might decide that performance is acceptable. JPT tuning, however, changes the picture considerably. The executive will see accuracy triple, but the system administrator will see a decrease in accuracy of more than three orders of magnitude. The executive and system administrator may now have different opinions.

Another problem with selecting an inappropriate summary statistic can be seen in Table 11. Not all measures have the same optimum threshold. An end user relying on an inappropriate summary statistic to determine a useful boundary for masquerade detection may be disappointed with their results.

After a classifier is selected, the two perspectives can lead to different system optimizations. When made available to end users, TAR and F-score values can help stakeholders such as executives and IT managers make more informed decisions. Since TAR/TOR and F-score/ΩF-score may have different optimum boundaries, practitioners and decision makers may benefit from having both values reported for each optimum boundary over an rCS range. That way, end users will have an appreciation of the tradeoff associated with selecting a particular solution.

7. Conclusion

This paper is a first step in identifying the structure of CPD problems faced by end users. Using that structure, we characterize how CPD evaluation measures are relevant to end users and identify end user relevant evaluation tools. To that end, we have defined rCS's importance to end user problems, identified measures that are efficacious for end users, and shown how JPT normalization and JPT tuning are useful for end user CPD evaluation.

Depending upon whether the end user is interested in the cumulative output or each individual CPD output, rCS is either an important factor or confounding. For maximum end user utility, research reports should include information efficacious for both problem types:

(i) for "rCS is confounding" problems, end users need a summary statistic, EPA $= ((T_+\overline{Y})/(F_+Y) + (T_-Y)/(F_-\overline{Y}))/2$ and the underlying measurement suite, PPV $= (T_+\overline{Y})/(F_+Y)$, NPV $= (T_-Y)/(F_-\overline{Y})$. All three values are based on normalized JPTs. If the values used are from normalized JPTs, then Y and $\overline{Y}$ both equal one, thus are unnecessary.

(ii) For "rCS is important" problems, end users must be able to tailor results to suit their individual rCS environments. We identify one appropriate summary statistic; the total accuracy odds ratio TOR $= (T_+ + T_-)/(F_+ + F_-)$. Another, F-score, is already in use: $F_\beta = ((1 + \beta^2)(\text{precision})(\text{recall}))/((\beta^2)(\text{precision} + \text{recall}))$, where β is the relative weight of precision and recall: β is the importance of precision relative to the importance of recall. End users can apply JPT tuning to tailor results for their environment. To do so, they will require the base JPT values ($\{T_+, F_+, F_-, T_-\}$).

Consolidating these findings, we propose that end users will be better served if research reports include PPV, NPV, EPA (or F_β, if it is prevalent in the domain), and the four normalized base JPT values.

Future work will continue to develop a CPD problem structure. The disparity between TAR and F-score suggests that at least one more characteristic exists. Also, without compensating for the effect of the shift in optimum boundary, JPT tuning does not fully address the end user's need to tailor research results. We will be considering means of addressing that deficiency.

Appendices

A. Restating F_1 in Terms of JPT Values

As defined,

$$F_1 = 2\frac{(\text{precision})(\text{recall})}{\text{precision} + \text{recall}}, \tag{A.1}$$

where

$$\text{precision} = \frac{T_+}{T_+ + F_-},$$
$$\text{recall} = \frac{T_+}{T_+ + F_+}. \tag{A.2}$$

Substituting, we have

$$F_1 = 2\frac{(T_+/(T_+ + F_-))(T_+/(T_+ + F_+))}{(T_+/(T_+ + F_-)) + (T_+/(T_+ + F_+))}. \tag{A.3}$$

Multiplying and creating common denominators,

$$F_1 = \frac{2T_+^2/((T_+ + F_-)(T_+ + F_+))}{(T_+(T_+ + F_+) + T_+(T_+ + F_-))/((T_+ + F_-)(T_+ + F_+))}. \tag{A.4}$$

Multiplying numerator and denominator by $(T_+ + F_-)(T_+ + F_+)/T_+$ leaves

$$F_1 = \frac{2T_+}{2T_+ + F_+ + F_-} = \frac{T_+}{T_+ (F_+/2) + (F_-/2)}. \tag{A.5}$$

B. Restating DP in Terms of JPT Values

$$\text{DP} = \frac{\sqrt{3}}{\pi}(\log X + \log W), \tag{B.1}$$

where

$$X = \frac{\text{sensitivity}}{1 - \text{sensitivity}},$$
$$Y = \frac{\text{specificity}}{1 - \text{specificity}},$$
$$\text{sensitivity} = \frac{T_+}{Y},$$
$$1 - \text{sensitivity} = \frac{F_-}{Y}, \tag{B.2}$$
$$\text{specificity} = \frac{T_-}{\overline{Y}},$$
$$1 - \text{specificity} = \frac{F_+}{\overline{Y}}.$$

Combining the logs, we get

$$\text{DP} = \frac{\sqrt{3}}{\pi}(\log(XY)). \tag{B.3}$$

Then, substituting for X and Y,

$$\text{DP} = \frac{\sqrt{3}}{\pi}\left(\log\left(\frac{\text{sensitivity}}{1-\text{sensitivity}}\,\frac{\text{specificity}}{1-\text{specificity}}\right)\right). \quad (B.4)$$

Substituting for sensitivity and specificity,

$$\text{DP} = \frac{\sqrt{3}}{\pi}\log\left(\frac{T_+/Y}{F_-/Y}\,\frac{T_-/\overline{Y}}{F_+/\overline{Y}}\right). \quad (B.5)$$

Multiplying top and bottom by $Y\overline{Y}$, we are left with

$$\text{DP} = \frac{\sqrt{3}}{\pi}\log\left(\frac{T_+T_-}{F_-F_+}\right). \quad (B.6)$$

C. Derivation of Normalized MCC Equation

An important side note is that MCC, as commonly calculated,

$$\text{MCC} = \frac{(T_+T_-)-(F_+F_-)}{\sqrt{Y\overline{Y}Z\overline{Z}}} \quad (C.1)$$

is not rCS-invariant as is sometimes reported [28–34]; it must use normalized JPT values (as in Table 13).

Substituting the normalized JPT values in (C.1) and collecting terms, the rCS-invariant MCC is

normalized MCC

$$= \frac{(T_+T_-)-(F_+F_-)}{\sqrt{Y\overline{Y}\left(\overline{Y}T_+ + YF_+\right)\left(YT_- + \overline{Y}F_+\right)}}. \quad (C.2)$$

Equation (C.2) can be used in lieu of normalizing JPTs prior to calculating MCC.

D. Measures with Intrinsic rCS Invariance

Although the AUC, Youden index and DOR/DP are distinctly different measures; they all have one key similarity: normalized input. The AUC and Youden index both are (TPR, FPR), and since TPR and FPR are conditional probabilities $P(T_+\mid Y)$ and $P(F_+\mid \overline{Y})$, likewise, TNR and FNR are conditional probabilities $P(T_-\mid Y)$ and $P(F_-\mid \overline{Y})$. If, in the JPT, we replace T_+ by TPR, F_+ by FPR, T_- by TNR, F_- by FNR, then the marginal totals Y and $\overline{Y}$ are replaced by 1 s and N becomes 2. This is shown in Table 15. Since the two marginal totals representing class size are equal, this process compensates for rCS: the CPD output JPTs have been normalized. In this paper, calculations and discussion using the rCS invariant JPT form shown in Table 14 will refer to "normalized" versions. Any discussions not referring to "normalization" are of measures using the "raw" JPT form as presented in Section 3, Table 1.

Regardless of the actual test set rCSs, the input values for the AUC and Youden index incorporate JPT normalization. Although not as evident, this is also true for DOR and DP. Any JPT can be defined in terms of the TPR and FPR. This is illustrated in Table 14. Using Table 14 definitions,

$$\text{DOR} = \frac{(c_Y \text{TPR})(c_{\overline{Y}}(1-\text{FPR}))}{(c_Y(1-\text{TPR})(c_{\overline{Y}}\text{FPR}))}. \quad (D.1)$$

TABLE 13: The values in this JPT have been normalized.

Actual target classification		Y	$\overline{Y}$	
Test result	Positive	T_+/Y	$F_+/\overline{Y}$	
	Negative	F_-/Y	$T_-/\overline{Y}$	
Normalized totals		1	1	2

TABLE 14: JPTs can be defined in terms of the TPR and FPR. c_Y and $c_{\overline{Y}}$ are the class sizes in the test set.

		Source population		
		Y	$\overline{Y}$	Totals ↓
Test result	Positive	$c_Y * \text{TPR}$	$c_{\overline{Y}} * \text{FPR}$	Z
	Negative	$c_Y * (1-\text{TPR})$	$c_{\overline{Y}} * (1-\text{FPR})$	$\overline{Z}$
	Totals	c_Y	$c_{\overline{Y}}$	N

TABLE 15: A normalized JPT has class sizes adjusted to one. The four classification categories are expressed as proportions of the test set class of which they are actually members.

		Source population		
		Y	$\overline{Y}$	
Test result	Positive	TPR	FPR	
	Negative	$\text{FPR}=1-\text{TPR}$	$\text{TNR}=1-\text{FPR}$	
	Totals	1	1	2

After simplification,

$$\text{DOR} = \frac{\text{TPR}(1-\text{FPR})}{\text{FPR}(1-\text{TPR})}. \quad (D.2)$$

Thus, we find that DOR and DP are based on normalized JPTs as well.

From the literature, we see that MCC is rCS-invariant when calculated on normalized JPTs. Presumably, other rCS-sensitive measures will be rCS-invariant when calculated on normalized JPTs as well. We tested this hypothesis by calculating accuracy, F-score, and MCC values on normalized versions. Figure 11 displays the peak Accuracy rate and F-score on normalized JPTs and compares them to the output of the established rCS-invariant measures, AUC, DOR,[29] and Youden index (DP, being just a log expression of DOR was left out.) The graphs are provided solely to compare their response to rCS. Any conclusions from Figure 11 beyond that must be made with care.

Figure 11 brings out some interesting points.

(i) Confidence interval response to rCS seems to fall into two categories. All of the normalized measures (including AUC, Youden index, DOR, and DP) have relatively stable CIs below rCS = 2^6. Above rCS = 2^6, there is an observable trend away from the stable value. This is due to a well-known issue with absolute sample size related to the strong law of large numbers. In our tests, the problem became statistically significant when the smaller sample had less than four hundred members.

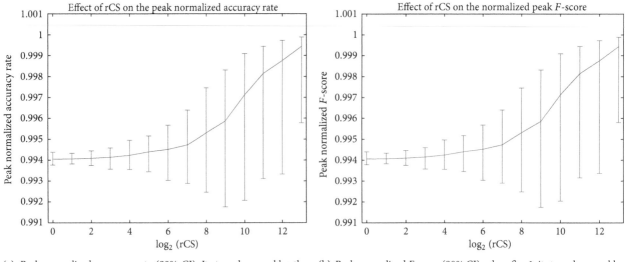

(a) Peak normalized accuracy rate (90% CI). It strongly resembles the Figures 11(b), 11(c), and 11(d)

(b) Peak normalized F-score (90% CI). when $\beta = 1$, it strongly resembles Figures 11(a), 11(c) and 11(d)

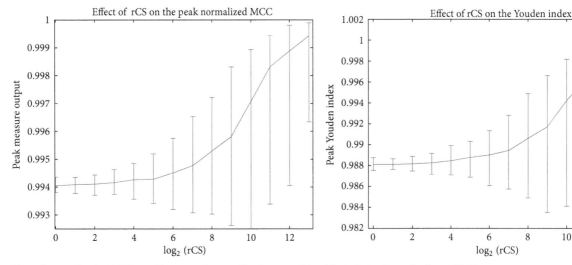

(c) Peak normalized MCC (90% CI): it strongly resembles Figures 11(a), 11(b) and 11(d)

(d) Peak Youden index (90% CI). This measure turns out to be related to the normalized accuracy rate

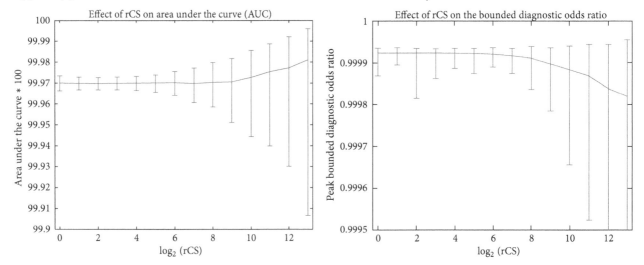

(e) Peak AUC (90% CI). It appears somewhat less sensitive to absolute sample size

(f) Best DOR (90% CI). As rCS invariance weakens, the DOR value drops

FIGURE 11: All of the normalized summary statistics exhibit rCS invariance. All of the lines vary from the horizontal, indicating that rCS invariance weakens when $rCS > 2^6$. This is a well-known absolute sample size issue. In our tests, the problem became statistically significant when $|A| < 400$.

For normalized accuracy rate, Youden index, normalized F-score, and normalized MCC, the 90% confidence interval generally increases as rCS increases. Analyzing the CIs is difficult because (all but DOR) are measured on scales with an upper bound, their scales are not linear. The CI changes observed, however, are consistent with expectations. In general, as the positive class size decreases, normalization magnifies any changes in T_+ and F_- far more than normalization of the negative class makes offsetting reductions (the positive class decreases by a factor of 2^{14}, while the negative class increases by a factor of less than 2^1).

(ii) Measure families have been found in the summary statistics evaluated. As discussed earlier, DOR and DP are related. The test also reveals a similarity between the normalized accuracy rate and Youden index:

$$\text{Youden index} = \text{TPR} - \text{FPR}$$

$$\text{norm accuracy rate} = \frac{\text{TPR} + 1 - \text{FPR}}{2} \quad \text{(D.3)}$$

so that

$$\text{norm accuracy rate} = \frac{\text{Youden Index} + 1}{2}. \quad \text{(D.4)}$$

Thus, we see that normalized accuracy rate and Youden index are related.

(iii) JPT normalization can inflate reported process accuracy. Each graph in Figure 11 exhibits rCS stability when rCS $< 2^6$. However, when rCS $> 2^6$, rCS invariance seems to weaken. This turns out to be a function of the absolute size of the smaller class and is a consequence of the strong law of large numbers. As class sample size decreases, its representation of the source population decreases. The problem is that as sample size decreases, distribution tails lose their definition. When a sample size is magnified by JPT normalization, the undefined tails do not reappear, thus causing the sample to represent a source population with a smaller variance. This means the class overlap is underrepresented. Since process accuracy is inversely related to class overlap, a reduction in estimated class overlap will result in process accuracy overestimation. In our tests, the difference became statistically significant when sample sizes fell below four hundred members.

Violating the strong law of large numbers also affects the optimum boundary. As the apparent source population variance decreases, the boundary shifts toward that class. This can be seen in all of the contour graphs. In order to increase rCS, our protocol decreases $|A|$. A has the lower mean; thus, as rCS increases, the calculated optimum boundary starts shifting toward μ_A. In our tests, when rCS $> 2^6$, the shift becomes statistically significant.

Acknowledgments

The authors are thankful for the insightful comments in the early days of this work by Dr. Lynda Ballou, Mathematics Department, NM, USA Institute of Mining and Technology, Socorro, New Mexico. They are also indebted to Dr. Andrew Barnes, Applied Statistics Lab, General Electric Global Research, Niskayuna, NY, USA for taking the time to discuss this work. The journal reviewer's comments strengthened the paper considerably.

Endnotes

1. There are two levels of tool development. If development is "basic research," then evaluation is application-agnostic. If it is "applied research," then the focus is application-specific and evaluation needs tend to align with practitioner needs. For the purpose of this discussion, researchers do basic research; end users consist of practitioners and applied researchers.

2. CPD are a subset of the more general group of categorical problems. Our investigations apply to both.

3. The measure suite members quantify some particular aspect of CPD performance, thus providing greater CPD performance detail. These measure suite elements tend to be monotonic; thus, they are difficult to use individually to quantify overall CPD performance.

4. If the summary statistic only generates a single value, it is by definition B^*. B^* can also be a range. If there are multiple B^*s, they need not be continuous.

5. For example, measures used for CPD evaluation have been tested for invariance to various JPT perturbations [6]. Sokolova and Lapalme claim to be the first to comprehensively assess invariance to JPT perturbations; no boundary invariance assessments are known and only one summary statistic, AUC, claims boundary invariance. This study observes boundary effect on the metrics, but does not look for a basis for boundary invariance. This is left for future work.

6. The receiver operating characteristic originated in signal theory and gained its name from that problem domain. ROC, however, is now commonly used to analyze categorical data represented in JPTs. Although "receiver operating characteristic" may be the most commonly seen label in the literature, "relative operating characteristic," being less domain specific, has been proposed as a more appropriate name.

7. End user knowledge regarding actual input population probabilities for their environment may vary. As pointed out later, such information may be either important or confounding.

8. The example in Section 6 presents a case with two physician's offices. One was a general practitioner, where patients tested for RA had an rCS of 0.01 (RA$_+$/RA$_-$). The other was a rheumatologist. In that office, patients tested for RA had an rCS of 100 (RA$_+$/RA$_-$).

9. MCC is often touted as being rCS-invariant. This, however, is only true in a special case. This and related implications are discussed in Section 5.
10. IC is also considered to be rCS-invariant. As with MCC, this is only true in a special case.
11. Or their complements, the probability that desired observations are incorrectly identified and the probability that desired observations are mistakenly labeled as undesired.
12. A Google scholar search for "Matthews correlation coefficient" turned up well over one thousand articles. The publications cited are but a small sample.
13. Using the results shown in Figures 5(a) and 5(b) as an example, if a test was run on a sample with rCS $= 2^8$ on raw JPTs, the MCC $\simeq 0.33$ and $B^* \simeq 1.1$. Recalculating MCC for the normalized JPT observed at rCS $= 2^8$ and $B^* \simeq 1.1$, results in MCC < 0.69. However, the actual peak is MCC > 0.85.
14. Independence is a highly overloaded term. In this context, it means that any change to T_+ will not affect T_-.
15. DOR and DP are seen frequently in medical studies. In this problem domain, the inappropriate boundary risk may not always be present. The risk would exist in a study of heart attacks versus cholesterol levels; cholesterol level is a continuous variable. However, in a study of heart attacks versus family history, family history could be binary (a close relative died/did not die). In this type of test, boundary sensitivity is not an issue; care must be taken, however, in test design. Just by changing the test to a count ("how many close relatives died/did not die," for instance) causes the problem to reappear.
16. DP and DOR are measured on different scales than the other summary statistics. In order to facilitate comparison, DOR was converted from an "odds ratio" type measure (bounded by $[0, \infty]$) to a "probability" type measure (bounded by $[0, 1]$). The relation between the two forms is

$$\text{probability measure} = 1 - \frac{1}{\text{odds measure} + 1}. \quad \text{(D.5)}$$

17. There is a similar measurement suite the "detection error tradeoff" (DET) [56]. DET plots the missed detection rate instead of the correct detection rate on the y axis. Since the two values are each other's complement, comments herein regarding ROC apply equally to DET. Interestingly, DET is plotted using log scales. This is a real challenge for measures with a lower bound of zero.
18. Since all of the inherently rCS-invariant measures studies have {TPR, FPR} as measurement suites, the ROC curve could be presented for each of them as well.
19. We noticed a similar effect on the measure's values. The values started becoming overly optimistic (once again, excepting DOR, the values of which dropped). The cause turned out to be a well-known issue with absolute sample size. The effect became significant when class A's size fell below 400 elements.
20. Pdf standardization is confounding when evaluating a problem where rCS is important; thus, standardization is not appropriate for all problems. The set of all CPD problems is greater than the set of problems where pdf standardization is useful. Likewise, the set of all pdf comparisons includes problems with other than overlapping (or potentially overlapping) probability distribution functions, hence, the CPD problem domain intersects with the pdf comparison domain, but is neither a superset nor a subset.
21. This expression does not require that rCS $= 1$ initially. With the exception of Y or $\overline{Y}$ equaling zero, any JPT can be transformed (tuned) from one rCS to another.
22. There may be a solution to this deficiency; we will investigate this in future work.
23. As nicely summarized by [57], meta-analysis is a statistical technique for combining the findings from independent studies. Meta-analysis is most often used to assess the clinical effectiveness of healthcare interventions; it does this by combining data from two or more randomized control trials. Meta-analysis of trials provides a precise estimate of treatment effect, giving due weight to the size of the different studies included. The validity of the meta-analysis depends on the quality of the systematic review on which it is based. Good meta-analyses aim for complete coverage of all relevant studies, look for the presence of heterogeneity, and explore the robustness of the main findings using sensitivity analysis.
24. Anti-CCP refers to an assay using cyclic citrullinated peptide (CCP) to detect the anti-CCP antibody.
25. RF is an initialism referring to rheumatoid factor, an antibody used as a marker for RA.
26. On a single tailed test as used here, only one bound is relevant; thus, the bound indicates a 97.5% confidence.
27. In a CPD setting where rCS is important, JPT tuning enables a capability previously unavailable: sensitivity analysis. For the practitioner, this means that CPD performance can be evaluated for the expected rCS. Moreover, CPD performance can be identified over the rCS range the practitioner might expect.
28. The implications of the difference between TAR and T_+ F-score will be addressed in future work.
29. All of the other measures are bound. In order to facilitate comparison, DOR was transformed from an "odds" format to the equivalent "probability" format.

References

[1] A. Jamain and D. J. Hand, "Mining supervised classification performance studies: a meta-analytic investigation," *Journal of Classification*, vol. 25, no. 1, pp. 87–112, 2008.

[2] R. P. W. Duin, "A note on comparing classifiers," *Pattern Recognition Letters*, vol. 17, no. 5, pp. 529–536, 1996.

[3] D. J. Hand, *Measurement Theory and Practice: The World Through Quantification*, Oxford University Press, New York, NY, USA, 2004.

[4] D. Böhning, W. Böhning, and H. Holling, "Revisiting Youden's index as a useful measure of the misclassification error in meta-analysis of diagnostic studies," *Statistical Methods in Medical Research*, vol. 17, no. 6, pp. 543–554, 2008.

[5] R. Caruana and A. Niculescu-Mizil, "Data mining in metric space: an empirical analysis of supervised learning performance criteria," in *Proceedings of the 10th ACM SIGKDD International Conference on Knowledge Discovery and Data Mining (KDD'04)*, pp. 69–78, August 2004.

[6] J. Davis and M. Goadrich, "The relationship between precision-recall and ROC curves," in *Proceedings of the 23rd International Conference on Machine Learning (ICML'06)*, pp. 233–240, June 2006.

[7] J. M. Fardy, "Evaluation of diagnostic tests," *Methods in Molecular Biology*, vol. 473, pp. 127–136, 2009.

[8] C. Ferri, J. Hernández-Orallo, and R. Modroiu, "An experimental comparison of performance measures for classification," *Pattern Recognition Letters*, vol. 30, no. 1, pp. 27–38, 2009.

[9] V. García, R. A. Mollineda, and J. S. Sánchez, "Theoretical analysis of a performance measure for imbalanced data," in *Proceedings of the 20th International Conference on Pattern Recognition (ICPR'10)*, pp. 617–620, Istanbul, Turkey, August 2010.

[10] Q. Gu, L. Zhu, and Z. Cai, "Evaluation measures of the classification performance of imbalanced data sets," *Communications in Computer and Information Science*, vol. 51, pp. 461–471, 2009.

[11] N. Japkowicz, "Why question machine learning evaluation methods?" in *Proceedings of the AAAI Evaluation Methods for Machine Learning Workshop*, pp. 6–11, July 2006.

[12] R. Potolea and C. Lemnaru, "A comprehensive study of the effect of class imbalance on the performance of classifiers," 2012, http://search.utcluj.ro/articole/Comprehensive Study.pdf.

[13] M. Sokolova, N. Japkowicz, and S. Szpakowicz, "Beyond accuracy, F-score and ROC: a family of discriminant measures for performance evaluation," in *Proceedings of the AI 2006: Advances in Artificial Intelligence*, pp. 1015–1021, July 2006.

[14] M. Sokolova and G. Lapalme, "A systematic analysis of performance measures for classification tasks," *Information Processing and Management*, vol. 45, no. 4, pp. 427–437, 2009.

[15] W. J. Youden, "Index for rating diagnostic tests," *Cancer*, vol. 3, no. 1, pp. 32–35, 1950.

[16] A. S. Glas, J. G. Lijmer, M. H. Prins, G. J. Bonsel, and P. M. M. Bossuyt, "The diagnostic odds ratio: a single indicator of test performance," *Journal of Clinical Epidemiology*, vol. 56, no. 11, pp. 1129–1135, 2003.

[17] D. D. Blakeley, E. Z. Oddone, V. Hasselblad, D. L. Simel, and D. B. Matchar, "Noninvasive carotid artery testing. A meta-analytic review," *Annals of Internal Medicine*, vol. 122, no. 5, pp. 360–367, 1995.

[18] B. W. Matthews, "Comparison of the predicted and observed secondary structure of T4 phage lysozyme," *Biochimica et Biophysica Acta*, vol. 405, no. 2, pp. 442–451, 1975.

[19] T. Fawcett, "An introduction to ROC analysis," *Pattern Recognition Letters*, vol. 27, no. 8, pp. 861–874, 2006.

[20] J. A. Swets, "Measuring the accuracy of diagnostic systems," *Science*, vol. 240, no. 4857, pp. 1285–1293, 1988.

[21] P. Baldi, S. Brunak, Y. Chauvin, C. A. F. Andersen, and H. Nielsen, "Assessing the accuracy of prediction algorithms for classification: an overview," *Bioinformatics*, vol. 16, no. 5, pp. 412–424, 2000.

[22] B. Rost and C. Sander, "Prediction of protein secondary structure at better than 70% accuracy," *Journal of Molecular Biology*, vol. 232, no. 2, pp. 584–599, 1993.

[23] K. H. Brodersen, C. S. Ong, K. E. Stephan, and J. M. Buhmann, "The balanced accuracy and its posterior distribution," in *Proceedings of the 20th International Conference on Pattern Recognition (ICPR'10)*, pp. 3121–3124, Istanbul, Turkey, August 2010.

[24] A. Frank and A. Asuncion, "UCI machine learning repository," 2010, http://archive.ics.uci.edu/ml/.

[25] S. S. Stevens, "On the theory of scales of measurement," *Science*, vol. 103, no. 2684, pp. 677–680, 1946.

[26] C. J. van Rijsbergen, "Information Retrieval," 1979, http://www.dcs.gla.ac.uk/Keith/Preface.html.

[27] C. W. Cleverdon, "The critical appraisal of information retrieval systems," 1968, http://hdl.handle.net/1826/1366.

[28] E. O. Cannon, A. Bender, D. S. Palmer, and J. B. O. Mitchell, "Chemoinformatics-based classification of prohibited substances employed for doping in sport," *Journal of Chemical Information and Modeling*, vol. 46, no. 6, pp. 2369–2380, 2006.

[29] O. Carugo, "Detailed estimation of bioinformatics prediction reliability through the fragmented prediction performance plots," *BMC Bioinformatics*, vol. 8, article 380, 2007.

[30] P. Chatterjee, S. Basu, M. Kundu, M. Nasipuri, and D. Plewczynski, "PSP_MCSVM: brainstorming consensus prediction of protein secondary structures using two-stage multiclass support vector machines," *Journal of Molecular Modeling*, vol. 17, no. 9, pp. 2191–2201, 2011.

[31] P. Dao, K. Wang, C. Collins, M. Ester, A. Lapuk, and S. C. Sahinalp, "Optimally discriminative subnetwork markers predict response to chemotherapy," *Bioinformatics*, vol. 27, no. 13, pp. i205–i213, 2011.

[32] K. K. Kandaswamy, K. C. Chou, T. Martinetz et al., "AFP-Pred: a random forest approach for predicting antifreeze proteins from sequence-derived properties," *Journal of Theoretical Biology*, vol. 270, no. 1, pp. 56–62, 2011.

[33] T. Y. Lee, C. T. Lu, S. A. Chen et al., "Investigation and identification of protein-glutamyl carboxylation sites," in *Proceedings of the 10th International Conference on Bioinformatics. 1st ISCB Asia Joint Conference 2011: Bioinformatics*, 2011.

[34] G. Mirceva, A. Naumoski, and D. Davcev, "A novel fuzzy decision tree based method for detecting protein active sites," *Advances in Intelligent and Soft Computing*, vol. 150, pp. 51–60, 2012.

[35] M. S. Cline, K. Karplus, R. H. Lathrop, T. F. Smith, R. G. Rogers, and D. Haussler, "Information-theoretic dissection of pairwise contact potentials," *Proteins*, vol. 49, no. 1, pp. 7–14, 2002.

[36] C. Kauffman and G. Karypis, "An analysis of information content present in protein-DNA interactions," *Pacific Symposium on Biocomputing*, pp. 477–488, 2008.

[37] M. Kulharia, R. S. Goody, and R. M. Jackson, "Information theory-based scoring function for the structure-based prediction of protein-ligand binding affinity," *Journal of Chemical Information and Modeling*, vol. 48, no. 10, pp. 1990–1998, 2008.

[38] T. J. Magliery and L. Regan, "Sequence variation in ligand binding sites in proteins," *BMC Bioinformatics*, vol. 6, article 240, 2005.

[39] C. S. Miller and D. Eisenberg, "Using inferred residue contacts to distinguish between correct and incorrect protein models," *Bioinformatics*, vol. 24, no. 14, pp. 1575–1582, 2008.

[40] O. G. Othersen, A. G. Stefani, J. B. Huber, and H. Sticht, "Application of information theory to feature selection in protein docking," *Journal of Molecular Modeling*, vol. 18, no. 4, pp. 1285–1297, 2012.

[41] A. D. Solis and S. Rackovsky, "Information and discrimination in pairwise contact potentials," *Proteins*, vol. 71, no. 3, pp. 1071–1087, 2008.

[42] B. Sterner, R. Singh, and B. Berger, "Predicting and annotating catalytic residues: an information theoretic approach," *Journal of Computational Biology*, vol. 14, no. 8, pp. 1058–1073, 2007.

[43] A. M. Wassermann, B. Nisius, M. Vogt, and J. Bajorath, "Identification of descriptors capturing compound class-specific features by mutual information analysis," *Journal of Chemical Information and Modeling*, vol. 50, no. 11, pp. 1935–1940, 2010.

[44] J. Francois, H. Abdelnur, R. State, and O. Festor, "Ptf: passive temporal fingerprinting," in *Proceedings of the 12th IFIP/IEEE International Symposium on Integrated Network Management*, pp. 289–296, Dublin, UK, 2011.

[45] T. M. Cover and J. A. Thomas, *Elements of Information Theory*, Wiley Series in Telecommunications, John Wiley & Sons, New York, NY, USA, 1991.

[46] R. W. Yeung, *A First Course in Information Theory. Information Technology: Transmission, Processing and Storage*, Kluwer Academic, New York, NY, USA, 2002.

[47] J. A. Swets, "Form of empirical ROCs in discrimination and diagnostic tasks. Implications for theory and measurement of performance," *Psychological Bulletin*, vol. 99, no. 2, pp. 181–198, 1986.

[48] J. A. Swets, "Indices of discrimination or diagnostic accuracy. Their ROCs and implied models," *Psychological Bulletin*, vol. 99, no. 1, pp. 100–117, 1986.

[49] D. Johnson, "Performance evaluation," 2003, http://cnx.org/content/m11274/1.3/content_info.

[50] J. M. Lobo, A. Jiménez-valverde, and R. Real, "AUC: a misleading measure of the performance of predictive distribution models," *Global Ecology and Biogeography*, vol. 17, no. 2, pp. 145–151, 2008.

[51] D. J. Hand, "Measuring classifier performance: a coherent alternative to the area under the ROC curve," *Machine Learning*, vol. 77, no. 1, pp. 103–123, 2009.

[52] S. Vanderlooy and E. Hüllermeier, "A critical analysis of variants of the AUC," *Machine Learning*, vol. 72, no. 3, pp. 247–262, 2008.

[53] M. Majnik and Z. Bosnic, "ROC analysis of classifers in machine learning: survey," Tech. Rep. MM-1/2011, Faculty of Computer and Information Science, University of Ljubljana, 2011.

[54] K. Nishimura, D. Sugiyama, Y. Kogata et al., "Meta-analysis: diagnostic accuracy of anti-cyclic citrullinated peptide antibody and rheumatoid factor for rheumatoid arthritis," *Annals of Internal Medicine*, vol. 146, no. 11, pp. 797–808, 2007.

[55] M. Schonlau, W. DuMouchel, W. H. Ju, A. F. Karr, M. Theus, and Y. Vardi, "Computer intrusion: detecting masquerades," *Statistical Science*, vol. 16, no. 1, pp. 58–74, 2001.

[56] A. Martin, G. Doddington, T. Kamm, M. Ordowski, and M. Przybocki, "The DET curve in assessment of detection task performance," in *Proceedings of the 5th European Conference on Speech Communication and Technology*, pp. 1895–1898, Rhodes, Greece, 1997.

[57] I. K. Crombie and H. T. Davies, "What is meta-analysis?. 'What is ... ?,'" series NPR09/1112, Hayward Medical Communications, 2009.

9

Tree Pruning for New Search Techniques in Computer Games

Kieran Greer

Distributed Computing Systems, Belfast, UK

Correspondence should be addressed to Kieran Greer; kgreer@distributedcomputingsystems.co.uk

Academic Editor: Srinivas Bangalore

This paper proposes a new mechanism for pruning a search game tree in computer chess. The algorithm stores and then reuses chains or sequences of moves, built up from previous searches. These move sequences have a built-in forward-pruning mechanism that can radically reduce the search space. A typical search process might retrieve a move from a Transposition Table, where the decision of what move to retrieve would be based on the position itself. This algorithm stores move sequences based on what previous sequences were better, or caused cutoffs. The sequence is then returned based on the current move only. This is therefore position independent and could also be useful in games with imperfect information or uncertainty, where the whole situation is not known at any one time. Over a small set of tests, the algorithm was shown to clearly out perform Transposition Tables, both in terms of search reduction and game-play results. Finally, a completely new search process will be suggested for computer chess or games in general.

1. Introduction

This paper describes a new way of dynamically linking moves into sequences that can be used to optimise a search process. The context is to optimise the search process for the game of computer chess. Move sequences are returned during the searching of the chess game tree that cause a cutoff, or determine that certain parts of the tree do not need to be searched further. These move sequences are usually stored in Transposition Tables [1, 2], but instead, they can be stored in a dynamic linking structure and reused in the same way. They can return an already evaluated sequence of moves, which removes the need to search the tree structure that would have resulted in this move sequence. The term "chain" instead of "sequence" will be used to describe the new structure specifically. Move sequence is a more general term that can be used to describe any searched move sequence.

This research has been carried out using an existing computer chess game-playing program called Chessmaps. The Chessmaps Heuristic [3] was created as part of a DPhil research project that was completed in 1998. The intention was to try and add some intelligence into a chess game-playing program. If the goal is to build the best possible chess program, then the experience-based approach has probably solved the problem already, as the best programs are now

better or at least equal to the best human players. Computer chess can also be used, however, simply as a domain for testing AI-related algorithms. It is still an interesting platform for trying to mimic the human thought process or add human-like intelligence to a game-playing program. Exactly this argument, along with some other points made in this paper, are also written or thought about in [4, 5]. While chess provides too much variability for the whole game to be defined, it is still a small enough domain to make it possible to accurately evaluate different kinds of search and evaluation processes. It provides complete information about its environment, meaning that the evaluation functions can be reliable, and is not so complex that trying to encapsulate the process in a comprehensive manner would be impossible.

The rest of the paper is structured as follows: Section 2 describes the original Chessmaps Heuristic that can be used to order moves as part of a search process. Section 3 describes the dynamic move-linking mechanism that is the new research of this paper. Section 4 describes some other AI-related chess game-playing programs. Section 5 describes some test results from tests performed using the new linking mechanism. Section 6 describes how the linking mechanism could lead to other types of research, while Section 7 gives some conclusions on the work.

2. Chessmaps Heuristic

The Chessmaps Heuristic [3] uses a neural network as a positional evaluator for a search heuristic. The neural network is taught to recognise what areas of the board a piece should be moved to, based on what areas of the board each side controls. The piece move is actually calculated based on what squares it attacks, or influences, after it has moved, which therefore includes the long range influence of the piece.

The neural network can be trained on saved game scores for any player, including grandmaster games. The chess position can be converted into a board that defines what squares each side controls and this is then used as the input to training the neural network. The move played in that position can be converted into the squares that the move played influences. These are the squares that the moved piece attacks, and these are used as the output that the neural network then tries to recognise. The theory behind this is that there is a definite relation between the squares that a player controls and the squares that the player moves his/her pieces to, or the areas the player then plays to, when formulating a plan. The neural network by itself proved not to be accurate enough, but as it required the control of the squares to be calculated, this allowed several other move types to be recognised. One division would be to split the moves into safe and unsafe. Unsafe moves would lead to loss of material on the square the piece was moved to, while safe moves would not. It was also possible to recognise capture, forced, and forcing moves. Forced moves would be ones where the piece would have to move because it could be captured with a gain of material. Forcing moves were moves that forced the opponent to move a piece because it could then be captured with a gain of material. This resulted in moves being looked at as part of a search process in the following order:

    (1) safe capture moves;

    (2) safe forced moves;

    (3) safe forcing moves;

    (4) safe other moves;

    (5) unsafe capture moves;

    (6) unsafe forced moves;

    (7) unsafe forcing moves;

    (8) unsafe other moves.

The Chessmaps Heuristic is therefore used as the move-ordering heuristic at each position in the tree search. The neural network was really only used to order the moves in the "other" moves category, although this would still be a large majority of the moves. The research therefore resulted in a heuristic that was knowledge based, but also still lightweight enough to be used as part of a brute-force alpha-beta (α-β) search. Test results showed that it would reduce the search by more than the History Heuristic [1], but because of its additional computational requirements; it would use more time to search for a move and would ultimately be inferior. The heuristic, however, proved difficult to optimize in code, for example, trying to create quick move generators through

bitmap boards, and so the only way to reduce the search time would probably be to introduce more AI-related techniques into the program. This has led to the following new suggestion for dynamic move sequences.

3. Dynamic Move Sequences

Two of the most popular experience-based approaches to minimising the search process are the History Heuristic and Transposition Tables [1, 2]. Tests have shown that using combinations of heuristics can produce a search reduction that is close to the minimal tree. This means that it is possible to reduce the size of an exhaustive or full search, close to what a perfect move ordering would produce. Perfect move ordering would select the best move first, second best second, and so on, at every node in the search tree. Transposition Tables, however, replace part of the search process with a result that has already been stored and so in effect forward prune, or remove, parts of the search tree. This means that it would be able, in theory, to produce a search tree size that was less than this minimum value. The History Heuristic is attractive because of its simplicity and also its compact form. It can represent all of the moves in a single 64-square board array. Transposition Tables can become very large in size, therefore requiring an indexing system to search over thousands of entries or more, to find a position that relates to the one currently being searched. The question arises could it not be possible to represent the Transposition Table information in a more compact form, if all of the moves can be represented in a 64-square board array? This might not be possible for Transposition Tables, as they need to index position descriptions themselves, but the dynamic move sequences will use this sort of structure.

The main structure for storing dynamic move sequences is a 64-square board array. During a normal α-β search, when a move sequence is found that causes a cutoff in the search process, it can be stored in this array by storing the first move in the array element, representing the first move's "move from" square. The entry then also stores all of the other move information, such as the "move to" square or the piece type. Multiple entries for different pieces can then be stored individually for the same square. This first move then stores a link to the second move, which stores a link to the next move, and so on. Each move could also have a weight value associated with it that would be incremented or decremented, based on whether the move sequence is subsequently found to be useful or not. The current implementation, however, does not require this, as any stored moves are automatically used again.

There are differences and similarities between the move chains and Transposition Tables. One thing is that these move sequences can be removed as well as added. Another is that Transposition Tables retrieve a move sequence for the "position" being currently searched, whereas the move chains do not consider the position but retrieve a possible move sequence for the "move" currently being looked at. The transformation processes are related, however, where any move played will lead to a position that could be stored in

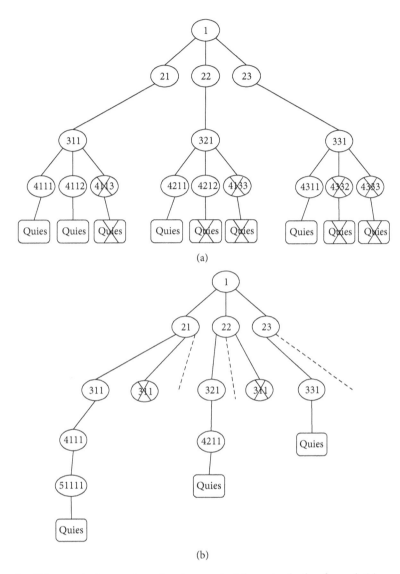

FIGURE 1: Diagram showing the difference in the number of nodes searched for a standard α-β search (a) or a search with dynamic move sequences (b).

a table, or any position evaluation retrieved from a table will result in a move that could be stored in a move chain. The difference then is that the position evaluation is exact and static, whereas the move path evaluation is dynamic and needs to be checked again before it can be used.

The argument for storing general information in experience-based heuristics is the fact that positions in a search tree vary only slightly from one ply to the next and so if some information is retrieved, it is likely to be useful again, even if it does not exactly match the current position. Dynamic move sequences can also use this argument. The positions that the move chains are used in (over a single search) should be closely related to each other, so if the move sequence is legal, it might be useful in a different position as well. Unreliable sequences then need to be removed when necessary, and this is helped by constantly updating the information on the stored move chains. Figure 1 is a diagram showing the potential difference in the number of nodes searched using a

standard α-β search or using dynamic move sequences. Note that this is only illustrative and is not meant to be accurate. Table 1 gives more accurate numbers. The figure is intended to show simply that the standard search is much broader and exhaustive. It will prune more, from the first branch to the last, as the window of acceptable moves narrows. The new algorithm will produce much narrower and deeper searches on every branch. The dashed lines show where possibly forward pruning has taken place. With fewer moves being considered; this is prone to miss critical moves, however.

Figure 1(a) shows a game tree searched to a particular depth, with certain nodes being pruned through the α-β minimax algorithm. These nodes are crossed out with Xs. Considering the nodes in the subtree of the node labeled "21", for example, the diagram shows that there are 5 standard node evaluations and a further two quiescence searches after this. Note that a node must be evaluated before its sub tree can be discarded. The quiescence search is much deeper but

TABLE 1: Comparison of node count for 98 game positions with the Chessmaps Heuristic, plus either transposition tables or dynamic move sequences.

	Chessmaps	Chessmaps + TT	Chessmaps + DMS
Depth 5	653134.3918	438067.3505	15365.72165
Reduction	0%	33%	97.5%
Depth 6	3263162.34	2467462.031	18920.76289
Reduction	0%	24.5%	99%

considers only forcing or capture moves, until a quiescent or stable position is reached. If Figure 1(b) represents the same tree, but including dynamic move sequences, then the valid move sequences forward prune the tree by replacing large parts of it. Only the paths in the move chains are considered and not the full sub tree with multiple branches. This can occur at any level in the tree. It is also dynamic, where an incorrect evaluation will remove the chain and allow for a full search the next time the move is encountered.

4. Related Work

The brute-force programs are still the most successful. They rely more on program optimization and speed, to search more positions and therefore obtain a more accurate evaluation. There are also, however, a number of strong AI-related programs, some of which are listed here. A summary of recent advances in AI game playing can be found in [6]. KnightCap [7] is possibly one of the best AI attempts at playing computer chess, based on its playing strength. It uses a variation of the Temporal Difference machine learning algorithm called TD Leaf (λ). The core idea of TD learning is that we adjust predictions to match other, more accurate, predictions about the feature. Accuracy can be obtained through deeper searches (more time) or evaluations of models that are closer to the known result. A similar mechanism was used in the NeuroChess program [8]. Blondie25 [9] is another example of a chess game-playing program that uses an evolutionary method to learn to play, as does [5]. These programs try to learn the evaluation function through feedback from playing a number of games, to adjust weight values related to features, to fine tune the evaluation criteria. They are therefore flexible in the sense that the criteria are not hard coded beforehand and are improved through machine learning. In [4] they use a Bayesian network to adapt the program's game-playing strategy to its opponent, as well as to adapt the evaluation function.

As the tree search process is almost optimised, the most important aspect of the computer chess program now is probably the evaluation function. The optimisation results, however, are compared to the brute-force α-β search, but with forward pruning it is possible to produce even smaller search trees. The smaller the search tree, the more information that can be added to the evaluation function, and so trying to minimise the search further is still important. While not directly related to computer chess, the paper [10] describes recent advances in dynamic search processes. Their algorithm called Learning Depth-First Search (LDFS) aims to be both

general and effective. It performs iterated depth-first searches enhanced with learning. They claim that LDFS shows that the key idea underlying several existing heuristic-search algorithms over various settings is the use of iterated depth-first searches with memory, for improving the heuristics over certain relevant states until they become optimal. Storing move chains is also a memory structure that is dynamic and built up over time. The dynamic moves approach also probably has similar intentions to the UCT search algorithms [11, 12]. These search to variable depths, select what branches to expand further, and are able to deal with large search trees or uncertainty. The paper [11] describes how TD learning is offline, while UCT is online. It also states

> At every time-step the UCT algorithm builds a search tree, estimating the value function at each state by Monte-Carlo simulation. After each simulated episode, the values in the tree are updated online and the simulation policy is improved with respect to the new values. These values represent local knowledge that is highly specialised to the current state.

The move chains mechanism, however, appears to be very different. The process does not require the intelligence that something comparing states might do but is more automatic. In this research that means simply: if they are legal move sequences and evaluated as better through the evaluation function. The bandit algorithms, such as UCT, appear to rely on aggregating statistical values, to build up a more knowledgeable picture of what nodes are good or bad.

5. Testing

5.1. Search to Fixed Depth for Different Algorithm Versions. This set of tests tried three different search algorithms on the same set of positions but to fixed depths of 5 or 6 ply for each position. The search process automatically applies a minimal window and iterative deepening to each search that is performed. As well as this, the three algorithms tested included: either the Chessmaps Heuristic by itself, the Chessmaps Heuristic and Transposition Tables, with 1000000 entries for each side, or the Chessmaps Heuristic with Dynamic Move Sequences. Table 1 gives the results of the test searches.

The first line of numbers is the actual search results, while the second line is the percentage difference between Chessmaps by itself and the other mechanism that it is compared to. The reduction row describes the amount of extra search reduction that either the Transposition Tables or the move chains produce over just the Chessmaps Heuristic. The Transposition Tables that are implemented as part of the Chessmaps program can be considered as a standard variation of the mechanism. They produce a significant reduction in the number of nodes searched, as shown in the table. The move chains then produce an even larger search reduction by radically forward pruning the search tree. Most of the generated move chains were in fact only to a depth of 1 move but could be to depth of 3 or 4 moves. Algorithm 1

```
moveList = generateMoves();

while (moveList not empty) {
        nextMove = getNextMove();

        if (nextMove in moveChains) {
                moveSequence = getMoveSequence(nextMove, moveChains);
                if (isValid(moveSequence)) {
                        linkPath = moveSequence;
                        nextEval = evalSearch(linkPath, then rest of a-b plus quies);
                } else {
                        remove moveSquence from moveChains;
                        linkPath = null;
                }
        } else {
                linkPath = null;
        }

        if (linkPath == null) {
                nextEval = evalSearch(full a-b search + quies);
        }

        if (nextEval > bestEval) {
                bestEval = nextEval;
                bestMove = nextMove;
        }

        if (bestEval > alpha) {
                alpha = bestEval;
                bestPath = serchPath;
                if (linkPath != null) update linkPath in moveChains;
        }
}
always add final bestPath to moveChains;


function update_linkPath {
        if (path exists under move key) {
                replace with linkPath;
        } else {
                add linkPath as new path with first move as key;
        }
}
```

ALGORITHM 1: Search algorithm with move chains, highlighting where move chains are used.

describes how the move chains are used as part of a search process.

In words this could be:

(1) When playing a move at a node, check for an exact match in the move chains structure. This can include to/from squares, move type, and pieces on the squares.

(2) If a move sequence exists as a link path then:

    (a) retrieve the link path and play the sequence to make sure that it is legal;

    (b) if it is legal then:

        (i) perform a search that is: the link path first, then a standard α-β search plus quiescence. Search depths for full searches can be cut if they exceed the current maximum allowed;

    (c) if it is illegal then:

        (i) remove the path from the move chains structure;

        (ii) perform a standard α-β search to the desired depth plus quiescence.

(3) If the current evaluation is better than the best for this node:

    (a) set the node's best value to the current evaluation;

    (b) set the node's best path to the current search path;

    (c) if the node's best value is better than alpha:

       (i) set alpha to the current best value;

       (ii) if the link path is valid, update the move chains structure to store the path.

(4) Always add any final path to the move chains structure.

This is probably just one variation of what could be a more flexible algorithm and mainly outlines where the move chains are used. This would be integrated as part of an α-β minimax algorithm, where the minimax values determine the cutoffs. In this version, the move chains replace almost exactly where the Transposition Table would be used. Any entry is automatically used if legal, and any new entry automatically overwrites an existing entry, as it is considered to be closer to the final solution. Any entry found not to be legal is automatically removed. The traditional assumption is that this should invalidate the search process, because the search tree can be different, and so critical moves are likely to be missed. The results of playing the two algorithms against each other, as described in Section 5.2, however, show that this is not the case. So can an argument be made for why these shallow move chain searches might work? Suppose that a move chain is stored that is only one move deep. It is only stored if the move was evaluated as better or caused a cutoff, which is only after a stabilizing quiescence search as well. Also, consider the fact that only the first positions in a search process are searched to the full depth. The leaf nodes are only searched to a depth of 1, plus the extensions. So this algorithm is treating more of the nodes like this. Because it is dynamic, the evaluations of the stored moves are constantly changing and being updated, which will help to maintain its accuracy. There might in fact be quite a lot of consistency between the nodes in the search tree, primarily because they originate from the same position and differ only slightly. The previous search results will then compensate for the shallow depth of a move chain plus forward pruning.

5.2. Playing the Different Algorithms against Each Other. The computer program is able to play different algorithms against each other. In these tests, the Chessmaps algorithm with Transposition Tables and a standard brute-force α-β search, was played against the Chessmaps algorithm with the Dynamic Move Sequences search algorithm. Both versions used an iterative deepening search with minimum window as well. There is also a random opening selector, so each game started from a different position. Tests were run over 100 games—50 with Chessmaps plus Transposition Tables as White and 50 with Chessmaps plus Dynamic Move Sequences as White. This test was repeated three times. Each side was allowed 30 minutes to play each game, with the results shown in Table 2.

These results are not meant to be definitive but should show that the new search algorithm is a viable alternative,

TABLE 2: Results of three hundred 30 minute games between transposition tables versus dynamic move sequences.

Draw	MinWin + CM + TT	MinWin + CM + DMS
102	80	118

with the idea of using dynamic move sequences being a sound one. These results show that using the dynamic move sequences with the Chessmaps Heuristic outperforms using Transposition Tables with the Chessmaps Heuristic, with the move chains version winning more games. The Chessmaps program is still only a prototype program and is missing modules or functions that would be included in a complete program. There is no real knowledge of endgame play, for example, where the program will tend to play more aimlessly and be happy to concede a draw by repetition, in a clearly winning position. On the other hand, in certain middlegame positions where its positional evaluator should work well, it does play strongly. It is still a bit buggy and can produce errors, but the testing and results have been performed under reliable circumstances. So a rough evaluation of playing strength might be a strong club player, although, this is not particularly strong for computer chess programs these days.

5.3. Longer Games. In half-hour games, the dynamic linking mechanism was better. In hour-long games, however, the standard brute-force α-β search appears to be improved. While either variation could win, the general standard of play was possibly equal. Unfortunately, it was difficult to quantify this accurately through multiple runs, as a bug could creep in, particularly around king checks and further on in the game. Viewing play before the program became buggy, however, showed an equal strength, with only minor things changing the game state and final result. A limit on the maximum depth allowed for the move chains' α-β search, helped a bit, but did not remove the bug completely. These results also suggest improvements that could be made to the search process, which are described in Section 6.

Because the bug was relatively easy to spot, through watching the play, and it never happened during the half-hour games, this suggests that the half-hour games were played correctly. The variation that used move chains could search to a depth of 20 ply or more, but there is not much benefit in searching this deep. The evaluation function is unlikely to generate a better evaluation, especially from a narrow search. The standard broader search, however, would really benefit from searching one or two ply more. It would therefore be able to make more of the extra time and produce a better evaluation during the hour-long games. So if the move chains statistically won again, the conclusion would be definitive, but as the two variations are instead more equal, the argument is that this actually helps to validate the earlier results. It also suggests that there should be a limit put on the maximum search depth and points out some failings that would occur against stronger searches.

5.4. Other Statistical Results. Some other statistical results were as follows. If considering the move chains, a quiescence search could search 15 to 40 times more nodes than the α-β search. For the search process, dynamic move chains would be retrieved only during the α-β search and for possibly 1/3 to 1/2 of the nodes searched in that part. This is, however, comparing moves to nodes but means that when a set of moves was evaluated at a node, a chain would be retrieved this number of times. It is estimated that on average, 6 moves are evaluated in a middlegame position, so a move chain would be retrieved possibly 1 in 12 to 1 in 18 times. The move chain would then be used possibly 1/2 to 3/4 of the time that a chain was retrieved. This is quite a high value and suggests some reliability behind the move chain and therefore also the relation between the nodes in the search tree. One other point to note is that the dynamic approach does not appear to use its time as well as the full α-β search and usually has more time left at the end of a game. Even for the half-hour games, the dynamic approach would have maybe 40–50% more time left over at the end. So it would be able to freely add extra evaluations without a time penalty. It would therefore benefit more from broadening its search and not deepening it further.

6. Future Work

The dynamic move sequences are a bit like dynamic chunking, where a player would recognise and play combinations he/she has seen before. In this case, the table stores move sequences instead of positions that can maybe be thought of as tactical chunks. Why compare to a tactical chunk? The aim of these chunks is to suggest relevant moves in a position. Tactics are about moves, not positional evaluation, and so move sequences known to be good could be thought of as chunks of tactical knowledge. Being able to react to individual moves would be useful for games with imperfect information as well.

6.1. Feature Extraction. Early work on knowledge-based approaches to playing computer chess tried to recognise key features in a chess position that would be used to determine what the best move might be. It is argued that stronger players are able to recognise these features, or chunks of knowledge [13], and use them better to analyse a position. One knowledge-based approach to building a computer chess program was to ask an expert to manually define these features in many different positions, but this proved impractical. One future research direction would be to store the positions that each move sequence was played in, with the move sequence itself. The set of positions can then be analysed to try and determine what the key features are. This is similar, but the process is slightly automated, and there is some help in determining what to analyse. The move sequences and the positions that the moves were played in are already defined, and so the problem is now to recognise the key difference or similarities in the related positions and not to redefine these key features from previous knowledge. This is still very challenging, however, and it is not clear how it might be done. Figure 2 describes this sort of process again.

In the figure, there is a move sequence and also the two positions that it was played in. These positions share

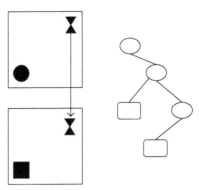

FIGURE 2: Move chain related to two different positions. The similarity in the positions is shown by the hour-glass feature.

one common feature shown by the hour-glass object. If this similarity can be automatically recognised, then the process of storing move chains gives an automatic process both for recognizing what the critical move sequences in a game are and also what the critical features that allowed the moves to be played are. One paper that describes using a predefined set of features is [4] where a relatively simplistic feature set contained 840 different variables, while nearly 6000 features are used in [7].

6.2. New Search Process. Section 5.3 showed how the dynamic move sequences algorithm was inferior for larger searches. It also suggested that a broader search was required for it, while the standard α-β search benefited from a deeper one. As the aim is to produce a more intelligent (and human-like) program, the following suggestions can now be made. Iterative deepening is also an often used heuristic, where a search is performed to, for example, 3 ply. It returns a best path, which is then the first path searched at 4 ply, and so on. If the best path is searched first, then the search is reduced by the greatest amount. Dynamic move sequences search deep enough, so to broaden them, why not try another complete search, but one that largely "excludes" the first search path. The justification would be that the narrow search would miss other legitimate lines of play, and a human also performs this type of task. A player would evaluate a move sequence to some depth and determine if it was good or not. The player would then check a completely new or different line, to see if some other plan was in fact better. The dynamic move sequences search could be widened by performing more than one full search but with the rule that they are mostly exclusive. There might have to be some overlap for single moves or smaller move sequences, and so research would need to determine the practical details of that. This process is also appealing in uncertain games, because full searches are returned up to the time limit. This would allow for full evaluations of something, when alternative plans might be missed completely—a more probabilistic and human approach.

The resulting separate but related narrow full searches suggest a number of potential solutions that can then be evaluated further as the start to new searches. The process could even use a genetic algorithm to take current solutions or searched paths and with evolution combine them into other ones. For this, both negative and positive search paths should be stored, so it would be paths with something critical or important in them. The resulting new paths would also have to be integrated with other full searches but starting from a more limited set of positions. So a different type of iterative process can be performed. The first phase, which is the traditional search using move chains, is almost a knowledge-extraction process that is then reasoned over in the second phase. Note that the positions still need to be stored, to define valid evolutions between existing move sequences, and feature selection would help to define when to crossover or what to mutate. This could still be largely a mechanical process and therefore implementable as part of a computer program.

So this is almost the opposite of what is currently done in more traditional searches, but of course, it uses an α-β variant for its tree searches first. These sorts of processes are also being attempted in general, see for example [10]. This also requires the idea of a "plan", possibly more than other search processes, to intelligently combine solution paths. To help with this, there should be more underlying knowledge, and statistics can also help, by removing bad or poor evolved plans automatically. More intelligence and reasoning appear to be part of new search processes now, in any case.

7. Conclusions

These tests are based on a relatively small number of examples, but they show the potential of the algorithm and confirm that dynamic move sequences are at least reliable. That is, they can be added to a search process and used without returning unreliable moves. Playing against the algorithm also confirms that it is not likely to make a poor move any more often than the other algorithms. So in this respect, move sequences or chains are a viable alternative to Transposition Tables. They also offer a compact solution to indexing the moves and offer new opportunities for research into other more knowledge-based or intelligent ways of playing the game of computer chess. The main danger is probably simply the loss in evaluation quality because of the reduction in the search space. Most of the generated move chains were only to depth 1 but could be to depth 3 or 4, for example. So it is the ability to dynamically update them, the similarity between positions in a search, and the quiescence search that keep the search result accurate.

The test results suggest that the potential of the move chains might be the fact that it can provide a basis for new ways to search a game tree and even under different circumstances. It is shown to be at least equal to the other variants tested, but the different way that it stores information could lead to different search mechanisms that might ultimately prove better in certain types of game. It is not completely clear if this process can be mapped to a human thought process when playing the game. Retrying a combination that a player thought of previously usually requires some positional judgment first. So it might simply be the statistical argument

that supports the other experience-based heuristics. The position changes only slightly from one ply to the next and so if a move is found to be good, then there is a reasonable chance that it will be good in a future position as well. The intention of this research has been to reduce the search process so much that the evaluation function can be made more substantial, to make the whole game-playing process more human like. In this respect, the research has certainly achieved its goal. The future work section describes a new search process that requires additional directed intelligence, but this is now being looked at for other search processes as well.

Disclosure

This paper is a revised version of a white paper "Dynamic Move Chains—a Forward Pruning Approach to Tree Search in Computer Chess", originally published on DCS and Scribd, March 2011.

References

[1] J. Schaeffer, "The history heuristic and alpha-beta search enhancements in practice," *IEEE Transactions on Pattern Analysis and Machine Intelligence*, vol. 11, no. 11, pp. 1203–1212, 1989.

[2] J. Schaeffer and A. Plaat, "New advances in alpha-beta searching," in *Proceedings of the 25th ACM Computer Science Conference*, pp. 124–130, February 1996.

[3] K. Greer, "Computer chess move-ordering schemes using move influence," *Artificial Intelligence*, vol. 120, no. 2, pp. 235–250, 2000.

[4] A. Fernández and A. Salmerón, "BayesChess: a computer chess program based on Bayesian networks," *Pattern Recognition Letters*, vol. 29, no. 8, pp. 1154–1159, 2008.

[5] A. Iqbal, "What computer chess still has to teach us—the game that will not go," *Electronic Journal of Computer Science and Information Technology*, vol. 2, no. 1, pp. 23–29, 2010.

[6] J. Fürnkranz, "Recent advances in machine learning and game playing," *Oesterreichische Gesellschaft fuer Artificial Intelligence Journal*, vol. 26, no. 2, pp. 19–28, 2007.

[7] J. Baxter, A. Tridgell, and L. Weaver, "KnightCap: a chess program that learns by combining TD(lambda) with gametree search," in *Proceedings of the 15th International Conference on Machine Learning*, pp. 28–36, 1998.

[8] S. Thrun, "Learning to play the game of chess," in *Advances in Neural Information Processing Systems 7*, G. Tesauro, D. Touretzky, and T. Leen, Eds., Morgen Kaufmann, San Fransisco, Calif, USA, 1995.

[9] D. B. Fogel, T. J. Hays, S. L. Hahn, and J. Quon, "A self-learning evolutionary chess program," *Proceedings of the IEEE*, vol. 92, no. 12, pp. 1947–1954, 2004.

[10] B. Bonet and H. Geffner, "Learning depth-first search: a unified approach to heuristic search in deterministic and non-deterministic settings, and its application to MDPs," in *Proceedings of the 16th International Conference on Automated Planning and Scheduling (ICAPS'06)*, D. Long, S. F. Smith, D. Borrajo, and L. Mc-Cluskey, Eds., pp. 142–151, June 2006.

[11] S. Gelly and D. Silver, "Combining online and offline knowledge in UCT," in *Proceedings of the 24th International Conference on Machine Learning (ICML'07)*, pp. 273–280, Corvallis, Ore, USA, June 2007.

[12] Y. Wang and S. Gelly, "Modifications of UCT and sequence-like simulations for Monte-Carlo Go," in *Proceedings of the IEEE Symposium on Computational Intelligence and Games (CIG'07)*, pp. 175–182, Honolulu, Hawaii, USA, April 2007.

[13] J. Fürnkranz, "Machine learning in computer chess: the next generation," *The International Computer-Chess Association Journal*, vol. 19, no. 3, pp. 147–161, 1995.

10

Learning to Translate: A Statistical and Computational Analysis

Marco Turchi,[1,2] **Tijl De Bie,**[2] **Cyril Goutte,**[3] **and Nello Cristianini**[2]

[1] *European Commission-Joint Research Centre (JRC), IPSC, GlobeSec, Via Fermi 2749, 21020 Ispra, Italy*
[2] *Intelligent Systems Laboratory, University of Bristol, MVB, Woodland Road, Bristol BS8 1UB, UK*
[3] *Interactive Language Technologies, National Research Council Canada, 283 Boulevard Alexandre-Taché, Gatineau, QC, Canada J8X 3X7*

Correspondence should be addressed to Marco Turchi, marco.turchi@gmail.com

Academic Editor: Peter Tino

We present an extensive experimental study of Phrase-based Statistical Machine Translation, from the point of view of its learning capabilities. Very accurate Learning Curves are obtained, using high-performance computing, and extrapolations of the projected performance of the system under different conditions are provided. Our experiments confirm existing and mostly unpublished beliefs about the learning capabilities of statistical machine translation systems. We also provide insight into the way statistical machine translation learns from data, including the respective influence of translation and language models, the impact of phrase length on performance, and various unlearning and perturbation analyses. Our results support and illustrate the fact that performance improves by a constant amount for each doubling of the data, across different language pairs, and different systems. This fundamental limitation seems to be a direct consequence of Zipf law governing textual data. Although the rate of improvement may depend on both the data and the estimation method, it is unlikely that the general shape of the learning curve will change without major changes in the modeling and inference phases. Possible research directions that address this issue include the integration of linguistic rules or the development of active learning procedures.

1. Introduction

Traditional approaches to machine translation (MT) [1] relied to a large extent on linguistic analysis. The (relatively) recent development of statistical approaches [2] and especially phrase-based machine translation, or PBMT [3, 4], has put the focus on the intensive use of large parallel corpora. In that statistical framework, translation is essentially viewed as the process of associating an input, the source sentence, with an output, the target sentence. Estimating a machine translation system is therefore similar to learning the mapping between the source/input and the target/output, a problem which has been extensively studied in statistics and in machine learning. This justifies our view of a typical phrase-based machine translation model as a learning system and motivates our analysis of the performance on that system.

A learning system typically considers a class of models, or hypotheses, and tries to find the one element in that class that provides the best prediction of the output on future,

unseen input examples. The performance of every learning system is the result of (at least) two combined effects: the representation power of the hypothesis class, determining how well the system can approximate the target behaviour; statistical effects, determining how well the system can approximate the best element of the hypothesis class, based on finite and noisy training information. The two effects interact with richer classes being better approximators of the target behaviour but requiring more training data to reliably identify the best hypothesis. The resulting trade-off, equally well known in statistics and in machine learning, can be expressed in terms of bias versus variance, capacity control, or model selection. Various theories on learning curves have been proposed to deal with it, where a learning curve is a plot describing performance of a learning system as a function of some parameters, typically training set size. In practice this trade-off is easily observed, by noticing how the training error can be driven to zero by using a rich hypothesis class, which typically results into overfitting and increased test error.

In the context of statistical machine translation (SMT), where large bilingual corpora are used to train adaptive software to translate text, this task is further complicated by the peculiar distribution underlying the data, where the probability of encountering new words or expressions never vanishes. If we want to understand the potential and limitations of the current technology, we need to understand this interplay between the two factors affecting performance. In an age where the creation of intelligent behaviour is increasingly data driven, this is a question of great importance to all of artificial intelligence. These observations lead us to an analysis of learning curves in machine translation, and to a number of related questions, including an analysis of the flexibility of the representation class used, an analysis of the stability of the models with respect to perturbations of the parameters, and an analysis of the computational resources needed to train these systems.

In phrase-based approaches to statistical machine translation, translations are generated in response to some input source text. The quality of the output translation depends on the correctness of the generated language (*fluency*) as well as on how faithful it is to the original meaning (*adequacy*). This is reflected in the two main components of the typical SMT model: the language model and the translation model. While these will be formally defined in Section 2, let us mention that the translation model relies on a bilingual table of corresponding "phrases" (sequences of words), with an associated probability which reflects how likely it is that the source phrase will be translated as the target phrase. The language model is typically built using a table of n-grams, with associated probabilities, which is sufficient to define a Markov chain. Note that the overall behaviour of the translation system is largely controlled by the content of those two tables. They are automatically filled during the training phase, when a bilingual corpus is used to identify both phrases and their probabilities. Since future translations are produced by maximizing a scoring function estimating translation quality, using the content of the two tables, we see that the contents of the translation and language models tables correspond to the tunable parameters of the learning system. The hypothesis space of SMT systems is then the class of all possible "translation functions" that can be implemented, for all possible choices of language and translation tables. As this is an enormous search space, it is no wonder that both algorithmic and statistical challenges are encountered when training these systems.

From a statistical learning point of view, this raises interesting questions: How much of the overall error of the translation system is due to representation limitations, and how much to the difficulty of extracting suitable Translation and Language model tables from a finite sample? And what quantities control the trade off between the approximation and estimation errors, essentially playing the role of model selection?

We have undertaken a large scale experimental and theoretical investigation of these questions. Using the open source packages Moses [5] and Portage [6], and three different corpora: the Spanish-English Europarl [7], the UN Chinese-English, and the Giga Corpus French-English [8],

we have performed a detailed investigation of the influence of data sizes and other design choices in training various components of the system, both on the quality of translations and on the computational cost. We use this data to inform a discussion about learning curves. We have also investigated the model-selection properties of n-gram size, where the n-grams are the phrases used as building blocks in the translation process. Note that our experiments have been performed using English as target language. Although many language pairs would yield different translation performance, in this paper, we are not interested in the translation performance *per se*: we focus our attention on analyzing the SMT system as a learning system.

Since our goal was to obtain high-accuracy learning curves, that can be trusted both for comparing different system settings and to extrapolate performance under unseen conditions, we conducted a large-scale series of tests, to reduce uncertainty in the estimations and to obtain the strongest possible signals. This was only possible, to the degree of accuracy needed by our analysis, by the extensive use of a high-performance computer cluster over several weeks of computation.

One of our key findings is that the current performance of phrase-based statistical machine translation systems is not limited by the representation power of the hypothesis class, but rather by model estimation from data. In other words, we demonstrate that parameter choices exist that can deliver significantly higher performance, but that inferring them from finite samples is the problem. We also suggest that increasing dataset size is not likely to bridge that gap (at least not for realistic amounts in the i.i.d. setting), nor is the development of new parameter estimation principles. The main limitation seems to be a direct consequence of Zipf's law, and the introduction of constraints from linguistics seems to be an unavoidable step, to help the system in the identification of the optimal models without resorting to massive increases in training data, which would also result in unmanageable training times, and model sizes. This is because the rate of improvement of translation performance is at best logarithmic with the training set size. We estimate that bridging the gap between training and test error would require about 10^{15} paired bilingual sentences, which is larger than the current estimated size of the web.

Parts of the results reported in this paper were presented at the third workshop on statistical machine translation [9]. Work related to our learning curve experiments can also be found in [10].

It is important to remark that while there are many discussions about automatic evaluation of SMT systems, this work does not consider them. We work within the well-defined setting where a loss function has been agreed upon, that can measure the similarity between two sentences, and a paired training set has been provided. The setting prescribes that the learning system needs to choose its parameters so that it can identify high-quality (low expected loss) translations. We investigate the learning-theoretic implications of this setting, including the interplay between approximation error and estimation error, model selection, and accuracy in parameters estimation. We do not address more general themes about the opportunity for SMT to be evaluated by automatic metrics.

2. Phrase-Based Machine Translation

What is the best function class to map Spanish documents into English documents? This is a question of linguistic nature and has been the subject of a long debate. With the growing availability of bilingual parallel corpora, the 1990 s saw the development of *statistical* machine translation (SMT) models. Given a source ("foreign") language sentence $\mathbf{f}$ and a target ("English") language translation $\mathbf{e}$, the relationship between $\mathbf{e}$ and $\mathbf{f}$ is modelled using a statistical or probabilistic model such as $p(\mathbf{e} \mid \mathbf{f})$.

The first statistical models were word based [2, 11], combining a Markovian language model with a generative word-to-word translation model, in a noisy channel model inspired by speech recognition research.

Current state-of-the-art SMT uses *phrase-based* models, which generalized and superseded word-based models. They rely on three key ideas:

(i) the use of *phrases* (sequences of consecutive words) as basic translation units instead of words;

(ii) the use of a log-linear model instead of a simple product of the language and translation models;

(iii) the use of minimum error-rate training in order to estimate the parameters of the log-linear model, instead of maximum likelihood.

Many additional ideas contribute to the efficiency of these models, such as efficient hypothesis search, rescoring, or improved feature functions. The underlying log-linear model may be interpreted as a maximum entropy model:

$$p(\mathbf{e} \mid \mathbf{f}) = \frac{\exp(\sum_i \lambda_i h_i(\mathbf{e}, \mathbf{f}))}{Z(\mathbf{f})}, \qquad (1)$$

where $Z(\mathbf{f})$ is the normalization factor, and h_i are the feature functions, which we will discuss further in a moment.

Note that finding the best target translation $\mathbf{e}$ given a source sentence $\mathbf{f}$ amounts to maximizing the conditional probability $p(\mathbf{e} \mid \mathbf{f})$ with respect to $\mathbf{e}$, which yields

$$\hat{\mathbf{e}} = \arg \max_{\mathbf{e}} \sum_i \lambda_i h_i(\mathbf{e}, \mathbf{f}) \approx \arg \max_{\mathbf{e}} \sum_i \lambda_i h_i(\mathbf{e}, \mathbf{a}, \mathbf{f}). \qquad (2)$$

The *feature functions* $h_i(\mathbf{e}, \mathbf{a}, \mathbf{f})$ involve both the source and target sentences, and the approximation gives these feature functions access to $\mathbf{a}$, the alignment connecting $\mathbf{e}$ and $\mathbf{f}$. This model for $\mathbf{e}$ given $\mathbf{f}$ is linear in the log domain, which motivates the description of this framework as "log-linear model" [3, 4, 12]. In addition, many feature functions are defined as logarithms of probabilities. The search for the optimal translation in (2) is also referred to as *decoding* as, in the original analogy of the noisy channel, it corresponds to retrieving the clean message $\mathbf{e}$ from a noisy or encrypted observation $\mathbf{f}$.

One key aspect of the log-linear model in (2) is that it can take into account almost arbitrary feature functions, as long as they can be defined in terms of $\mathbf{e}$, $\mathbf{f}$, and $\mathbf{a}$. However, in order to be able to efficiently search for the optimal translation $\hat{\mathbf{e}}$, we usually assume that the feature functions decompose linearly across basic constituents of the sentences. In phrase-based MT, the sentences are decomposed into basic translation units called *phrases*. Note that these are not phrases in the linguistic sense, but simply subsequences of words. For a sentence $\mathbf{e}$ composed of the sequence of words $w_1, \ldots w_{|\mathbf{e}|}$, phrases e_k can be any contiguous subsequence of words w_j (and similarly for $\mathbf{f}$). A feature function that linearly decomposes across phrases takes the form $h_i(\mathbf{e}, \mathbf{a}, \mathbf{f}) = \sum_k h_i(e_k, a_k, f_k)$, where e_k and f_k are phrases from $\mathbf{e}$ and $\mathbf{f}$ (resp.), and a_k is the alignment that connects them.

Typical examples of feature function that compose a basic phrase-based MT system are:

(i) one or several phrase translation features: $h_T(\mathbf{e}, \mathbf{a}, \mathbf{f}) = \sum_k \log p(f_k \mid e_k)$;

(ii) one or more language model features: $h_L(\mathbf{e}, \mathbf{a}, \mathbf{f}) = \log p(\mathbf{e}) = \sum_j \log p(w_j \mid w_{j-1}, \ldots w_1)$;

(iii) distortion feature $h_D(\mathbf{e}, \mathbf{a}, \mathbf{f}) = \sum_k -\|\text{start}(f_k) - \text{end}(f_{k-1}) - 1\|$;

(iv) word penalty and/or phrase penalty features.

The phrase translation probabilities $p(f_k \mid e_k)$ are defined over a set of phrase pairs (e_k, f_k) referred to as a *phrase table*. Part of the overall MT training process is to estimate this table and the associated probabilities. This is typically done by first aligning each sentence pair at the word level, and then extracting all phrase pairs that are compatible with the word alignment. Statistics on the phrase pair are accumulated over the entire corpus. In our experiments below, we rely on word-to-word IBM models [2] for alignment. Although more elaborate techniques have appeared more recently [13, 14], their impact on the resulting machine translation quality is still unclear [15].

The standard language model feature such as used below relies on an *n*-gram language model, combining the probabilities of each word in the target hypothesis given the preceding *n*-gram language models, combined with appropriate smoothing, are very efficient and naturally decomposable across words (and phrases), making them particularly well suited in this framework. Again, more recent alternatives exist, but their actual impact on MT performance is not always obvious.

The distortion feature controls the reordering between phrases. Note that only very short-range reordering may be handled within phrases. Long-range reordering must be handled by target phrase permutations. This feature allows to regulate the amount of reordering depending on, for example, the language pair.

The word length (or word penalty) feature regulates the length of the target sentence. This is useful because the language model feature typically favours shorter sentences (because each additional trigram can only lower the language model probability). This is a simple, yet effective feature.

The process of training a machine translation system involves estimating the various parameters of the model: the log-linear parameters λ_i as well as the parameters internal to the feature functions, such as the phrase translation probabilities and language model n-gram and backoff probabilities. In a typical phrase-based system such as used in our work, training is modularized by first estimating the later on various corpora, for example, a large bilingual corpus for translation probabilities and a possibly larger monolingual corpus for the language model parameters.

The log-linear parameters are then estimated by *minimum error rate training* (MERT). The weights λ_i are tuned to optimize an automatic MT metric such as BLEU [16] over a number of bilingual sentence pairs from a development corpus:

$$\hat{\lambda} = \arg\max_{\lambda} BLEU(\hat{\mathbf{e}}(\mathbf{f}), \mathbf{e}; \ (\mathbf{e}, \mathbf{f}) \in \mathcal{D}), \qquad (3)$$

where $\hat{\mathbf{e}}(\mathbf{f})$ is the translation produced by solving (2) for source sentence $\mathbf{f}$, and $\mathbf{e}$ is the corresponding reference translation. $\mathcal{D}$ is the set of sentence pairs over which MERT is performed. Solving (3) is difficult because the decoding necessary to produce the hypothesis translation is expensive. The standard solution [17] is to approximate the exhaustive search in (2) by a search over a smaller set of n-best candidate translations for $\mathbf{f}$. For each new value of λ tried by MERT, new hypothesis translations are added to the list. As the number of hypotheses produced by the decoder is finite, this is guaranteed to converge, and in practice, it does fairly quickly. An additional difficulty is that the landscape of the cost, for example, BLEU, is piecewise constant and highly irregular. In practice, the optimization in (3) is done using the Powell's method [18], a straightforward coordinate descent method where optimization is performed along each λ_i in turn. The key observation is that when optimization is approximated as described above by a search over a list of n translations, there are at most $n - 1$ points along the line search where BLEU can change. This yields an efficient algorithm for obtaining the exact solution of each line search in Powell's method and therefore provides a way to iteratively optimize the log-linear weights λ using MERT. A number of alternatives have been proposed, such as on-line discriminative training [19, 20]. However, the two systems we use here both use a fairly traditional implementation of MERT.

This *phrase-based machine translation* approach relies on a specific representation of the translation process, such as the choice of contiguous word sequences (phrases) as basic units in the language and translation models. How far can this representation take us towards the target of improving translation quality? Are the current limitations due to the approximation error of this representation, or to estimation errors originating from insufficient training data? How much space for improvement is there, given new data or new statistical estimation methods or given different models with different complexities?

Before we present experimental results that address these questions, we will describe the setup that was used to obtain these results.

3. Experimental Setup

3.1. Data. We used three different sentence-aligned corpora, covering different language pairs and sizes:

(1) Europarl Release v3 Spanish-English [7],

(2) UN Chinese-English corpus provided by the Linguistic Data Consortium,

(3) Giga corpus French-English [8].

The details of these three corpora are given in Table 1. The language pairs cover European as well as non-European languages, and the sizes range from 1.2 M to 22.5 M sentence pairs. We expect that translation between European languages will be easier than from Chinese to English; however, we are not so much interested in the actual translation performance as in the way this performance evolves with increasing data and under a number of conditions.

The Europarl corpus contains material extracted from the proceedings of the European parliament, and the UN data contains material from the United Nations. Both therefore cover a wide range of themes, but are fairly homogeneous in terms of style and genre. The Giga corpus, on the other hand, was obtained through a targeted web crawl of bilingual web sites. These sites come from the Canadian government, the European Union, the United Nations, and other international organizations. In addition to covering a wide range of themes, they also contain documents with different styles and genres. We estimate that the rate of misaligned sentence pairs was around 13%.

These corpora are each divided in three sets, each with a different role. The *training* part is used to obtain the language model and phrase tables. The *development* set is used to estimate the log-linear weights λ using MERT, and the *test* set is set aside during the estimation process in order to provide an unbiased estimate of the translation performance.

This work contains several experiments on different types and sizes of data set. To be consistent and to avoid anomalies due to overfitting or particular data combinations, each set of pairs of sentences has been randomly sampled. The number of pairs is fixed, and a program selects them randomly from the whole original training, development, or test set using a uniform distribution. This process is iterated a certain number of time and redundancy of pairs is allowed inside each subset (bootstrap, see [18, 21, 22] for an application to PBSMT).

3.2. Software. Several software packages are available for training PBSMT systems. In this work, we use both Moses [5] and Portage [6]. Moses is a complete open-source phrase-based translation toolkit for academic purposes, while Portage is a similar package available to partners of the National Research Council Canada. Both provide all the state-of-the-art components needed to create a phrase-based machine translation system from one language to another. They contain different modules to preprocess data and train the language models and the translation models. These models can be tuned using minimum error rate training [17]. Both use standard external tools for training

TABLE 1: Number of total and distinct words in training, development, and test sets.

			Training	Development	Test
Europarl		No. of Sentences	1,259,914	2,000	2,000
	English	Total words	35,284,052	58,762	59,147
		Distinct words	124,080	6,551	6,429
	Spanish	Total words	36,695,628	60,536	61,160
		Distinct words	164,920	8,182	8,239
UN corpus		No. of Sentences	4,968,857	1,000	10,000
	English	Total words	146,980,344	29,545	295,085
		Distinct words	485,494	5,210	17,105
	Chinese	Total words	138,045,740	27,764	278,4256
		Distinct words	530,295	4,353	13,193
Giga corpus		No. of Sentences	22,515,400	2,000	3,000
	English	Total words	636,113,866	51,549	90,474
		Distinct words	2,603,907	8,691	12,580
	French	Total words	772,104,558	62,682	109,197
		Distinct words	2,512,286	10,124	14,614

the language model, such as SRILM [23], and Moses also uses GIZA++ [24] for word alignments. Moses and Portage are very sophisticated systems, capable of learning translation tables, language models, and decoding parameters from data. We will later analyze the contribution of each component to the overall score.

The typical processing pipeline is as follows. Given a parallel training corpus, long sentences are filtered out, and the remaining material is lowercased and tokenized. These sentences are used to train the language and translation models. Training the translation models requires several steps such as aligning words, computing the lexical translation, extracting and scoring the phrases, and creating the reordering model. When the models have been created, the development set is used to run the minimum error rate training (MERT) algorithm [17] to optimize their weights. We refer to that step as the optimization step in the rest of the paper. The test set is used to evaluate the quality of models on the data.

All experiments using Moses have been run using the default parameter configuration. GIZA + + used IBM models 1, 2, 3, and 4 with number of iterations for model 1 equal to 5, model 2 equal to 0, and model 3 and 4 equal to 3; SRILM used n-gram order equal to 3 and the Kneser-Ney smoothing algorithm; MERT has been run fixing to 100 the number of n best target sentence for each developed sentence, and it stops when none of the weights changed more than 1e-05 or the n best list does not change.

The training, development, and test set sentences are tokenized and lowercased. The maximum number of tokens for each sentence in the training pair has been set to 50, whilst no limit is applied to the development or test set. TMs were limited to a phrase length of 7 words, and LMs were limited to 3.

3.3. Hardware.
All the experiments have been run on high-performance clusters of machines.

The first cluster (at U. Bristol) includes 96 nodes each with two dual-core Opteron processors, 8 GB of RAM per node (2 GB per core) and 4 thick nodes each with four dual-core Opteron processors, 32 GB of RAM per node (4 GB per core), for a total of 416 CPUs. Additional information: ClearSpeed accelerator boards on the thick nodes; SilverStorm Infiniband high-speed connectivity throughout for parallel code message passing; General Parallel File System (GPFS) providing data access from all the nodes with a total of 11 terabytes of storage. Each experiment has been run using one core and allocating 4 Gb of RAM.

The second cluster (at NRC) includes 29 nodes each with two dual-core processors and 16 GB RAM per node (4 GB per core) and 8 "fat" nodes with 4 quad-core processors each and 128 GB RAM per node (8 GB per core), for a total of 244 CPUs. The file system is Ibrix and provides data access from all nodes, with a total of 17 TB of storage. Experiments using Portage are distributed over several CPUs, the total number of which depends on the various stages in the estimation process.

3.4. Evaluation Metrics.
The evaluation of a machine translation system is a lively and hotly debated topic in this

TABLE 2: Correlation coefficient between evaluation scores.

	BLEU	NIST	METEOR	TER
BLEU	1	0.724	0.8633	−0.866
NIST	0.724	1	0.6171	−0.8702
METEOR	0.8633	0.6171	1	−0.8173
TER	−0.866	−0.8702	−0.8173	1

field. Ideally, human beings can evaluate the quality of a translated sentence. However, this is unfeasible for rapid development of automatically trained systems with multiple parameter tuning, as human evaluation is expensive, slow, and sometimes inconsistent and subjective.

Therefore, instead of reporting human judgement of translation quality, various automatic measures have been proposed. An automatic score measures the quality of machine-translated sentences by comparing them to a set of human translations, called reference sentences. The score needs to be able to discriminate good translations from bad ones, whilst considering aspects such as adequacy and fluency.

Several metrics have been introduced: BLEU [16], NIST [25], Meteor [26, 27], and TER [28] are among the most well known. BLEU and NIST are based on averaging n-gram precisions, combined with a length penalty which penalizes short translations containing only sure words. These metrics differ on the way the precisions are combined and on the length penalty.

Meteor evaluates a translation by computing a score based on the word alignment between the translation and a given reference translation. TER relies on the computation of an edit distance, and it is defined as the minimum number of edit operations (insertions, deletions, substitutions, *and shifts*) needed to change an automatically translated sentence into one of the references, normalized by the average length of the references.

Table 2 reports the correlation coefficients between the measures (details on how these values have been computed are in Section A.3). Clearly, all measures correlate strongly with each other, such that the choice of the performance measure is fairly arbitrary, as long as one is consistent. For this reason, we have chosen to use BLEU throughout this paper as it is the most widely used automatic score in machine translation.

4. Learning Curve Analysis

4.1. Role of Training Set Size on Performance on New Sentences. In this section, we analyze how training set size affects the performance by creating learning curves (BLEU score versus training set size).

The general framework for this set of experiments consists of creating subsets of the complete corpus by sub-sampling from a uniform distribution without replacement. We have created 10 random subsets for each of the 20 chosen sizes, where each size represents 5%, 10%, and so forth

TABLE 3: Different settings used to create the Learning Curves. Due to the large dimension of the Giga corpus, only three random subsets have been built.

Language pairs	Data	SMT system	No. random subsets
Es − En	Europarl	Moses	10
Es − En	Europarl	Portage	10
Fr − En	Giga	Moses	3
Zh − En	UN	Portage	10

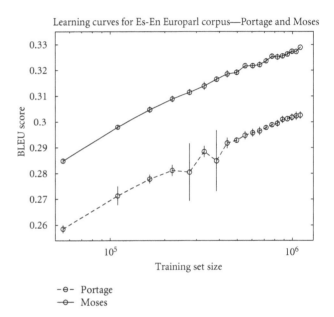

FIGURE 1: Spanish-English learning curve obtained using Europarl corpus, Portage and Moses.

of the complete corpus. For each subset, a new instance of the PBSMT system has been created, for a total of 200 models. Two hundred experiments have then been run on an independent test set (of 2,000 sentences, also not included in any other phase of the experiment).

In these experiments, we focus our attention on the growth rate of the learning curve, in particular we are interested to check if the learning curve has a logarithmic behaviour. In fact, a common belief in SMT is that learning curves follow logarithmic laws; to analyze this in our experiments, we show all the learning curves in the linear log scale, where we can study if the curve has a linear behaviour.

Note that sampling without replacement, error bar dimension reduces according to the increment of the training set size. We also believe that in this particular situation, the presence of the error bars may help to better understand the stability of the system.

Using the framework described above, four different settings have been set to produce learning curves, see Table 3. In Figures 1, 2, and 3, the learning curves are shown.

In all the figures, the curves are increasing linearly or slightly more slowly than that, suggesting a learning curve

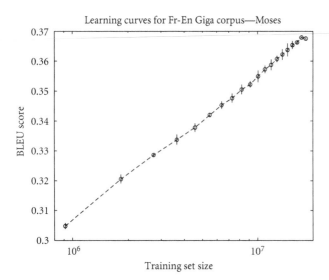

FIGURE 2: French-English learning curve obtained using Giga corpus and Moses.

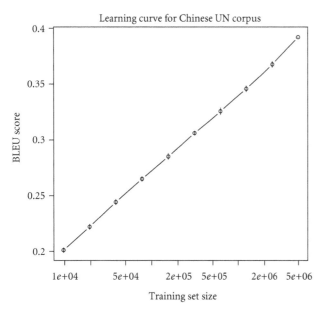

FIGURE 3: Chinese-English learning curve obtained using UN corpus and Portage.

that is "at best" logarithmically increasing with the training set size. Shape of the learning curves is comparable across different data size and language pairs. In any case, the addition of massive amounts of data from the same distribution will result in small improvements in the performance.

The small error bars that we have obtained also allow us to regard the stability of the SMT when trained on the same training set size.

Due to the large amount of data in the Giga corpus, Fr-En learning curve has been obtained running only three subsamples for training set size.

4.2. Relative Importance of TM and LM. In the previous section, experiments have been run using the same training set size for language and translation models. In general, there is a large difference in terms of cost of retrieving training data for language and translation models; the former can be trained using monolingual data, while the second needs bilingual texts. In recent years, several parallel corpus have been produced, for example, Europarl [7], JRC Acquis [29], and others, but they are not comparable to the amount of freely available monolingual datasets.

Google in [30] has shown that performance improves logarithmically in the linear scale with the number of tokens in the language model training set when this quantity is huge (from billions to trillions of tokens). In this section, we are interested to understand whether there is a trade-off between the training data size used to build language and translation models and how performances are affected by their differences. We propose a mathematical model to estimate the BLEU score's variations according to the language and translation training data sizes. Performance of an SMT system is a function of the dimension of the training data that can be logarithmic as seen in the previous section. We have modelled this relation in the following way:

$$\text{BLEU}(d) = \alpha_{\text{LM}} \times \log_2(d_{\text{LM}}) + \alpha_{\text{TM}} \times \log_2(d_{\text{TM}}) + \epsilon \,,$$

(4)

where d is the amount of training data, d_{LM} is the amount of training data used to build the language model, d_{TM} is the amount of training data used to build the translation model, α_{LM} and α_{TM} are weighting factors that identify the contribution of language and translation training data to the BLEU score, and ϵ is the residual. To evaluate the relation between the amount of training data used to build language and translation models, we estimated α_{LM} and α_{TM}.

Subsets of the training data have been selected using 10% of the data as increasing set size. For each training set size, one random set has been created without replacement. Development and test sets are fixed. One instance of the SMT system has been run for each of all possible combinations of the language and translation training data sizes. BLEU score value has been associated to each pair: language and translation set size. Multiple linear regression based on least squares [31] has been performed using the BLEU score values as response observations and the logarithmic values of the training set sizes as observations. This setting has been applied to Europarl and Giga corpus datasets using Moses as SMT system.

We performed two sets of experiments: in the first one, we estimated the weighting factors using all the data, see Table 4, and in the second, we tested the prediction capability of our model randomly splitting the data in training (80%) and test (20%) sets.

The results in Table 4 empirically confirm the common belief that adding data to the translation model is more important than to the language model ($\alpha_{\text{TM}} > \alpha_{\text{LM}}$). The values of α_{LM} and α_{TM} vary across the datasets and correspond to an increase of 1.3 to 1.5 BLEU point for the LM and 1.8 to 1.9 for the TM, for each doubling of the data. However, their ratio is rather stable.

For the second set of experiments, data has been randomly sampled in training and test sets one thousand

TABLE 4: Empirical estimation of the weighing factors α_{LM} and α_{TM}. Experiments have been performed independently on the Europarl and Giga corpus datasets.

Data	α_{LM}	α_{TM}	$\alpha_{\mathrm{TM}}/\alpha_{\mathrm{LM}}$	ϵ
Europarl	0.0147	0.0193	1.313	2×10^{-4}
Giga Corpus	0.0133	0.0182	1.368	4×10^{-6}

times. Training set has been used to estimate the alphas and the residual, and test set to predict the BLEU score values. At each iteration, estimation error was computed. Average α and error on the Europarl and Giga corpus datasets are shown in Table 5. The proposed model is able to approximate well enough the BLEU score using Moses as translation system and in-domain test sets. According to this setting and assuming that we are in the standard case where d_{LM} is equal to d_{TM}, it is possible to use our model to estimate the amount of training data needed to reach a certain Bleu score for example, more than 150 million sentences to obtain a Spanish-English Bleu score equal to 0.45.

4.3. Role of Phrase Length in the Translation Table (Model Selection).

The richness of the hypothesis class controls the trade-off between training and test error. Richer hypothesis classes can fit the training data more accurately but generalize less well than poorer classes, a phenomenon known as overfitting. The choice of the appropriate expressive power, within a parametrized class of models, is called model selection and is one of the most crucial steps in the design of learning systems.

In phrase-based SMT, this is controlled by selecting the maximum length of phrases to be used as building blocks for translation. Using long phrases will help when the system has to translate sequences of words that match what was encountered in the training corpus, but this becomes increasingly unlikely as the phrases become longer. On the other hand, short sentences are more often reused, but may also be more ambiguous and lead to errors more often. This is where the trade-off between representation and estimation errors is controlled. When extracting longer phrases, we expect training set performance to be higher, but test performance to drop (overfitting). Optimizing test performance requires the right trade-off.

In this section, we analyze how the phrase length can affect the performance in terms of BLEU score. We also report the distribution of the phrase lengths in the translation table, as well as how the system uses the phrases of different length during the translation of both training and test material. We have created 10 random subsets of the complete Europarl corpus containing 629,957 pairs of sentences. For each subset, ten PBMT systems have been estimated. Each instance of Moses has been trained using a different maximum phrase length, from 1 to 10. Each model was then tested on the 2000 sentence test set, and on a random subset of 2000 training sentences. Translation of training sentences allows us to estimate the training error.

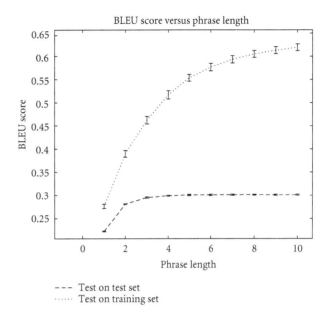

FIGURE 4: BLEU versus n-gram length. "Test on test set" has been obtained using a fixed test set and no optimization phase. "Test on training set" is a test set selected by the training set for each training set size and no optimization phase.

The learning curves in Figure 4 illustrate how the performance is affected by the phrase length. The "test on test set" curve is less influenced by the phrase length than the "test on training set" curve. The latter shows a large upward bias in translation performance, which is expected from a learning system when testing on material that has been used for training. Both learning curves show a big improvement when moving from the word-to-word translation (phrase length equal to one) to the phrase-based model (higher phrase lengths).

In the "test on test set" learning curve, there seems to be no significant advantage to using phrases longer than 4 words. By contrast, when testing on the subset of the training material, the performance continues to grow. This unrealistic case is not affected by the Zipf's law, because almost all the words necessary to translate the training material have, by definition, already been observed. The model is therefore able to match long phrases when producing the "test on training set" translations.

In order to explore this further, we also compute the distribution of the entries in the translation table as a function of the length of the source language phrases. Figure 5 shows that the number of phrases peaks around 4-grams and 5-grams, then steadily decreases. This means that the phrase extraction algorithm finds it more and more difficult to extract longer phrases.

We investigate this further by plotting the distribution of phrases actually used while translating. We randomly select 2 sets of 500 sentences, one from the training and one from the test material. In each case, we count the number of phrases of each length that were actually used to produce the translation. The right panel of Figure 5 reports these distribution. It shows that, while the models use a fair

TABLE 5: Performance obtained training the regressor on 80% of the data and testing on 20%. This process has been iterated 1,000 times. Experiments have been performed independently on the Europarl and Giga corpus dataset.

Data	α_{LM}	α_{TM}	*Estimation Error*
Europarl	$0.0102 \pm 2 \times 10^{-4}$	$0.0134 \pm 2 \times 10^{-4}$	$5.45 \times 10^{-5} \pm 14 \times 10^{-4}$
Giga Corpus	$0.0092 \pm 7 \times 10^{-5}$	$0.0126 \pm 7 \times 10^{-5}$	$-5.57 \times 10^{-5} \pm 2 \times 10^{-4}$

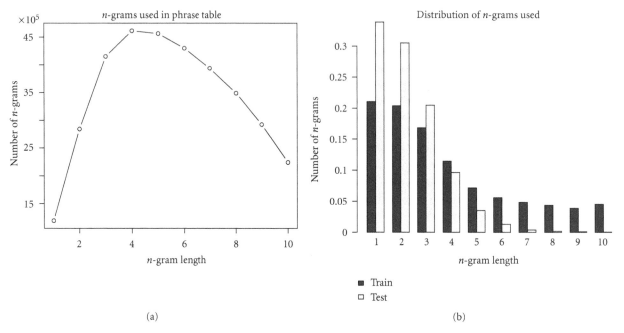

(a) (b)

FIGURE 5: N-gram statistics: (left) number of n-grams of each size in the translation table; (right) distribution of phrase size used for translating training and test material, for $n = 1, \ldots, 10$.

amount of longer phrases to translate the training material, these longer phrases are essentially never used for translating the test set: 98% of the phrases are 5-grams or shorter. Again this is related to Zipf's law: while the model is able to match longer sequences from material it has already seen, test data is usually too different to reliably match beyond 4 or 5 consecutive words.

These experiments suggest that the phrase length has a limited impact on actual test performance. Going to larger n-grams seems to bring little benefit in terms of performance as the model continues to prefer short phrases during the decoding phase. This is due to both the diminishing number of longer phrases in the table and to the lower probability that these longer sequences match the test material.

5. Model Perturbation: Analysis and Unlearning Curves

Much research has focused on devising improved principles for the statistical estimation of the parameters in language and translation models. The introduction of discriminative graphical models has marked a departure from traditional maximum likelihood estimation principles, and various approaches have been proposed.

The question is how much information is contained in the probabilities estimated by the model? Does the performance improve with more data because certain parameters are estimated better, or just because the lists are growing? In the second case, it is likely that more sophisticated statistical algorithms to improve the estimation of probabilities will have limited impact.

In this section, we analyze what we call "unlearning curves." These are obtained by increasingly perturbing the parameters inferred by the system, in order to observe how performance deteriorates. This can either represent the effect of insufficient statistics in estimating them, or the use of imperfect parameter estimation biases. These parameters are probabilities, phrases, and associations between source/target phrases contained inside translation and language model tables.

We have performed two different types of perturbation.

(i) *Unlearning by Adding Noise.* A percentage of noise has been added to each probability, $\tilde{p}$, in the Language model, including conditional probability, and translation model, bidirectional phrase translation probabilities and lexicalized weighting. The aim of this set of experiments is to test how robust the system is with respect to a reduced accuracy of its numeric parameters.

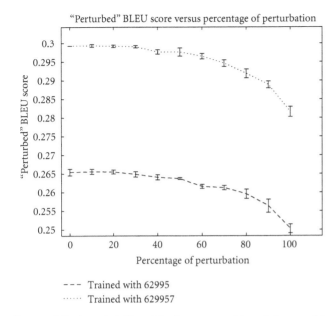

"Perturbed" BLEU score versus percentage of perturbation

--- Trained with 62995

······ Trained with 629957

FIGURE 6: Each probability of the language and translation models has been perturbed adding a percentage of noise. This learning curve reports BLEU score versus the percentage of perturbation applied. These results have been obtained using a fixed training set size equal to 62,995 and 629,957 pairs of sentences and Moses as translation system.

The noised probability is obtained as $p' = \min(1, \tilde{p} + \nu)$, where $\nu = \text{rand}(-\tilde{p} \times k, +\tilde{p} \times k)$ with percentage of noise $k \in [0,1]$. Different noise levels k have been used. For each value of k, ten experiments have been run. In this case, we randomly select two fixed training set sizes equal to 62,995 and 629,957 pairs of sentences form the Europarl corpora and use Moses as translation system. The unlearning curves are shown in Figure 6.

(ii) *Unlearning by Randomization of Parameters*. The second kind of noise that we add to the model is based on a swap of a particular quantity inside two entries of language or translation model. This is meant to test how robust the system is to perturbations of the all-important associations between phrases/numbers and to the associations between source/target phrases.

We refer to "numerical swap" when, given two entries, probabilities are swapped. While we refer to "words swap" when, given two entries of the translation model, we swap the target language phrases.

Three different sets of experiments have been run applying "numerical swap" only to the language model, "numerical swap" only to the translation model and "words swap" only to the translation model. Different values of percentage of noise between 0 and 1 have been used. For each percentage value, ten experiments have been run. All the perturbations have been applied on a model trained with

629,957 pairs of sentences randomly selected form the Europal data using Moses as translation system. The unlearning curves are shown in Figure 7.

Various observations can be made based on these experiments. The first unlearning curve (Figure 6), obtained by adding to each parameter a random number (sampled from within a range) proportional to its size, is meant to test the role of detailed tuning of parameters. While the orders of magnitude are respected, the fine structure of the parameter set is randomized. The gentle decline in performance seems to suggest that fine tuning of parameters is not what controls the performance here, and that perhaps advanced statistical estimation or more observations of the same n-grams would not lead to much better performance. This is also compatible with what is seen in the learning curve.

It is important to notice, however, that introducing a more aggressive type of noise (Figure 7(b)) that essentially replaces entire parameters with random values does lead to a more significant decline in performance. This was obtained by swapping random entries, and so after 100 percent of swaps essentially every entry is a random number (because the locations to swap are chosen with replacement). It is interesting to see that the decline of the language model is much less pronounced than that of the translation model.

The set of experiments in Figure 7(a) is harder to explain without discussing the inner workings of the translation model and Moses. Here, we swapped n-grams in the translation table, essentially breaking the connection between words and their translation. A rapid decline should be expected. However, the mapping between words is stored in a very redundant way within the TM, and this depends on the way the translation table is created, based on sentence alignments. Once an alignment has been found between two sentences, essentially every n-gram (for every value of n) is a candidate for insertion in the translation table. So very often, longer n-grams are inserted, alongside shorter segments of the same n-grams, and are added to different entries of the table. So if we remove an n-gram, chances are that other similar (longer or shorter) n-grams are present and can take over. In this way, it is not possible to directly compare the unlearning curve for the n-grams part with that for the numeric part of the tables.

6. Discussion

The impressive capability of current machine translation systems is not only a testament to an incredibly productive and creative research community, but can also be seen as a paradigm for other artificial intelligence tasks. Data-driven approaches to all main areas of AI currently deliver the state-of-the-art performance, from summarization to speech recognition to machine vision to information retrieval. And statistical learning technology is central to all approaches to data-driven AI. Understanding how sophisticated behaviour can be learnt from data is hence not just a concern for machine learning, or to individual applied communities, such as statistical machine translation, but rather a general concern for modern artificial intelligence. The analysis of learning curves and the identification of the various

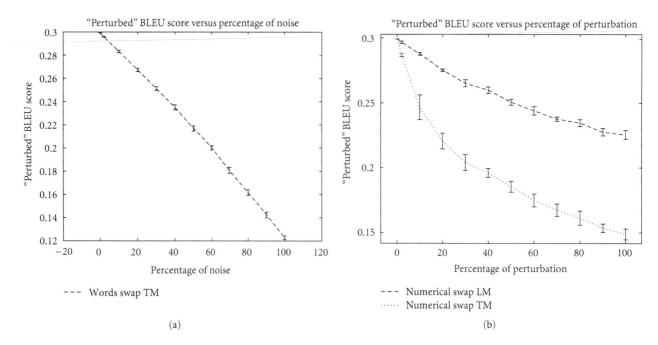

(a)   (b)

FIGURE 7: Unlearning curves. These results have been obtained using a fixed training set size equal to 629,957 pairs of sentences and Moses as translation system. In (a), "words swap TM" has been obtained by swapping the target phrases inside the TM. In (b), two unlearning curves have been compared. "Numerical swap LM" has been obtained applying numerical swaps only to the LM and "numerical swap TM" applying numerical swaps only to the LM.

limitations to performance are a crucial part of the machine learning method, and one where statistics and algorithms interact closely.

Using state-of-the-art phrase-based statistical machine translation packages and high-performance computing, we derived very accurate learning curves for a number of language pairs and domains. Our results suggest that performance, as measured by BLEU, increases by a constant factor for each doubling of the data. Although that factor varies depending on corpus and language pair, this result seems consistent over all experimental conditions we tried. Our findings confirm the results reported, for example, by [30, 32]. Authors in [30] reported "almost linear" improvements in BLEU score by doubling the training set size. In the presentation [32], the claim is that BLEU increases with each doubling of the training set size, by 0.5 and 2.5 BLEU points for the language and translation models, respectively, in the context of Arabic-English translation. Both claims seem to be qualitatively compatible with our observation of improvements that are at best logarithmic in the training set size, although our estimates are closer to 1.4 and 1.9 BLEU points for the LM and TM, respectively.

Our findings are also consistent with the curves presented by [33], although their results are limited to a much lower data set size (less than 10^5 sentences) and presented on a linear scale. Incidentally, that paper also presents a recent attempt into using active learning for improving MT and meets the challenge of "diminishing returns" identified in the learning curves: a constant performance improvement requires increasing amounts of data. Active learning is well-known in machine learning as an attempt to bypass the

distribution-sampling limitations by actively seeking new examples. One way to achieve this could be to either introduce an oracle to which the system can ask for annotation when needed or a process that uses linguistic knowledge to create new table entries based on existing table entries and some grammatical rules. An oracle could be formed by a web agent capable of locating useful bilingual sentences, for any given task, or even a linguistic-based system that could turn SMT models into richer ones by essentially generating new entries and removing unreliable ones. Any way to enforce linguistic constraints might result in a reduced need for data, and ultimately in more complete models, given the same corpus [34]. Neither approach would change the statistical nature of the system, but they would help it bypass the phrase acquisition bottleneck. Note however that the development of active learning systems for statistical MT raises the issue of confidence estimation, which is typically at the heart of many classical active learning procedures. This is an active area of research in machine translation [35–37].

The results of the perturbation analysis in Section 5 suggest that the limiting factor in the translation tables is not in the numeric part of the model—the parameters being estimated—but in the phrases contained in it, the entries of the phrase table. Together these observations point to limitations to the phrase-acquisition process, that under i.i.d. conditions is controlled by a Zipf law and hence leads to very slow rate of discovery of new phrases. In other words, the essential limiting factor for phrase-based SMT systems seems to be the Zipf law found in natural language.

Our large-scale analysis also suggests that the current bottleneck of the phrase-based SMT approach is the lack of sufficient data, not the function class used for the representation of translation systems. We reach this conclusion by noting that within a fixed class of parameters, an instance of the model has been trained on a set of sentences that includes also the test set (while limiting the phrase length to 7 words, to prevent full-sentence memorization), and this yields much improved performance. In addition, we also observed that the larger phrases (beyond 5 words) are in fact seldom used.

The high performance observed in the train-on-test conditions shows that there exists at least one choice of tunable parameters with which the phrase-based translation system can deliver much higher performance. This is useful to bound the space of "possible performances," although in ideal situations. The clear gap between performances on training and test set, together with the rate of the learning curves and our perturbation experiments, suggest that improvements in BLEU score are theoretically possible, if the right entries were present in the translation and language models. Unfortunately, current estimation procedures are unable to reach such high-performing regions of the parameter space. This was also noted by a recent paper by Wisniewski et al. who note that *"the current bottleneck of translation performances is not the representation power of the [phrase-based translation systems] but rather in their scoring functions"* [38].

Finally, let us note that we have not addressed the thorny issue of the reliability of automatic MT metrics. Some will be quick to point out that maximizing, for example, BLEU may neither be necessary for, nor guarantee good translation performance. Although we acknowledge that automatic MT metrics may not tell the whole story as far as translation quality is concerned, our systematic study aims at characterizing the behaviour of SMT systems that are built by maximizing such metrics. Deriving learning curves using human-generated translation quality score would definitely be interesting, but we are not aware of such effort, which would currently involve an overwhelming amount of human annotation.

7. Conclusion

Data-driven solutions to classic AI problems are now commonplace, ranging from computer vision to information retrieval tasks, and machine translation is one of the main successes of this approach. The idea of putting learning systems at the centre of all AI methodologies introduces however the need to understand the properties and limitations of these learning components. In this study, we have produced very accurate learning curves for the class of phrase-based SMT systems, using different implementations, different language pairs, and different datasets. In each case, we found the same overall behaviour, of a logarithmic growth in performance with training set size. The question becomes as follows: on which aspect of these systems should we act to achieve better performance? We have performed an extensive series of experiments to separately measure how different factors affect the performance of phrase-based SMT systems. Our first concerns were to distinguish between

approximation and estimation error: the performance limitations due to the use of a limited language model versus those due to the need to estimate the parameters of that model from a finite sample. Our experiments show that the estimation part of the error is the dominant one, suggesting that performance can still improve if the appropriate entries were available in the language and translation models. The second concern was to distinguish between the role of the numerical and lexical parts in the language and translation models. Various perturbation experiments show that the accuracy in estimating the numerical parameters is not a crucial aspect of performance, while the estimation of the lexical parts of the tables is a major factor in determining performance. In a third set of experiments, we determined that the estimation of the translation model has a bigger effect than the estimation of the language model, on performance.

We therefore reach the conclusion that estimating entries in the phrase translation tables is the dominant factor in determining performance. What controls the creation of phrase-translation tables? This is mostly limited by Zipf's law, since the probability of encountering phrases that have not been seen in the training set does not vanish even after observing very large corpora. The question therefore becomes as follows: how can we fill translation tables with phrase pairs while Zipf's law seems to prevent us from generating them from the data alone? Among possible methods, two stand out as particularly promising. The first is to generate phrase pairs by using grammatical or various linguistic rules (e.g., turning existing entries into new entries, by applying various forms of inflection). The second is to allow the system to make queries, active learning style, in order to produce phrase-table entries without having to wait for them to appear by sampling additional textual data. Both of these ideas of course are being pursued at the moment. It is of course important to remark that these limitations only refer to the current systems, where language is modelled as a Markov chain, and by entirely changing language model, different limitations could be found.

Appendix

A. Supplementary Results

A.1. Effect of Data Size in Optimization Set. In this section, we study the role of the optimization/development set with regard to the quality of translation. In particular, we analyze how different sizes of the development set affect the performance and the computational cost of the optimization phase.

The whole Europarl training set has been randomly split into two parts without replacements. One, containing 1,159,914 pairs of sentences, has been used to train the model. This step has been done only once, and all the experiments use the same translation, language, and reordering models. The second set has 100,000 pairs of sentences, and it is used to randomly select the development sets. The test set contains 2,000 pairs of sentences and is the same for all the experiments.

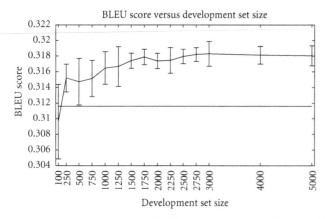

FIGURE 8: BLEU score versus development set size. The horizontal line is the BLEU score without any optimization. It is equal to 0.3116.

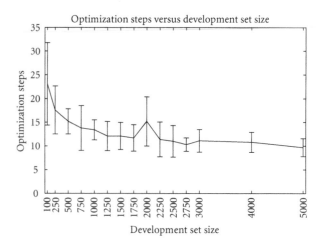

FIGURE 10: Optimization steps versus development set size.

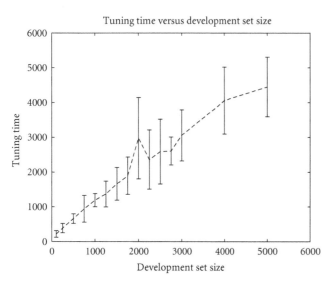

FIGURE 9: Tuning CPU times versus development set size.

Different sizes of the development set (100, 250, 500, 750, 1,000, 1,250, 1,500, 1,750, 2,000, 2,250, 2,500, 2,750, 3,000, 4,000, and 5,000 pairs of sentences) have been chosen, focusing our attention on small, rather than large dimensions. Replacements are not allowed. These choices also depend on the high computational cost of the tuning algorithm. For each size, ten random sets have been selected. For each set, an instance of the system has been run. The optimized model is used to test, and the results are evaluated.

In Figure 8, BLEU score as function of the development size is reported. The optimization procedure increases the quality of the translations. This improvement does not seem to be significant after a certain size of the development set. In fact, when we increase the development set size beyond 2,000 sentence pairs, BLEU does not change significantly. On the other hand, optimization is really expensive in terms of computational cost. In Figure 9, it increases roughly linearly with the development set size. It is nice to note how the

computational time is strongly related to the number of optimization steps in Figure 10.

A.2. Role of the Unknown Words. Understanding the most important reasons for failure of a PBSMT system is a fundamental task. In [39], a classification of different types of error has been proposed. In this section, we focus our attention on a particular type of error: unknown words. This type of error is considered a source error because it depends on the source sentence and not the translation process. It has been distinguished between truly unknown words (or stems) and unseen forms of known stems. The unknown words are the direct effect of Zipf's law in a language, as new words can come, but the training set is not flexible enough to cover them.

We have created 10 random subsets for each of the 10 chosen sizes, where each size represents 10%, 20%, and so forth of the complete corpus. For each subset, a new instance of the PBSMT system has been created, for a total of 100 models. Each model has been tested on the test set and on a subset of 2,000 pairs the training set. The optimization step has not been run. For each model, we count the unknown words.

Figure 11 shows unknown words as function of the training model. It is clear that small training sets are able to cover a small part of the word space. When increasing the dimension of the training set, the number of unknown words decreases. These curves reflect how machine translation is strongly affected by Zipf's law and confirm the results of the previous sections. A briefly discussion about the presence of unknown words when we test on a subset of the training set is given by Section 4.3.

A.3. Role of Test Set Size on Measuring Performance. BLEU score, the metric used in this work to evaluate the quality of the translation, is test set dependent. It means that different test sets regardless of the dimension can produce variation in the value of the BLEU score. In this section, we investigate how BLEU is affected by the test set size.

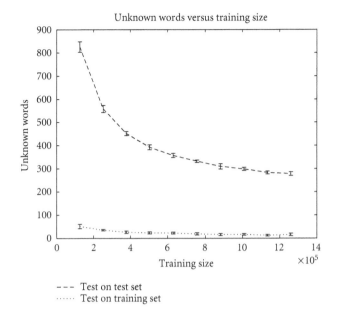

FIGURE 11: Number of unknown words translating training and test sets versus training set size.

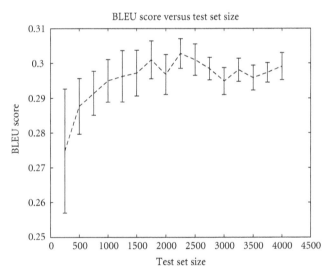

FIGURE 12: BLEU score versus test set size.

We have isolated 4,000 pairs of sentences from the Europarl training set, and we have selected from the remaining part 629,957 pairs. A Moses model is trained using this set. Using the 4,000 sentences pairs, we have created 10 random subsets for each of the 16 chosen sizes, where each size can contain a number of pairs from 250 to 4,000 by a step of 250 pairs. The model is tested over all these subsets, and the learning curve is reported in Figure 12. Small test set sizes produce a big variance in BLEU score. When increasing the test set size, the error bars tend to reduce.

In this work, a test set with 2,000 sentences pairs has been used. In the learning curve in Figure 12, the average value and standard deviation for this size are equal to 0.29677 ± 0.0057. This implies that differences in BLEU score smaller than 1.9% using two different test sets of the same size depend on the test set choice and not on different techniques. In recent years, this trouble has been partially solved using a standard test set obtained by the Europarl corpus.

In Section 3.4, we report the correlation coefficient between all the measures. Each correlation coefficient is computed using the results of the 160 experiments described above.

Acknowledgments

The authors thank Callum Wright, Bristol HPC Systems Administrator (http://www.acrc.bris.ac.uk/acrc/hpc.htm), Moses mailing list, Philip Koehn for various advices and for making available the Europarl corpus, Alessia Mammone, Omar Ali, and George Foster for many useful comments and for help with Portage. This work is supported by the EU IST Project SMART (FP6-033917).

References

[1] W. Locke and A. Booth, *Machine Translation of Languages*, MIT Press, Cambridge, Mass, USA, 1955.

[2] P. F. Brown, S. D. Pietra, V. J. D. Pietra, and R. L. Mercer, "The mathematic of statistical machine translation: parameter estimation," *Computational Linguistics*, vol. 19, no. 2, pp. 263–311, 1994.

[3] P. Koehn, F. J. Och, and D. Marcu, "Statistical phrase-based translation," in *Proceedings of the Conference of the North American Chapter of the Association for Computational Linguistics on Human Language Technology*, pp. 48–54, Edmonton, Canada, 2003.

[4] R. Zens, F.-J. Och, and H. Ney, "Phrase-based statistical machine translation," in *Proceedings of the 25th Annual German Conference on AI (KI '02)*, pp. 18–32, Springer, London, UK, 2002.

[5] P. Koehn, H. Hoang, A. Birch et al., "Moses: open source toolkit for statistical machine translation," in *Proceedings of the Annual Meeting of the Association for Computational Linguistics, Demonstration Session*, pp. 177–180, Columbus, Ohio, USA, 2007.

[6] N. Ueffing, M. Simard, S. Larkin, and J. H. Johnson, "NRC's PORTAGE system for WMT," in *Proceedings of ACL 2nd Workshop on Statistical Machine Translation*, pp. 185–188, Prague, Czech Republic, 2007.

[7] P. Koehn, "Europarl: a parallel corpus for statistical machine translation," in *Proceedings of the 10 th Machine Translation Summit*, pp. 79–86, Phuket, Thailand, 2005.

[8] C. Callison-Burch, P. Koehn, C. Monz, and J. Schroeder, "Findings of the 2009 Workshop on Statistical Machine Translation," in *Proceedings of the Fourth Workshop on Statistical Machine Translation*, C. Callison-Burch, P. Koehn, C. Monz, and J. Schroeder, Eds., pp. 263–311, Association for Computational Linguistics, Athens, Greece, 2009.

[9] M. Turchi, T. DeBie, and N. Cristianini, "Learning performance of a machine translation system: a statistical and computational analysis," in *Proceedings of the 3rd Workshop on Statistical Machine Translation*, pp. 35–43, Columbus, Ohio, USA, 2008.

[10] Y. Al-Onaizan, J. Curin, M. Jahr et al., "Statistical machine translation: final report," Tech. Rep., Johns Hopkins University, Summer Workshop on Language Engineering, Center for Speech and Language Processing, Baltimore, Md, USA, 1999.

[11] F. J. Och and H. Weber, "Improving statistical natural language translation with categories and rules," in *Proceedings of the 17th International Conference on Computational Linguistics*, vol. 2, pp. 985–989, Stroudsburg, Pa, USA, 1998.

[12] F. J. Och and H. Ney, "Discriminative training and maximum entropy models for statistical machine translation," in *Proceedings of the 40th Annual Meeting on Association for Computational Linguistics*, pp. 295–302, Philadelphia, Pa, USA, 2001.

[13] Y. Liu, Q. Liu, and S. Lin, "Discriminativeword alignment by linear modeling," *Computational Linguistics*, vol. 36, no. 3, pp. 303–339, 2010.

[14] R. C. Moore, W.-T. Yih, and A. Bode, "Improved discriminative bilingual word alignment," in *Proceedings of the 21st International Conference on Computational Linguistics and the 44th annual meeting of the Association for Computational Linguistics (ACL '06)*, pp. 513–520, Sydney, Australia, 2006.

[15] A. Fraser and D. Marcu, "Measuring word alignment quality for statistical machine translation," *Computational Linguistics*, vol. 33, no. 3, pp. 293–303, 2007.

[16] K. Papineni, S. Roukos, T. Ward, and W. J. Zhu, "Bleu: a method for automatic evaluation of machine translation," in *Proceedings of the 40th Annual Meeting on Association for Computational Linguistics*, pp. 311–318, Philadelphia, Pa, USA, 2001.

[17] F. J. Och, "Minimum error rate training in statistical machine translation," in *Proceedings of the 41st Annual Meeting on Association for Computational Linguistics*, pp. 160–167, Sapporo, Japan, 2003.

[18] W. H. Press, S. A. Teukolsky, W. T. Vetterling, and B. P. Flannery, *Numerical Recipes in C++*, Cambridge University Press, Cambridge, Mass, USA, 2002.

[19] A. Arun and P. Koehn, "Online learning methods for discriminative training of phrase based statistical machine translation," in *Proceedings of 11th the Machine Translation Summit*, Copenhagen, Denmark, 2007.

[20] D. Chiang, Y. Marton, P. Resnik, and P. Resnik, "Online large-margin training of syntactic and structural translation features," in *Proceedings of the Conference on Empirical Methods in Natural Language Processing (EMNLP '08)*, pp. 224–233, Association for Computational Linguistics, Stroudsburg, Pa, USA, 2008.

[21] B. Efron and R. J. Tibshirani, *An Introduction to the Bootstrap*, CRC Press, Boca Raton, Fla, USA, 1994.

[22] P. Koehn, "Statistical significance tests for machine translation evaluation," in *Proceedings of the Conference on Empirical Methods in Natural Language Processing*, pp. 388–395, Barcelona, Spain, 2004.

[23] A. Stolcke, "Srilm—an extensible language modeling toolkit," in *Proceedings of the International Conference on Spoken Language Processing*, Denver, Colo, USA, 2002.

[24] F. J. Och and H. Ney, "A systematic comparison of various statistical alignment models," *Computational Linguistics*, vol. 29, no. 1, pp. 19–51, 2003.

[25] G. Doddington, "Automatic evaluation of machine translation quality using n-gram co-occurrence statistics," in *Proceedings of the 2nd International Conference on Human Language Technology Research*, pp. 138–145, Morgan Kaufmann Publishers, San Francisco, Calif, USA, 2002.

[26] S. Banerjee and A. Lavie, "Meteor: an automatic metric for mt evaluation with improved correlation with human judgments," in *Proceedings of the 43rd Annual Meeting on Association for Computational Linguistics*, Ann Arbor, Mich, USA, 2005.

[27] A. Lavie and A. Agarwal, "Meteor: an automatic metric for mt evaluation with high levels of correlation with human judgments," in *Proceedings of 45th Annual Meeting of the Association for Computational Linguistics*, pp. 228–231, Association for Computational Linguistics, Prague, Czech Republic, 2007.

[28] M. Snover, B. Dorr, R. Schwartz, L. Micciulla, and J. Makhoul, "A study of translation edit rate with targeted human annotation," in *Proceedings of the 7th Conference of the Association for Machine Translation in the Americas*, pp. 223–231, Association for Machine Translation in the Americas, Los Angeles, Calif, USA, 2006.

[29] R. Steinberger, B. Pouliquen, A. Widiger et al., "The jrc-acquis: a multilingual aligned parallel corpus with 20+ languages," in *Proceedings of the 5th International Conference on Language Resources and Evaluation*, pp. 2142–2147, Genova, Italy, 2006.

[30] T. Brants, A. C. Popat, P. Xu, F. J. Och, and J. Dean, "Large language models in machine translation," in *Proceedings of the Joint Conference on Empirical Methods in Natural Language Processing and Computational Natural Language Learning (EMNLP-CoNLL '07)*, pp. 858–867, Association for Computational Linguistics, Prague, Czech Republic, 2007.

[31] N. Draper and H. Smith, *Applied Regression Analysis*, John Wiley & Sons, New York, NY, USA, 1981.

[32] F. J. Och, "Statistical machine translation: foundations and recent advances," in *Proceedings of the Tutorial at MT Summit*, 2005.

[33] M. Bloodgood and C. Callison-Burch, "Bucking the trend: large-scale cost-focused active learning for statistical machine translation," in *Proceedings of the 48th Annual Meeting of the Association for Computational Linguistics (ACL '10)*, pp. 854–864, Association for Computational Linguistics, Stroudsburg, Pa, USA, 2010.

[34] P. Koehn and H. Hoang, "Factored translation models," in *Proceedings of the Joint Conference on Empirical Methods in Natural Language Processing and Computational Natural Language Learning (EMNLP-CoNLL '07)*, pp. 868–876, 2007.

[35] J. Blatz, E. Fitzgerald, G. Foster et al., "Confidence estimation for machine translation," in *Proceedings of the 20th international Conference on Computational Linguistics (COLING '04)*, vol. 315, Association for Computational Linguistics, Morristown, NJ, USA, 2004.

[36] L. Specia, M. Turchi, Z. Wang, J. Shawe-Taylor, and C. Saunders, "Improving the confidence of machine translation quality estimates," in *Proceedings of 12th the Machine Translation Summit*, 2009.

[37] N. Ueffing and H. Ney, "Word-level confidence estimation for machine translation using phrase-based translation models," in *Proceedings of the Conference on Human Language Technology and Empirical Methods in Natural Language Processing (HLT '05)*, pp. 763–770, Association for Computational Linguistics, Morristown, NJ, USA, 2005.

[38] G. Wisniewski, A. Allauzen, and F. Yvon, "Assessing phrase-based translation models with oracle decoding," in *Proceedings of the Conference on Empirical Methods in Natural Language Processing (EMNLP '10)*, pp. 933–943, Association for Computational Linguistics, Stroudsburg, Pa, USA, 2010.

[39] D. Vilar, J. Xu, L. F. D'Haro, and H. Ney, "Error analysis of statistical machine translation output," in *Proceedings of the 5th International Conference on Language Resources and Evaluation (LREC '06)*, Genova, Italy, 2006.

11

A Cultural Algorithm for the Representation of Mitochondrial Population

Athanasios Alexiou and Panayiotis Vlamos

Department of Informatics, Ionian University, Plateia Tsirigoti 7, 49100 Corfu, Greece

Correspondence should be addressed to Athanasios Alexiou, alexiou@ionio.gr

Academic Editor: Catalina Cocianu

We propose a novel Cultural Algorithm for the representation of mitochondrial population in mammalian cells as an autonomous culture. While mitochondrial dysfunctions are highly associated with neurodegenerative diseases and related disorders, an alternative theoretical framework is described for the representation of mitochondrial dynamics. A new perspective of bioinspired algorithm is produced, combining the particle-based Brownian dynamics simulation and the combinatorial representation of mitochondrial population in the lattice, involving the optimization problem of ATP production in mammalian cells.

1. Introduction

Considering the latest researches, disruptions in the regulation of mitochondrial dynamics, low-energy production, increased reactive oxygen species, and mtDNA damage are relevant to human diseases, mainly in neurogenerative diseases and cancer. Recent discoveries have highlighted that neurons are reliant particularly on the dynamic properties of mitochondria. In addition, mitochondria are actively recruited to subcellular sites, such as the axonal and dendritic processes of neurons. Defects in mitochondrial dynamics are associated with neurodegenerative disease. For example, Charcot-Marie-Tooth type 2A, a peripheral neuropathy, and dominant optic atrophy, an inherited optic neuropathy, result from a primary deficiency of mitochondrial fusion. Moreover, several major neurodegenerative diseases including Parkinson's, Alzheimer's, and Huntington's diseases involve disruption of mitochondrial dynamics.

On the other hand, cultural algorithms are a class of population concepts, principles, mechanisms, and optimization techniques that work on a principle inspired by nature: evolution of species [1]. These algorithms are very useful tools in a large number of applications in optimization, control, signal processing, or machine learning [2].

Lately, researchers attempted to model the cultural evolution process from both a microevolutionary perspective in terms of the transmission of behaviors or traits between individuals in a population and a macroevolutionary perspective in terms of the formation of generalized beliefs based upon individual experiences. These generalized beliefs can serve to constrain the behaviors of individuals within the associated population [3].

According to Reynolds, Cultural Algorithms are a class of computational models of cultural evolution that support such a dual inheritance perspective. This approach provides a framework in which to describe all of the current models of cultural evolution from a computational point of view since any of the single inheritance systems can be produced as a special case [3].

Cultural Algorithms, are based on the supposition that one can get better learning rates for an evolutive genetic algorithm [4] adding to it one more element of evolutive pressure—called Belief Space, a mechanism of cultural pressure. Therefore, a system of double inheritance, both genetic and cultural, could better respond to a large number of problems, while cultural evolution enables societies to evolve or adapt to their environments at rates that exceed that of biological evolution based upon genetic inheritance alone [5, 6].

In this paper we investigate the application of Cultural Algorithms on the representation of mitochondrial population in mammalian cells, a biological system with high complexity, different capabilities and operations, and great importance for the human health.

2. The Mitochondrial Population and Dynamics

The number of mitochondria in a cell is regulated to match the cell's requirements for ATP, while fusions and fissions play a functional role in maintenance of proper inner membrane electrical potential. Mitochondria provide most of the ATP for cellular reactions. ATP production in mitochondria is coupled to an electron transport system in which the passage of electrons down the various electron carriers is associated with the transport of protons from the matrix into the intermembrane space. The majority of these protons reenter the mitochondrial matrix by the ATP syntheses, thereby generating ATP.

Mitochondria are involved in numerous metabolic and cellular processes [7]. Besides the citric acid cycle and the oxidative phosphorylation, these processes also include the urea cycle and the oxidation of fatty acids. Other reactions carried out and orchestrated are the biosynthesis of heme, several amino acids, and vitamin cofactors, as well as the formation and export of iron-sulphur clusters [8]. Beyond these metabolic functions, mitochondria are also involved in the programmed cell death [9] and in case of their dysfunction in ageing [10] and several diseases [11].

2.1. Mitochondrial Structure. Found in most eukaryotic cells, mitochondria are subcellular organelles that play a central role in energy metabolism. The key feature of the mitochondrion is the presence of two membranes that encapsulate a protein-rich central matrix. Specifically, this organelle is compartmentalized by two membranes into four compartments. A smooth outer membrane surrounds and isolates the organelle from the cytosol while the inner membrane with several invaginations, called cristae, divides them further into the mitochondrial intermembrane space and the matrix. The organization of the inner membrane was dissected in recent studies using improved electron microscopic and tomographic techniques [12, 13]. The inner membrane contains the protein complexes and redox cofactors involved in electron transfer and ATP synthesis.

Besides the outer membrane, an inner boundary membrane is connected by several tubular junctions to the cristae, creating a distinction between the intermembrane and the intercristal space. This basic concept of the inner membrane is structurally dynamic with respect to cristae connection to each other or with the inner membrane and can be considerably varied among different organisms' tissues or physiological conditions [12]. The mitochondrial matrix contains a highly concentrated mixture of enzymes involved in all aspects of metabolism, in addition to the mitochondrial genome which, in mammalian mitochondria, encodes 39 genes involved in mitochondrial function. Families of mitochondrial carriers, of which approximately 50 have been identified in the human genome, are present to enable exchange between the intermembrane space and the matrix [14].

The fact that many central processes in eukaryotic cells are functionally linked to this double membrane shielded organelle requires an interface between the mitochondrial compartment and the cytoplasm. To achieve this intracellular exchange the two membranes include a variety of transport and receptor proteins [15–17] as well as a specific subset of translocases involved in the import and assembly of mitochondrial proteins [18].

2.2. Mitochondrial Processes: Fusion, Fission, Motility, and Mitophagy. The number of mitochondria in a cell is regulated to match the cell's requirements for ATP, while fusions and fissions play a functional role in maintenance of proper inner membrane electrical potential. Without the mitochondrial dynamics, the mitochondrial population consists of autonomous organelles that have impaired function [19]. In a wild type cell, high rates of fusion and fission are independent events, which constantly change the identity of individual mitochondria, as well as the motility and the mitophagy.

An individual mitochondrion is not an autonomous organelle. The hundreds of mitochondria within a typical cell undergo continual cycles of fusion and fission. Because mitochondria have an outer lipid membrane as well as an inner one, each fusion event requires the coordinated fusion of the membranes [20, 21]. Fusion is likely to protect function by providing a chance for mitochondria to mix their contents, thus enabling protein complementation, mtDNA repair, and equal distribution of metabolites, helping the isolation of damaged-mitochondrial segments and promoting their autophagy [22, 23]. In contrast, fission acts in order to facilitate equal segregation of mitochondria into daughter cells during cell division and to enhance distribution of mitochondria along cytoskeletal tracks [24].

Intuitively, it is easy to imagine how mitochondrial fusion and fission can change the morphologic characteristics of mitochondria [20–22]. Fusion results in fewer and longer mitochondria, whereas fission results in more and shorter mitochondria. Indeed, genetic studies indicate that cells with mutations in the genes required for mitochondrial fusion have fragmented mitochondria instead of the tubular mitochondrial network observed in normal cells [24]. Similarly, cells with mutations in genes required for mitochondrial fission have excessively elongated and interconnected mitochondria because of unopposed fusion. Peroxisomal shape is also controlled by fission; the role of fusion is less clear [20].

Additional studies have also shown that mitochondrial fission precedes apoptosis [25]. Defects in mitochondrial fusion cause neurodegenerative disease [23, 24]. Charcot-Marie-Tooth disease type 2A, an autosomal dominant neuropathy of long peripheral nerves, is caused by mutations in MFN2. Moreover, dominant optic atrophy, the most commonly inherited optic neuropathy, is caused by mutations in OPA1. This apparent sensitivity of neurons to defects in mitochondrial dynamics probably depends on the special requirements of neurons for mitochondrial function [20]. An ultrastructural hallmark of the synapse is the presence of abundant mitochondria, which maintains calcium homeostasis and levels of ATP production that, in turn, are critical to nerve transmission. Neurons have extraordinarily long cellular processes, and tight control of mitochondrial dynamics is probably necessary for distributing active mitochondria to dendrites and axon terminals. Given the important roles of mitochondrial dynamics in human physiologic processes, it would not be surprising to find additional diseases caused by mutations in genes that control mitochondrial fusion and fission [20].

Another aspect of mitochondrial dynamics beyond fusion and fission is the motility of mitochondria [21]. This aspect is critically important in highly polarized cells, such as neurons [26], which require mitochondria at sites distant from the cell body, but can also be crucial to cellular function in smaller cells [27]. Defects in both fusion and fission have been shown to decrease mitochondrial movement. In neurons lacking mitochondrial fusion, both increased mitochondrial diameter due to swelling and aggregations of mitochondria seem to block efficient entry into neurites, resulting in a dearth of mitochondria in axons and dendrites [28]. These defects result in improperly developed neurons or gradual neurodegeneration.

Autophagy is a mechanism whereby eukaryotic cells degrade their own cytoplasm and organelles [29]. Autophagy functions as a homeostatic nonlethal stress response mechanism for recycling proteins to protect cells from low supplies of nutrients and as a cell death mechanism. This degradation of organelles and long-lived proteins is carried out by the lysosomal system; thus, a hallmark of autophagy is accumulation of autophagic vacuoles of lysosomal origin [23]. Autophagy has been seen in developmental and pathological conditions. Mitophagy denotes the degradation of mitochondria through autophagy. Although the existence of mitophagy has been known for some time, it has been unclear whether mitochondria are randomly or selectively targeted for mitophagy [21].

3. An Alternative Biological Culture

3.1. Mitochondrial Civilization Associated with Neurogenerative Diseases. From a geometrical point of view, a number of (un)correlated factors can affect the mitochondrial shape. This illustrates a more complex problem, while morphological changes in mitochondrial structure are associated with biological dysfunctionalities and electrophysiology problems [30]. These effects are directly or indirectly correlated with human neurodegenerative diseases. While fusions and fissions contribute to the wide variety of mitochondrial morphologies, a discrete mitochondrion at one point in time will be changed at a later time by the addition of new mitochondrial material through fusion or by the removal of material through division. It is a logical consequence of high probability that after a certain period of successful events (fusions and fissions) the inner structure will totally lose its initial characteristics in a nonreversible way, restricting the inner space and reducing the corresponding area and energy [30]. It is obvious that any failure in inner membrane mitochondrial fissions can easily generate unstable electric potential, effecting functionality and reduce voltage gradient. Fusion and fission seems to be required

to maintain mitochondrial function, as independent and different mechanisms. Fusion is likely to protect function by providing a chance for mitochondria to mix their contents, thus enabling protein complementation, mtDNA repair, and equal distribution of metabolites, helping the isolation of damaged mitochondrial segments and promoting their autophagy. In contrast, fission acts in order to facilitate equal segregation of mitochondria into daughter cells during cell division and to enhance distribution of mitochondria along cytoskeletal tracks. The failure in this biological machinery may also promote apoptosis.

Even though, these four processes are independent, it is clear that any interactions will be critically important in neurons. For example, defects in both fusion and fission have been shown to decrease mitochondrial movement. The large tangle of highly interconnected mitochondria in fission-deficient cells prevents efficient movement, especially into small pathways such as neuronal processes. While mitophagy denotes the degradation of mitochondria through autophagy, recent findings indicate that mitophagy can selectively degrade defective mitochondria.

Especially in the case of Alzheimer's Disease, scientists used brain tissue from cases with a diagnosis of AD [31, 32], as well as control cases with no clinical or pathological history of neurological disease, applying cytological *in situ* hybridization, immunocytochemistry, and morphometry [33] techniques, showing that the area of intact mitochondria is significantly decreased in AD. While AD can be genetically classified as familiar or sporadic, researchers proposed that the case of sporadic AD is not caused by the accumulation of amyloid-β ($A\beta$), but instead is a consequence of a decline in mitochondrial function with age [34, 35]. Additionally, the overexpression of $A\beta$ causes an alteration in the mitochondrial fission and fusion proteins resulting in mitochondrial dysfunction, mitochondrial fragmentation, increase in reactive oxygen species (ROS) and ATP production, and reduced mitochondrial membrane potential [36].

3.2. A New Cultural Algorithm. From the philosopher Aristotle to the anthropologist Geertz [37], any civilization consists of citizens, where besides the variation of their genetic characteristics, they participate to the social evolution through their behaviour and several others mechanisms, rules, principles, or even more principles.

Additionally researchers [38] introduce the term Artificial Culture where, a new knowledge domain tries to connect the models found in complex adaptive systems to the models found in the domain of culture. According to this terminology Artificial Culture is a population of individual agents, with its own sense, with its own cognition and performance, interacting in a social ambient with others agents in a physical environment of artifacts and others objects [38].

According to Holland [39], a complex system usually has the following characteristics, which obviously in the case of mitochondrial populations are adapted in most of the cases.

(i) Relationships in complex system are nonlinear.

(ii) Complex systems contain feedback loops.

$t \leftarrow 1$
Generate Civilization: N individuals are distributed
        in the parametric space, assuming that correspond
        to a local martingale
        Initialize Population $P(t)$
        Initialize Belief Space $BS(t)$
While (ATP Production = Acceptant) and ($t <$ constant value) do
{
Evaluate $P(t)$
Evolve $((P(t), Merging(P(t), Combine(P(t)))), Influence(BLF(t)))$
Vote $(BS(t), Accept(P(t)))$
Evaluate $(P(t), Adjust(BS(t)))$
Update $(BS(t), Accept(P(t)))$
$t \leftarrow t + 1$
Select $P(t)$ from $P(t-1)$
}
End

ALGORITHM 1: Cultural Algorithm.

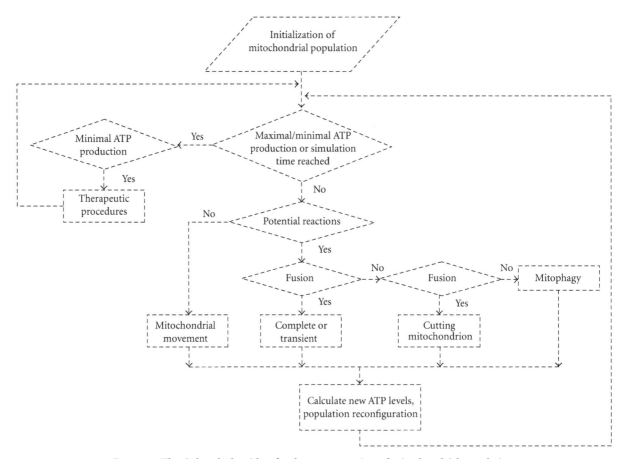

FIGURE 1: The Cultural Algorithm for the representation of mitochondrial population.

(iii) Complex systems are open.

(iv) Complex systems have memory (even though mitochondria seem to obey the memoryless phenomenon [30]).

(v) Complex system may produce emergent phenomena.

The proposed Cultural Algorithm for the representation of the mitochondrial population is an extended version of Reynolds [3], adapted in mitochondrial terminology (operations) where $P(t)$ represents the population and $BS(t)$ the Belief Space at time t.

The algorithm starts with the generation of the civilization, where the initialization of both the Population and

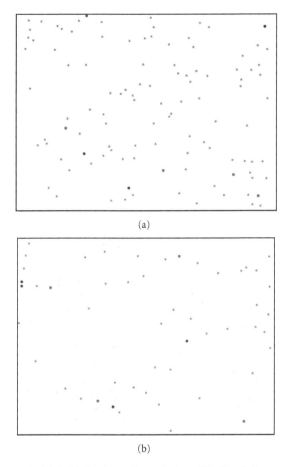

FIGURE 2: (a) Initialization of population. (b) Simulation results after N Steps.

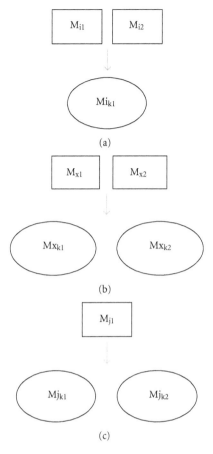

FIGURE 3: (a) Complete fusion. (b) Transient fusion. (c) Fission.

the Belief Space, occurs. Due to the biological identities of mitochondria in mammalian cells, and their stochastic distribution in the lattice space, we assumed that they produce a local martingale limiting their ATP production within the normal measurement limits. The proposed algorithm enters the evolution loop until the ATP production is decreased in a level likely to result in a neurological disorder. At the beginning of each generation, individuals in the Population Space are first evaluated and then interact to each other through the operation factors "Merging" and "Combine" (representing in a way the mitochondrial dynamics and the communication paths between them in order to exchange their contents) resulting a new selection of individuals through the Influence function.

Additionally, the two feedback functions Accept and Influence, give the opportunity to the population component and the Belief Space to interact with each other in the way that human culture evolve [40–42].

The pseudocode of the proposed bioinspired algorithm is given in Algorithm 1.

By the mechanism of mitochondrial dynamics these organelles can undergo exchange their contents for desired morphology and topology. The above algorithm is a more sophisticated control of mitochondrial proper functioning, setting as population belief a total optimum in the cell space.

Empirically, fusion-deficient mitochondria display loss of directed movement, instead hovering in a manner reminiscent of Brownian motion [43]. It is well known that particle-based Brownian dynamics simulations offer the opportunity to not only simulate diffusion of particles but also the reactions between them. Particle-based simulations naturally incorporate the concepts of space, crowding, and stochasticity [44, 45]. Those methods treat proteins or other reactants explicitly, and the time-evolution of particle positions is sampled at discrete time intervals by Brownian dynamics simulations [46, 47]. The basic motion of a particle undergoing diffusion can be described by Einstein's diffusion equation [48] as follows:

$$\frac{\partial}{\partial t} P(r, t \mid r_0, t_0) = D\nabla^2 P(r, t \mid r_0, t_0), \tag{1}$$

where $P(r, t \mid r_0, t_0)$ is the probability that the particle will be at position r at time t given the particle was initially at position r_0 at time t_0. The rate of diffusion is given by the parameter D. When the diffusive motions of multiple particles are simulated, in a traditional Brownian dynamics algorithm the distribution of particle displacements $P(r, t)$ is sampled for each particle every time step [49].

Algorithm 1 is a a novel theoretical approach in order to represent mitochondrial population of mammalian cells as an independent culture. We assigned a random walk in these subcellular compartments of a neural cell as follows: viruses to destroyed mitochondria, infected individuals to mitochondria with decreased ATP production, and uninfected individuals to healthy mitochondria.

A more informative representation of the above pseudocode can be seen in Figure 1, where the main feature involves the optimization level of ATP production. In this Cultural Algorithm the stochastic evolution function is performed until the solution has reached a total optimum, the maximal or minimal ATP level, responsible for several human diseases.

We tested our algorithmic representations in a multi-agent simulation environment called MASON, which is a single-process discrete-event simulation core and visualization library for biological systems [50].

The population is represented by the colour dots [50], brown for the healthy mitochondria, green for the mitochondria with decreased functionality, and the red for the destroyed mitochondria. There are also some cases of healthy mitochondria, which are represented with black dots with red cross, where destroyed mitochondria can be disinfected through the operation of fusion (Figure 2).

It is obvious that the formulation of mitochondrial population as a biological culture, gives us the potentiality of visualization of the two main observed classes of fusion events in mammalian cells. The complete fusion and the transient fusion events [51], wherein two mitochondria came into close apposition, exchanged soluble intermembrane space and matrix proteins, and reseparated, preserving the original morphology.

In this phase, we are more focused in the three main mitochondrial operations: the complete fusion, the transient fusion of two mitochondria, and the fission of one mitochondrion (Figure 3).

It is obvious that further simulation testing of these dependent operations will give us the opportunity of modelling efficiently the mitochondrial dysfunctions over age and figure more accurate the potential safe boundaries of healthy mitochondrial population against the early diagnosis of neurogenerative diseases. Genes, proteins interactions, and mtDNA quality, shall be taken into consideration in future work as the main factors of the proposed representation affecting the mitochondrial population and its functionality.

4. Conclusions and Future Work

Cultural Algorithms will definitely offer a powerful evolutionary algorithmic tool for many biological diseases at both the levels of diagnosis and treatment. In the case of mitochondrial populations and their association with several neurogenerative disorders, this computation technique will lead us to a more formalistic representation of experimental results concerning subcellular measurements and mitochondrial population. In this paper we presented a new combined version of Cultural Algorithms, using the basic notions of evolutionary algorithms on mitochondrial dynamics.

Future research includes more computational tests and a detailed analysis of the performance on real biological data and case studies, concerning mammalian cells.

References

[1] K. J. Batenburg, "An evolutionary algorithm for discrete tomography," *Discrete Applied Mathematics*, vol. 151, no. 1-3, pp. 36–54, 2005.

[2] K. J. Batenburg and W. J. Palenstijn, "A new exam timetabling algorithm," in *Proceedings of the 15th Belgium-Netherlands Artificial Intelligence Conference (BNAIC'03)*, T. Heskes, P. Lucas, L. Vuurpijl, and W. Wiegerinck, Eds., pp. 19–26, 2003.

[3] R. G. Reynolds, "An introduction to cultural algorithms," in *Proceedings of the 3rd Annual Conference on Evolutionary Programming*, pp. 131–139, 1994.

[4] D. E. Goldberg, *Genetic Algorithms*, Addison-Wesley Longman, USA, 1998.

[5] R. G. Reynolds, "An introdution to cultural algorithms," Cultural Algorithms Repository, 1998.

[6] R. G. Reynolds, E. Zannoni, and R. M. Posner, "Learning to understand software using cultural algorithms," Cultural Algorithms Repository, 1998.

[7] A. S. Reichert and W. Neupert, "Mitochondriomics or what makes us breathe," *Trends in Genetics*, vol. 20, no. 11, pp. 555–562, 2004.

[8] R. Lill and G. Kispal, "Maturation of cellular Fe-S proteins: an essential function of mitochondria," *Trends in Biochemical Sciences*, vol. 25, no. 8, pp. 352–356, 2000.

[9] G. Vandecasteele, G. Szabadkai, and R. Rizzuto, "Mitochondrial calcium homeostasis: mechanisms and molecules," *IUBMB Life*, vol. 52, no. 3-5, pp. 213–219, 2002.

[10] A. Trifunovic, "Mitochondrial DNA and ageing," *Biochimica et Biophysica Acta*, vol. 1757, no. 5-6, pp. 611–617, 2006.

[11] D. C. Wallace, "Mitochondrial diseases in man and mouse," *Science*, vol. 283, no. 5407, pp. 1482–1488, 1999.

[12] C. A. Mannella, "The relevance of mitochondrial membrane topology to mitochondrial function," *Biochimica et Biophysica Acta*, vol. 1762, no. 2, pp. 140–147, 2006.

[13] G. Perkins, C. Renken, M. E. Martone, S. J. Young, M. Ellisman, and T. Frey, "Electron tomography of neuronal mitochondria: three-dimensional structure and organization of cristae and membrane contacts," *Journal of Structural Biology*, vol. 119, no. 3, pp. 260–272, 1997.

[14] E. R. S. Kunji, "The role and structure of mitochondrial carriers," *FEBS Letters*, vol. 564, no. 3, pp. 239–244, 2004.

[15] R. Lill and G. Kispal, "Mitochondrial ABC transporters," *Research in Microbiology*, vol. 152, no. 3-4, pp. 331–340, 2001.

[16] B. O'Rourke, "Mitochondrial ion channels," *Annual Review of Physiology*, vol. 69, pp. 19–49, 2007.

[17] L. Palmieri, F. M. Lasorsa, A. Vozza et al., "Identification and functions of new transporters in yeast mitochondria," *Biochimica et Biophysica Acta*, vol. 1459, no. 2-3, pp. 363–369, 2000.

[18] W. Neupert and J. M. Herrmann, "Translocation of proteins into mitochondria," *Annual Review of Biochemistry*, vol. 76, pp. 723–749, 2007.

[19] D. C. Chan, "Mitochondrial fusion and fission in mammals," *Annual Review of Cell and Developmental Biology*, vol. 22, pp. 79–99, 2006.

[20] D. C. Chan, "Mitochondrial dynamics in disease," *New England Journal of Medicine*, vol. 356, no. 17, pp. 1707–1709, 2007.

[21] H. Chen and D. C. Chan, "Mitochondrial dynamics—fusion, fission, movement, and mitophagy—in neurodegenerative diseases," *Human Molecular Genetics*, vol. 18, no. 2, pp. R169–176, 2009.

[22] G. Twig, A. Elorza, A. J. A. Molina et al., "Fission and selective fusion govern mitochondrial segregation and elimination by autophagy," *EMBO Journal*, vol. 27, no. 2, pp. 433–446, 2008.

[23] A. Alexiou, J. Rekkas, and P. Vlamos, "Modeling the mitochondrial dysfunction in neurogenerative diseases due to high H+ concentration," *Bioinformation*, vol. 6, no. 5, pp. 173–175, 2011.

[24] L. J. Martin, "Mitochondrial and cell death mechanisms in neurodegenerative diseases," *Pharmaceuticals*, vol. 3, pp. 839–915, 2010.

[25] R. J. Youle and M. Karbowski, "Mitochondrial fission in apoptosis," *Nature Reviews Molecular Cell Biology*, vol. 6, no. 8, pp. 657–663, 2005.

[26] P. J. Hollenbeck and W. M. Saxton, "The axonal transport of mitochondria," *Journal of Cell Science*, vol. 118, no. 23, pp. 5411–5419, 2005.

[27] S. Campello, R. A. Lacalle, M. Bettella, S. Mañes, L. Scorrano, and A. Viola, "Orchestration of lymphocyte chemotaxis by mitochondrial dynamics," *Journal of Experimental Medicine*, vol. 203, no. 13, pp. 2879–2886, 2006.

[28] H. Chen, J. M. McCaffery, and D. C. Chan, "Mitochondrial fusion protects against neurodegeneration in the cerebellum," *Cell*, vol. 130, no. 3, pp. 548–562, 2007.

[29] D. J. Klionsky and S. D. Emr, "Autophagy as a regulated pathway of cellular degradation," *Science*, vol. 290, no. 5497, pp. 1717–1721, 2000.

[30] A. T. Alexiou, P. M. Vlamos, and K. G. Volikas, "A theoretical artificial approach on reducing mitochondrial abnormalities in Alzheimer's disease," in *Proceedings of the 10th International Conference on Information Technology and Applications in Biomedicine: Emerging Technologies for Patient Specific Healthcare (ITAB'10)*, Corfu, Greece, November 2010.

[31] Z. S. Khachaturian, "Diagnosis of Alzheimer's disease," *Archives of Neurology*, vol. 42, no. 11, pp. 1097–1105, 1985.

[32] S. S. Mirra, A. Heyman, D. McKeel et al., "The Consortium to establish a registry for Alzheimer's disease (CERAD). Part II. Standardization of the neuropathologic assessment of Alzheimer's disease," *Neurology*, vol. 41, no. 4, pp. 479–486, 1991.

[33] K. Hirai, G. Aliev, A. Nunomura et al., "Mitochondrial abnormalities in Alzheimer's disease," *Journal of Neuroscience*, vol. 21, no. 9, pp. 3017–3023, 2001.

[34] R. H. Swerdlow and S. M. Khan, "A "mitochondrial cascade hypothesis" for sporadic Alzheimer's disease," *Medical Hypotheses*, vol. 63, no. 1, pp. 8–20, 2004.

[35] R. H. Swerdlow and S. M. Khan, "The Alzheimer's disease mitochondrial cascade hypothesis: an update," *Experimental Neurology*, vol. 218, no. 2, pp. 308–315, 2009.

[36] X. Wang, B. Su, H. Fujioka, and X. Zhu, "Dynamin-like protein 1 reduction underlies mitochondrial morphology and distribution abnormalities in fibroblasts from sporadic Alzheimer's disease patients," *American Journal of Pathology*, vol. 173, no. 2, pp. 470–482, 2008.

[37] C. Geert, *A Interpretação Das Culturas*, Editora Guanabara, Rio de Janeiro, Brazil, 1989.

[38] N. Gessler, *Artificial Culture—Experiments in Synthetic Anthropology*, 1999.

[39] J. Holland, *Adaptation in Natural and Artificial Systems*, MIT Press, Cambridge, Mass, USA, 1992.

[40] J. Barkow, L. Cosmides, and J. Tooby, *The Adapted Mind: Evolutionary Psychology and the Generation of Culture*, Oxford University Press, USA, 1992.

[41] A. Johnson and T. Earle, *The Evolution of Human Societies: from Foraging Group to Agrarian State*, Stanford Univ Press, 2000.

[42] P. Richerson and R. Boyd, *Not by Genes Alone: How Culture Transformed Human Evolution*, University of Chicago Press, 2005.

[43] H. Chen, S. A. Detmer, A. J. Ewald, E. E. Griffin, S. E. Fraser, and D. C. Chan, "Mitofusins Mfn1 and Mfn2 coordinately regulate mitochondrial fusion and are essential for embryonic development," *Journal of Cell Biology*, vol. 160, no. 2, pp. 189–200, 2003.

[44] M. Dobrzyński, J. V. Rodríguez, J. A. Kaandorp, and J. G. Blom, "Computational methods for diffusion-influenced biochemical reactions," *Bioinformatics*, vol. 23, no. 15, pp. 1969–1977, 2007.

[45] M. Długosz and J. Trylska, "Diffusion in crowded biological environments: applications of Brownian dynamics," *BMC Biophysics*, vol. 4, no. 1, Article no. 3, 2011.

[46] D. L. Ermak and J. A. McCammon, "Brownian dynamics with hydrodynamic interactions," *The Journal of Chemical Physics*, vol. 69, no. 4, pp. 1352–1360, 1978.

[47] S. H. Northrup and H. P. Erickson, "Kinetics of protein-protein association explained by Brownian dynamics computer simulation," *Proceedings of the National Academy of Sciences of the United States of America*, vol. 89, no. 8, pp. 3338–3342, 1992.

[48] H. Kim and K. J. Shin, "Exact solution of the reversible diffusion-influenced reaction for an isolated pair in three dimensions," *Physical Review Letters*, vol. 82, no. 7, pp. 1578–1581, 1999.

[49] Z. Frazier and F. Alber, "A computational approach to increase time scales in Brownian dynamics-based reaction-diffusion modeling," *Journal of Computational Biology*, vol. 19, no. 6, pp. 606–618, 2012.

[50] S. Luke, C. Cioffi-Revilla, L. Panait, K. Sullivan, and G. Balan, "MASON: a multiagent simulation environment," *Simulation*, vol. 81, no. 7, pp. 517–527, 2005.

[51] X. Liu, D. Weaver, O. Shirihai, and G. Hajnóczky, "Mitochondrial kiss-and-run: interplay between mitochondrial motility and fusion-fission dynamics," *EMBO Journal*, vol. 28, no. 20, pp. 3074–3089, 2009.

12

A Method for Identifying Japanese Shop and Company Names by Spatiotemporal Cleaning of Eccentrically Located Frequently Appearing Words

Yuki Akiyama[1] and Ryosuke Shibasaki[2]

[1] Center for Spatial Information Science, The University of Tokyo, Cw-503 Shibasaki Laboratory, 4-6-1 Komaba, Meguro-ku, Tokyo 153-8505, Japan
[2] Center for Spatial Information Science, The University of Tokyo, 5-1-5 Kashiwanoha, Kashiwa City, Chiba 277-8568, Japan

Correspondence should be addressed to Yuki Akiyama, aki@iis.u-tokyo.ac.jp

Academic Editor: Mohamed Afify

We have developed a method for spatiotemporally integrating databases of shop and company information, such as from a digital telephone directory, spatiotemporally, in order to monitor dynamic urban transformations in a detailed manner. To realize this, an additional method is necessary to verify the identicalness of different instances of Japanese shop and company names that might contain fluctuations of description. In this paper, we discuss a method that utilizes an n-gram model for comparing and identifying Japanese words. The processing accuracy was improved through developing various kinds of libraries for frequently appearing words, and using these libraries to clean shop and company names. In addition, the accuracy was greatly and novelty improved through the detection of those frequently appearing words that appear eccentrically across both space and time. By utilizing natural language processing (NLP), our method incorporates a novel technique for the advanced processing of spatial and temporal data.

1. Introduction

Spatiotemporal changes of shop and company locations have a major effect on the vitality and attraction of urban space. It is a significant challenge to monitor these changes, quantitatively and in as detailed as manner as possible, for use in various fields including urban engineering, geography, and economics. However, it is difficult to comprehensively monitor urban spaces, because much general regional and statistical information (e.g., the population census, commercial statistics) is compiled by separate administrative or city block units.

On the other hand, detailed information on shop and company locations and names can be collected using telephone directories and web information. Fortunately, this is possible in Japan, because of the availability of digital telephone directories and detailed digital maps which can monitor almost all residents and tenants in a given building.

The yearly continuations and changes in tenants or residents can be monitored for a certain location, and we can integrate these data across multiple years. The same can be done for shop and company locations over multiple years, by measuring changes in shop and company names. However, this measure is not easy because of name fluctuations between different two years or different kinds of data. Therefsore, we have been developing a dataset that can monitor the time-series changes of each shop and company and a system that can develop such data as to resolve this challenge [1, 2]. This paper focuses on a particular method of name identification, pertinent to shop and company names—that is, an identification method for Japanese words.

1.1. Previous Studies: About Spatial and Temporal Data Developments. There have been many previous studies that have attempted to monitor changes in urban spaces using time-series information of shops, companies, and buildings.

A Method for Identifying Japanese Shop and Company Names by Spatiotemporal Cleaning of Eccentrically
Located Frequently Appearing Words

163

For example, the locations of open and closed shops were extracted using digital maps and the results of field surveys by Ato et al. [3], and time-series changes of building locations were extracted and applications were developed using digital residential maps by Ai et al. [4]. However, the processing methods used in almost all of these previous studies are inappropriate for large quantities of data (e.g., the whole area of one city or prefecture) because the researchers developed their time-series data by manual, time-intensive processing.

On the other hand, Ito and Magaribuchi have developed a completely automated method of spatiotemporal integration of digital residential maps, which is capable of processing large volumes of data [5]. However, this method has been applied to only one specific kind of digital map. In addition, the method encounters difficulties when dealing with problems of so-called noise word cleaning and local frequently appearing words (to be described below) because of the focus of this study was only Tokyo's 23 wards. As result, we consider that there are some limitations to apply this method over a broad area.

1.2. Previous Studies: About Language Processing.

For this study, a method to recognize name entities (i.e., compound noun) is necessary. There have been many previous studies that worked in various ways to develop this method. Florian et al. presented a statistical language-independent framework for identifying and tracking named, nominal, and pronominal references to entities within unrestricted text documents, then chaining them into clusters corresponding to each logical entity present in the text [6]. Tri Tran et al. applied a support-vector-machine- (SVM-) based NER model to the Vietnamese language [7]. Tjong Kim Sang and Meulder processed named entity data from English and German using sixteen different kinds of systems to recognize the entities' identities, and they obtained the best result using a combined learning system that applied Maximum Entropy to each language [8]. In addition, there have been many studies that have attempted to recognize name entities from other kinds of languages [9–13].

There have also been many previous studies focusing on the processing of Japanese words. Sato et al. developed a method to predict the authors of a text based on frequencies of word usage within it [14]. Kawakami and Suzuki presented a method to calculate word similarities in random texts using a decision list [15]. Mishina et al. evaluated word similarities using n-grams. Similarly, we will use n-grams in this study in order to recognize and identify shop and company names [16].

However, it has been difficult for previous methods to deal with local frequently appearing words (LFAW). Our approach to managing this problem is introduced in Section 3.5 in detail.

1.3. About This Paper.

This paper and our system focus on Japanese language processing. Our system can monitor the time-series changes of each shop and company, integrating them to create a dataset containing their names and locations, that is, address, longitude, and latitude across two years spatially and to measure identifications of their names. In

TABLE 1: Example of description of Kanji by Hiragana.

	Described by Kanji	Described by Hiragana/Katakana
Japanese characters	日本	にほん
Pronunciations	Nihon	Ni Ho Nn
Meaning in English	Japan	Japan

TABLE 2: Pronunciations by Chinese and Japanese of the same characters.

Chinese/Japanese character	中	山	本
Pronunciations in Chinese	Zhōng	Shān	Běn
Pronunciations in Japanese (only common readings)	Naka Chūuu	Yama San Sen	Hon Bon Pon Moto

this paper, we focus on how to measure identifications of Japanese words.

There are two remarkable and novel points our paper introduces. The first is that it utilizes natural language processing (NLP) for the advanced processing of spatial and temporal data. There are few studies that have processed data using NLP in the field of spatial information science. Some studies in this field have partly utilized NLP [17, 18]; however, there are no studies that have utilized NLP for the processing of spatial and temporal data to the same extent as our study. In Japan, Ito and Magaribuchi [5] have accomplished a similar trial to our study, as detailed in Section 1.1. However, their method has been applied only in central Tokyo. Our study is the first to develop a spatiotemporal dataset for throughout Japan. The second is that our method can deal with LFAW. It is a novel method that recognizes so-called pure shop and company names ("Pure" refers to the elements of a character string which identifies a tenant uniquely.) and detects words that are eccentrically-located spatially and temporally (LEAW) and also cleans shop and company names of LFAW.

In Japan, there are many kinds of data that contain name and location information. One of the largest and most complete datasets for shops and companies all over Japan comprises residential and tenant information from digital residential maps (Zenrin CO., Ltd.; in Japanese, "Zyutaku-Chizu") and digital telephone directories (e.g., "Town Page Database" by NTT Business Information Service, Inc. and "Telepoint Data" by Zenrin CO., Ltd.). Other data are data of each companies and enterprises, for example, the quarterly journal of companies and enterprises of Japan, or shop information on the Web collectable by API services. Therefore, our method can be adapted across various fields of data development.

Our system should be able to process data in various regions and times. Therefore, the test data used in the development of our system was the residential and tenant information in the digital residential maps and telephone

TABLE 3: Example of Japanese without blanks.

	Text	Translation from English to Japanese
Japanese	東京証券取引所	
English	Tokyo Stock Exchange	Tokyo = 東京 Stock = 証券 Exchange = 取引所

TABLE 4: Examples of description of loanwords by katakana.

		Example 1	Example 2	Example 3
Words	Loanwords	Notebook (En)	Baumkuchen (De)	Château (Fr)
	Japanese	ノートブック	バームクーヘン	シャトー
Pronunciations	Loanwords	nóutbuk	baʊmˈkuːxn̩	ʃætóʊ
	Japanese	nōtobukku	Bāmukūhen	Shatō

TABLE 5: Examples of noise words in shop and company names.

	Example 1	Example 2
Shop and company names		
Japanese	マクドナルド下北沢店	スターバックスコーヒー六本木ヒルズ店
English	McDonalds Shimokitazawa shop	Starbucks Coffee Roppongi Hills shop
Noise words		
Japanese	下北沢店	六本木 ヒルズ店
English	Shimokitazawa shop	Roppongi Hills shop
Kind of noise words	Station/geographic name	Building name

TABLE 6: Examples of fluctuations of description between old and new names.

Name (in 2005)	Name (in 2000)	Address
20世紀フォックス映画	20世紀フオツクス映画会社	東京都港区六本木3丁目16-33
55ステーション江戸川橋店	55分DPEステーション江戸川橋店	東京都文京区関口1丁目6-10
747サウンドポート新宿南口本店	サウンドポートIN747新宿南口本店	東京都新宿区新宿3丁目36-16
ABC新宿クッキングスタジオ	ABCクッキングスタジオ新宿店	東京都新宿区西新宿1丁目26-2
Antsケントレーディング	ケントレーディングブレイン株式会社	東京都中央区銀座1丁目14-10
ARAトラベル合宿インフォメーション	ARAトラベルガッシュクインフォメーション	東京都新宿区新宿3丁目12-4
auショップ六本木交差点	IDOプラザ六本木交差点	東京都港区六本木4丁目8-7
BA—RU	BA・RU	東京都文京区千石4丁目38-10
B—マリエ	ビーマリエ	東京都港区白金1丁目29-15
CLAN・PaPa	ビアレストランP	東京都文京区根津2丁目11-8
COM陶芸教室	コム（COM）陶芸教室	東京都新宿区西新宿7丁目6-6
Di・マーレ	ディマーレー	東京都台東区浅草橋3丁目20-18
ELEC英語研修所	エレック英語研修所	東京都千代田区神田錦町3丁目20
ESPギタークラフト・アカデミー東京	ESPギタークラフトアカデミー東京	東京都千代田区神田錦町1丁目8
IDC大塚家具・新宿ショールーム	IDC大塚家具新宿ショールーム	東京都新宿区新宿3丁目33-1
KAZUKIスパゲティ専門店	スパゲティ専門店KAZUKI	東京都千代田区内神田1丁目4-12
KOJI・VANCOUVER・赤坂	KOJI・VANCOUVER赤坂	東京都港区赤坂2丁目14-27
MKミッシェルクラン新宿小田急店	ミッシェルクランエムケー	東京都新宿区西新宿1丁目1-3

A Method for Identifying Japanese Shop and Company Names by Spatiotemporal Cleaning of Eccentrically
Located Frequently Appearing Words

165

directory mentioned above, because these data can cover all of Japan with a homogeneous resolution.

2. Characteristic Features of Japanese

Japanese is a language used throughout Japan. There are about 130 million speakers in the world, mainly in East Asia [19].

One of the main characteristics of Japanese is its use of three kinds of characters: hiragana, katakana, and kanji. Hiragana and katakana are phonograms, while kanji are ideograms. The origin of kanji is Chinese characters, while hiragana and katakana are unique characters originating in Japan. Kanji are mainly used to write nouns, roots of verbs and adjectives, and personal names of Japanese and Chinese people. Kanji can be described by hiragana and katakana because the pronunciations of kanji can be written phonetically, as seen in Table 1. In addition, there are multiple pronunciations in kanji, unlike Chinese characters (Table 2). In such cases, the pronunciation of a given kanji is decided by the context of the surrounding words and texts.

A notable characteristic of written Japanese is that it does not have blanks between single words. Because of this, it is difficult to divide one text into its component single words without an adequate understanding of word meaning or class (Table 3). This is a common characteristic of major languages in East Asia. Klein et al. have also pointed this out and tried to recognize Chinese name entities using the character sequences [20].

In addition, one of the interesting features of Japanese is that it typically writes loanwords with similarly pronounced katakana (Table 4). Chinese also has this same feature. When it is difficult to write loanwords with katakana because of inadequate or incompatible phonemic inventories, loanwords are sometimes written in the original languages and script [21].

2.1. Difficulty in Verifying the Identity of Shop and Company Names. It is not easy to verify that two Japanese words are identical or even similar because of the above features of Japanese. For example, character string lengths tend to be longer than English or French, because Japanese is written without blanks between single words. In addition, there are many fluctuations of description, because Japanese uses three kinds of characters and changes word order frequently.

Moreover, one kind of character string that appears frequently in shop and company names is branch names. These strings become noise words, making name identification difficult if a shop and company name contains long geographic or building names (Table 5). We realize the necessity of solving these kinds of problems if we wish to verify the identicalness of different instances of shop and company names adequately.

3. Development

We identify and verify the time-series changes of shops and companies between two different years based on location (i.e., address, longitude, and latitude) and name information (i.e., shop, company, or building names). Then, we can assess the kind of time-series change—that is, continuation, change, emergence, and demise—of each shop or company between different two years, for monitoring purposes.

3.1. Input Data. The input data consisted of name and location information separated by commas (e.g., in csv or txt format) containing an address at minimum. When more specific information is provided in the source data—building names, floors, and room numbers—our system can integrate input data more accurately than without. Figure 1 shows an image of some sample input data and their resultant output.

3.2. Processing Flow. Figure 2 shows the processing flow of our method and all potential results of time-series integration. At first, new and old data are integrated spatially for each shop and company unit. Shops and companies found at the same location are integrated into a set, and after subsequent time-series integration, they are labeled either "continuation" or "change." The time-series results of shop and companies that exist only as new data are labeled "emergence" and those that exist only as old data are labeled "demise."

In this paper, we introduce a method to verify whether or not two spatially integrated names refer to the same tenant, and then to decide whether the time-series change is best classified as "continuation" or "change." The details of spatial integration have been described in our previous studies [1, 2].

In this study, the time-series changes of each shop and company were monitored based on the "name" changes within the same location. In other words, our method monitors time-series changes of buildings and their floors and rooms. Therefore, our method will not identify transfers of shop or company ownership, whether by merger or acquisition. However, we expect that interested parties will be able to track changes of ownership at the same "continuation" location by using other data or statistics more relevant to company mergers and acquisitions, such as the Japan Company Handbook (Toyo Keizai Inc.).

3.3. Verification of Name Identification. It is not easy to verify that a new name and old name refer to the same company at a given location, because simply determining whether each name is exactly the same returns inadequate results. There are subtle fluctuations of description between the names in new data versus old data, even though they may actually be the same shops or companies. Table 6 shows some examples of fluctuations of description between old and new names of the same business. The shops and companies listed in Table 6 were taken from the 2000 and 2005 Tokyo telephone directories. Each shop or company is located at the same location in 2000 and 2005, and this fact can be verified via human manual processing. However, each name is subtly different.

In order to solve this problem, we must meaningfully quantify similarities between the words of the shop and company names.

TABLE 7: Appearance frequencies of FAW in tenant names in 2005.

FAW in Japanese	FAW in English	Appearance frequency	Ratio of appearance (%)
（株）	Co.	532007	13.88
（有）	Ltd.	322517	8.42
株式会社	Corporation	151421	3.95
有限会社	Limited company	69205	1.81
センター	Center	54179	1.41
（事）	Office	39617	1.03
美容室	Beauty salon	32534	0.85
（営）	Business office	28489	0.74
ビル	Building	27510	0.72
クリニック	Clinic	19028	0.50
東京	Tokyo	18702	0.49
駐車場	Parking	17703	0.46
ハイツ	Heights	17679	0.46
サービス	Service	17542	0.46
クリーニング	Cleaning	17432	0.45
スナック	Snack bar	14308	0.37
コーポ	Cooperative	13716	0.36

▪RThe ratio of appearance is calculated as the appearance frequency divided by the tenant total.
▪The full library contains 963 words.
Tenants in the 2005 residential maps: 3,141,434
Tenants the 2005 telephone directory: 690,183
Total tenants: 3,831,617.

TABLE 8: Examples of noise words in shop and company names.

Names (Japanese/English)	Noise words	Kind of noise word
株式会社ゼンリン/ Zenrin Co., Ltd.	株式会社/Co., Ltd.	FAW
サーティワンアイスクリーム麻布店/ 31 ice cream Azabu shop	麻布店/Azabu shop	Geographic name
かつや代々木駅前店/ Katsuya in front of Yoyogi station	新橋駅前店/in front of Yoyogi station	Station name
株式会社ホブソンズジャパン西麻布店/ Hobsons Japan Co. Nishiazabu office	株式会社/Co.	FAW
	西麻布店/Nishiazabu office	Geographic name
アコム株式会社新橋駅前支店/Acom Co., Ltd in front of Shinbashi station	株式会社/Co., Ltd.	FAW
	新橋駅前支店/in front of Shinbashi station	Station name
喫茶室ルノアール赤坂見附店/ Coffee shop Renoir Akasaka Mitsuke shop	喫茶室/Coffee shop	FAW
	赤坂見附店/Akasaka Mitsuke shop	Geographic name

In this study, this word quantification has been realized by the "n-gram." The n-gram is one method of natural language processing that can quantify the degree of similarity between different two words [22]. The method has been attracting attention in fields as diverse as literature, linguistics, and computer science [23–25].

We use the bigram (2-gram) to calculate name similarity in this study. The bigram extracts string blocks constructed of 2 characters from new and old names and then compares them. This method can resolve the problem of fluctuations of description. Figure 3 depicts the bigram calculation method as applied to our word similarity problem. A name similarity between word i and word j is defined by

$$S_{ij}^{(n)} = \frac{n_{ij}^{(n)} + n_{ji}^{(n)}}{m_i^{(n)} + m_j^{(n)}}, \qquad (1)$$

where $S_{ij}^{(n)}$ is the name similarity between word i and word j, $m_i^{(n)}$ is the number of string blocks extracted from word i, $m_j^{(n)}$ is the number of string blocks extracted from word j, and $n_{ij}^{(n)}$ and $n_{ji}^{(n)}$ are the number of string blocks within $m_i^{(n)}$ matching within $m_j^{(n)}$, and vice versa, respectively.

A Method for Identifying Japanese Shop and Company Names by Spatiotemporal Cleaning of Eccentrically
Located Frequently Appearing Words

167

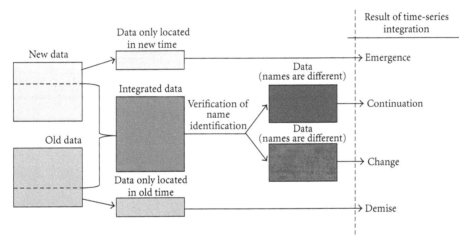

New data

Name	Location Information			
	Address	Bldg information	Longitude	Latitude
ロッテリア大通店	北海道札幌	大通ビル1階	141.35	43.06
養老の瀧	北海道札幌	大通ビルB1階	141.35	43.06
札幌観光（株）	北海道札幌	大通ビル303号	141.35	43.06
北海道食品	北海道札幌	鉄北会館2A	141.34	43.07
札幌かに道場	北海道札幌	薄野タワー202	141.35	43.05
セイコーマート琴似	北海道札幌	ハイム琴似1F	141.31	43.07

Old data

Name	Location Information			
	Address	Bldg information	Longitude	Latitude
ロッテリア札幌大通店	北海道札幌	大通りビル1F	141.35	43.06
つぼ八大通り店	北海道札幌	大通りビルB1F	141.35	43.06
北洋商事	北海道札幌	大通りビル202	141.35	43.06
北海道食品（株）	北海道札幌	鉄北会館3B号	141.34	43.07
かに道場	北海道札幌	薄野タワー2階	141.35	43.05
セイコーマート	北海道札幌		141.31	43.07

Result of time-series integration

Name in new time	Name in old time	Location information						Result of time-series integration
		Address	Bldg info	floor	Room No.	Lon	Lat	
ロッテリア大通店	ロッテリア札幌大通店	北海道札幌	大通ビル	1		141.35	43.06	Continuation
養老の瀧	つぼ八大通り店	北海道札幌	大通ビル	-1		141.35	43.06	Change
札幌観光（株）		北海道札幌	大通ビル	3	303	141.35	43.06	Emergence
	北洋商事	北海道札幌	大通りビル	2	202	141.35	43.06	Demise
北海道食品		北海道札幌	鉄北会館	2	A	141.34	43.07	Emergence/imigration
	北海道食品（株）	北海道札幌	鉄北会館	3	B	141.34	43.07	from other floor
札幌かに道場	かに道場	北海道札幌	薄野タワー	2	202	141.35	43.05	Continuation (add floor info)
セイコーマート琴似	セイコーマート	北海道札幌	ハイム琴似	1		141.31	43.07	Continuation (add bldg info)

Note: All information in this table is fictional.

FIGURE 1: Image of sample input data and resultant output (time-series integration).

FIGURE 2: Processing flow of time-series integration by our method.

It was necessary to designate a minimum threshold for the similarity metric $S_{ij}^{(n)}$ experimentally. First, 3,000 shops and companies were randomly extracted from the 2005 Tokyo telephone directory, and then integrated with the shops and companies in their respective spaces from the 2000 directory. Next, the name similarities between shops and offices in the integrated dataset were calculated using the method above, using a comprehensive range of values for $S_{ij}^{(n)}$. We then compared these automated results with results obtained via manual processing that were verified as correct. Figure 4 shows the results of this comparison. Accordingly, a value of about 0.4 was determined to be optimal for the threshold of $S_{ij}^{(n)}$. Integrated data over the threshold $S_{ij}^{(n)}$ are considered to accord. As a result, we set the default value of $S_{ij}^{(n)}$ as 0.4 for our system.

3.4. Removal of Noise Words. Shop and company names may often contain frequently appearing words (FAWs), geographic names, and station names. Because of the confounding and pseudosimilar effects of these words and names,

appropriate verification that similar names refer to the same tenant is difficult to achieve. Sagara and Kitsuregawa have also pointed out this difficulty in recognizing pure shop and company names using computers [26]. A method that can remove these so-called "noise words" from name information is necessary.

We solved this problem by creating dictionaries of noise words and using them to remove noise words from shop and company names prior to n-gram analysis. The FAW dictionary developed in this study was developed by applying an automated system of Japanese morphological analysis called "Chasen" [27] to tenant names that had been extracted from the 2005 residential maps and telephone directory covering the South Kanto region. Tenant names were divided into parts of speech by the Chasen, and these data were combined with manually culled FAWs to develop our library. Table 7 shows examples of FAWs taken from tenant names by automated morphological analysis of the Chasen. The library of geographic names was developed using the "Nihon Gyosei Kukaku Binran Data File" published by Nihon Kajo-Syuppan Corporation. The library of station names was developed

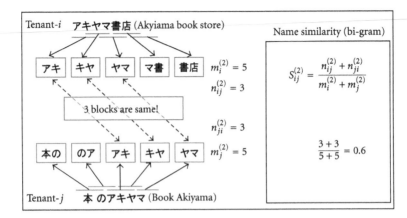

FIGURE 3: Calculation method for word similarity using a bigram.

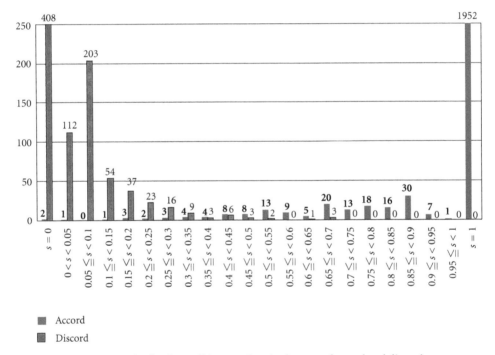

FIGURE 4: Distributions of bigram values in the case of accord and discord.

using railroad timetables of Japan. Table 8 shows some examples of noise words, and Table 9 shows the number of words present in each library.

Only those character strings that contain the geographic and station name structures depicted in Figure 5 are removed from shop and company names. The processing in Figure 5 is necessary because it decreases the risk that character strings which have no relation with geographic and station names might be removed from shop and company names. This risk increases to remove noise words in shop and company names to use only geographic and station names. We consider one geographic name, "Nakagawa (中川)", as an example. This name is common in Adachi ward in Tokyo Prefecture, where it refers to a geographic name. However, it is strongly expected that there will also be many shops and companies that contain "Nakagawa" even outside of the Nakagawa area, because it is a very popular family name

in Japan: in fact, in the 2005 telephone directory, there are 311 shops and companies that do. Almost all of the shops and companies extracted were this nongeographical Nakagawa (Figure 6). Table 10 shows some examples of shop and company names containing an instance of Nakagawa unrelated to its geographic and station usages.

On the other hand, using the removal procedure in Figure 5 diminishes the risks associated with removing character strings unrelated to geographic and station names, that is, used for the n-gram similarity metric. Figure 7 shows the results of a search for shops and companies containing "Nakagawa" in their names using this rule. Two shops were found, and Table 11 shows that the "Nakagawa" in their names refers to the geographic Nakagawa.

Eventually, pure shop and company names remain after removing the various kinds of noise words through the above processing. This process is demonstrated in Figure 8.

A Method for Identifying Japanese Shop and Company Names by Spatiotemporal Cleaning of Eccentrically
Located Frequently Appearing Words

169

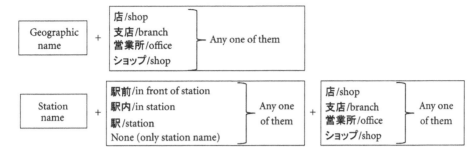

FIGURE 5: Character strings removed from shop and company names.

FIGURE 6: Locations of shops and companies in the 2005 telephone directory containing "Nakagawa (中川)" in Tokyo's 23 wards.

3.5. Removal of Local Frequently Appearing Words.

Nonetheless, there are cases that cannot be processed well, even when all of the above methods and libraries are incorporated. This is because there are frequently appearing words that are eccentrically located both spatially and temporally. We refer to such words as "Local Frequently Appearing Words (LFAW)" in this study.

We explain about the LFAWs using three examples, depicted in Figure 9. "Shinjuku Nishiguchi" (the western exit of Shinjuku terminal) and "Yaesu-guchi" (Yaesu exit) are not geographic names. In addition, "Yaesu-guchi" is not a station name. However, there are many shops and companies whose names contain these character strings, because they are located in the western area of Shinjuku terminal or the eastern area of Tokyo terminal, respectively. These are examples of FAWs, which are eccentrically located in space: that is, they are concentrated only around a particular area. Figure 10 shows the locations of shops and companies whose names contain "Shinjuku Nishiguchi-ten" (Shinjuku terminal western exit shop) taken from the 2005 telephone directory. There are many data points in the western area outside Shinjuku terminal that fit this category.

Tenants containing Nakagawa in their names

Location of Nakagawa district

FIGURE 7: Search results of shops and companies containing "Nakagawa" as a geographic name.

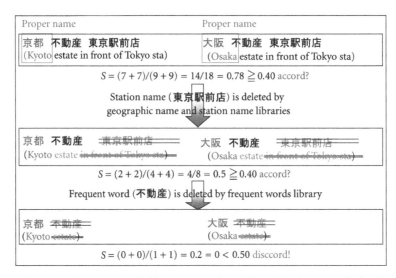

FIGURE 8: Accuracy improvement in bigram processing achieved by the removal of noise words.

A Method for Identifying Japanese Shop and Company Names by Spatiotemporal Cleaning of Eccentrically Located Frequently Appearing Words

171

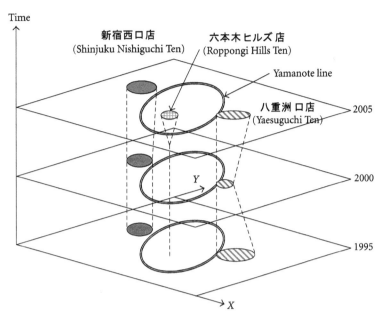

Figure 9: Image of LFAWs.

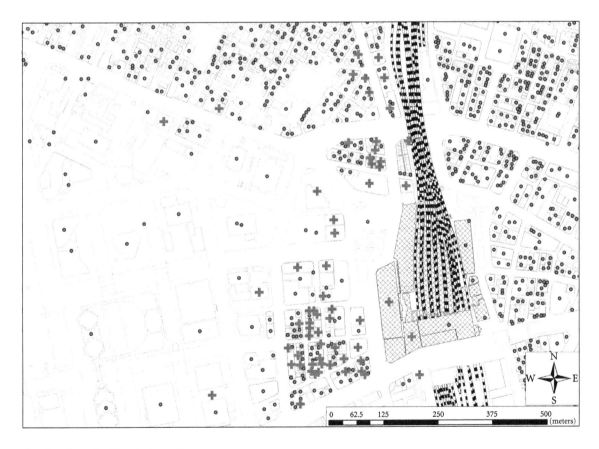

Figure 10: Data distribution of locations containing "Shinjuku Nishiguchi-ten" ("Nichiguchi-ten" means western exit shop/branch).

The list of LFAW (GridID: 13970035686)

Number of characters	LFAW list	Frequency	Examples	
			Names before removal of LFAW (red strings = LFAW)	Names after removal of LFAW
9	新宿西口国際通り店	2	福善新宿西口国際通り店	福善
8	新宿エステック店	3	ちよだ鮨新宿エステック店	ちよだ鮨
8	エステック情報店	3	そじ坊新宿エステック情報店	そじ坊新宿
7	ク新宿南口支店	2	ディック新宿南口支店	ディツ
6	ト新宿南口店	2	協和コンタクト新宿南口店	協和コンタク
6	新宿駅西口店	2	ミニストップ新宿駅西口店	ミニストップ
5	新宿南口店	3	山頭火新宿南口店	山頭火
4	新宿南口	12	天狗新宿南口	天狗
4	新宿西口	12	ボーダフォン新宿西口	ボーダフォン
4	新宿支社	3	ジャパンプロテック新宿支社	ジャパンプロテック
4	西口本店	2	ヨドバシカメラ西口本店	ヨドバシカメラ
4	東京支社	4	近畿設備東京支社	近畿設備

· The search area is 3/1000° square (the SW edge is N35.685, E139.699 and the NE edge is N35.688, E139.702.).

· The names before LFAW removal have already had other noise words removed.

FIGURE 11: Examples of LFAWs and their removal from shop and company names in one grid covering an area west of Shinjuku terminal (taken from the 2005 telephone directory).

On the other hand, "Roppongi Hills" (one of the largest and most famous skyscraper complexes in Tokyo and Japan) in Figure 9 is an example of an FAW, which is eccentrically-located not only spatially but also temporally. There are almost no shop or company names from before 2003 containing "Roppongi Hills," because Roppongi Hills was only opened in that year. There are 105 shops and companies in 2005 and 141 in 2009 that contain "Roppongi Hills" in their names: however, there was zero such shops in the 2000 Tokyo telephone directory, as Roppongi Hills opened only in 2003. Thus, a method to remove these kinds of LFAWs was necessary.

We constructed grids measuring millidegree square along longitude and latitude, and all source data were allocated to this grid. Frequently appearing character strings were searched for in the shop and company names within each grid using the n-gram method. For each grid, n-grams created strings measuring from $n = 4$ to $n = 9$ based on both the shop and company names within the targeted grid itself and the neighboring 8 grids on all sides. It was necessary to search in the neighboring grids as well, so that shops or companies located near the grid borders could be incorporated into the LFAW identification process. Finally, the identified LFAWs were removed from the shop and company names in each grid. For our purposes, LFAWs are only 4- to 9-gram-constructed strings that appear multiple times, and whose endings comprise "店/ten" (shop), "支社/sisya" (branch), "営業所/eigyosyo" (office), "東口/higashiguchi" (eastern exit), "西口/nishiguchi" (western exit), "南口/Minamiguchi" (southern exit), and "北口/kitaguchi" (northern exit). Also, long LFAWs are removed earlier than short LFAWs. In other words, those LFAWs created by the 9-gram are removed first, those created by the 8-gram next, and so on through the 4-gram.

To this effect, Figure 11 shows the results from these example LFAWs and their removal in one grid west of Shinjuku terminal. Almost all of the shop and company names were processed adequately. In addition, even when

A Method for Identifying Japanese Shop and Company Names by Spatiotemporal Cleaning of Eccentrically Located Frequently Appearing Words

173

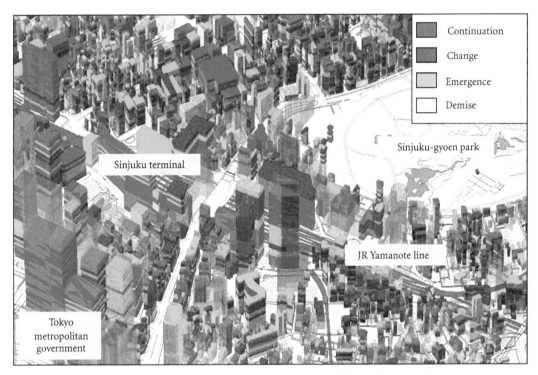

FIGURE 12: Time-series 3D map of tenants around Shinjuku terminal.

TABLE 9: The number of words in each noise word dictionary.

Regions of Japan	Number of words		
	Geographic names	Station names	FAW
Hokkaido	48570	1519	
Tohoku	135436	1314	
North Kanto	12224	678	
South Kanto	35869	2625	
Koshinetsu	16677	785	
Hokuriku	14248	721	963
Tokai	76361	2008	
Kinki	66681	2290	
Chugoku	21554	1081	
Shikoku	17303	580	
Kyusyu	28868	1717	
Okinawa	1835	19	

Each region contains the following prefectures.
- Hokkaido: Hokkaido
- Tohoku: Aomori, Iwate, Akita, Miyagi, Yamagata, and Fukushima
- North Kanto: Ibaraki, Tochigi, and Gunma
- South Kanto: Saitama, Chiba, Tokyo, and Kanagawa
- Koshinetsu: Niigata, Nagano, and Yamanashi
- Hokuriku: Toyama, Ishikawa, and Fukui
- Tokai: Shizuoka, Aichi, Gifu, and Mie
- Kinki: Siga, Kyoto, Nara, Wakayama, Osaka, and Hyogo
- Chugoku: Tottori, Shimane, Okayama, Hiroshima, and Yamaguchi
- Shikoku: Kagawa, Tokushima, Kochi, and Ehime
- Kyusyu: Fukuoka, Nagasaki, Saga, Oita, Kumamoto, Miyazaki, and Kagoshima
- Okinawa: Okinawa

TABLE 10: Examples of shop and company names containing Nakagawa unrelated by geography or station name.

Names	
In Japanese	In English
株式会社中川印刷所	Nakagawa Printing Press Co., Ltd.
中川金属株式会社	Nakagawa Metal Co., Ltd.
中川歯科クリニック	Nakagawa Dental Clinic
中川屋カレーうどん	Nakagawa-ya Curry Udon

TABLE 11: Shop names of search results from Figure 7.

Names	
In Japanese	In English
あいちや中川店	Aichiya Nakagawa shop
西沢薬局中川支店	Nishizawa pharmacy, Nakagawa branch

parts of noise words remained in the pure shop or company names, or when parts of the pure name were erroneously removed, the effects can be largely ignored because the n-gram can still calculate name similarity effectively as in Figure 3.

Tables 12 and 13 show some example test results of our method for removing noise words. For telephone directory data (Table 12), there are 654 shops and companies from which noise words should be removed, out of 1000 extracted by random sampling. 92.4% of these 654 shops and companies had their noise words successfully removed without damaging the character strings of pure names. For web information (Table 13), the fluctuation of shop and company names seems larger than in the telephone

TABLE 12: Processing accuracy of removal of noise words (Data consists of 1000 samples extracted randomly from the 2005 Tokyo prefecture telephone directory).

Number of samples					1000			
Is it necessary to remove noise words from names, as determined by a manual check?		Yes: 654				No: 346		
Can we get the same result as manual processing using the FAW dictionary?	**Yes: 513**		No: 141					
Can we get the same result as manual processing using the dictionary of geographic names and station names?		**Yes: 70**		No: 71				
Can we get the same result as manual processing after LFAW removal?			**Yes:11**		**No:60**			
Do pure names remain after all noise word removal processing?						**Yes: 330**	**No: 16**	**Sum total**
Number of data processed successfully	513	70	11		0	330	0	924
Processing accuracy (%)								92.40

TABLE 13: Processing accuracy of removal of noise words (Data consists of 1000 samples extracted randomly from web data using the Hot Pepper API from within Tokyo prefecture).

Number of samples					1000			
Is it necessary to remove noise words from names, as determined by a manual check?		Yes: 545				No: 455		
Can we get the same result as manual processing using the FAW dictionary?	**Yes: 67**		No: 478					
Can we get the same result as manual processing using the dictionary of geographic names and station names?		**Yes: 237**		No: 241				
Can we get the same result as manual processing after LFAW removal?			**Yes:81**		**No:160**			
Do pure names remain after all noise word removal processing?						**Yes: 409**	**No: 46**	**Sum total**
Number of data processed successfully	67	237	81		0	409	0	794
Processing accuracy (%)								79.40

"Hot Pepper" is a famous free coupon magazine in Japan, produced by Recruit Co., Ltd. Using the Hot Pepper API, we can collect information about many kinds of shops, companies, restaurants, and so forth.

directory, with 79.4% of the locations having their noise words removed successfully. In addition, the FAW dictionary exerts the largest discriminative effect within each test.

There are cases where noise words still remain partly in shop and company names or where important character strings are erroneously removed after the LFAW processing. These are indicated by the blue numbers in Table 12 (76 shops and companies: 7.6%) and Table 13 (206 shops and companies: 20.6%) and the blue character strings in the "Name after removal of LFAW" row within Figure 11.

A Method for Identifying Japanese Shop and Company Names by Spatiotemporal Cleaning of Eccentrically
Located Frequently Appearing Words

175

TABLE 14: Sample areas and their numbers of data.

| Sample areas | | The number of data | | | |
| | | in 2005 | | in 2000 | |
Locations of area	Area types	Z	T	Z	T
Part of Kabukicho, Shinjuku-ku, Tokyo	Bustling shopping area in city center	191	88	210	94
Nodai dori shopping street, Setagaya-ku, Tokyo	Old shopping street around train station	276	130	247	141
Vicinity of Amatsu port, Kamogawa city, Chiba	Port town	121	82	136	94
Nakanogo and Kashidate districts, Hachijo island, Tokyo	Settlements in an isolated island	140	105	144	121
	Sum total	728	405	737	450

"Z" in number of data denotes residential map tenant data.
"T" in number of data denotes telephone directory data.

TABLE 15: Processing accuracy of time-series integration for residential map tenant data.

| | | System results | | | | | |
		Sum total	Co	Ch	Em	De	FSI	Accuracy (%)
Manual results	Continuation	467	443	4	22	0	2	94.86
	Change	129	4	121	8	0	0	93.80
	Emergence	132	4	2	126	0	0	95.45
	Demise	141	8	3	0	130	0	92.20
						Sum total		94.36

"Co": continuation, "Ch": change, "Em": emergence, and "De": demise
"FSI" means failure of spatial integration.

However, these effects are negligibly small, because n-gram processing can nonetheless verify name similarity despite the incompleteness of the pure character string. Tables 15, 16, and 17 in Section 4 will demonstrate that our method can process data with sufficiently high accuracy.

4. Processing Accuracy

So far, we have developed a method for removing various kinds of noise words from shop and company names, and one for verifying that differing names may refer to the same tenant, by calculating the name similarity. In this section, the processing accuracy of our system achieved by these methods is discussed.

We compared the results of time-series data produced by our system with results created manually (and verified for correctness) in some sample areas in the South Kanto region of Japan. Input data for this verification of identity were taken from the telephone directories and digital residential maps as described in Section 1.3. Table 14 shows our sample areas: two each of urban and rural areas.

First, telephone directory and residential map tenant data from 2000 were integrated spatiotemporally with the same data from 2005 over the whole South Kanto region. Then, sample data were extracted from the results of time-series integration. Finally, these automated results were compared with results manually obtained and verified as correct.

Tables 15 and 16 show the processing accuracy achieved by our system's time-series integration. Each table begins with the manually verified total of all the time-series changes observed in each of the sample areas. The system

accomplished a processing accuracy of 94.36% (820/869) in integrating the old and new residential map tenant data spatiotemporally (Table 15), and one of 95.22% (478/502) in integrating the old and new telephone directory data (Table 16). The reason why the sum totals here are discordant with their respective sum totals in Table 14 is because the "Demise" results are counted instead of obscured by subtraction. That is, the sum total in Table 15 not including "Demise" data is the same as the sum total of the number of tenants in the 2005 residential maps. The most remarkable and salient point from Tables 15 and 16 is the high accuracy achieved for continuation and change results. We could not have acquired such high values without not only accurate spatial integration but also a robust method for identifying differing names as referring to the same tenant. We demonstrate that the Japanese language processing methodology introduced in this paper is effective for the realization of time-series integration.

In addition, Table 17 shows the processing accuracy for the residential map tenant data in each sample area. For example, in the Continuation column of "Kabukicho," "79 (87)" means that 87 data points were judged as "Continuation" through manual analysis, and 79 out of those 87 were judged to be the same time-integration category by our system. Processing accuracies in urban areas were slightly lower than in rural areas, because of high density of shops and companies and frequent transfers of them. Processing accuracies in rural areas were almost 100%.

It has been shown in Tables 15, 16, and 17 that there is about a 5% error rate when creating time-series data manually. Compared to this rate, the processing accuracy of

TABLE 16: Processing accuracy of time-series integration for telephone directory data.

		System results						
		Sum total	Co	Ch	Em	De	Sim	Accuracy (%)
Manual results	Continuation	**307**	**293**	4	10	0	0	**95.44**
	Change	**46**	1	**43**	2	0	0	**93.48**
	Emergence	**52**	0	3	**49**	0	0	**94.23**
	Demise	**97**	2	2	0	**93**	0	**95.88**
							Sum total	**95.22**

TABLE 17: Comparison of processing accuracy in each sample area.

Sample area	Number of data		Processing accuracy of time-series integration					Accuracy (%)
	in 2005	in 2000	Co	Ch	Em	De	FSI	
Part of Kabukicho, Shinjuku-ku, Tokyo	191	210	79(87)	67(74)	28(30)	44(49)	2	**94.58**
Nodai-dori shopping street, Setagaya-ku, Tokyo	276	247	137(154)	48(51)	67(71)	38(42)	0	**92.45**
Vicinity of Amatsu port, Kamogawa city, Chiba	121	136	116(116)	0(1)	4(4)	19(19)	0	**99.29**
Nakanogo and Kashidate districts, Hachijo island, Tokyo	140	144	106(110)	2(3)	27(27)	29(31)	0	**97.66**

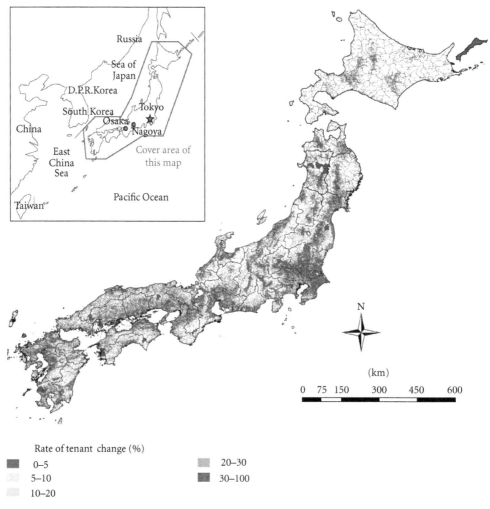

Rate of tenant change (%)
- 0–5
- 5–10
- 10–20
- 20–30
- 30–100

FIGURE 13: Grid map of rate of tenant change all over Japan (1 km square grid).

A Method for Identifying Japanese Shop and Company Names by Spatiotemporal Cleaning of Eccentrically Located Frequently Appearing Words

177

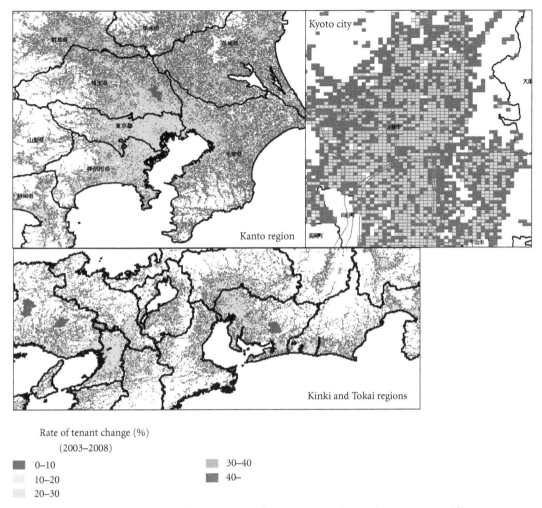

Rate of tenant change (%)
(2003–2008)

▪ 0–10		▪ 30–40
░ 10–20		▪ 40–
░ 20–30		

FIGURE 14: Grid map of rate of tenant change in parts of Japan (500 m square grid).

our system is certainly practical and robust, considering the inevitable human error and large amounts of labor and time necessary when performing such work manually.

The high processing accuracy observed with our system was achieved not only with accurate spatiotemporal integration—the method we developed, which identifies two different names as referring to the same tenant by calculating of word similarity, was essential. The results detailed in this section demonstrate that our method for name identification discussed in this paper performs at a reliable level.

5. Examples of Data Graphics Developed Using Our System

In this section, we will briefly discuss some examples and applications of detailed time-series datasets that can be developed by our system.

Figure 12 shows a 3D time-series map of tenant changes around Shinjuku terminal between 2000 and 2005. This map was constructed so as to integrate the residential map time-series datasets with the respective telephone ones for the years 2000 and 2005. It is possible to find buildings that were newly built between 2000 and 2005 by searching for buildings where all tenants are categorized as "Emergence," and conversely, to find vacant sites or sites under construction by searching for buildings where all tenants are categorized as "Demise." In addition, we can easily see that many of the "Change" tenants are (in 2005) located in low floors around Shinjuku terminal.

Figure 13 shows a grid map (500 m square length) of various "Change" rates based on the results of time-series integration of residential map tenant data from 2003 and 2008 from all over Japan. This is calculated as the number of "Change" tenants divided by the total number of tenants. It is readily apparent from Figure 14 that grids with high "Change" rates are located in urban areas: this may be expected, since competition among shops and companies is usually intense in such areas. In addition, it is interesting to be able to monitor the variability of the "Change" rate across many different areas in the same city.

This is the first instance where such a detailed time-series dataset with such homogenous resolution over this broad of an area has been realized in Japan. This kind of data can make a valuable contribution in solving the problems encountered in previous studies, as introduced in Section 1.

6. Conclusion

In this paper, we discussed a method for identifying Japanese names, by quantitatively analyzing their true, "pure" similarities while ignoring pseudosimilar "noise words" within them. The most remarkable achievement of this study was its removal of eccentricallylocated LFAW located both spatially and temporally by an n-gram-adapted methodology. This novel approach integrates knowledge bases from both linguistics and spatial information science. In addition, we can further conjecture that this study is predictive of how the demands for natural language processing will increase more and more in the fields of spatial information science and geography.

There are some future challenges to improve the identification of Japanese words. One challenge is to develop an environment that can convert effortlessly between kanji, hiragana, and katakana. Mutual conversion between hiragana and katakana is very easy because both sets of characters comprise the same set of phonograms. However, it seems difficult to convert kanji directly into hiragana or katakana because kanji are ideograms. In addition, almost all kanji in Japanese have multiple kinds of pronunciation. The development of a method to accurately and robustly convert kanji into hiragana or katakana is one of the most important tasks facing our research. Another important challenge is that of converting loanwords into katakana. We have already realized a simplified system that can do this. However, the processing accuracy of this system is inadequate, with this system converting only some English and French words into katakana precisely. Both are very difficult challenges, yet nonetheless very interesting and exciting directions for future research.

Acknowledgments

The authors were given the digital telephone directory by ZENRIN CO., LTD (Telepoint Pack!) and NTT Business Information Service, Inc. (Town Page Databese) and the digital residential maps by ZENRIN CO., LTD (Zmap TOWN II). Publication of this paper was supported by Earth Observation Data Integration and Fusion Research Institute (EDITORIA). They would like to thank ZENRIN CO., LTD, NTT Business Information Service, Inc., and EDITORIA for their contribution.

References

[1] Y. Akiyama and R. Shibasaki, "Development of detailed spatio-temporal urban data through the integration of digital maps and yellow page data and feasibility study as complementary data for existing statistical information," in *Proceedings of the Computers in Urban Planning and Urban Management (CUPUM '09)*, 187, 2009.

[2] Y. Akiyama, T. Shibuki, and R. Shibasaki, "Development of three dimensional monitoring dataset for tenants variations in broad urban area by spatio-temporal integrating digital house maps and yellow page data," in *Proceedings of the 4th International Conference on Intelligent Environments (IE '08)*, 2008.

[3] T. Ato, K. Omura, T. Arata, and S. Hujii, "The stagnation of commercial accumulation districts in front of the stations in the suburbs of the Tokyo metropolitan area: a study of honatsugi and odawara," *City Planning Review*, vol. 41, no. 3, pp. 1037–1042, 2006.

[4] H. Ai, Y. Sadahiro, and Y. Asami, "Spatio-temporal analysis of building location and building use in middle scale commercial accumulation districts," *City Planning Review*, vol. 43, no. 3, pp. 103–108, 2008.

[5] K. Ito and H. Magaribuchi, "Method for making spatio-temporal data from accumulated information: using the identification by resolving geometric and non-geometric ambiguity," in *Proceedings of the Geographic Information Systems Association*, vol. 10, pp. 147–150, 2001.

[6] R. Florian, H. Hassan, A. Ittycheriah et al., "A statistical model for multilingual entity detection and tracking," in *Proceedings of the Human Language Technologies Conference (HLT-NAACL '04)*, pp. 1–8, May 2004.

[7] Q. Tri Tran, T. X. Thao Pham, Q. Hung Ngo, D. Dinh, and N. Collier, "Named entity recognition in Vietnamese documents," *Progress in Informatics*, no. 4, pp. 5–13, 2007.

[8] E. F. Tjong Kim Sang and F. D. Meulder, "Introduction to the CoNLL-2003 Shared task: language-independent named entity recognition," in *Proceedings of the 7th Conference on Natural Language Learning (HLT-NAACL '03)*, vol. 4, pp. 142–147, 2003.

[9] R. Florian, A. Ittycheriah, H. Jing, and T. Zhang, "Named entity recognition through classifier combination," in *Proceedings of the 7th Conference on Natural Language Learning at (HLT-NAACL '03)*, vol. 4, pp. 168–171, 2003.

[10] H. L. Chieu and H. T. Ng, "Named entity recognition: a maximum entropy approach using global information," in *Proceedings of the 19th International Conference on Computational Linguistics*, vol. 1, pp. 1–7, 2002.

[11] R. Steinberger and B. Pouliquen, "Cross-lingual named entity recognition," *Lingvisticae Investigationes*, vol. 30, no. 1, pp. 135–162, 2007.

[12] T. Bogers, *Dutch named entity recognition: optimizing features, algorithms, and output*, Ph.D. thesis, University of Van Tilburg, 2004.

[13] C. Sporleder, M. V. Erp, T. Porcelijn, A. V. Bosch, and P. Arntzen, "Identifying named entities in text databases from the natural history domain," in *Proceedings of the 5th International Conference on Language Resources and Evaluation*, pp. 1742–1745, 2006.

[14] S. Sato, M. Harada, and K. Kazama, "Measuring similarity among information sources by comparing string frequency distributions," *Information Processing Society of Japan Digital Document*, vol. 2002, no. 28, pp. 119–126, 2002.

[15] T. Kawakami and H. Suzuki, "A calculation of word similarity using decision list," *IPSJ SIG Technical Report*, vol. 2006, no. 94, pp. 85–90, 2006.

[16] K. Mishina, S. Tsuchita, S. Kurokawa, and R. Huji, "An emotion similarity calculation using N-gram frequency," *IEICE Technical Report*, vol. 107, no. 158, pp. 37–42, 2007, NLC2007-7.

[17] D. Cali, A. Condorelli, S. Papa, M. Rata, and L. Zagarella, "Improving intelligence through use of natural language processing. A comparison between NLP interfaces and traditional visual GIS interfaces," *Procedia Computer Science*, vol. 5, pp. 920–925, 2011.

[18] B. Bitters, "Geospatial reasoning in a natural language processing (NLP) environment," in *Proceedings of the 25th International Cartographic Conference*, CO-253, July 2011.

A Method for Identifying Japanese Shop and Company Names by Spatiotemporal Cleaning of Eccentrically
Located Frequently Appearing Words

179

[19] S. Miyagawa, "The Japanese Language," MIT JP NET, 2011, http://web.mit.edu/jpnet/articles/JapaneseLanguage.html.

[20] D. Klein, J. Smarr, H. Nguyen, and C. D. Manning, "Named entity recognition with character-level models," in *Proceedings of the 7th Conference on Natural Language Learning (HLT-NAACL '03)*, vol. 4, pp. 180–183, 2003.

[21] S. Kuno, *The Structure of the Japanese Language. Current Studies in Linguistics*, MIT Press, 1 edition, 1973.

[22] C. E. Shannon, *A Mathematical Theory of Communication*, University of Illinois Press, 1948.

[23] M. Kondo, *An Analysis of Japanese Classical Literature Using Character-Based N-Gram Model*, vol. 29, Chiba University, Zinbun Kenkyu, 2000.

[24] T. Odaka, T. Murata, J. Gao et al., "A proposal on student report scoring system using N-gram text analysis method," *Journal of Institute of Electronics, Information, and Communication Engineers*, vol. 86, no. 9, pp. 702–705, 2003.

[25] J. B. Marino, R. E. Banchs, J. M. Crego et al., "N-gram-based machine translation," *Computational Linguistics*, vol. 32, no. 4, pp. 527–549, 2006.

[26] T. Sagara and M. Kitsuregawa, "Cleaning shop names by its location information for shop information retrieval from the web," *Journal of Institute of Electronics, Information, and Communication Engineers*, vol. 91, no. 3, pp. 531–537, 2008.

[27] Chasen legacy—an old morphological analyzer, http://chasen-legacy.sourceforge.jp/.

13

RPCA: A Novel Preprocessing Method for PCA

Samaneh Yazdani,[1] Jamshid Shanbehzadeh,[2] and Mohammad Taghi Manzuri Shalmani[3]

[1] *Department of Computer Engineering, Science and Research Branch, Islamic Azad University, Tehran, Iran*
[2] *Department of Computer Engineering, Faculty of Engineering, Kharazmi University, Tehran, Iran*
[3] *Electronic Research Center, Sharif University of Technology, Tehran, Iran*

Correspondence should be addressed to Samaneh Yazdani, samaneh.yazdani@gmail.com

Academic Editor: Wolfgang Faber

We propose a preprocessing method to improve the performance of Principal Component Analysis (PCA) for classification problems composed of two steps; in the first step, the weight of each feature is calculated by using a feature weighting method. Then the features with weights larger than a predefined threshold are selected. The selected relevant features are then subject to the second step. In the second step, variances of features are changed until the variances of the features are corresponded to their importance. By taking the advantage of step 2 to reveal the class structure, we expect that the performance of PCA increases in classification problems. Results confirm the effectiveness of our proposed methods.

1. Introduction

In many real world applications, we faced databases with a large set of features. Unfortunately, in the high-dimensional spaces, data become extremely sparse and far apart from each other. Experiments show that in this situation once the number of features linearly increases, the required number of examples for learning exponentially increases. This phenomenon is commonly known as the curse of dimensionality. Dimensionality reduction is an effective solution to the problem of curse of dimensionality [1, 2]. Dimensionality reduction is to extract or select a subset of features to describe the target concept. The selection and extraction are based on finding a relevant subset of original features and generating a new feature space through transformation, respectively [1, 3]. The proper design of selection or extraction process improves the complexity and the performance of learning algorithms [4].

Feature selection concerns representing the data by selecting a small subset of its features in its original format [5]. The role of feature selection is critical, especially in applications involving many irrelevant features. Given a criterion function, feature selection is reduced to a search problem [4, 6]. Exhaustive search, when the number of the features is too large, is infeasible and heuristic search can be employed. These algorithms, such as sequential forward and/or backward selection [7, 8], have shown successful results in practical applications. However, none of them can provide any guarantee of optimality. This problem can be alleviated by using feature weighting, which assigns a real-value number to each feature to indicate its relevancy to the learning problem [6]. Among the existing feature weighting algorithms, ReliefF [5] is considered as one of the most successful ones due to its simplicity and effectiveness [9]. A major shortcoming of the feature weighting is its inability to capture the interaction of correlated features [4, 10]. This drawback can be solved by some feature extraction techniques.

The basis of feature extraction is a mathematical transformation that changes data from a higher dimensional space into a lower dimensional one. Feature extraction algorithms are generally effective [11]. However, their effectiveness will be degraded when they are used for processing large-scale datasets [12]. In addition, the features extracted from the mathematical transformation usually concern with all original features. So the extracted features may contain

ReliefF Algorithm

(1) Initialization: given $D = \{(x_j, y_j)\}_{j=1}^{N}$, y is the label of classes between $1 \ldots c$.
c number of class, set $w_i = 0$, $\ 1 \leq i \leq t$, number of iteration T;
(2) for $l = 1$ to T
    (3) Randomly select a pattern x_r from D with class y_r;
    (4) Find k nearest hits H_j from class y_r
    (5) For each class $y \neq y_r$
      (6) from class y find k nearest misses $M_j(y)$
    (7) For $i = 1$ to t
      (8) compute: $w_i = w_i - \sum_{j=1}^{k} \dfrac{|x_{ri} - H_{ji}|}{T \cdot k} + \sum_{y \neq y_r} \left(\dfrac{p(y)}{1 - p(y_r)} \sum_{j=1}^{k} \dfrac{|x_{ri} - M_{ji}(y)|}{T \cdot k} \right)$
    (9) end
(10) end

PSEUDOCODE 1: Pseudocode of ReliefF [2].

information originated from the irrelevant information in the original space [3, 13].

Principal Component Analysis (PCA) is an effective feature extraction approach and has successfully been applied in recognition applications such as face, handprint, and human-made object recognition [14–16] and industrial robotics [17]. The traditional PCA is an orthogonal linear transformation and operates directly on a whole pattern represented as a vector and acquires a set of projections to extract global feature from a given training pattern [18]. PCA reduces the dimension such that the representation is as faithful as possible to the original data [2]. PCA employs all features in the original space, regardless their relevancy, to produce new features. This may result in features containing information originated from irrelevant features in the original space. A side effect is misclassification results. Some works have been done to improve the performance of PCA via the feature weighting. In [19, 20], feature weighting has been used for eliminating irrelevant features or using the weight of features in its calculation. In [19], rank is used instead of the original data for copying the outliers and noises. Honda et al. used weights of features in PCA-guided formulation, while in our proposed method we utilize weights of features to properly change the dataset.

The main objective of this paper is to improve the accuracy of classification using features extracted by PCA. PCA is the best-known unsupervised linear feature extraction algorithm; but it is used for classification tasks too. Since PCA do not pay any particular attention to the underlying class structure, it is not always an optimal dimensionality-reduction procedure for classification purposes, and the projection axes chosen by PCA might not provide the good discrimination power. However, the study in [21] illustrates that PCA might outperform LDA which is one of the best supervised dimensionality reduction method, when the number of samples per class is small or when the training data nonuniformly samples the underlying distribution. In the present work, we propose a novel preprocessing method composed of two steps. In the first step, the qualities of features are computed via a feature weighting algorithm. The

selected relevant features, features with weights larger than a predefined threshold, are then subject to the second step. In the second step, the variances of features are modified until the most relevant ones become the most important ones for PCA. Finally, PCA is performed on them to generate uncorrelated features.

The rest of this paper is organized as follows. Section 2 reviews ReliefF, PCA, and its associated problems in brief. Section 3 describes the proposed algorithm. Section 4 presents our experiments on both synthetic and real data and the final section is Conclusion.

2. Review of the ReliefF and PCA Methods

This section reviews ReliefF and PCA briefly and presents the drawbacks of PCA.

2.1. ReliefF. Relief [5] is one of the most successful algorithms to assess the quality of features. The main idea of Relief is to iteratively estimate the weights of features according to how well values distinguish among instances that are near each other. The original Relief limits into two classes problems and deals with complete data [22]. In particular, it has no mechanism to eliminate redundant features [23]. This paper utilizes an extension of Relief called ReliefF [22] that solves the two first problems of Relief. In contrast to Relief, which uses the 1-nearest-neighbor algorithm, ReliefF uses an approach based on K-nearest-neighbor algorithms. Pseudocode 1 presents the pseudocode of this algorithm. It is assumed that $D = \{(x_j, y_j)\}_{j=1}^{N}$ denotes a training dataset with N samples in which each sample consists of t features $x = (x_1, \ldots, x_t)$ and the known class label y_j. In each iteration, ReliefF randomly selects a sample (pattern) x and then searches k of its nearest neighbors from the same class, termed nearest hits H_j, and also the nearest neighbors from each of different classes, called nearest misses $M_j(y)$. To compute the weight of each feature, ReliefF uses the contribution of all the hits and misses.

TABLE 1: Centroids and standard deviations of classes in different variables.

Class	Class centroids	Standard deviations	No. of points
1	(0.547, 0728, 0.424, 0.492, 0561)	(0.054, 0.044, 0.071, 0.288, 0.302)	100
2	(0.299, 0.585, 0.318, 0.555, 0.455)	(0.061, 0.044, 0.069, 0.269, 0.274)	100
3	(0.422, 0.452, 0.636, 0.520, 0.536)	(0.055, 0.050, 0.075, 0.263, 0.274)	100

In ReliefF algorithm, T is a parameter defined by users and determines the number of process repeats to estimate the weight of each feature. x_{ri} is the ith feature of sample x_r and $p(y)$ is the prior probability of class y.

2.2. Principle Component Analysis. PCA is a very effective approach of extracting features. It is successfully applied to various applications of pattern recognition such as face classification [18]. As mentioned above, N and t are the number of samples and their dimension of dataset D, respectively. PCA finds a subspace whose basis vectors correspond to the maximum-variance direction of the original space. As mentioned before, PCA is a linear transform. Let W represents the linear transformation that maps the original t-dimensional space into an f-dimensional feature space where normally $f \ll t$. Equation (1) shows the new feature vectors, $z_j \in R^f$

$$z_j = W^T x_j, \quad j = 1, 2, \ldots, N. \tag{1}$$

Columns of W are the eigenvectors e_i obtained by solving (2):

$$\lambda_j e_j = Q e_j \quad \text{where } Q = XX^T, \ X = \{x_1, \ldots, x_N\}. \tag{2}$$

Here Q is the covariance matrix and λ_j the eigenvalue associated with the eigenvector e_j. The eigenvectors are sorted from high to low according to their corresponding eigenvalues. The eigenvector associated with largest eigenvalue is the most important vector that reflects the greatest variance [21].

PCA employs the entire features and it acquires a set of projection vectors to extract global feature from given training samples. The performance of PCA is reduced when there are more irrelevant features than the relevant ones. On the other hand, PCA has no preknowledge about the class in a given data. So, it is not efficient to determine the classes in the subspace of a given dataset.

We present an example to confirm the mentioned points. This example uses a dataset with five variables and 300 records. The number of classes is three and each class has 100 points. The last two variables represent uniform distributed noise points and irrelevant features. Table 1 shows the centroids and the standard deviations of the three classes [24].

The centroids of two noise variables (x_3 and x_4), against other three variables, are very close and their standard deviations are larger than those of the other three variables. Figure 1, illustrates the 300 points in different two-dimensional subspaces. We can find no class structure in subspaces with two noisy features. Now, PCA is applied on the database presented in Table 1. Figure 2 shows the results obtained by using two significant eigenvectors extracted by PCA.

Figure 2 shows that the obtained result is not suitable for classification, because there is no mechanism in PCA algorithm to determine irrelevant features. As mentioned before, PCA finds projections of the data with maximum variance. Observably, in this example, there are two irrelevant features with the largest variance. Now, PCA is just performed on three relevant variables x_1, x_2, x_3. Figure 3 illustrates the new data by applying the PCA. Notice that the class structures can be found in Figure 3. Because of removing irrelevant features, it is suitable for classification. The next section presents the proposed algorithm to solve this problem.

3. RPCA Feature Extraction

As shown in Figure 2, the directions founded by PCA are not proper for classification if the variances of features are not corresponding with their importance. For example, if the variances of irrelevant features are large, then the extracted features via PCA are not suitable for classification. Therefore, it is expected that if the importance of features are proper with their variances then the extracted features using PCA are more likely suitable for classification. In this paper, a new preprocessing method is proposed which involves two connected steps: relevance analysis and variance adjustment as shown in Figure 4.

In the step of the relevant analysis, weights of features are calculated through one feature weighting approach (like Relief or its extension for multiclass dataset called ReliefF). Assume that $W = [w_1, w_2, \ldots, w_t]$ be the weight vector, estimated by using ReliefF, for the t variables in the original space. Since the weights indicate the level of relevancy, the feature with the largest weight has the largest relevancy. The relevancy level is close to zero or negative when the feature is irrelevant [5]. In this work, features with the weights larger than the threshold defined by user y are the subject to the next step. Therefore, W vector is changed as follows:

$$w_i = \begin{cases} w_i & w_i > \gamma, \\ 0 & \text{otherwise.} \end{cases} \tag{3}$$

After removing the irrelevant features, we do not need to collect all the features. In the variance adjustment step, the variances of features have been changed so that the most important feature becomes the most important feature for PCA. A key idea for this step is motivated from this characteristic of PCA: a feature with maximum variance has the most important for PCA. The new variance of ith feature is calculated as follows:

$$\delta_{\text{new}i} = m - (w_{k(m)} - w_i)(m - k(i)), \tag{4}$$

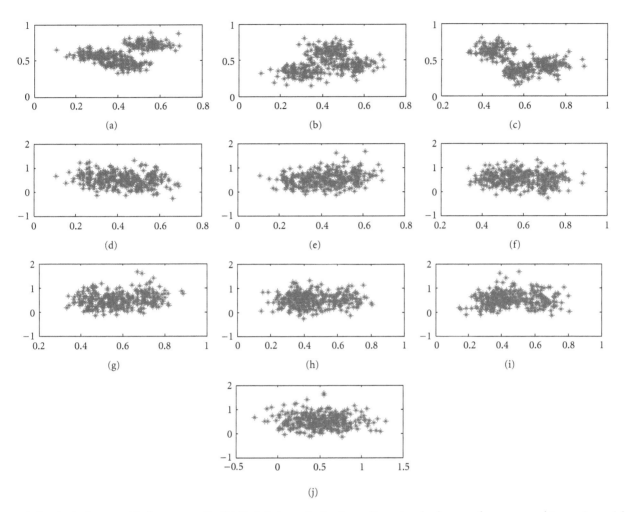

FIGURE 1: Synthetic dataset with three normally distributed classes in the three-dimensional subspace of x_0, x_1, x_2 and two noise variables x_3, x_4. (a) The subspace of x_0, x_1. (b) The subspace of x_0, x_2. (c) The subspace of x_1, x_2. (d) The subspace of x_0, x_3. (e) The subspace of x_0, x_4. (f) The subspace of x_1, x_3. (g) The subspace of x_1, x_4. (h) The subspace of x_2, x_3. (i) The subspace of x_2, x_4. (j) The subspace of x_3, x_4 [24].

where m is the number of features that their weight are more than threshold (number of relevant features). $w_{k(m)}$ is the weight of most important feature and $k(i)$ is the weight rank of i-th feature (1 is least importance and m is most importance). Since $w_{k(m)} - w_i > 0$, and $(m - k(i)) \geq 0$, δ_{newi} is always positive. It is important to mention that $w_{k(m)} > w_i$ because $w_{k(m)}$ is the largest weight. Then, to modify the variance of i-th feature to δ_{newi}, the values of it should be multiplied by the number specified for it. So, it is calculated as follows:

$$\delta_{newi} = \frac{1}{N-1} \sum_{j=1}^{N} \left(nx_{ji} - n\vec{x}_i\right)^2,$$

$$\delta_{newi}(N-1) = \sum_{j=1}^{N} \left(nx_{ji} - n\vec{x}_i\right)^2, \qquad (5)$$

$$n = \sqrt{\frac{\delta_{newi}(N-1)}{\sum_{j=1}^{N} \left(x_{ji} - \vec{x}_i\right)^2}}.$$

Equation (5) shows the way that can obtain n for each feature where σ_{newi} is the new variance of ith feature and calculated using (4). N is the number of samples and $x_{ji}, \vec{x}_i$ are ith feature of jth sample and mean of ith feature, respectively. After this adjustment, PCA is employed on data. We call our proposed method RPCA that refers to applying ReliefF in the first step for weighting features.

Notice that each feature weighting method can be utilized in the first step. Since the output of the first step is used as a subject for the second step (variance adjustment), more effective feature weighting methods lead to better results. Hence, if we use a feature weighting more effective than ReliefF, the obtained result is better than we use ReliefF. Further, the type of feature weighting is very important. For example, if we replace ReliefF with another unsupervised feature weighting method like SUD [25], the proposed method can be utilized for the unsupervised dataset as a dimensionality reduction. The advantages of our preprocessing method are summarized as follows.

(i) The extracted features are formed only by using relevant features.

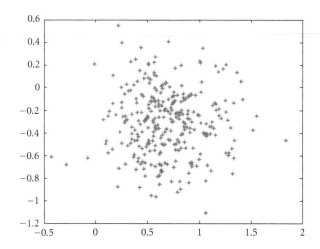

FIGURE 2: A plot of a new data point by applying the PCA using two significant eigenvectors.

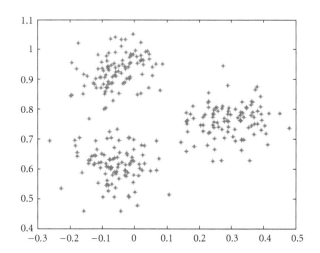

FIGURE 3: A new data point by applying the PCA using two significant eigenvectors after removing irrelevant features.

(ii) The preprocessing steps have low time complexity.

(iii) The preprocessing steps reveal the underlying class structure for PCA approximately.

4. Simulation Results

This section presents the experimental results to show the effectiveness of RPCA on four UCI datasets and synthetic data introduced in Section 2.2. Table 2 summarizes the data information of the four UCI datasets. We applied ReliefF, which employs M instead of just one nearest hit and miss, in our experiment. The value of M was set to 10 as suggested in [22].

In order to provide a platform where PCA and RPCA can be compared, KNN classification errors are used. The number of nearest neighbors is achieved by trial and error. To eliminate statistical variation, each algorithm is run 20 times for each dataset. In each run, a dataset is randomly

FIGURE 4: Proposed preprocessing steps.

TABLE 2: Summary of four UCI data sets.

Database	Training	Testing	Features
Twonorm	400	7000	20
Waveform	400	4600	21
Ringnorm	400	7000	20
Breast cancer	100	545	9

TABLE 3: The testing errors.

Database	PCA	RPCA
Synthetic data	0.5787	0.0083
Twonorm	0.2529	0.0349
Waveform	0.6653	0.2496
Ringnorm	0.5021	0.1797
Breast cancer	0.3581	0.0434

partitioned into training and testing. Also, 50 irrelevant features with Gaussian distributions are added to UCI datasets. The mean of Gaussian distribution is equal to zero and the standard deviation is set based on dataset.

Table 3 shows the testing errors. The number of extracted features is five expected in syntactic dataset which is two in this dataset. The number of training and testing instances for synthetic dataset are 100 and 200, respectively. The performance of KNN is degraded significantly in the presence of the large number of irrelevant features [6]. Figure 5 illustrates the average testing errors of PCA and RPCA as a function of the number of extracted features for 20 runs. This figure reveals that RPCA significantly outperforms PCA in terms of classification errors and effectiveness in reducing dimensionality. These results show that RPCA can significantly improve the performance of KNN. As discussed in Section 3, using a feature weighting better than ReliefF in the first step can lead to better results.

5. Conclusion

We propose a new preprocessing method comprised two steps to improve the performance of PCA in classification task. After weighting features and selecting relevant features in the first step, the variances of features are adjusted based on their importance in the second step until the most important feature has the most variance. Finally, PCA is applied to the modified data. Since, in the first step, ReliefF is used for feature weighting, we nominate our proposed preprocessing technique RPCA. Moreover, we can utilize another type of feature weighting method instead of ReliefF. For example, SUD [25] can be employed in unsupervised data. The simulation results show that the RPCA significantly improves the efficiency of PCA in classification purposes.

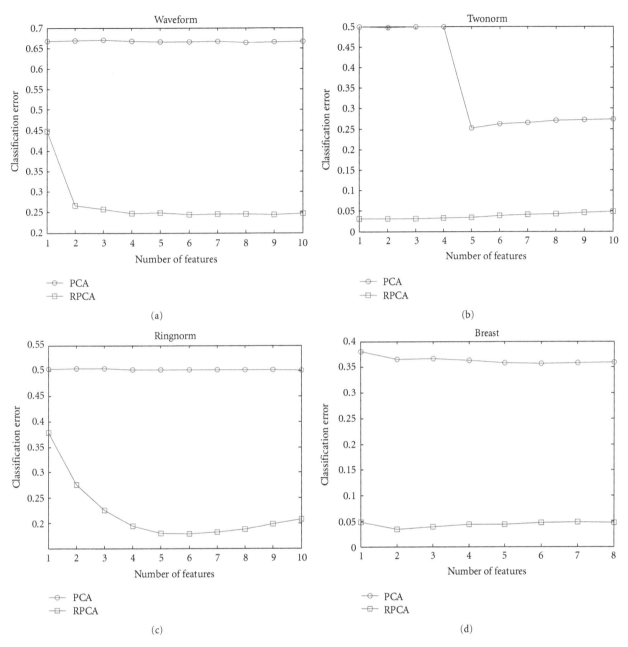

FIGURE 5: Classification errors of PCA and RPCA on the four UCI datasets.

Acknowledgment

This research is supported by Iran Telecommunication Research Center (ITRC).

References

[1] M. Dash and H. Liu, "Dimensionality reductionin," in *Encyclopedia of Computer Science and Engineering*, B. W. Wah, Ed., vol. 2, pp. 958–966, John Wiley & Sons, Hoboken, NJ, USA, 2009.

[2] H. Liu and H. Motoda, *Computational Methods of Feature Selection*, Taylor & Francis Group, 2008.

[3] M. Yang, F. Wang, and P. Yang, "A novel feature selection algorithm based on hypothesis-margin," *Journal of Computers*, vol. 3, no. 12, pp. 27–34, 2008.

[4] Y. Sun and D. Wu, "A RELIEF based feature extraction algorithm," in *Proceedings of the 8th SIAM International Conference on Data Mining*, pp. 188–195, April 2008.

[5] K. Kira and L. A. Rendell, "A practical approach to feature selection," in *Proceedings of the 9th International Conference on Machine Learning*, pp. 249–256, 1992.

[6] Y. Sun, "Iterative RELIEF for feature weighting: algorithms, theories, and applications," *IEEE Transactions on Pattern Analysis and Machine Intelligence*, vol. 29, no. 6, pp. 1035–1051, 2007.

[7] S. C. Yusta, "Different metaheuristic strategies to solve the feature selection problem," *Pattern Recognition Letters*, vol. 30, no. 5, pp. 525–534, 2009.

[8] P. Pudil and J. Novovičová, "Novel methods for subset selection with respect to problem knowledge," *IEEE Intelligent Systems and Their Applications*, vol. 13, no. 2, pp. 66–74, 1998.

[9] T. G. Dietterich, "Machine-learning research: four current directions," *AI Magazine*, vol. 18, no. 4, pp. 97–136, 1997.

[10] D. Wettschereck, D. W. Aha, and T. Mohri, "A review and empirical evaluation of feature weighting methods for a class of lazy learning algorithms," *Artificial Intelligence Review*, vol. 11, no. 1–5, pp. 273–314, 1997.

[11] J. Yan, B. Zhang, N. Liu et al., "Effective and efficient dimensionality reduction for large-scale and streaming data preprocessing," *IEEE Transactions on Knowledge and Data Engineering*, vol. 18, no. 3, pp. 320–332, 2006.

[12] R. Jensen and Q. Shen, *Computational Intelligence and Feature Selection Rough and Fuzzy Approach*, Press Series on Computational Intelligence, John Wiley & Sons, 2008.

[13] I. T. Jolliffe, *Principal Component Analysis*, Wiley, 2nd edition, 2002.

[14] M. Turk and A. Pentland, "Eigenfaces for recognition," *Journal of Cognitive Neuroscience*, vol. 3, no. 1, pp. 71–86, 1991.

[15] H. Murase, F. Kimura, M. Yoshimura, and Y. Miyake, "An improvement of the autocorrelation matrix in pattern matching method and its applicationto handprinted 'HIRAGANA'," *IECE Transactions*, vol. 64, no. 3, pp. 276–283, 1981.

[16] H. Murase and S. K. Nayar, "Visual learning and recognition of 3-d objects from appearance," *International Journal of Computer Vision*, vol. 14, no. 1, pp. 5–24, 1995.

[17] S. K. Nayar, S. A. Nene, and H. Murase, "Subspace methods for robot vision," *IEEE Transactions on Robotics and Automation*, vol. 12, no. 5, pp. 750–758, 1996.

[18] S. Chen and Y. Zhu, "Subpattern-based principle component analysis," *Pattern Recognition*, vol. 37, no. 5, pp. 1081–1083, 2004.

[19] J. F. Pinto Da Costa, H. Alonso, and L. Roque, "A weighted principal component analysis and its application to gene expression data," *IEEE/ACM Transactions on Computational Biology and Bioinformatics*, vol. 8, no. 1, pp. 246–252, 2011.

[20] K. Honda, A. Notsu, and H. Ichihashi, "Variable weighting in PCA-guided κ-means and its connection with information summarization," *Journal of Advanced Computational Intelligence and Intelligent Informatics*, vol. 15, no. 1, pp. 83–89, 2011.

[21] A. M. Martinez and A. C. Kak, "PCA versus LDA," *IEEE Transactions on Pattern Analysis and Machine Intelligence*, vol. 23, no. 2, pp. 228–233, 2001.

[22] I. Kononenko, "Estimating attributes: analysis and extensions of RELIEF," in *Proceedings of the European Conference on Machine Learning (ECML '54)*, pp. 71–182, 1994.

[23] R. Gilad-Bachrach, A. Navot, and N. Tishby, "Margin based feature selection—theory and algorithms," in *Proceeding of the 21st International Conference on Machine Learning (ICML '04)*, pp. 337–344, July 2004.

[24] J. Z. Huang, M. K. Ng, H. Rong, and Z. Li, "Automated variable weighting in k-means type clustering," *IEEE Transactions on Pattern Analysis and Machine Intelligence*, vol. 27, no. 5, pp. 657–668, 2005.

[25] M. Dash, H. Liu, and J. Yao, "Dimensionality reduction of unsupervised data," in *Proceedings if the 9th IEEE International Conference on Tools with Artificial Intelligence (ICTAI '97)*, pp. 532–539, November 1997.

14

Discrete Artificial Bee Colony for Computationally Efficient Symbol Detection in Multidevice STBC MIMO Systems

Saeed Ashrafinia, Muhammad Naeem, and Daniel Lee

School of Engineering Science, Simon Fraser University, Burnaby, BC, Canada V5A 1S6

Correspondence should be addressed to Saeed Ashrafinia; saa62@sfu.ca

Academic Editor: Jun He

A Discrete Artificial Bee Colony (DABC) is presented for joint symbol detection at the receiver in a multidevice Space-Time Block Code (STBC) Mutli-Input Multi-Output (MIMO) communication system. Exhaustive search (maximum likelihood detection) for finding an optimal detection has a computational complexity that increases exponentially with the number of mobile devices, transmit antennas per mobile device, and the number of bits per symbol. ABC is a new population-based, swarm-based Evolutionary Algorithms (EA) presented for multivariable numerical functions and has shown good performance compared to other mainstream EAs for problems in continuous domain. This algorithm simulates the intelligent foraging behavior of honeybee swarms. An enhanced discrete version of the ABC algorithm is presented and applied to the joint symbol detection problem to find a nearly optimal solution in real time. The results of multiple independent simulation runs indicate the effectiveness of DABC with other well-known algorithms previously proposed for joint symbol detection such as the near-optimal sphere decoding, minimum mean square error, zero forcing, and semidefinite relaxation, along with other EAs such as genetic algorithm, estimation of distributions algorithm, and the more novel biogeography-based optimization algorithm.

1. Introduction

Multi-Input Multi-Output (MIMO) communication systems can offer spatial diversity gains in the fading channels and have significantly higher channel capacity than the Single-Input Single-Output (SISO) systems for the same total transmission power and bandwidth [1, 2]. The system proposed in this paper comprises of one receiving station and multiple transmitting devices. The receiver's front end has multiple antennas, and each transmitting device has multiple transmit antennas. Employing the Space Time Block-Code (STBC) is realized to increase the capacity of MIMO systems and consequently improves data throughput and spectral efficiency [3]. Multiantenna systems are widely used because of their ability of dramatically increasing the channel capacity in fading channels [4]. Each transmit device uses an STBC; the receiver side performs the joint signal detection. Such a system is referred to as a multidevice (MD) STBC-MIMO system. Generally in an MD-STBC-MIMO system, the number of receive antennas is typically smaller than the cumulative number of transmit antennas used by all transmitting devices in the system. An example of MD-STBC-MIMO, with a smaller number of antennas at the base station or access point, would be the uplink multiple access communication in cellular systems.

This paper addresses the symbol detection in MD-STBC-MIMO systems. The Maximum A Posteriori (MAP) detection, which reduced to the Maximum Likelihood (ML) detection in the case of a priori equally likely symbol blocks, minimizes the probability of detection error, and thus is optimal and is further explained in Section 3. However, a computationally efficient algorithm for achieving MAP or ML detection is not known. Some studies with Sphere Decoding (SD) algorithms exhibit that their expected computational complexity grows polynomially with the problem size M up to some value of M for the cases of small constellation sizes [5], but it grows exponentially for the cases of large constellation sizes. Also, for some SD algorithms, operation at a low SNR requires inordinately high computation; yet operation at a high SNR is efficient. In fact, [6] shows that even the expected computational complexity of the SD grows exponentially with the problem size in MIMO communication systems. In any case, an algorithm with polynomial growth of expected complexity for all values of the problem size M has not yet been found.

Due to the combinatorial nature of the problem, the ML detection is a choice to obtain the optimal solution; yet it has a high computational complexity. Taking advantage of heuristic algorithms, evolutionary algorithms (EAs) more specifically, and their ability to solve optimization problems efficiently facilitates finding an optimal solution with relatively low computational cost. evolutionary algorithms (EAs) are a subset of heuristic algorithms, which is inspired by biological evolution and mutation.

The Artificial Bee Colony (ABC) algorithm is one of the novel EAs that has been introduced by Karaboga in [7]. He presented the ABC algorithm for real (continuous) parameter optimization in unconstrained optimization problems in [8]. ABC is a population-based, stochastic global optimizer Evolutionary Algorithm. It is based on the theory of foraging bees searching for food sources for their nectar and sharing the information of food sources' locations to other bees in the hive. This algorithm demonstrates good accuracy and efficiency, compared with other mainstream EAs. In [8], Karaboga and Akay showed that ABC algorithm outperforms other EAs such as Differential Evolution (DE) [9], Particle Swarm Optimization (PSO) [10], and Genetic Algorithm (GA) [11] for numeric problems with multi-dimensions. In his recent paper [12], Karaboga compared the ABC programming with various genetic programming techniques and crossover methods available in [13] and demonstrated the superiority of ABC over these schemes through simulations. After introducing the ABC algorithm in 2007, some papers are published on the applications of ABC to different optimization problems [14–16], in addition to various real-world applications including filter design [17], image processing [18], control engineering [19], computer science [20, 21], neural networks [22], and even biology [23]. In these studies, ABC outperforms other EAs and is turned into a popular global optimization solver to the continuous optimization problems and applications.

The ABC algorithm discussed in [24] is primarily presented for continuous functions; yet the MD-STBC-MIMO detection problem is in the discrete domain. The impressive results of ABC implementation for continuous problems bring up the idea that a discretized versions of ABC can be a potential high-efficient low-complex solver for discrete or numerical optimization problems. In this paper we introduce a discrete ABC algorithm, in addition to some new features to enhance the overall algorithm's performance. Although there are a few discretized version of ABC in the literature, we will discuss in Section 4 that their efficiency is the result of their high complexity; thus they cannot be utilized for a real-time symbol detection problem such as MD-STBC-MIMO.

Our simulation results show that discrete ABC can meet the best known semi-optimal detector (i.e., SD) with less complexity and has better performance than other methods such as Minimum Mean Square Error (MMSE), Zero Forcing (ZF), and Semi-Definite Relaxation (SDR) [25], while it

outperforms other EAs such as GA, Estimation of Distributions Algorithm (EDA) [26], and the recently proposed Biogeography-Based Optimization (BBO) [27].

In the rest of this paper, the system model is presented in Section 2. The application of existing symbol detection algorithms is discussed in Section 3. The discrete ABC algorithm and its application to the symbol detection problem are presented in Section 4. The computational complexity comparison of EAs and other solvers is discussed in Section 5. The simulation results are presented in Section 6, and Section 7 contains the conclusion and the future work.

2. System Model

The system consists of K mobile devices transmitting signals and one receiver. This system can model the uplink communication of the cellular system. Each mobile device has N_T transmit antennas that apply STBC, whereas the receiver front end has N_R receive antennas. The multiple mobile devices in the proposed systems can cause cochannel interference. An IQ-modulation scheme (e.g., M-QAM, M-PSK) maps source information into complex numbers. Even if each transmit device employs an orthogonal space-time code, the absence of coding across different wireless devices cannot guarantee the orthogonality among their signals. In the case of a single mobile device $K = 1$, the wireless device transmits using N_T transmit antennas and communicates with a receiver that has N_R antennas. The number of time slots in the space-time block code is denoted by T. The channel is assumed to be quasistatic; that is, the channel gain remains constant during each time block of data. It is also assumed that the channel gain at each time block is known to the receiver. This assumption is often used in the literature and reasonable if training or pilot signals are used. A complex $N_T \times N_R$ dimensional matrix H represents the MIMO channel, and another complex $T \times N_T$ dimensional matrix S represents the input signal in a space-time block code. The relationship between the input and output signals can be expressed as

$$\widetilde{Y} = SH + \widetilde{Z}, \tag{1}$$

where $\widetilde{Y}$ is a $T \times N_R$ dimensional complex output matrix and $\widetilde{Z}$ denotes the additive white noise matrix.

Equation (1) describes the relation between the input transmitted signals and the output received signals in terms of complex-valued matrix equation. The relation between input and output of the channel in a system with linear dispersion space-time coding can be equivalently expressed in terms of a real-valued matrix equation. We now briefly discuss the real-valued matrix equation. The input signal in (1) in the case of the linear dispersion code [28] is denoted by a complex-valued matrix S that takes the following form:

$$S = \sum_{q=1}^{Q} \left[\left(\alpha_q + j\beta_q \right) C_q + \left(\alpha_q - j\beta_Q \right) D_q \right]. \tag{2}$$

Here, $\alpha_q + j\beta_q$ $(q = 1, \ldots, Q)$ is the complex number that represents the qth symbol, where α_q and β_q correspond to the real and imaginary parts of the symbol, respectively, and Q

indicates the number of symbols conveyed in a space-time code block. In the IQ constellation diagram, α_q and β_q are discrete-valued variables, such that $\alpha_q + j\beta_q$ corresponds to a symbol in the constellation diagram. In 4-QAM, for example, each of these two variables can take values of ± 1, and thus $\alpha + j\beta$ determines one of the four possible symbols arranged in the square grid of $(1, i)$, $(-1, i)$, $(-1, -i)$, and $(1, -i)$. These Q symbols $\alpha_q + j\beta_q$ can be represented as a $2Q$-dimensional real-valued row vector $\mathcal{X}$, whose components are constituted by $\alpha_q, \beta_q, q = 1, \ldots, Q$. The real and imaginary parts of matrix $\tilde{Y}$'s components can be arranged as a $2TN_R$-dimensional real-valued row vector y. The relation between $\mathcal{X}$ and y in this new alternative form can be expressed as

$$y = \mathcal{X}\Gamma + Z, \qquad (3)$$

where Z is a $2TN_R$-dimensional real-valued vector representing noise, and Γ is a $2Q \times 2TN_R$ real-valued matrix derived from the component of matrices $C_q, D_q, q = 1, \ldots, Q$, and H. Equation (1) in the case of multiple wireless devices can be expressed as

$$\tilde{Y} = \sum_{k=1}^{K} S_k H_k + \tilde{Z}, \qquad (4)$$

where S_k is a $T \times N_T$-dimensional complex matrix of the input signal from wireless device k and the $N_T \times N_R$-dimensional complex matrix H_k represents the channel from the kth device to the receiver. As a result, (3) can be written as

$$y = [\mathcal{X}_1 \mathcal{X}_2 \cdots \mathcal{X}_K] \begin{bmatrix} \Gamma_1 \\ \Gamma_2 \\ \vdots \\ \Gamma_K \end{bmatrix} + Z, \qquad (5)$$

where $\mathcal{X}_k, k = 1, 2, \ldots, K$ is a $2Q_k$-dimensional real-valued row vector that represents the Q_k complex symbols sent from the kth wireless device in a space-time code block. Note that (5) can model the case in which different wireless devices use different code rates Q_k/T and different space-time codes. The total number of symbols transmitted from all wireless devices in a space-time code block through all transmit antennas is denoted by $N_S = \sum_{k=1}^{K} Q_k$.

3. Signal Detection

The ML detection is known to yield the lowest symbol error probability in the case of a priori equally likely symbols. In the case of our problem, the detector at the receiver has to choose from M^{N_S} possible sequences of symbols transmitted in a space-time code block, where M is the size of the symbol constellation associated with the modulation scheme. ML detection chooses transmitted symbols $[\mathcal{X}_1, \mathcal{X}_2, \ldots, \mathcal{X}_K]$ that maximize $P(y \mid \mathcal{X}_1, \mathcal{X}_2, \ldots, \mathcal{X}_K)$. In the case of additive white Gaussian noise Z, the ML detection is reduced to choosing the vector $[\mathcal{X}_1, \mathcal{X}_2, \ldots, \mathcal{X}_K]$ from M^{N_S} possibilities

that has the shortest Euclidean distance $\hat{l}$, which is expressed as

$$\hat{l} = \left\| y - \sum_{k=1}^{K} \mathcal{X}_k \Gamma_k \right\|. \qquad (6)$$

The ML detection scheme can be implemented by searching through all $M^{N_S} = 2^{bN_S}$ possible symbol sequences, where $b = \log_2 M$ and M is the size of the symbol constellation. Performing such an exhaustive search to find the minimum Euclidean distance in (6) is computationally inefficient, especially for large N_S. Computational complexity increases exponentially with N_S, the number of bits per symbol, transmit antennas per device, and the number of wireless devices K. High-speed communication requirements demand a low-complexity detection scheme. For low-complexity near-optimal detection, in this paper the ABC algorithm is applied to this MD-STBC-MIMO detection problem. The MD-STBC-MIMO detection problem is converted into a discrete optimization problem that searches the space of $M^{N_S} = 2^{bN_S}$ symbol combinations. Section 4.2 describes how discrete ABC is applied to the signal detection. In the following sections, the performance of the discrete ABC-based detector is compared with other low-complexity suboptimal algorithms such as MMSE, ZF, SDR, and SD.

4. Discrete Artificial Bee Colony

This section presents the discrete Artificial Bee Colony (ABC) algorithm. A general description of ABC is given in the next subsection, followed by the modified discrete ABC algorithm in the subsequent section.

4.1. The Artificial Bee Colony Algorithm. evolutionary algorithms (EAs) have been often used to solve difficult optimization problems. Most of the EAs are inspired by the theory of biological evolution (e.g., selection, crossover, mutation, recombination, and reproduction). The ABC algorithm has been recently presented by Karaboga for real (continuous) parameter optimization in unconstraint optimization problems [24], which is based on a particular intelligent behavior of the honey bee swarms. This algorithm demonstrates good accuracy and efficiency compared to other EAs such as differential evolution (DE) [29], ant colony optimization (ACO) [30], PSO, and GA, for numeric problems with multidimensions [8].

Consider an optimization problem

$$\max_x F(x) \qquad (7)$$

$$\text{subject to:} \quad x \in C,$$

where $x \equiv (x_1, x_2, \ldots, x_D)^t$ is a vector and C is a constraint set. In the original ABC, each candidate solution is represented by a vector variable of the optimization problem. In the context of evolutionary algorithms, a candidate solution is also referred to as an "individual," and a group of candidate solutions is referred to as a "population" of individuals. In ABC, each individual (candidate solution to an optimization problem) is analogically considered as a food source position. The fitness value, $F(x)$, of each individual (food source) x corresponds to the nectar quality of the food source.

This algorithm imitates the behaviors of the real bees on finding food source locations and sharing the information of food sources to the other bees in the nest. In this algorithm colony bees are classified into three types with certain responsibilities: employed bees, onlooker bees, and scout bees. Employed bees are the bees that have already been assigned to a food source. Each of them saves the food source position and selects another food source in her neighbor and chooses out of two the one that has a better nectar. Then they return to the hive and start to dance based on the quality of the nectar of their associated food source. An onlooker bee watches the dance of employed bees at the hive and selects an employed bee based on the dances observed so that the probability of choosing an employee bee is proportional to the nectar quality of that employee bee. Then the onlooker bee receives the information of the chosen employed bee associated with food source (the food source position and its nectar quality) from her and becomes an employed bee associated with that food source. Since then, the new employed bee (former onlooker) performs the same act as the employed bee in the previous phase; that is, she searches for a new food source in the neighbor of her associated food source for higher nectar quality and saves the best food source and its nectar to her memory. Finally, scout bees are free bees responsible for finding new food sources and evaluating their nectar. As soon as a scout bee finds a food source, she turns into an employed bee.

The algorithm assumes that there is only one employed bee for every food source; thus the number of employed bees is equal to the number of individuals in the population N. If there is no improvement in the nectar quality of a food source after certain number of trials, the food source will be abandoned and the employed bee assigned to that food source will become a scout bee that looks for a new food source. A pseudocode of the ABC algorithm is given in Pseudocode 1.

At the first step, ABC generates randomly distributed initial food source positions of the size N, whereas each individual solution x^i, $i \in (1, 2, \ldots, N)$ is a D-dimensional vector of numbers. In this step each scout bee that finds a food source location saves the current location in her memory and becomes an employed bee. In the employed bees phase, each employed bee finds a new food source position v^i in the neighborhood of her current associated food source x^i, and if the new food source has a better nectar, she saves the new position to her memory. In the original ABC algorithm, an employed bee locates the new food source positions using the following expression [24]:

$$v_j^i = x_j^i + \phi_{ij} \left(x_j^i - x_j^l \right). \tag{8}$$

In this equation x_j^i is the jth component of the ith individual of the population, $l \in \{1, 2, \ldots, N\}$ is a randomly selected food source location (different from i), and $j \in \{1, 2, \ldots, D\}$ is a randomly chosen index. ϕ_{ij} is a random real number between $[-1, 1]$ that controls the production of a neighbor food source around x_j^i.

At the beginning of the onlooker bees phase, employed bees share their information about the quality of food sources with onlooker bees. An onlooker bee chooses an employed bee to take the food source information based on the following probability:

$$p_i = \frac{F\left(x^i\right)}{\sum_{i=1}^{N} F\left(x^i\right)}, \tag{9}$$

where $F(x^i)$ is the fitness value of the ith solution in the population x^i. After an onlooker bee selects a food source, she becomes an employed bee and locates a new food source in the neighborhood using (8), then she compares its nectar quality with the current food source, and saves the food source position that has a better nectar quality to her memory and returns back to the hive to share this information.

If the number of trials t^i of a food source x^i is not improved through a predetermined number of trials t, it will be removed from the population, and the employed bee assigned to that bee becomes a scout that searches for a new food source. Each component of the new food source is randomly selected from $[x_{\min}, x_{\max}]$, where $x_{\min}$ and $x_{\max}$ are the minimum and maximum of the allowable values in the problem domain. The previous steps are repeated until the termination condition is satisfied, which here is a preset maximum number of generations G.

4.2. Discrete ABC Algorithm for Joint Symbol Detection.

This subsection introduces a discrete version of the ABC algorithm. The ABC algorithm discussed in the previous subsection is for optimization problems in the continuous domain. However, some of the previous steps have to be modified because the decision variables, which in this case are the transmitted symbols of the MD-STBC-MIMO problem, are a set of nonnegative integer numbers. In the discrete ABC (DABC) algorithm, we define a new expression to search in the neighborhood of the current food source position as a replacement to expression (8):

$$v_j^i = \mathrm{randint}\left(x_j^l, 2x_j^i - x_j^l\right), \tag{10}$$

where "randint (a, b)" returns a random integer number between a and b (more specifically a random integer number starting from $\min\{a, b\}$ to $\max\{a, b\}$). Note that if the result of (10) falls beyond the problem's integer domain, that number is replaced with the closest integer defined within the boundaries. This expression is used in both employed bees and onlooker bees phases. Moreover, the onlooker bees select employed bees with the following probability:

$$p_i = \sqrt{\frac{F\left(x^i\right)}{\max_{i=1,\ldots,N} F\left(x^i\right)}}, \tag{11}$$

which has been observed to increase the efficiency of the algorithm more than other selection methods and the one in (9). The evaluation of (10) is explained in the appendix.

We have applied more enhancements to the algorithm in order to reduce its computational complexity. The most

```
(1) Send scouts (generate initial population)
(2) Repeat
(3)     Employed bees phase
(4)     Onlooker bees phase
(5)     Scout bee phase
(6)     Memorize the best food source found so far
(7) Until termination condition satisfied
```

PSEUDOCODE 1: Pseudocode of the general ABC algorithm.

```
(1) Initialize the population of solutions $x^i$, $i = 1, 2, \ldots, N$,
(2) Evaluate $F(x^i)$, $\forall i$,
(3) repeat
(4)     Run the DABC employed bee phase, (Pseudocode 3)
(5)     Run the DABC onlooker bee phase, (Pseudocode 4)
(6)     Run the DABC scout bee phase, (Pseudocode 5)
(7)     Save the best results,
(8) until termination condition satisfied,
```

PSEUDOCODE 2: The DABC algorithm pseudocode.

complex section of ABC, and most other EAs, is the fitness function evaluation. Therefore, if the number of these evaluation decreases, the algorithm runs faster. In this version of the discrete ABC, during the employed bees and onlookers bees phases, the algorithm is set to only evaluate those individuals that are modified during the greedy selection process. When the algorithm uses (10) to select a neighbor food source, it may not always return a new food source position due to the stochastic nature of (10). The DABC is set to check whether a food source has been modified prior to proceeding to the fitness function evaluation. In this case, it eliminates a number of fitness evaluations for some individuals that were already evaluated during the previous generations.

The last phase of the DABC is similar to the scout bee phase of the original ABC. In the scout bee phase of DABC, the algorithm selects only one food source x^i that exceeds maximum allowable number of trials t^i to abandon and sends one scout bee to explore new food source positions. The scout bee randomly selects one food source, evaluates its nectar quality, and saves it in her memory. This procedure helps the algorithm to explore the search space more effectively, which is an advanced version of the mutation process in GA and some other EAs that they randomly mutate any individual of the population. A detailed pseudocode for the discrete ABC algorithm is given in Pseudocodes 2, 3, 4, and 5.

We found a few articles in the literature that employ ABC for numerical optimization problem. In [31], Tsai et al. presented an enhanced ABC, which is applied to numerical optimization problems, and called it the interactive ABC (IABC). They have modified the way in which onlooker bees choose a neighboring food source position. IABC incorporates the concept of universal gravitation into the consideration of the affection between employed bees and onlooker bees, and their simulation results demonstrate the high performance of IABC compared with ABC and PSO. Note that the higher performance of their new method comes with the price of a significant increase in the complexity of the algorithm—there is heavy computational load for calculating the gravitation between n employed bees in (10) and (11) in [31] for every food source in every algorithm iteration. As mentioned before, an important aspect of EAs' implementation for wireless communication problems, specifically the MD-STBC-MIMO detection, is to have high performance results while maintaining low complexity.

There are other articles that apply ABC to optimization problems with a binary domain. Wang et al. have presented a binary selection method to the ABC algorithm in [32]. Their binary encoding method employs a sigmoid function of velocity as a logical choice for binary selection. However, because they are incorporating (8) with a sigmoid function, their method has a higher complexity than (10) presented in the present paper. Salim et al. introduce a discrete bee algorithm for numerical optimization. However, their algorithm includes binary operators ((8) and (11)–(13) in [33]). They show that their algorithm has better performance than ABC; but if this algorithm is applied to a numerical optimization problem, integer-to-binary and binary-to-integer built-in functions are required to convert all of the integer individuals of each population to binary for food source exploration, and they all have to be converted back into integer for fitness function evaluation after population modification. This procedure has to be done at least two times (during employed bee and onlooker bee phases) for all individuals in all generations, which dramatically increases the algorithm complexity. The algorithm in the present paper has two advantages over the aforementioned papers: it can be implemented for numerical optimization problems, including problems with a binary domain, and it clearly has less complexity

```
(1) t^i = 0, ∀i
(2) for each food source x^i, i = 1, 2, ..., N,
(3)     Select a random food source l, l ≠ i ∈ {1, 2, ..., N},
(4)     Select a random component j, j ∈ {1, 2, ..., D},
(5)     v^i_j = randint(x^l_j, 2x^i_j − x^l_j),
(6)     t^i = t^i + 1,
(7)     if v^i ≠ x^i then,
(8)         Evaluate F(v^i),
(9)         x^i ← v^i,
(10)        t^i = 0,
(11)    end if,
(12) end for,
```

PSEUDOCODE 3: The DABC employed bee phase pseudocode.

```
(1) Calculate probability values p_i for x^i, ∀i using (11),
(2) w = 1; i = 1;
(3) for w = 1, ..., N, %(w corresponds to the wth onlooker bee)%
(4)     if rand > p_i then, %(select the ith employed bee to follow)%
(5)         Select a random food source l, l ≠ i ∈ {1, 2, ..., N},
(6)         Select a random component j, j ∈ {1, 2, ..., D},
(7)         v^i_j = randint(x^l_j, 2x^i_j − x^l_j),
(8)         t^i = t^i + 1,
(9)         if v^i ≠ x^i then,
(10)            Evaluate F(v^i),
(11)            x^i ← v^i,
(12)            t^i = 0,
(13)        end if,
(14)        w = w + 1,
(15)    end if,
(16)    i = i + 1;
(17)    if i > N then i = 1; %(reset i)%
(18) end for,
```

PSEUDOCODE 4: The DABC onlooker bee phase pseudocode.

compared with algorithms presented in other papers. DABC's superior performance compared with other mainstream EAs is demonstrated through simulation results in Section 6.

4.3. Application of DABC to MD-STBC-MIMO Joint Symbol Detection. The aim of applying DABC to the MD-STBC-MIMO symbol detection problem is to minimize the Euclidian distance defined in (6). Therefore, the Euclidian distance in (6) represents the fitness function or nectar quality, and shorter Euclidian distance means better fitness. An individual of the discrete ABC algorithm corresponds to a possible solution to the joint symbol detection problem, that is, a set of conveyed symbols from the K transmit devices.

In the MD-STBC-MIMO system discussed in this paper, transmitted symbols are chosen from an IQ modulation such as M-QAM or M-PSK constellation diagram. We represent each of the M possible points in the constellation by a unique integer in the set $\{0, ..., M-1\}$. The system comprises K transmit devices, each device indexed by k transmitting Q_k M-QAM symbols in a space-time code block. Therefore,

a DABC individual x (a food source location) can be defined as a $N_S = \sum_{k=1}^{K} Q_k$-dimensional ($D = N_S$) integer row vector $x \triangleq [x_1, x_2, ..., x_{N_S}]$ where $x_v \in \{0, ..., M-1\}$, $v \in \{1, ..., N_S\}$. For DABC, the integer vector x represents the vector $[\mathscr{X}_1 \mathscr{X}_2 \cdots \mathscr{X}_K]$ in expression (6), and the fitness function is translated accordingly. Consequently, a scout bee generates a random vector of D integer numbers in $\{0, ..., M-1\}$ as a new individual (new food source location) in line 1 of Pseudocode 2 and line 3 of Pseudocode 5; that is, $x_{\min} = 0, x_{\max} = M - 1$.

5. Computational Complexity

A motivation for applying the proposed near-optimal algorithms to an MD-STBC-MIMO problem is their low computational complexity. In this section, the computational complexity of DABC for MD-STBC-MIMO symbol detection is compared with that of ZF, MMSE, SD, SDR, EDA, BBO, and GA. The computational complexity of the exhaustive search (an implementation of the ML detector) is $O(M^{N_S})$,

```
(1) if there exists some $x^i \mid \{t^i > t\}$,
(2) Select one such $x^i$ randomly,
(3)   for each component $j$, $j \in \{1, 2, \ldots, D\}$,
(4)     $v_j^i = \text{randint}[x_{\min}, x_{\max}]$,
(5)   end for,
(6) Evaluate $F(v^i)$,
(7) $x^i \leftarrow v^i$,
(8) $t^i = 0$,
(9) end if,
```

PSEUDOCODE 5: The DABC scout bee phase pseudocode.

so exhaustive search is usually impractical for real-time operations of symbol detection. A number of suboptimal detection schemes with better computational complexity have been presented in the literature.

The worst-case complexity of SD is exponential, and its expected complexity depends on the problem size and SNR [5]. SD has high complexity of $O(\tilde{n}^6)$ [34] at low SNRs, where $\tilde{n} = n \log_2 M$. However, it has polynomial complexity, often roughly cubic complexity, at high SNRs [5]. MMSE is one of the suboptimal detectors that involves inverting a matrix, and its computational complexity is $O(\tilde{n}^3)$ [35]. The computational complexity of SDR [36] in each iteration is $O(N_T^{3.5})$ where N_T stands for the number of transmit antennas.

Typically, the computational complexity of population-based algorithms is analyzed in terms of the number of fitness function evaluations, which in this paper would be (6). One important reason is that their complexity is highly dependent on their implementation and coding efficiency. The number of function evaluations in, BBO, GA, and EDA, is the same and equal to GN, where G and N represent the total number of generations and the population size, respectively [9]. The reason is that in all these algorithms, every individual is evaluated just once during one generation.

In the ABC algorithm however, there is more than one fitness function evaluation for each individual during a generation. During one generation in ABC, during the employed bees phase, each employed bee tests a neighbor food source for its quality; thus the fitness function evaluation has to be run for the whole N food source positions once. By the same token, during the onlooker bees phase there are N fitness function evaluations for every food source. So the overall number of fitness function evaluations for the algorithm for these two phases would be $2GN$. In the scout bees phase, the algorithm selects only one individual that exceeds t trials to abandon and replaces its employed bee with a scout. Hence the first individual to exceed t trials would be in the $(t/2)$th algorithm generation. After that, in order to determine a feasible number of function evaluations the worst case has to be considered, in which after the $(t/2)$th generation there is a maximum of one abandoned food source in every generation. As a result, the total number of fitness function evaluations for ABC would be as follows:

$$2GN + \left(G - \frac{t}{2}\right). \tag{12}$$

This complexity is higher than the complexity of other aforementioned EAs. However, the complexity of DABC presented in this paper is yet less than (12) because this algorithm does not run the function evaluation procedure for all the individuals in the employed bees and onlooker bees phases due to the conditions in line 7 of Pseudocode 3 and line 9 in Pseudocode 4. This stochastic behavior prevents DABC to have a closed-form number of fitness function evaluations.

6. Simulation Results

This section contains the simulation results of the proposed DABC-based detection and its comparison with other detection techniques applied to an MD-STBC-MIMO system. The channels are assumed to be quasistatic, and different channels in MD-STBC-MIMO are assumed to be independent. In all our simulations, it is assumed that the mobile data is transmitted in a form of 4-QAM modulation from all wireless devices ($M = 4$). For simulation experiments we assumed that each of the K devices transmits the same number of symbols $Q_k = Q$. Therefore, there are $N_S = KQ$ symbols conveyed from the K transmit devices to the receiver. Each point in the plots of Figures 1, 2, 3, 4, 5, 6, 7, and 8 is a value averaged over multiple independent runs. During each simulation runs, the set of symbols transmitted in a space-time code block are generated randomly and independently of other simulation run. Also the noise term is generated randomly and independently of other simulation trials.

In order to present a fair comparison between the EAs, they are tuned to their best performance, and they are sharing the same number of generations, population size, and initial population. Other EA parameters are kept constant during all simulation runs. A list of parameters set for each algorithm is presented in a table for each simulation result next to its figure. Moreover, GA employs a greedy selection scheme [11], and BBO uses a low complex emigration-based migration scheme with a constant emigration curve and linear immigration curve [9].

Each point in the plots of Figures 1–8 is a value averaged over multiple independent runs. In each simulation run, the set of transmitted symbols ($[\mathcal{X}_1, \mathcal{X}_2, \ldots, \mathcal{X}_K]$ in (5)), channel matrices ($[\Gamma_1, \Gamma_2, \ldots, \Gamma_K]^T$ in (5)), and noise (Z in (5)) are generated randomly and independently of other trials. Hence, in each simulation run the received signal y in (6) is set from those randomly generated variables in accordance

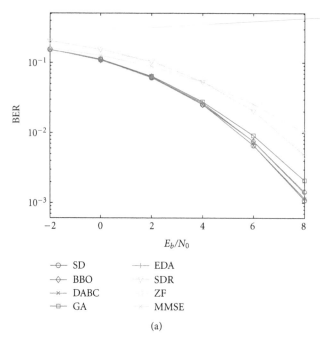

(a)

					System parameters						
K	N_T	N_R	M	T	Search space	STBC type	Channel type		No. of simulation runs		
4	2	6	4	2	4^8	Alamouti	Quasi-static fading		2000		

Shared EAs			BBO		DABC	GA			EDA		
Generation	Pop	I	m	Migration	t	P_{xover}	P_{mut}	P_{sel}	P_{xover}	P_{mut}	P_{sel}
60	60	1	0.015	Constant	$0.4 \times pop$	0.9	0.5	0.5	0.99	0.95	0.5

(b)

	−2	0	2	4	6	8
ZF	89	86	80	74	70	64
MMSE	96	92	86	78	74	66
SDR	84	84	80	78	78	77
GA	100	99	96	91	85	83
EDA	100	100	98	95	93	88
BBO	100	100	98	97	96	95
DABC	100	100	100	100	100	100

(c)

FIGURE 1: (a) BER performance comparison of $(K, N_T, N_R, M) = (4, 2, 6, 4)$, (b) simulation parameters, and (c) percentage of decoders with the SD results.

with (5). Then the algorithms are run to search for the value of the integer vector x (which represents $[\mathscr{X}_1, \mathscr{X}_2, \ldots, \mathscr{X}_K]$ as mentioned in Section 4.3) that minimizes $\hat{l}$. Therefore, the results averaged over different simulation runs are in fact averaged over the different channel and noise realizations and also different realizations of the algorithm's evolution in the case of probabilistic algorithms such as GA, DABC, EDA, and BBO. This experimental setup compares different algorithms in terms of the averaged performance over different channel and noise realizations.

The simulation results in Figures 1 through 8 show the BER performance comparison between ZF, MMSE, SDR, SD, GA, EDA, BBO, and DABC detectors. The MD-STBC-MIMO system configuration, (K, N_T, N_R, M, T), is set to $(4, 2, 6, 4, 2)$, $(5, 2, 8, 4, 2)$, $(6, 2, 10, 4, 2)$, and $(3, 4, 4, 4, 2)$ for Figures 1, 2, 3, and 4, respectively. The Alamouti space-time coding [24] is used in Figures 1, 2, and 3; but for Figure 4, a nonorthogonal four transmit antennas configuration is used for each mobile device.

EA's shared parameters (G, N), are set to $(60, 60)$, $(100, 100)$, $(100, 120)$, and $(120, 200)$ in Figures 1, 2, 3, and 4, respectively. For these figures, the total number N_S of symbols transmitted from all users is set to 8, 10, 12, and 14; the algorithms are searching through a search space of 4^8, 4^{10}, 4^{12}, and 4^{12} possible solutions, respectively. For each simulation run, the pair of (G, N) is selected not only to make the EAs' results close to SD's, but to choose the smallest possible G and N to reduce their computational complexity.

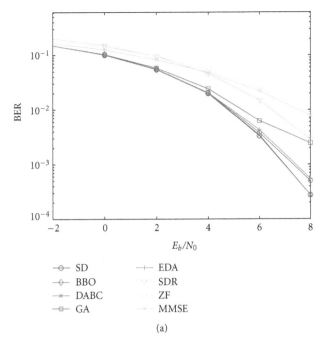

System parameters

K	N_T	N_R	M	T	Search space	STBC type	Channel type				No. of simulation runs	
5	2	8	4	2	4^{10}	Alamouti	Quasi-static fading				2000	

Shared EAs			BBO		DABC	GA			EDA		
Generation	Pop	I	m	Migration	t	P_{xover}	P_{mut}	P_{sel}	P_{xover}	P_{mut}	P_{sel}
100	100	1	0.015	Constant	$0.4 \times pop$	0.9	0.5	0.5	0.99	0.95	0.5

(b)

	−2	0	2	4	6	8
ZF	88	85	81	75	64	58
MMSE	95	90	85	78	67	59
SDR	85	82	81	79	74	71
GA	100	99	98	95	89	73
EDA	100	100	100	99	96	92
BBO	100	99	100	100	98	93
DABC	100	100	100	100	99	100

(c)

FIGURE 2: (a) BER performance comparison of $(K, N_T, N_R, M) = (5, 2, 8, 4)$, (b) simulation parameters, and (c) percentage of decoders with the SD results.

In these figures, three EAs (DABC, BBO, and EDA) return the closest results to the SDs. In most of the cases, DABC and SD exactly match together and seem as a united line. Observing these figures shows that the best algorithm that almost always returns the same result as the SD is DABC, followed by the BBO decoder that returns results with about 95% of SD. The third place is for EDA, followed by GA. All EAs outperform other suboptimal detection methods in all the five figures and can meet the optimal result by searching through a much smaller set of individuals by selecting a decent pair of (G, N).

Figures 1, 2, and 3 indicate that in the MD-STBC-MIMO, DABC has significant better BER performance than ZF,

MMSE, SDR, GA, EDA, and BBO, while it closely matches SD. In Figure 3, for example, although DABC and other EAs are searching over approximately $GN = 12,000$ individuals over the entire search space of $4^{12} \cong 1.7 \times 10^8$ possible solutions, DABC's BER performance meets the near-optimal SD. According to this figure, DABC matches SD, where BBO, EDA, and GA require about 0.1 dB, 0.5 dB, and 0.6 dB more SNRs than BBO to achieve BER of 10^{-2}, respectively.

The experiment in Figure 4 was performed on a nonorthogonal space-time code, whereas the experiments in the other figures were performed on the Alamouti code (simple and orthogonal). The total number of symbols N_S transmitted from all users in a space time code block is 12. Hence,

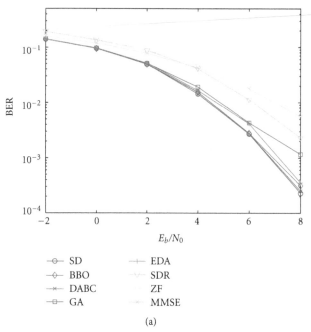

(a)

					System parameters							
K	N_T	N_R	M	T	Search space	STBC type	Channel type			No. of simulation runs		
6	2	10	4	2	4^{12}	Alamouti	Quasi-static fading			2000		
Shared EAs				BBO		DABC	GA			EDA		
Generation	Pop	I	m		Migration	t	P_{xover}	P_{mut}	P_{sel}	P_{xover}	P_{mut}	P_{sel}
100	120	1	0.015		Constant	$0.4 \times pop$	0.9	0.5	0.5	0.99	0.95	0.5

(b)

	−2	0	2	4	6	8
ZF	87	85	81	72	66	61
MMSE	93	90	85	74	68	62
SDR	84	84	81	75	76	72
GA	99	99	98	93	92	81
EDA	100	100	98	97	93	95
BBO	100	100	100	98	99	96
DABC	100	100	100	100	100	99

(c)

FIGURE 3: (a) BER performance comparison of $(K, N_T, N_R, M) = (6, 2, 10, 4)$, (b) simulation parameters, and (c) percentage of decoders with the SD results.

using 4-QAM, the size of the search space would be 4^{12}, while EAs only evaluate $GN = 24,000$ points in the search space, which is significantly smaller than the search space ML has to cover. Similar to other figures, SD and DABC have the best BER performance. In higher SNRs, GA's performance diminishes notably, while DABC pursues the near-optimal SD. It can be observed from the figure that BBO, EDA, and GA require 0.3, 0.4, and 1.5 dB less SNR than SD and DABC to achieve BER of 10^{-2}, respectively. DABC perceptibly behaves as the best detection algorithm among other suboptimal detection methods in all the four figures.

From the computational complexity point of view in EAs, finding the optimal pair of (G, N) is essential in order to minimize the processing power and the required memory. According to the computational complexity order of these algorithms, with a fixed population size N, more iterations until termination means more computation. Figure 5 shows the number of iterations required by each detection scheme to achieve a desirable BER. The MIMO system configuration is $(K, N_T, N_R, M) = (6, 2, 10, 4)$, it uses the Alamouti STBC and quasistatic channel, and the SNR is fixed to 8 dB. Figure 5 shows that the discrete ABC algorithm with the population size fixed to 100 is the first algorithm that can reach SD's performance in less than 65 iterations. Other EAs whether cannot reach the SD results, or require much more iterations to converge to the SD results. This improved performance

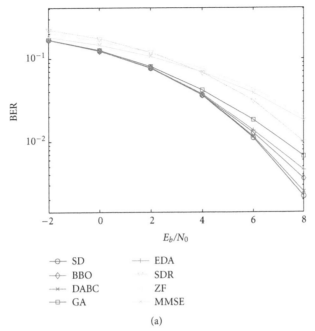

(a)

System parameters												
K	N_T	N_R	M	T	Search space	STBC type	Channel type			No. of simulation runs		
3	4	4	4	2	4^{12}	Alamouti	Quasi-static fading			2000		
Shared EAs				BBO		DABC	GA			EDA		
Generation	Pop	I		m	Migration	t	P_{xover}	P_{mut}	P_{sel}	P_{xover}	P_{mut}	P_{sel}
120	200	1		0.015	Constant	$0.4 \times pop$	0.9	0.5	0.5	0.99	0.95	0.5

(b)

	−2	0	2	4	6	8
ZF	88	85	81	75	64	58
MMSE	95	90	85	78	67	59
SDR	85	82	81	79	74	71
GA	100	99	98	95	89	73
EDA	100	100	100	99	96	92
BBO	100	99	100	100	98	93
DABC	100	100	100	100	99	100

(c)

FIGURE 4: (a) BER performance comparison of $(K, N_T, N_R, M) = (3, 4, 4, 4)$, (b) simulation parameters, and (c) percentage of decoders with the SD results.

is consistently observed in several other simulations with different system configurations. As a result, not only DABC algorithm outperforms other suboptimal algorithms, it delivers better results than other well-known EAs, such as GA, BBO, and EDA, and can reach SD.

Figures 6 to 8 show the trade-off between the population size and the iterations required to achieve a desired BER in GA, BBO, and DABC. The MIMO system configuration is $(K, N_T, N_R, M) = (4, 2, 4, 4)$, using the Alamouti STBC and quasistatic channel, and the SNR is set to 8 dB. The detailed system configuration is given in Table 1. This trade-off is useful from the system design point of view. If a hardware system has high processing capabilities and low memory,

then the population size can set lower to get same BER performance and vice versa. (Higher N and G need more memory.)

Finally, we compare the number of fitness function evaluations between EAs to demonstrate the superiority of DABC over other EAs. As mentioned in Section 5, BBO, EDA, and GA all have the same number of fitness function evaluations equal to GN. For the parameters of a system described in Figure 2 for instance, these EAs require $GN = 10,000$ fitness function evaluations. The original ABC requires $2GN + (G − t/2) = 20,080$, while DABC requires an average of 13,600 evaluations per independent simulation run, which is comparable to other EAs, less than the original ABC and

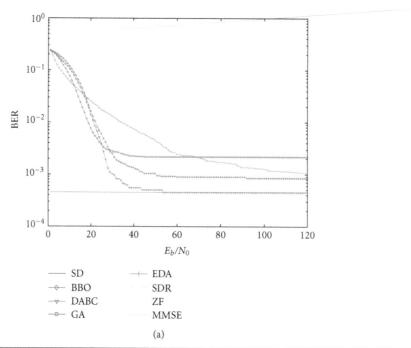

SD   EDA
BBO   SDR
DABC   ZF
GA   MMSE

(a)

System parameters									
K	N_T	N_R	M	T	Search space	STBC type	Channel type		No. of simulation runs
6	2	10	4	2	4^{12}	Alamouti	Quasi-static fading		2000

Shared EAs			BBO		DABC	GA			EDA		
Generation	Pop	I	m	Migration	t	P_{xover}	P_{mut}	P_{sel}	P_{xover}	P_{mut}	P_{sel}
1 ~ 150	100	1	0.015	Constant	$0.4 \times pop$	0.9	0.5	0.5	0.99	0.95	0.5

(b)

FIGURE 5: (a) BER performance comparison versus iterations for $(K, N_T, N_R, M) = (6, 2, 10, 4)$ and (b) simulation parameters.

TABLE 1: System parameters for iteration-population size trade-off.

System parameters									
K	N_T	N_R	M	T	Search space	STBC type	Channel type		No. of simulation runs
5	2	8	4	2	4^{10}	Alamouti	Quasi-static fading		2000

Shared EAs			BBO		DABC	GA			EDA		
Generation	Pop	I	m	Migration	t	P_{xover}	P_{mut}	P_{sel}	P_{xover}	P_{mut}	P_{sel}
1~120	100	1	0.015	Constant	$0.4 \times pop$	0.9	0.5	0.5	0.99	0.95	0.5

much less than the optimal ML detector with a search space of 4^{10} possible solutions. As a result, DABC would be a significantly considerable choice for joint symbol detection in MD-STBC-MIMO systems.

7. Conclusion and Future Work

In this paper, a modified version of the Artificial Bee Colony algorithm is presented for the optimization problems in discrete domain and is applied to a Multi Device (MD) Space-Time Block Code (STBC) Multi-Input Multi-Output (MIMO) system. The enhancements in this algorithm have reduced its complexity, which is much less as compared with optimal ML detector. Thus it is suitable for cost-effective high-speed real-time communications. In addition,

compared to other evolutionary algorithms like GA, EDA, and BBO, the presented discrete ABC (DABC) detection in MD-STBC-MIMO shows a significantly better performance. The proposed algorithm also has consistently better performance-complexity trade-offs at low SNRs, in comparison to the existing algorithms. Even at high SNRs, this algorithm has relatively good performance-complexity trade-offs. In conclusion, the proposed DABC is suitable for cost-effective high-speed real-time communications in MIMO systems.

DABC is a good candidate for solving the same type of computationally complex problems in wireless communication because of its simplistic model, low implementation complexity, and convergence to a nearly optimal solution with a small number of iterations. In this work, our main purpose was to employ a low-complexity algorithm that can

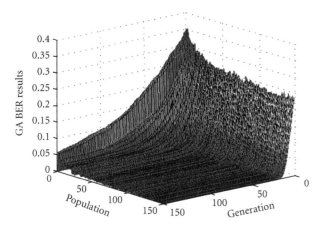

FIGURE 6: A tradeoff between population size and iterations for GA. $(K, N_T, N_R, M) = (4, 2, 6, 4)$.

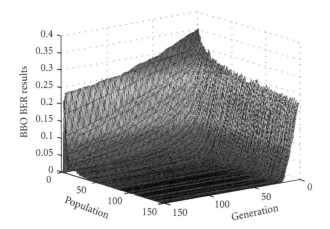

FIGURE 7: A trade-off between population size and iterations for BBO. $(K, N_T, N_R, M) = (4, 2, 6, 4)$.

beat the existing suboptimal detection schemes. To this end, some of the evolutionary procedures of the algorithm have been modified.

Currently, the authors are working on hybridizing DABC with other EAs to take the best aspects of each algorithm for specific applications. The authors are also working on applying DABC to other types of optimization problems, such as multiobjective or constrained optimization problems.

Appendix

Food Source Selection in a Neighborhood in DABC

In (8), ϕ_{ij} is a random number between $[-1, 1]$. We choose the minimum and maximum of this interval and apply it to (8). The minimum is $\phi_{ij} = -1$; hence:

$$v_j^i = x_j^i + (-1)\left(x_j^i - x_j^l\right)$$
$$v_j^i = x_j^l. \tag{A.1}$$

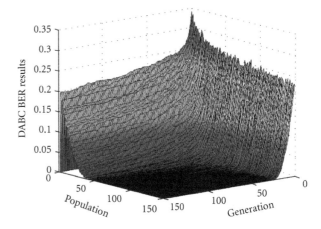

FIGURE 8: A trade-off between population size and iterations for ABC. $(K, N_T, N_R, M) = (4, 2, 6, 4)$.

The maximum is $\phi_{ij} = +1$; therefore:

$$v_j^i = x_j^i + (1)\left(x_j^i - x_j^l\right)$$
$$v_j^i = 2x_j^i - x_j^l. \tag{A.2}$$

Putting (A.1) and (A.2) together and using a random integer number generator function randint(a, b) that returns a random integer between a and b, for the integer values of x we obtain

$$v_j^i = \text{randint}\left[x_j^l, 2x_j^i - x_j^l\right]. \tag{A.3}$$

Acknowledgment

This work was supported in part by a discovery grant from the National Science and Engineering Research Council (NSERC) of Canada.

References

[1] G. J. Foschini and M. J. Gans, "On limits of wireless communications in a fading environment when using multiple antennas," *Wireless Personal Communications*, vol. 6, no. 3, pp. 311–335, 1998.

[2] E. Telatar, "Capacity of multi-antenna Gaussian channels," *European Transactions on Telecommunications*, vol. 10, no. 6, pp. 585–595, 1999.

[3] V. Tarokh, N. Seshadri, and A. R. Calderbank, "Space-time codes for high data rate wireless communication: performance criterion and code construction," *IEEE Transactions on Information Theory*, vol. 44, no. 2, pp. 744–765, 1998.

[4] A. Paulraj, R. Nabar, and D. Gore, *Introduction to Space-Time Wireless Communications*, Cambridge University Press, Cambridge, UK, 2003.

[5] B. Hassibi and H. Vikalo, "On the sphere decoding algorithm: part I, the expected complexity," *IEEE Transactions on Signal Processing*, vol. 53, no. 8, pp. 2806–2818, 2005.

[6] J. Jaldén and B. Ottersten, "On the complexity of sphere decoding in digital communications," *IEEE Transactions on Signal Processing*, vol. 53, no. 4, pp. 1474–1484, 2005.

[7] D. Karaboga, "An Idea Based on Honey Bee Swarm for Numerical Optimization," Tech. Rep. Tr06, Erciyes University, Engineering Faculty, Computer Engineering Department, 2005.

[8] D. Karaboga and B. Akay, "A comparative study of Artificial Bee Colony algorithm," *Applied Mathematics and Computation*, vol. 214, no. 1, pp. 108–132, 2009.

[9] S. Ashrafinia, U. Pareek, M. Naeem, and D. Lee, "Biogeography-based optimization for joint relay assignment and power allocation in cognitive radio systems," in *Proceedings of the Symposium Series on Computational Intelligence, IEEE SSCI 2011— IEEE Symposium on Swarm Intelligence (SIS '11)*, pp. 237–244, Paris, France, April 2011.

[10] J. Kennedy and R. Eberhart, "Particle swarm optimization," in *Proceedings of the IEEE International Conference on Neural Networks*, vol. 4, pp. 1942–1948, November/December 1995.

[11] D. Goldberg, *Genetic Algorithms in Search, Optimization, and Machine Learning*, Addison-Wesley, 1989.

[12] D. Karaboga, C. Ozturk, N. Karaboga, and B. Gorkemli, "Artificial bee colony programming for symbolic regression," *Information Sciences*, vol. 209, pp. 1–15, 2012.

[13] N. Q. Uy, N. X. Hoai, M. O'Neill, R. I. McKay, and E. Galván-López, "Semantically-based crossover in genetic programming: application to real-valued symbolic regression," *Genetic Programming and Evolvable Machines*, vol. 12, no. 2, pp. 91–119, 2011.

[14] S. N. Omkar, J. Senthilnath, R. Khandelwal, G. Narayana Naik, and S. Gopalakrishnan, "Artificial Bee Colony (ABC) for multi-objective design optimization of composite structures," *Applied Soft Computing Journal*, vol. 11, no. 1, pp. 489–499, 2011.

[15] J. D. Schaffer, *Multi-objective optimization with vector evaluated genetic algorithms [Ph.D. thesis]*, 1984.

[16] C. Xu, H. Duan, and F. Liu, "Chaotic artificial bee colony approach to Uninhabited Combat Air Vehicle (UCAV) path planning," *Aerospace Science and Technology*, vol. 14, no. 8, pp. 535–541, 2010.

[17] N. Karaboga, "A new design method based on artificial bee colony algorithm for digital IIR filters," *Journal of the Franklin Institute*, vol. 346, no. 4, pp. 328–348, 2009.

[18] J. Liang, M. Guo, Y. Fan, Y. Yin, and M. Ma, "SAR image segmentation based on Artificial Bee Colony algorithm," *Applied Soft Computing*, vol. 11, pp. 5205–5214, 2011.

[19] M. Cengiz Taplamacioglu and H. Gozde, "Comparative performance analysis of artificial bee colony algorithm for automatic voltage regulator (AVR) system," *Journal of the Franklin Institute*, vol. 348, pp. 1927–1946, 2011.

[20] M. Sonmez, "Artificial Bee Colony algorithm for optimization of truss structures," *Applied Soft Computing Journal*, vol. 11, no. 2, pp. 2406–2418, 2011.

[21] H. Narasimhan, "Parallel artificial bee colony (PABC) algorithm," in *Proceedings of the World Congress on Nature and Biologically Inspired Computing (NABIC '09)*, pp. 306–311, Coimbatore, India, December 2009.

[22] B. Akay, C. Ozturk, and D. Karaboga, "Artificial bee colony (ABC) optimization algorithm for training feed-forward neural networks," in *Proceedings of the 4th International Conference on Modeling Decisions for Artificial Intelligence (MDAI '07)*, Berlin, Germany, 2007.

[23] H. A. A. Bahamish, R. Abdullah, and R. A. Salam, "Protein tertiary structure prediction using artificial bee colony algorithm," in *Proceedings of the 3rd Asia International Conference on Modelling and Simulation (AMS '09)*, pp. 258–263, Bali, Indonesia, May 2009.

[24] D. Karaboga and B. Basturk, "A powerful and efficient algorithm for numerical function optimization: artificial bee colony (ABC) algorithm," *Journal of Global Optimization*, vol. 39, no. 3, pp. 459–471, 2007.

[25] M. Nekuii, M. Kisialiou, T. N. Davidson, and Z. Q. Luo, "Efficient soft demodulation of MIMO QPSK via semidefinite relaxation," in *Proceedings of the IEEE International Conference on Acoustics, Speech and Signal Processing (ICASSP '08)*, pp. 2665–2668, Las Vegas, Nev, USA, April 2008.

[26] J. A. Lozano, *Estimation of Distribution Algorithms: A New Tool for Evolutionary Computation*, Springer, 2002.

[27] D. Simon, "Biogeography-based optimization," *IEEE Transactions on Evolutionary Computation*, vol. 12, no. 6, pp. 702–713, 2008.

[28] B. Hassibi and B. M. Hochwald, "High-rate codes that are linear in space and time," *IEEE Transactions on Information Theory*, vol. 48, no. 7, pp. 1804–1824, 2002.

[29] R. Storn and K. Price, "Differential evolution—a simple and efficient heuristic for global optimization over continuous spaces," *Journal of Global Optimization*, vol. 11, no. 4, pp. 341–359, 1997.

[30] M. Dorigo, V. Maniezzo, and A. Colorni, "Ant system: optimization by a colony of cooperating agents," *IEEE Transactions on Systems, Man, and Cybernetics B*, vol. 26, no. 1, pp. 29–41, 1996.

[31] P. W. Tsai, J. S. Pan, B. Y. Liao, and S. C. Chu, "Enhanced artificial bee colony optimization," *International Journal of Innovative Computing, Information and Control*, vol. 5, no. 12, pp. 5081–5092, 2009.

[32] J. Wang, T. Li, and R. Ren, "Real time IDSs based on artificial bee colony-support vector machine algorithm," in *Proceedings of the 3rd International Workshop on Advanced Computational Intelligence (IWACI '10)*, pp. 91–96, Suzhou, China, August 2010.

[33] M. Salim and M. T. Vakil-Baghmisheh, "Discrete bee algorithms and their application in multivariable function optimization," *Artificial Intelligence Review*, vol. 35, no. 1, pp. 73–84, 2011.

[34] O. Damen, A. Chkeif, and J. C. Belfiore, "Lattice code decoder for space-time codes," *IEEE Communications Letters*, vol. 4, no. 5, pp. 161–163, 2000.

[35] C. Comaniciu, N. B. Mandayam, and H. V. Poor, *Wireless Networks: Multiuser Detection in Cross-Layer Design*, Springer, New York, NY, USA, 2005.

[36] M. Kisialiou and Z. Q. Luo, "Performance analysis of quasi-maximum-likelihood detector based on semi-definite programming," in *Proceedings of the IEEE International Conference on Acoustics, Speech, and Signal Processing (ICASSP '05)*, pp. III433–III436, March 2005.

Permissions

The contributors of this book come from diverse backgrounds, making this book a truly international effort. This book will bring forth new frontiers with its revolutionizing research information and detailed analysis of the nascent developments around the world.

We would like to thank all the contributing authors for lending their expertise to make the book truly unique. They have played a crucial role in the development of this book. Without their invaluable contributions this book wouldn't have been possible. They have made vital efforts to compile up to date information on the varied aspects of this subject to make this book a valuable addition to the collection of many professionals and students.

This book was conceptualized with the vision of imparting up-to-date information and advanced data in this field. To ensure the same, a matchless editorial board was set up. Every individual on the board went through rigorous rounds of assessment to prove their worth. After which they invested a large part of their time researching and compiling the most relevant data for our readers. Conferences and sessions were held from time to time between the editorial board and the contributing authors to present the data in the most comprehensible form. The editorial team has worked tirelessly to provide valuable and valid information to help people across the globe.

Every chapter published in this book has been scrutinized by our experts. Their significance has been extensively debated. The topics covered herein carry significant findings which will fuel the growth of the discipline. They may even be implemented as practical applications or may be referred to as a beginning point for another development. Chapters in this book were first published by Hindawi Publishing Corporation; hereby published with permission under the Creative Commons Attribution License or equivalent.

The editorial board has been involved in producing this book since its inception. They have spent rigorous hours researching and exploring the diverse topics which have resulted in the successful publishing of this book. They have passed on their knowledge of decades through this book. To expedite this challenging task, the publisher supported the team at every step. A small team of assistant editors was also appointed to further simplify the editing procedure and attain best results for the readers.

Our editorial team has been hand-picked from every corner of the world. Their multi-ethnicity adds dynamic inputs to the discussions which result in innovative outcomes. These outcomes are then further discussed with the researchers and contributors who give their valuable feedback and opinion regarding the same. The feedback is then collaborated with the researches and they are edited in a comprehensive manner to aid the understanding of the subject.

Apart from the editorial board, the designing team has also invested a significant amount of their time in understanding the subject and creating the most relevant covers. They scrutinized every image to scout for the most suitable representation of the subject and create an appropriate cover for the book.

The publishing team has been involved in this book since its early stages. They were actively engaged in every process, be it collecting the data, connecting with the contributors or procuring relevant information. The team has been an ardent support to the editorial, designing and production team. Their endless efforts to recruit the best for this project, has resulted in the accomplishment of this book. They are a veteran in the field of academics and their pool of knowledge is as vast as their experience in printing. Their expertise and guidance has proved useful at every step. Their uncompromising quality standards have made this book an exceptional effort. Their encouragement from time to time has been an inspiration for everyone.

The publisher and the editorial board hope that this book will prove to be a valuable piece of knowledge for researchers, students, practitioners and scholars across the globe.

List of Contributors

Lev V. Utkin and Yulia A. Zhuk
Department of Control, Automation and System Analysis, St. Petersburg State Forest Technical University, Institutski per. 5, St. Petersburg 194021, Russia

Kushan Ahmadian and Marina Gavrilova
Department of Computer Science, University of Calgary, Calgary, AB, Canada T2N 1N4

Tomoaki Yoshikai, Marika Hayashi, Yui Ishizaka, Hiroko Fukushima, Asuka Kadowaki, Takashi Sagisaka, Kazuya Kobayashi, Iori Kumagai and Masayuki Inaba
Department of Mechano-Informatics, The University of Tokyo, 7-3-1 Hongo, Bunkyo-ku, Tokyo 113-8656, Japan

Anamika Jain
Department of Electrical Engineering, National Institute of Technology, Raipur 492010, India

Ah-Lian Kor
Arts Environment and Technology Faculty, Leeds Metropolitan University, Headingley Campus, Leeds LS6 3QS, UK

Brandon Bennett
School of Computing, University of Leeds, Leeds LS2 9JT, UK

Pejman Kamkarian
Electrical and Computer Engineering Department, Southern Illinois University, Carbondale, IL 62901, USA

Henry Hexmoor
Department of Computer Science, Southern Illinois University, Carbondale, IL 62901, USA

Leandro Pereira dos Santos
Instituto Federal do Parana, Assis Chateaubriand, 80230-150 Curitiba, PR, Brazil

Guilherme Ernani Vieira
Petrobras S.A., 41770-395 Salvador, BA, Brazil
Doutor Jose Peroba 225, Apartment no. 1103, 41.770-235 Salvador, BA, Brazil
Department of Industrial Engineering, Pontifical Catholic University of Parana, 80215-901 Curitiba, PR, Brazil

Maria Teresinha Arns Steiner
Department of Industrial Engineering, Pontifical Catholic University of Parana, 80215-901 Curitiba, PR, Brazil

Higor Vinicius dos R. Leite
Department of Industrial Engineering, Pontifical Catholic University of Parana, 80215-901 Curitiba, PR, Brazil
Department of Management, Universidade Tecnol´ogica Federal do Paran´a, 80230-901 Curitiba, PR, Brazil

E. Earl Eiland and Lorie M. Liebrock
Computer Science and Engineering Department, New Mexico Institute of Mining and Technology, 801 Leroy Place, Socorro, NM 87801, USA

Kieran Greer
Distributed Computing Systems, Belfast, UK

Marco Turchi
European Commission-Joint Research Centre (JRC), IPSC, GlobeSec, Via Fermi 2749, 21020 Ispra, Italy
Intelligent Systems Laboratory, University of Bristol, MVB, Woodland Road, Bristol BS8 1UB, UK

Cyril Goutte
Interactive Language Technologies, National Research Council Canada, 283 Boulevard Alexandre-Tach´e, Gatineau, QC, Canada

Tijl De Bie and Nello Cristianini
Intelligent Systems Laboratory, University of Bristol, MVB, Woodland Road, Bristol BS8 1UB, UK

Athanasios Alexiou and Panayiotis Vlamos
Department of Informatics, Ionian University, Plateia Tsirigoti 7, 49100 Corfu, Greece

Yuki Akiyama
Center for Spatial Information Science, The University of Tokyo, Cw-503 Shibasaki Laboratory, 4-6-1 Komaba, Meguro-ku, Tokyo 153-8505, Japan

Ryosuke Shibasaki
Center for Spatial Information Science, The University of Tokyo, 5-1-5 Kashiwanoha, Kashiwa City, Chiba 277-8568, Japan

Samaneh Yazdani
Department of Computer Engineering, Science and Research Branch, Islamic Azad University, Tehran, Iran

Jamshid Shanbehzadeh
Department of Computer Engineering, Faculty of Engineering, Kharazmi University, Tehran, Iran

Mohammad Taghi Manzuri Shalmani
Electronic Research Center, Sharif University of Technology, Tehran, Iran

Saeed Ashrafinia, Muhammad Naeem and Daniel Lee
School of Engineering Science, Simon Fraser University, Burnaby, BC, Canada V5A 1S6

Printed in the USA
CPSIA information can be obtained
at www.ICGtesting.com
JSHW051441221024
72173JS00006B/1543

9 781632 403575